STOP!

This is the back of the book.
You wouldn't want to spoil a great ending!

This book is printed "manga-style," in the authentic Japanese right-to-left format. Since none of the artwork has been flipped or altered, readers get to experience the story just as the creator intended. You've been asking for it, so TOKYOPOP® delivered: authentic, hot-off-the-press, and far more fun!

1
2
3
4
5
6
7
8
9
10

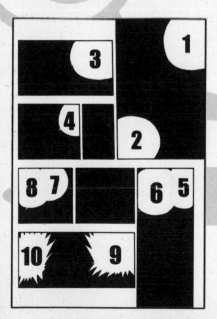

DIRECTIONS

If this is your first time reading manga-style, here's a quick guide to help you understand how it works.

It's easy... just start in the top right panel and follow the numbers. Have fun, and look for more 100% authentic manga from TOKYOPOP®!

THE MANGA REVOLUTION • LEADING • THE MANGA REVOLUTION • LEADING

漫画革命

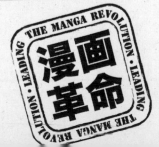

TOKYOPOP MANGA SUPPLEMENT

Learn From the Best!

Featuring the artists behind *Fruits Basket*, *Vampire Knight*, *Maid Sama* and many more!

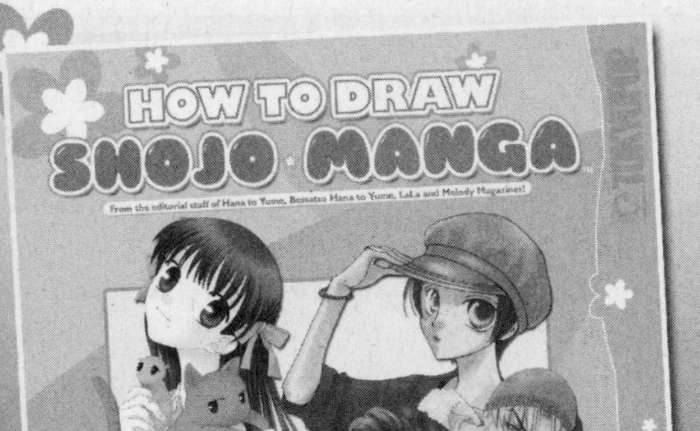
HOW TO DRAW SHOJO MANGA
From the editorial staff of Hana to Yume, Bessatsu Hana to Yume, LaLa and Melody Magazines!
Featuring many of the artists behind today's top shojo series!

Wanna draw your own shojo manga but not quite sure where to start? The editors at Hakusensha Publishing, home of such beloved shojo series as *Fruits Basket*, *Vampire Knight*, *Maid Sama* and *Ouran High School Host Club*, have assembled a book jam-packed with useful tips and practical advice to help you develop your skills and go from beginner to ready for the manga big leagues!

Join aspiring artist Ena as she strives to make her big break drawing manga. Aided by her editor, Sasaki, and some of the best shojo artists in Japan, follow along as Ena creates a short story from start to finish, and gets professional feedback along the way. From page layout and pacing to pencils and perspective, this guide covers the basics, and then challenges you to go to the next level! Does Ena (and you!) have what it takes to go pro? Pick up this book and learn from the best!

ROMANCE

FOR MORE INFORMATION VISIT: www.TOKYOPOP.com

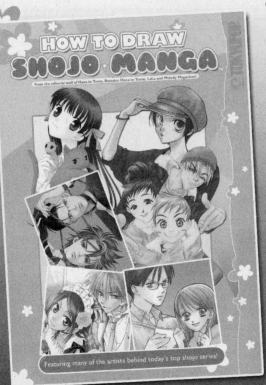

WARNING: Nosebleeds Ahead!!!

Karin is back!

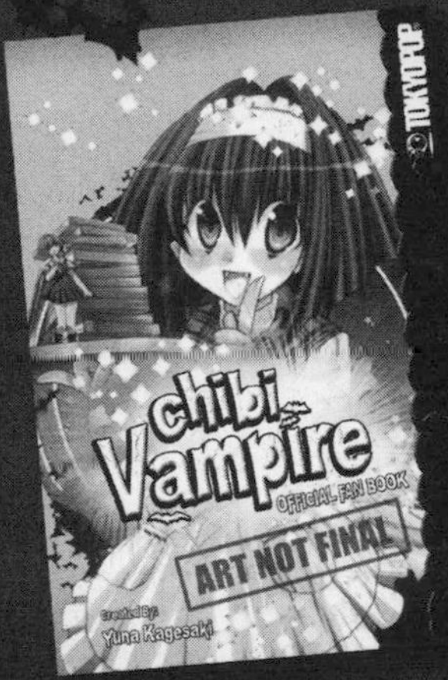
TOKYOPOP
chibi Vampire
OFFICIAL FAN BOOK
ART NOT FINAL
Created By:
Yuna Kagesaki

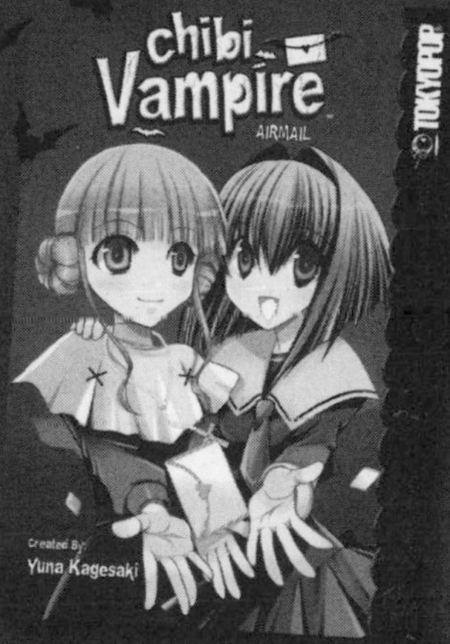
chibi Vampire
AIRMAIL
TOKYOPOP
Created By:
Yuna Kagesaki

Relive the laughter, romance and bittersweet moments in this must have book for Chibi Vampire fans. Loads of never before seen character sketches, maps and story highlights on the manga, anime and novels.

CHIBI VAMPIRE Official Fanbook available January 2011!

A collection of manga stories that follows the continuing adventures of our favorite vampire. Finally find out what happened to Karin and her friends in these sweet tales and scary legends!

CHIBI VAMPIRE: AIRMAIL available NOW in bookstores everywhere!

COMEDY | OT OLDER TEEN AGE 16+

BE SURE TO VISIT WWW.TOKYOPOP.COM/SHOP FOR EVERYTHING YOU COULD EVER WANT!

ReD HoT CHiLI SaMuRai

Created By: Yoshitsugu Katagiri

The **HOTTEST** manga in town is about to take a bite out of crime...and the nearest pepper!

ReD HoT CHiLI SaMuRai
Created By: Yoshitsugu Katagiri

Vol. 1

Kokaku is the hero and don't you forget it!

As the son of the local lord, his job is to stop evildoers in their tracks. But if he doesn't have a steady flow of the spiciest chili peppers, Kokaku isn't going to stop anything! Can he save his home town from corruption and wrong-doing? Only if you'll pay him in hot sauce!

ACTION

OT
OLDER TEEN
AGE 16+

FOR MORE INFORMATION VISIT: www.TOKYOPOP.com

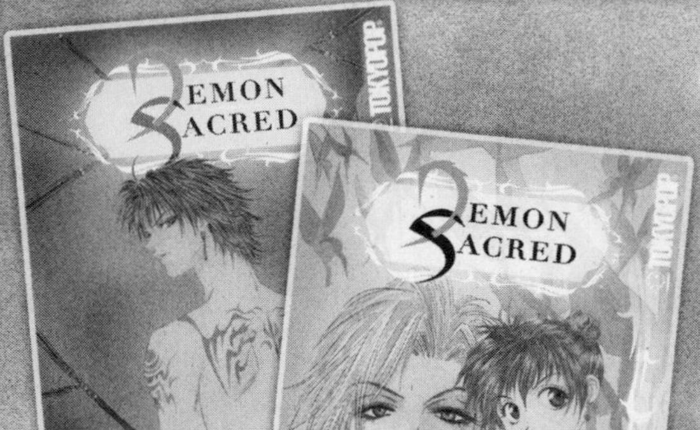
DEMON SACRED
2 Natsumi Itsuki
TOKYOPOP
DEMON SACRED
1 Natsumi Itsuki
TOKYOPOP

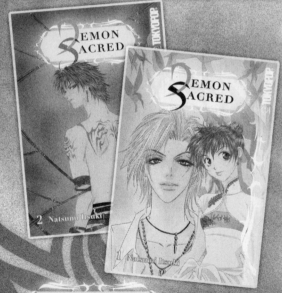

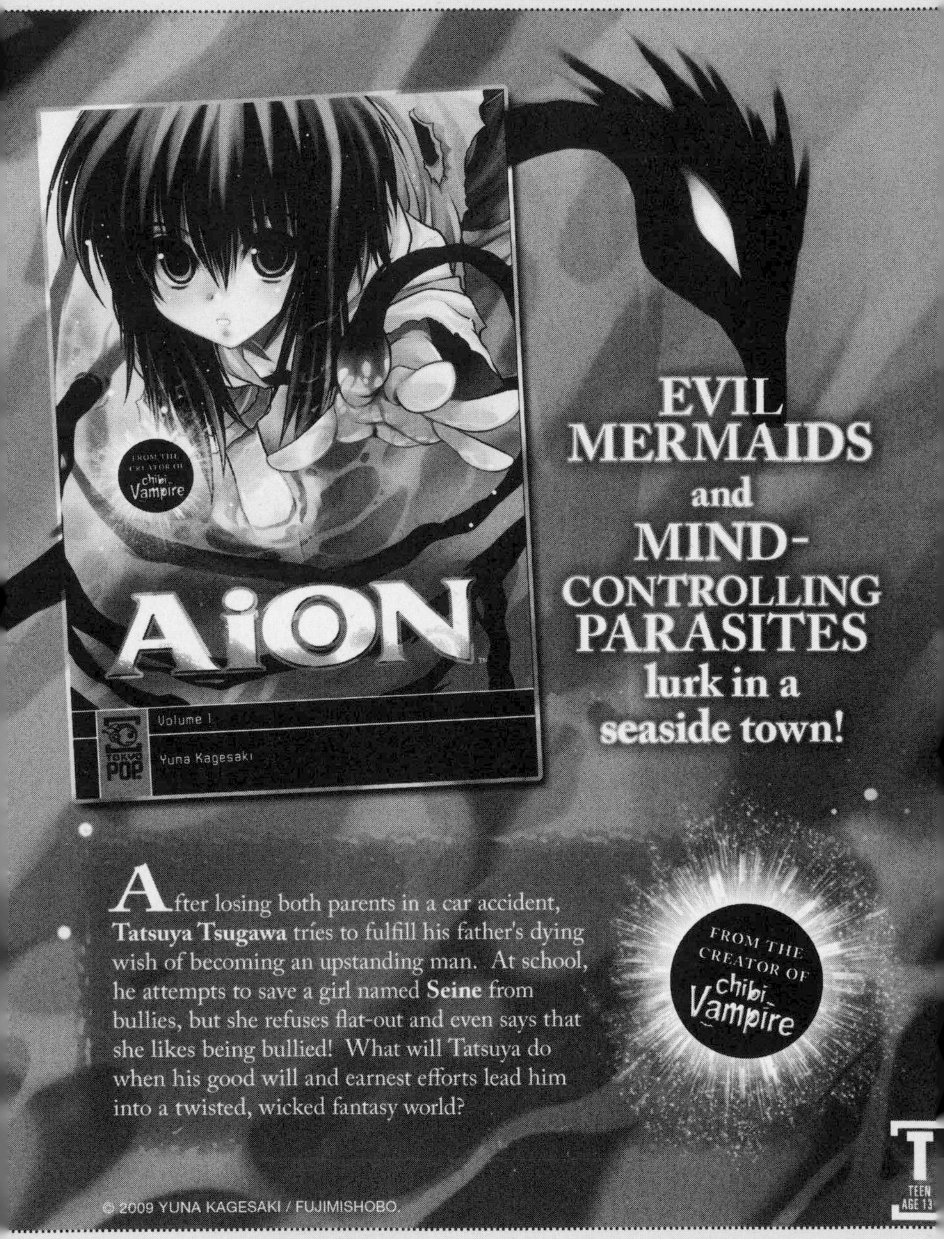
FROM THE CREATOR OF chibi Vampire
AiON
Volume 1
Yuna Kagesaki
TOKYOPOP
EVIL MERMAIDS and MIND-CONTROLLING PARASITES lurk in a seaside town!
After losing both parents in a car accident, Tatsuya Tsugawa tries to fulfill his father's dying wish of becoming an upstanding man. At school, he attempts to save a girl named Seine from bullies, but she refuses flat-out and even says that she likes being bullied! What will Tatsuya do when his good will and earnest efforts lead him into a twisted, wicked fantasy world?
FROM THE CREATOR OF chibi Vampire
T TEEN AGE 13+
© 2009 YUNA KAGESAKI / FUJIMISHOBO.

SKYBLUE SHORE

VOLUME 2

BY
Nanpei Yamada

HAMBURG // LONDON // LOS ANGELES // TOKYO

Skyblue Shore Volume 2
Created by Nanpei Yamada

Translation - Kristy Harmon
English Adaptation - Hope Donovan
Retouch and Lettering - Star Print Brokers

Editor - Daniella Orihuela-Gruber
Print Production Manager - Lucas Rivera
Managing Editor - Vy Nguyen
Senior Designer - Louis Csontos
Art Director - Al-Insan Lashley
Director of Sales and Manufacturing - Allyson De Simone
President and C.O.O. - John Parker
C.E.O. and Chief Creative Officer - Stu Levy

A  Manga

TOKYOPOP Inc.
5900 Wilshire Blvd. Suite 2000
Los Angeles, CA 90036

E-mail: info@TOKYOPOP.com
Come visit us online at www.TOKYOPOP.com

ISBN: 978-1-4278-2006-8

First TOKYOPOP printing: March 2011
10 9 8 7 6 5 4 3 2 1
Printed In the USA

SKYBLUE SHORE

Volume 2

Nanpei Yamada

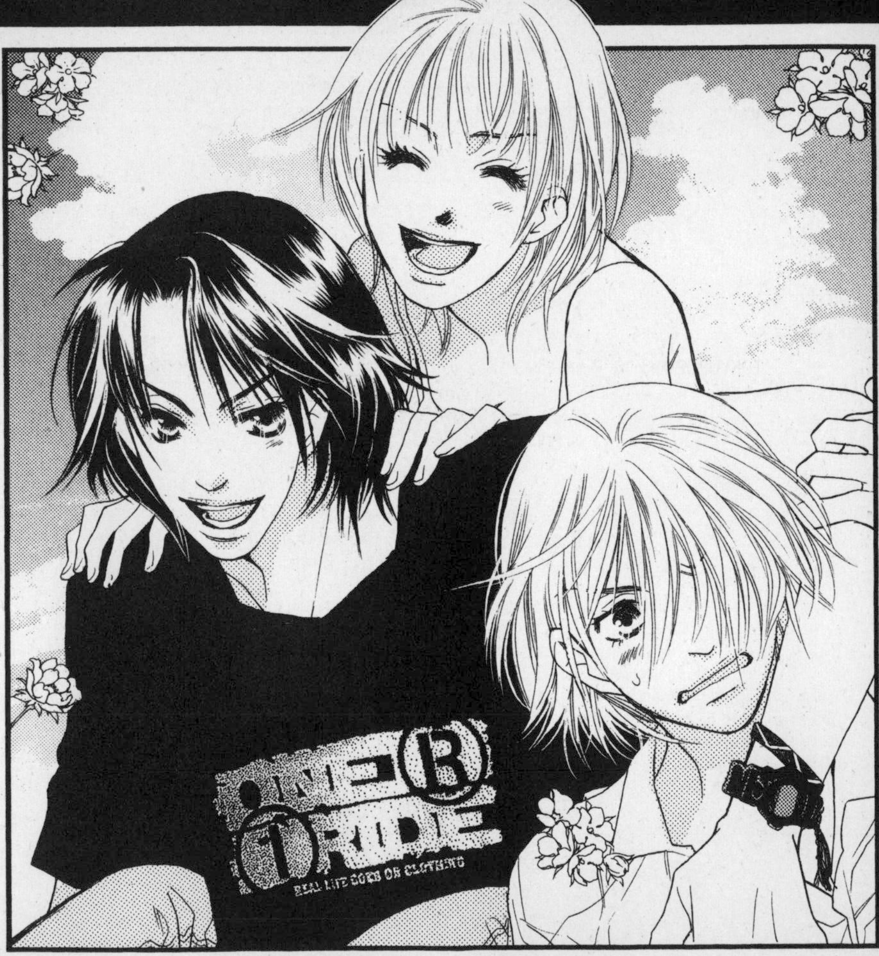

SKYBLUE SHORE

■ Contents ■

MAIN CHARACTER Q&A
Q. What's your name?
Tomo Sakurai!
Q. When is your birthday?
August 27th!
Q. What's your blood type?
Type O!
Q. Your favorite food?
Udon!
Q. If you could change one thing in your life, what would it be?
I'd love to lose 7 pounds over the summer!
I mean, I'm GOING to!

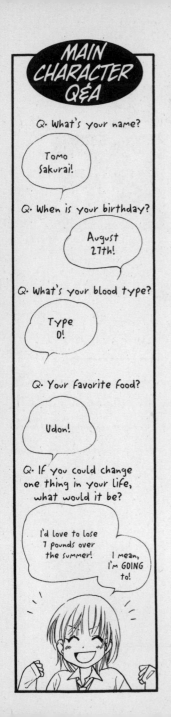

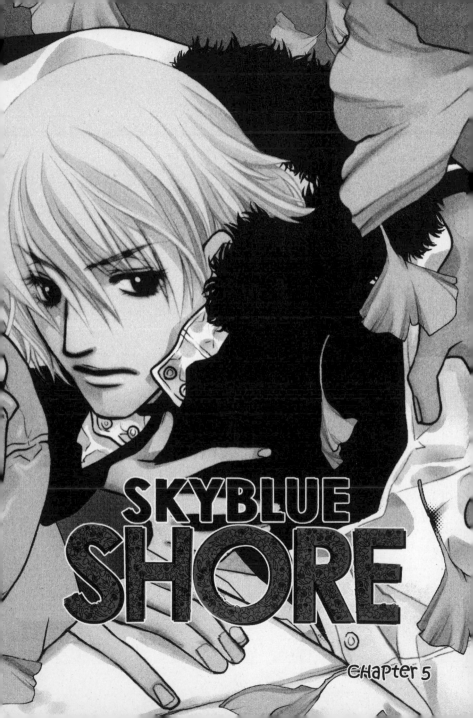

SKYBLUE SHORE

CHAPTER 5

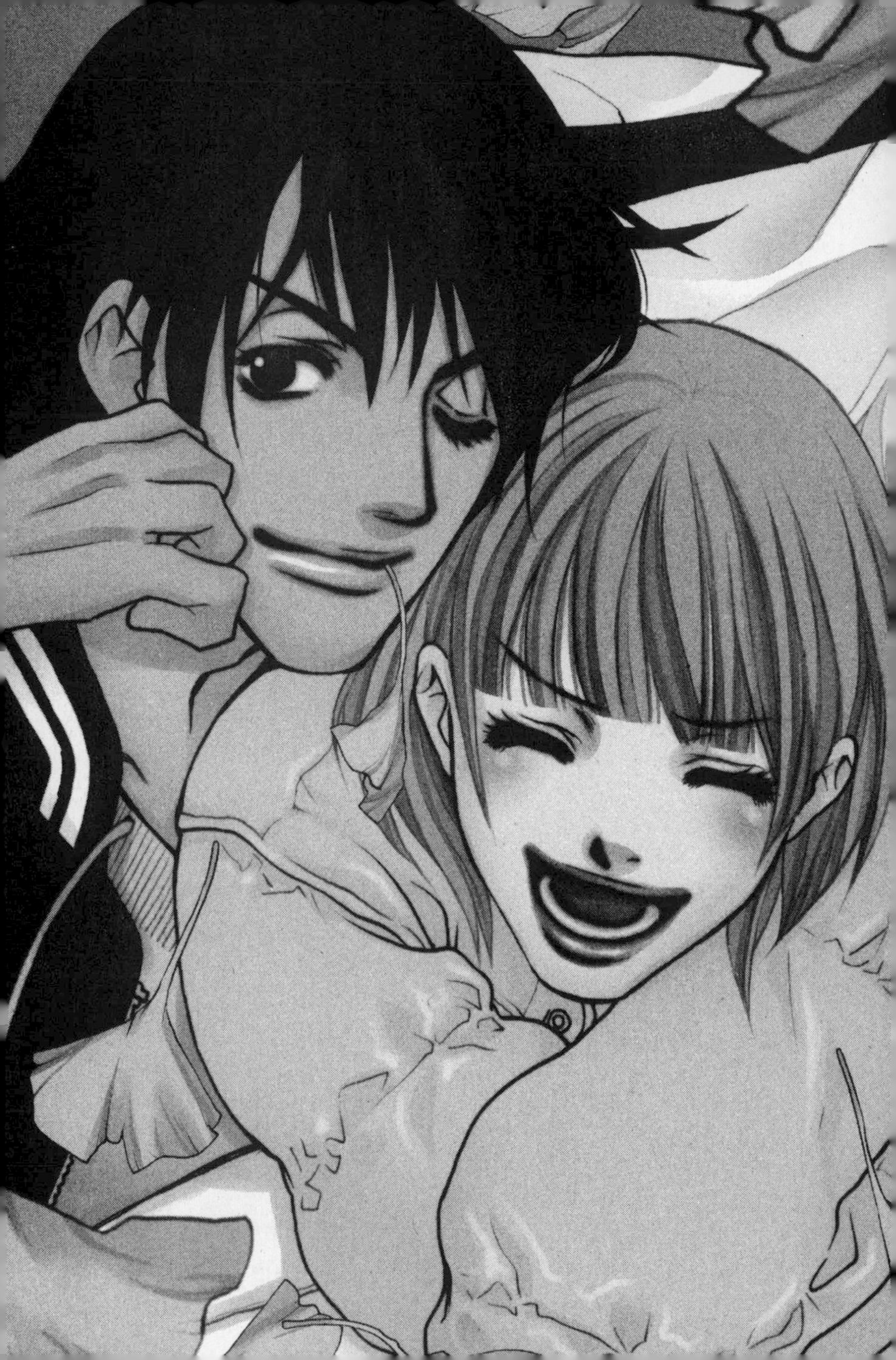

MAIN CHARACTER Q&A

Q. What's your name?

> Michiru Saeki.

Q. When is your birthday?

> None of your business.

Q. What's your blood type?

> I don't know.

Q. Your favorite food?

> Don't have any.

Q. If you could change one thing in your life, what would it be?

> Like I'd tell you. Not that I would change anything.

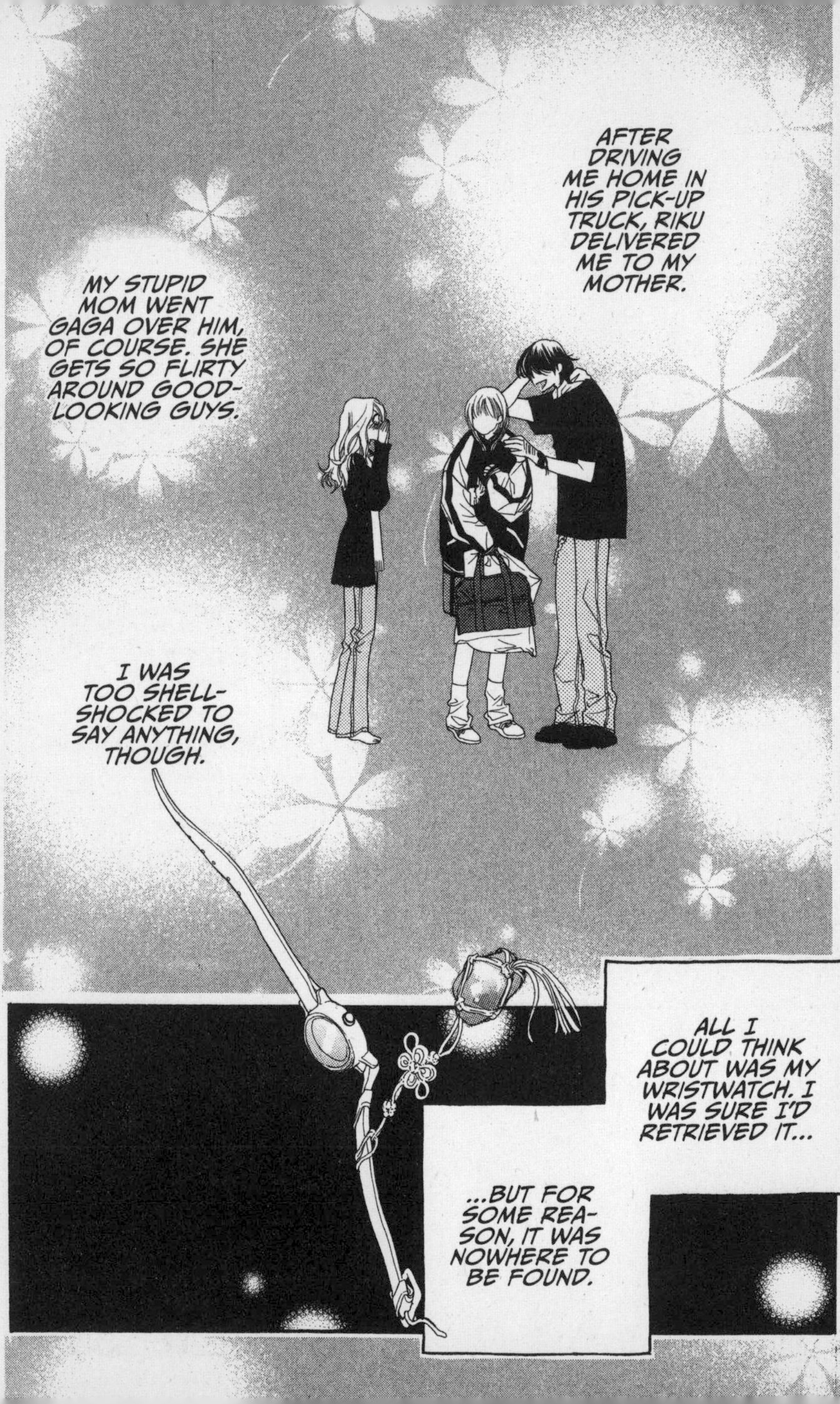
AFTER DRIVING ME HOME IN HIS PICK-UP TRUCK, RIKU DELIVERED ME TO MY MOTHER.
MY STUPID MOM WENT GAGA OVER HIM, OF COURSE. SHE GETS SO FLIRTY AROUND GOOD-LOOKING GUYS.
I WAS TOO SHELL-SHOCKED TO SAY ANYTHING, THOUGH.
ALL I COULD THINK ABOUT WAS MY WRISTWATCH. I WAS SURE I'D RETRIEVED IT...
...BUT FOR SOME REA-SON, IT WAS NOWHERE TO BE FOUND.

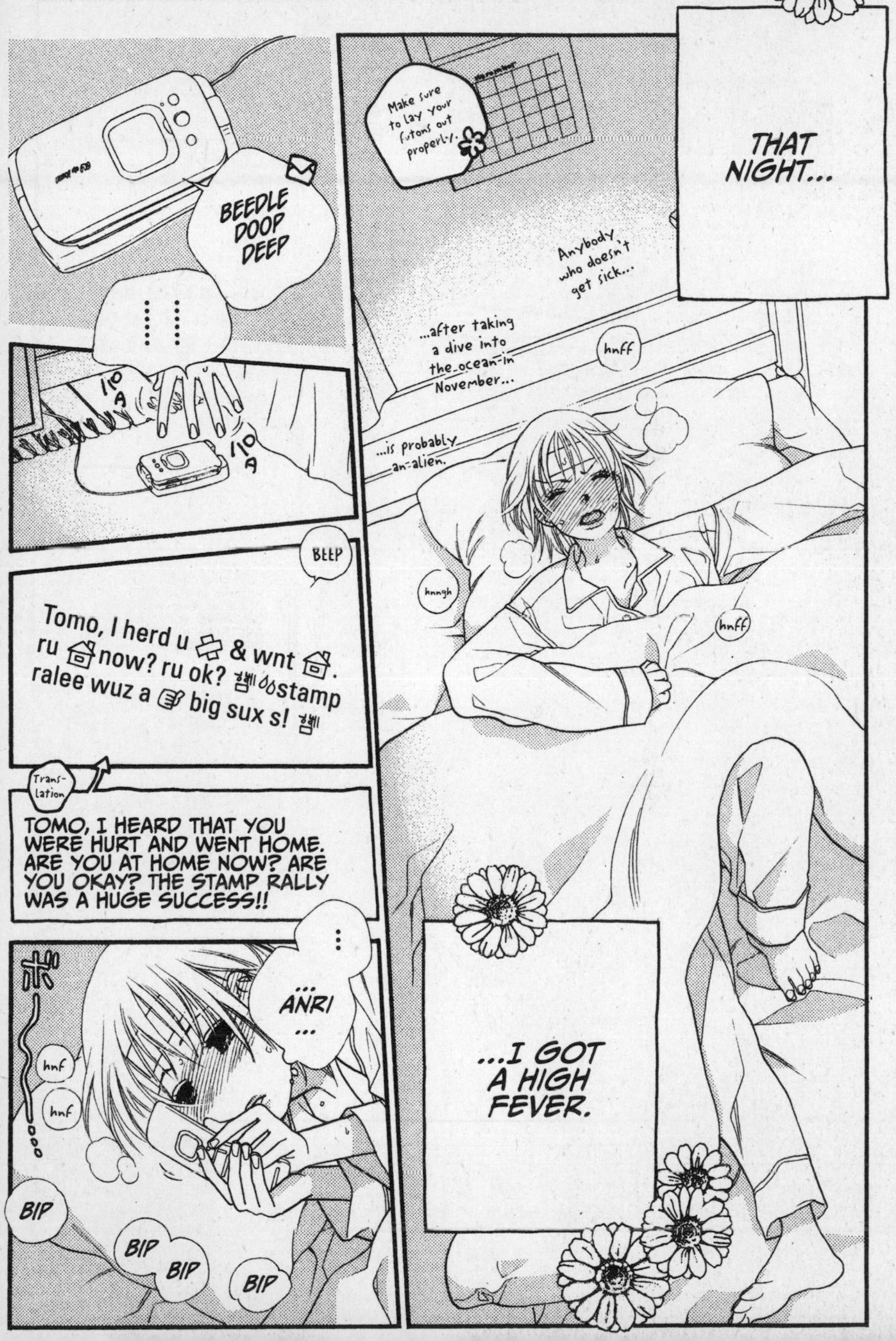

THAT NIGHT...
Make sure to lay your futons out properly.
Anybody who doesn't get sick...
...after taking a dive into the ocean in November...
...is probably an alien.
hnff
hnngh
hnff
...I GOT A HIGH FEVER.
BEEDLE DOOP DEEP
......
BEEP
Tomo, I herd u & wnt . ru now? ru ok? stamp ralee wuz a big sux s!
Trans-lation
TOMO, I HEARD THAT YOU WERE HURT AND WENT HOME. ARE YOU AT HOME NOW? ARE YOU OKAY? THE STAMP RALLY WAS A HUGE SUCCESS!!
...
...ANRI...
hnf
hnf
BIP
BIP
BIP
BIP

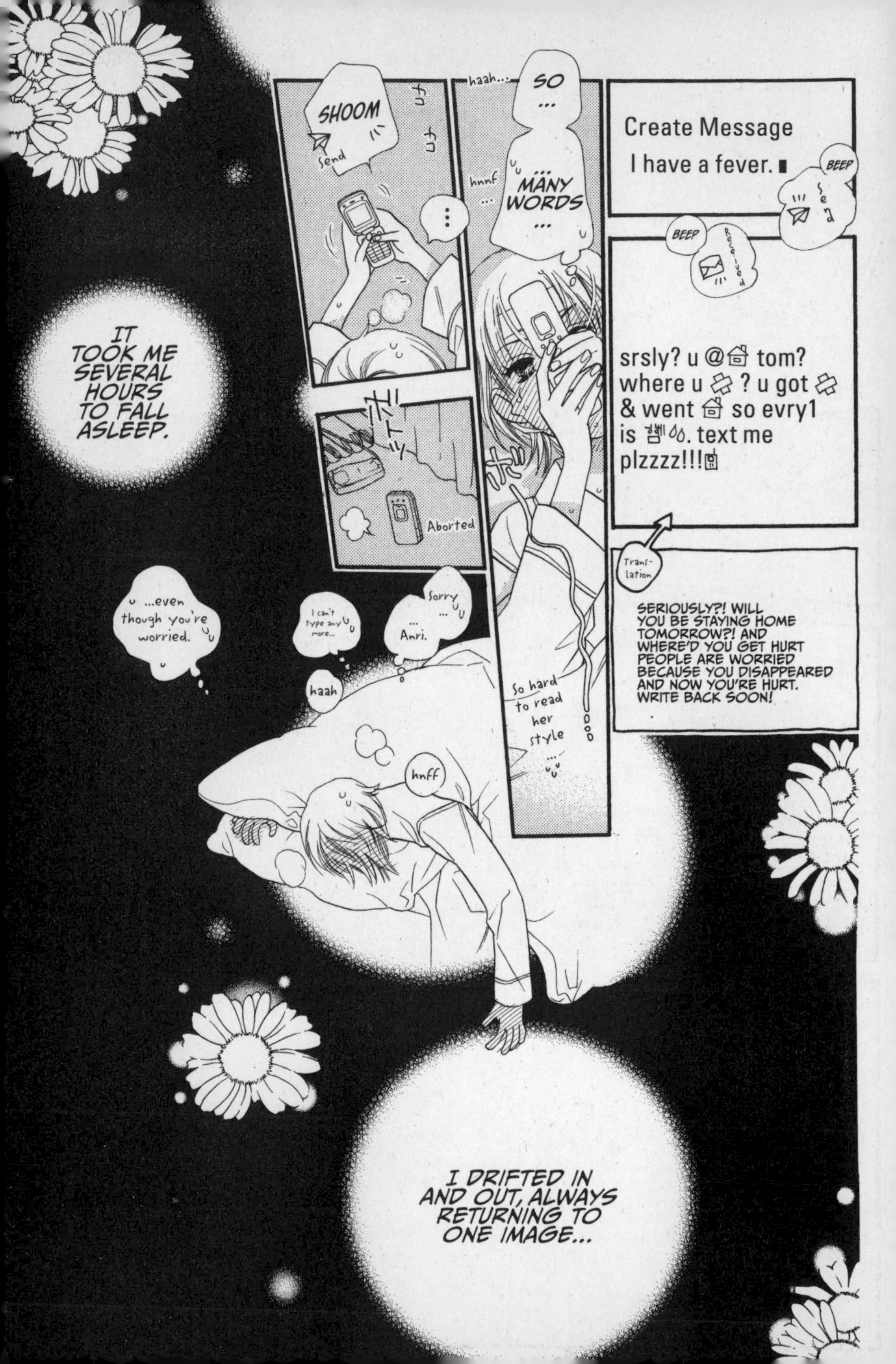
Create Message
I have a fever.
BEEP
send
BEEP
Received
srsly? u @🏠 tom? where u ✚? u got ✚ & went 🏠 so evry1 is 💦. text me plzzzz!!!
Translation
SERIOUSLY?! WILL YOU BE STAYING HOME TOMORROW?! AND WHERE'D YOU GET HURT PEOPLE ARE WORRIED BECAUSE YOU DISAPPEARED AND NOW YOU'RE HURT. WRITE BACK SOON!
haah...
SO ... ... MANY WORDS ...
hnnf ...
So hard to read her style ...
SHOOM
send
...
Aborted
IT TOOK ME SEVERAL HOURS TO FALL ASLEEP.
Sorry ... ... Anri.
I can't type any more...
...even though you're worried.
haah
hnff
I DRIFTED IN AND OUT, ALWAYS RETURNING TO ONE IMAGE...

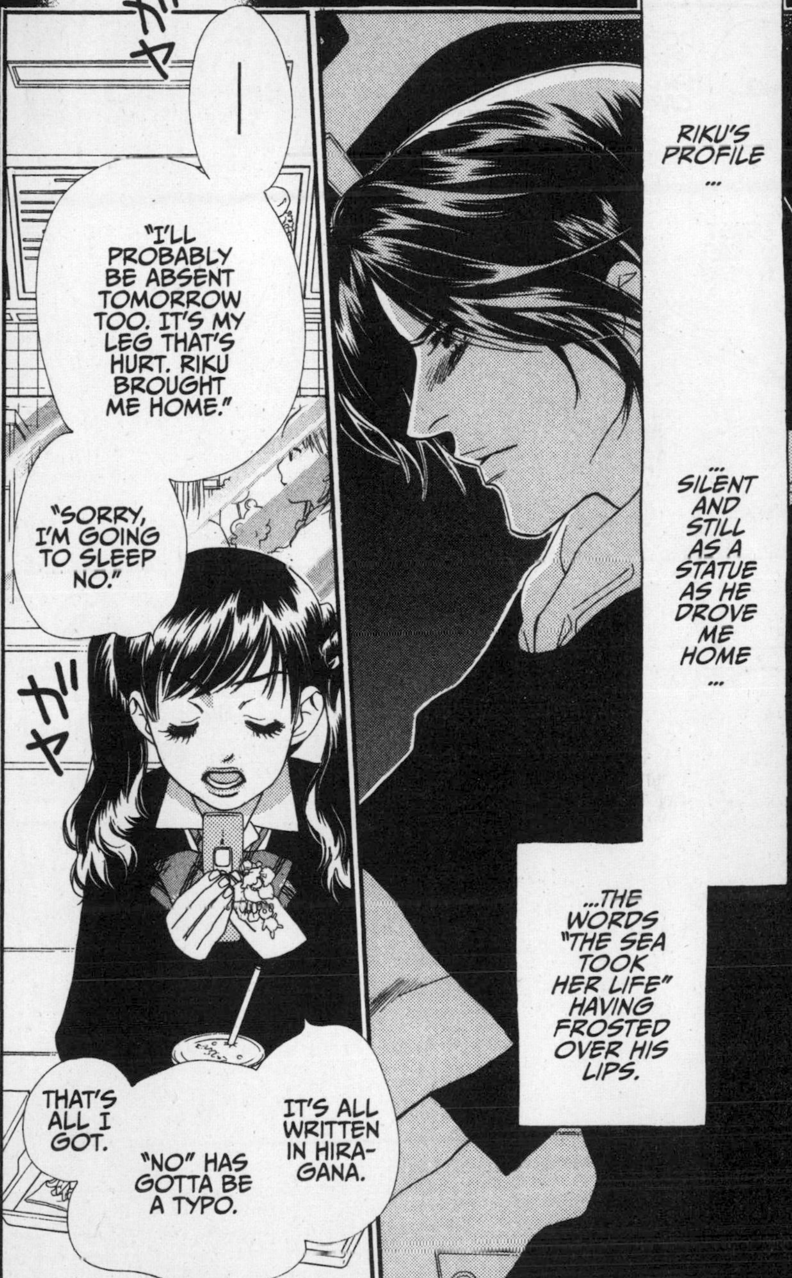
RIKU'S PROFILE ...
...SILENT AND STILL AS A STATUE AS HE DROVE ME HOME ...
...THE WORDS "THE SEA TOOK HER LIFE" HAVING FROSTED OVER HIS LIPS.
ガヤ
"I'LL PROBABLY BE ABSENT TOMORROW TOO. IT'S MY LEG THAT'S HURT. RIKU BROUGHT ME HOME."
"SORRY, I'M GOING TO SLEEP NO."
ガヤ
IT'S ALL WRITTEN IN HIRA-GANA.
"NO" HAS GOTTA BE A TYPO.
THAT'S ALL I GOT.

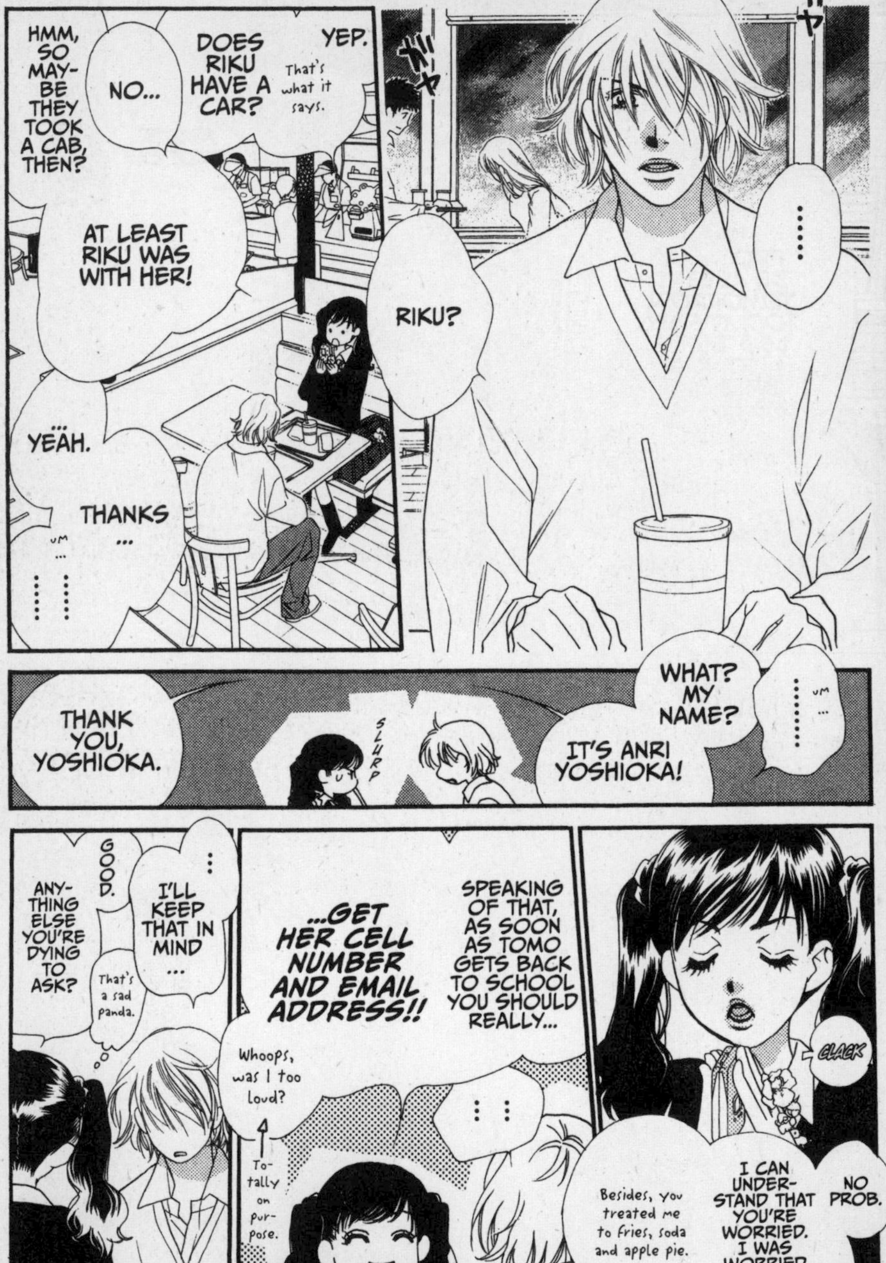
ガヤ
ガヤ
......
RIKU?
YEP.
That's what it says.
DOES RIKU HAVE A CAR?
NO...
HMM, SO MAYBE THEY TOOK A CAB, THEN?
AT LEAST RIKU WAS WITH HER!
...YEAH.
THANKS...
UM...
......
......
UM...
....
WHAT? MY NAME?
IT'S ANRI YOSHIOKA!
SLURP
THANK YOU, YOSHIOKA.
CLACK
NO PROB.
I CAN UNDERSTAND THAT YOU'RE WORRIED. I WAS WORRIED TOO.
Besides, you treated me to fries, soda and apple pie.
SPEAKING OF THAT, AS SOON AS TOMO GETS BACK TO SCHOOL YOU SHOULD REALLY...
...GET HER CELL NUMBER AND EMAIL ADDRESS!!
: :
Whoops, was I too loud?
Totally on purpose.
...
I'LL KEEP THAT IN MIND...
GOOD.
ANYTHING ELSE YOU'RE DYING TO ASK?
That's a sad panda.

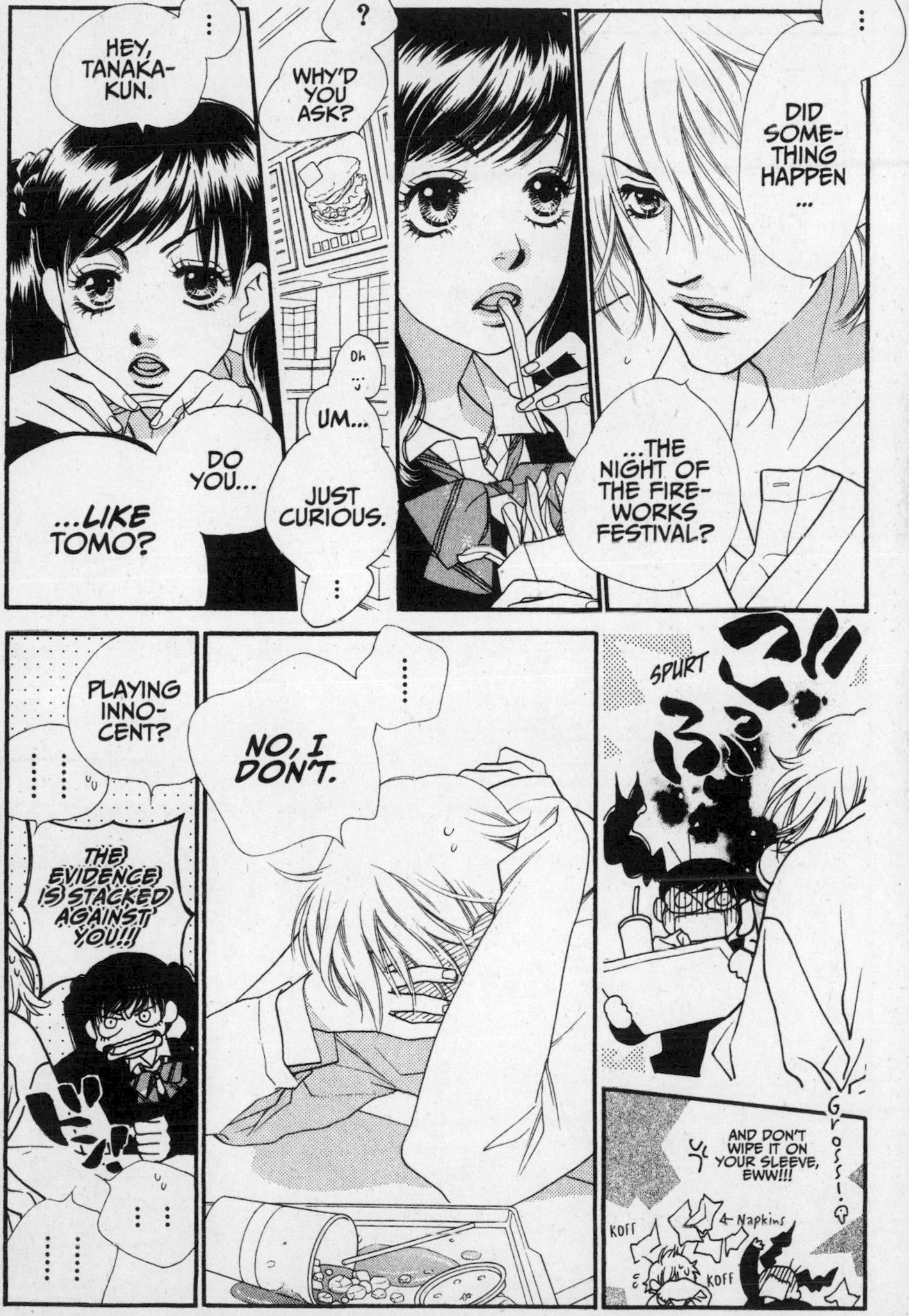

...
DID SOMETHING HAPPEN ...
...THE NIGHT OF THE FIRE-WORKS FESTIVAL?
?
WHY'D YOU ASK?
Oh ...
UM...
JUST CURIOUS.
...
...
HEY, TANAKA-KUN.
DO YOU...
...LIKE TOMO?
SPURT
Gross!
AND DON'T WIPE IT ON YOUR SLEEVE, EWW!!!
Napkins
KOFF
KOFF
......
NO, I DON'T.
PLAYING INNO-CENT?
......
THE EVIDENCE IS STACKED AGAINST YOU!!!
...
...

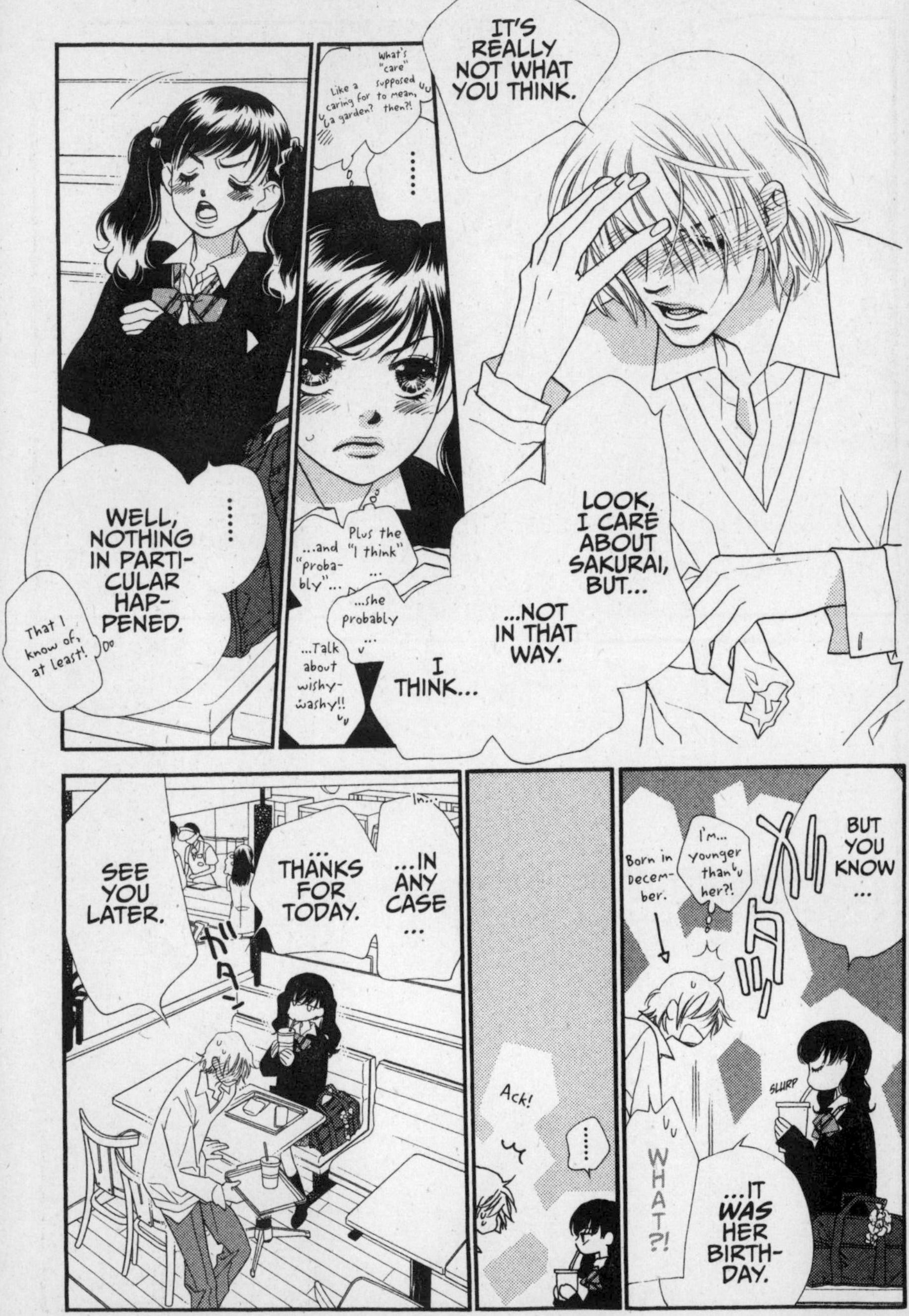
IT'S REALLY NOT WHAT YOU THINK.
LOOK, I CARE ABOUT SAKURAI, BUT...
...NOT IN THAT WAY.
I THINK...
What's "care" supposed to mean, then?!
Like a caring for a garden?
......
Plus the "I think" ...
...and "probably"...
...she probably ...
...Talk about wishy-washy!!
......
WELL, NOTHING IN PARTICULAR HAPPENED.
That I know of, at least!
BUT YOU KNOW ...
...IT WAS HER BIRTHDAY.
I'm... younger than her?!
Born in December.
WHAT?!
Ack!
......
SLURP
In...
...IN ANY CASE ...
...THANKS FOR TODAY.
SEE YOU LATER.

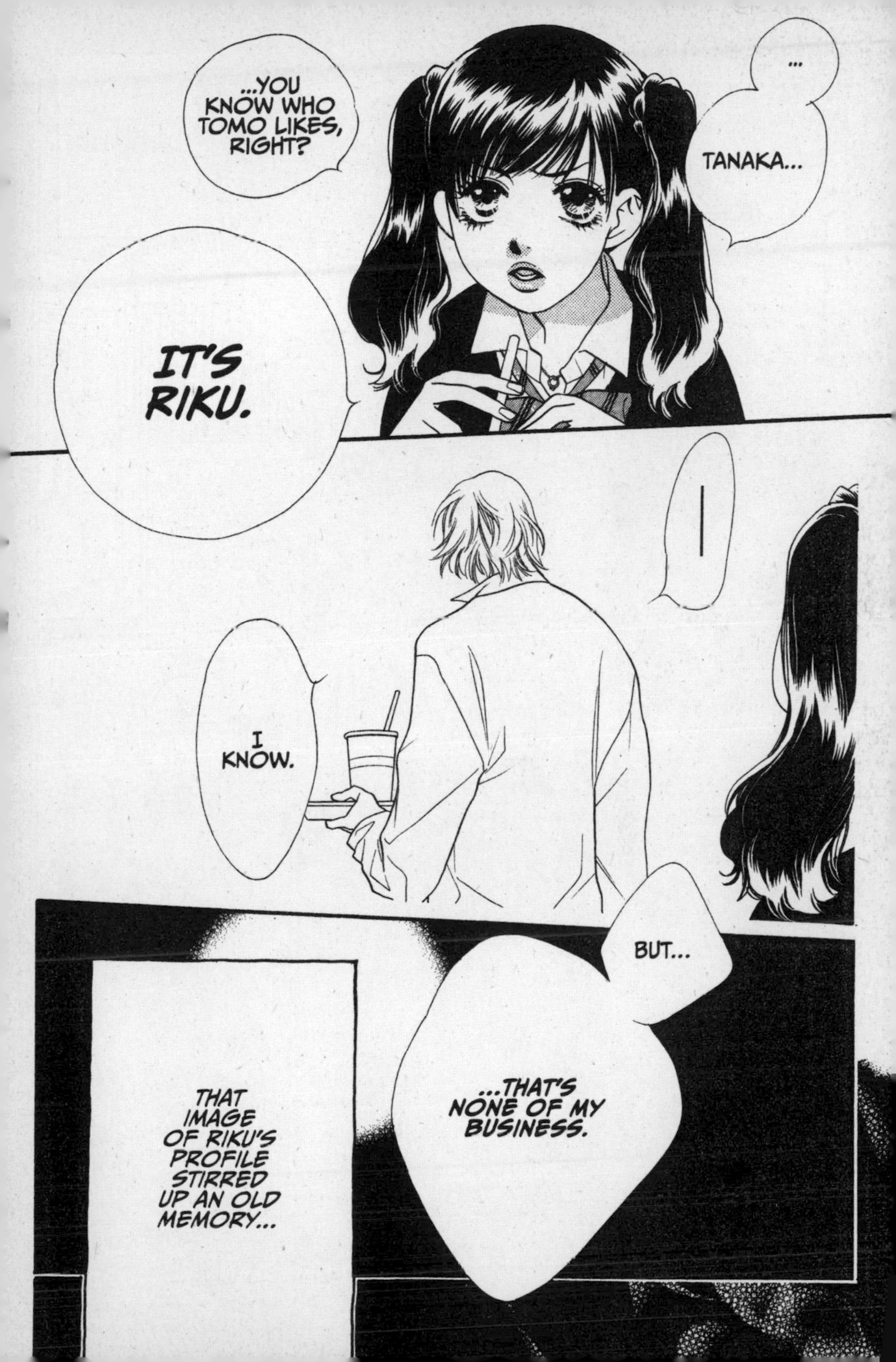
...
TANAKA...
...YOU KNOW WHO TOMO LIKES, RIGHT?
IT'S RIKU.
I KNOW.
BUT...
...THAT'S NONE OF MY BUSINESS.
THAT IMAGE OF RIKU'S PROFILE STIRRED UP AN OLD MEMORY...

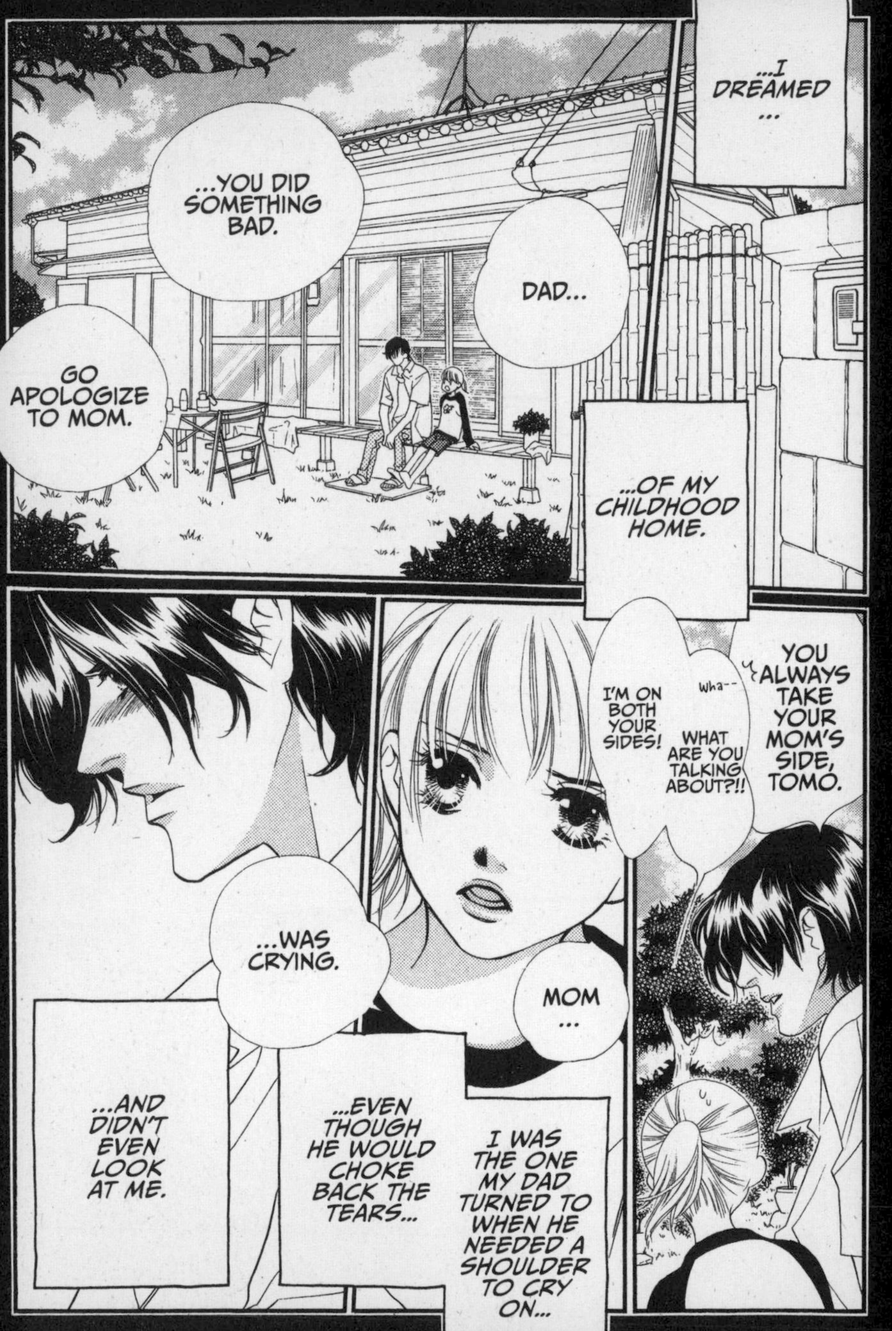
...I DREAMED ...
...OF MY CHILDHOOD HOME.
DAD...
...YOU DID SOMETHING BAD.
GO APOLOGIZE TO MOM.
YOU ALWAYS TAKE YOUR MOM'S SIDE, TOMO.
Wha--
WHAT ARE YOU TALKING ABOUT?!!
I'M ON BOTH YOUR SIDES!
MOM ...
...WAS CRYING.
I WAS THE ONE MY DAD TURNED TO WHEN HE NEEDED A SHOULDER TO CRY ON...
...EVEN THOUGH HE WOULD CHOKE BACK THE TEARS...
...AND DIDN'T EVEN LOOK AT ME.

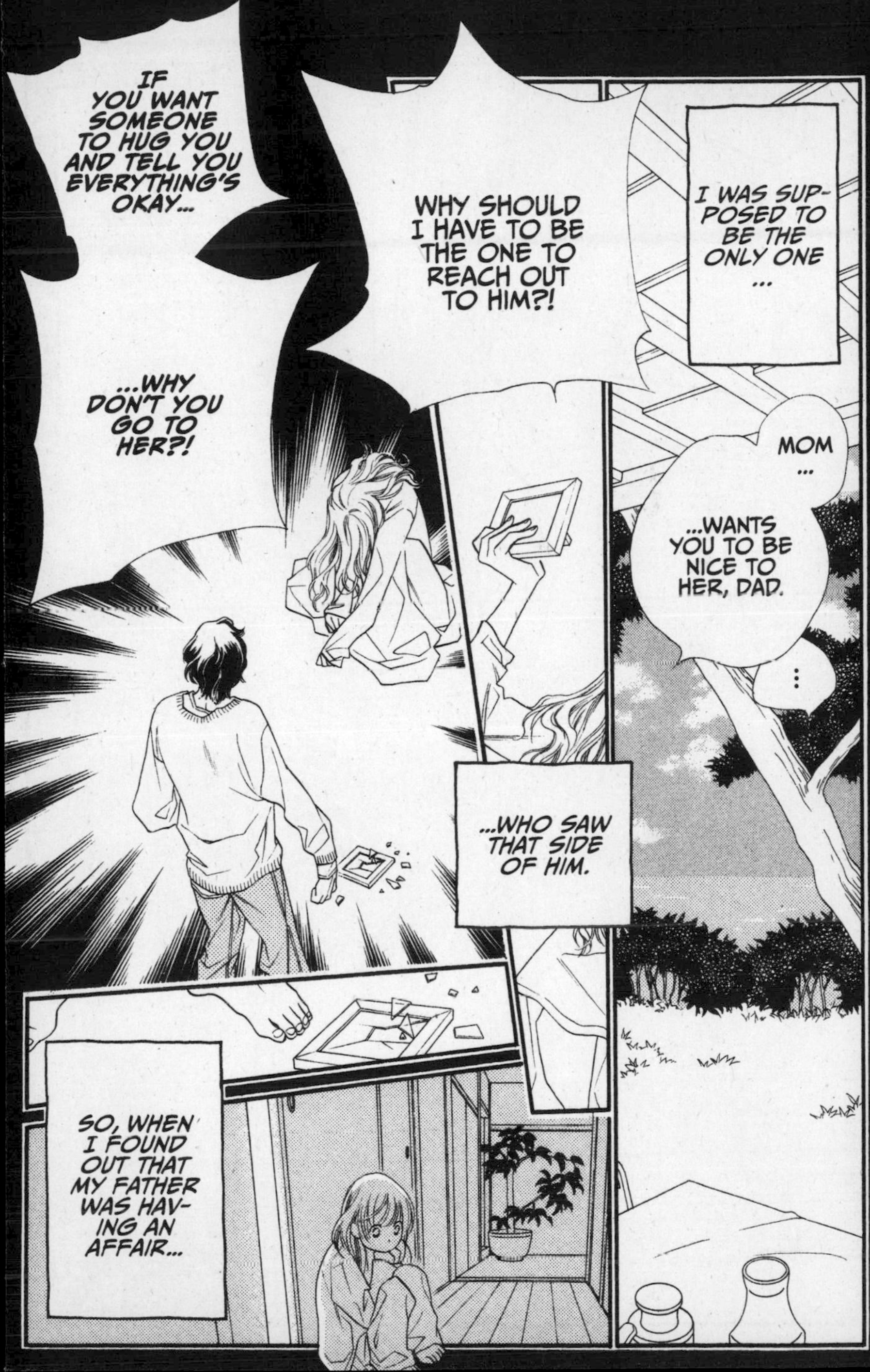
I WAS SUP-POSED TO BE THE ONLY ONE ...
MOM ...
...WANTS YOU TO BE NICE TO HER, DAD.
...
WHY SHOULD I HAVE TO BE THE ONE TO REACH OUT TO HIM?!
...WHO SAW THAT SIDE OF HIM.
IF YOU WANT SOMEONE TO HUG YOU AND TELL YOU EVERYTHING'S OKAY...
...WHY DON'T YOU GO TO HER?!
SO, WHEN I FOUND OUT THAT MY FATHER WAS HAV-ING AN AFFAIR...

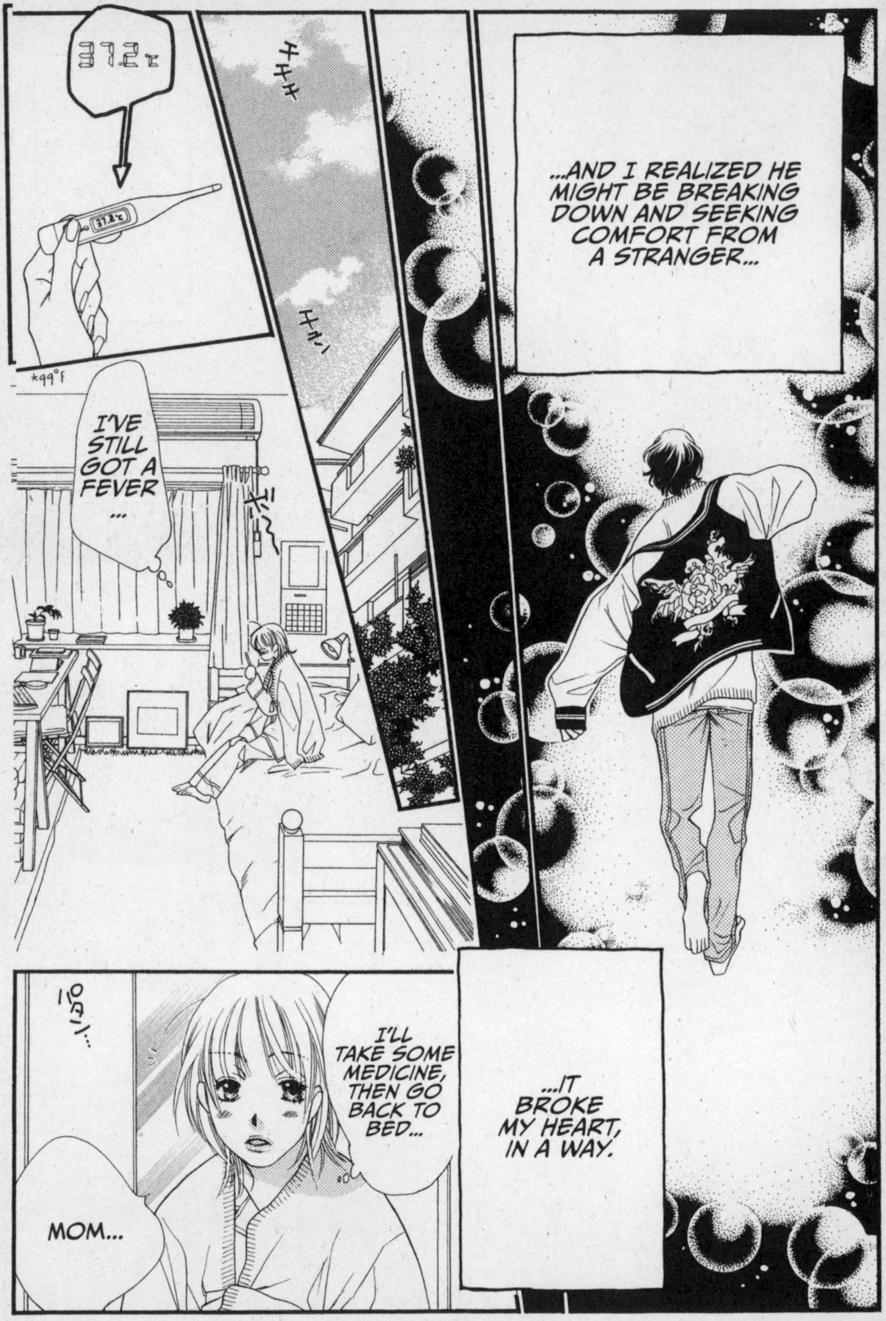
...AND I REALIZED HE MIGHT BE BREAKING DOWN AND SEEKING COMFORT FROM A STRANGER...
...IT BROKE MY HEART, IN A WAY.
37.2c
*99°F
I'VE STILL GOT A FEVER ...
I'LL TAKE SOME MEDICINE, THEN GO BACK TO BED...
MOM...

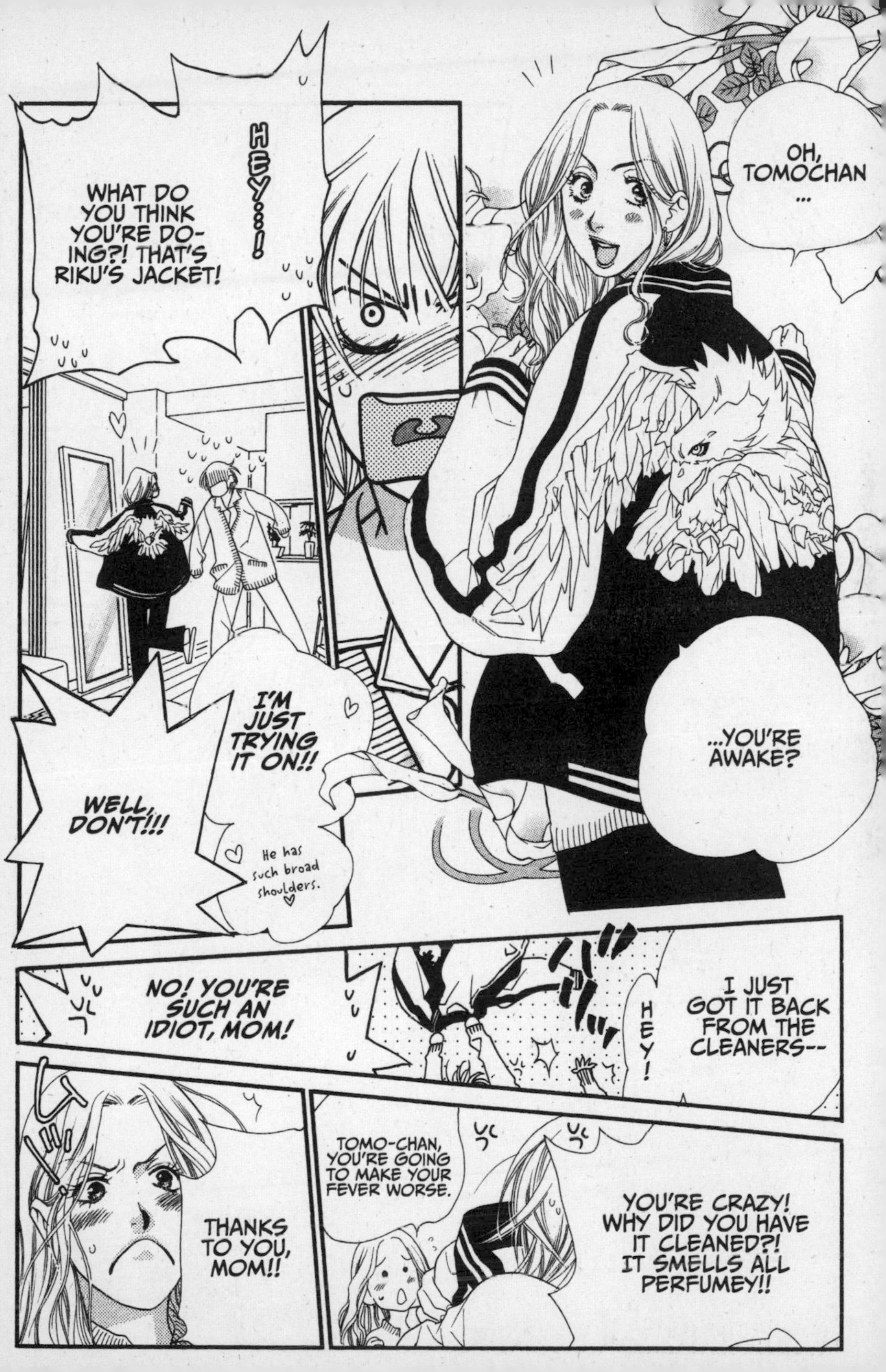
OH, TOMOCHAN ...
...YOU'RE AWAKE?
HEY...!!
WHAT DO YOU THINK YOU'RE DOING?! THAT'S RIKU'S JACKET!
I'M JUST TRYING IT ON!!
He has such broad shoulders.
WELL, DON'T!!!
I JUST GOT IT BACK FROM THE CLEANERS--
HEY!
NO! YOU'RE SUCH AN IDIOT, MOM!
YOU'RE CRAZY! WHY DID YOU HAVE IT CLEANED?! IT SMELLS ALL PERFUMEY!!
TOMO-CHAN, YOU'RE GOING TO MAKE YOUR FEVER WORSE.
THANKS TO YOU, MOM!!

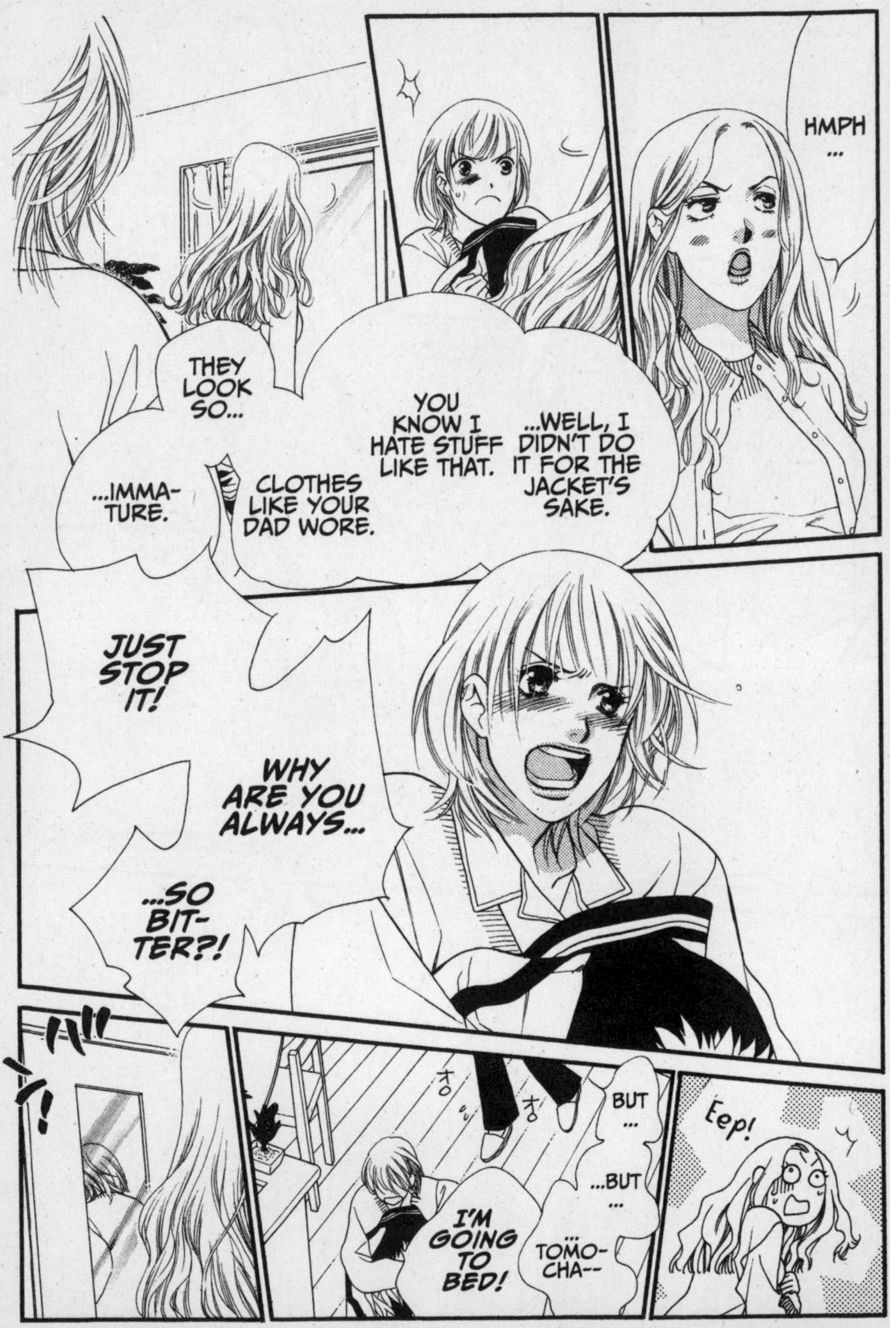
HMPH ...
...WELL, I DIDN'T DO IT FOR THE JACKET'S SAKE.
YOU KNOW I HATE STUFF LIKE THAT.
CLOTHES LIKE YOUR DAD WORE.
THEY LOOK SO...
...IMMA-TURE.
JUST STOP IT!
WHY ARE YOU ALWAYS...
...SO BIT-TER?!
Eep!
BUT ...
...BUT ...
... TOMO-CHA--
I'M GOING TO BED!
バッ

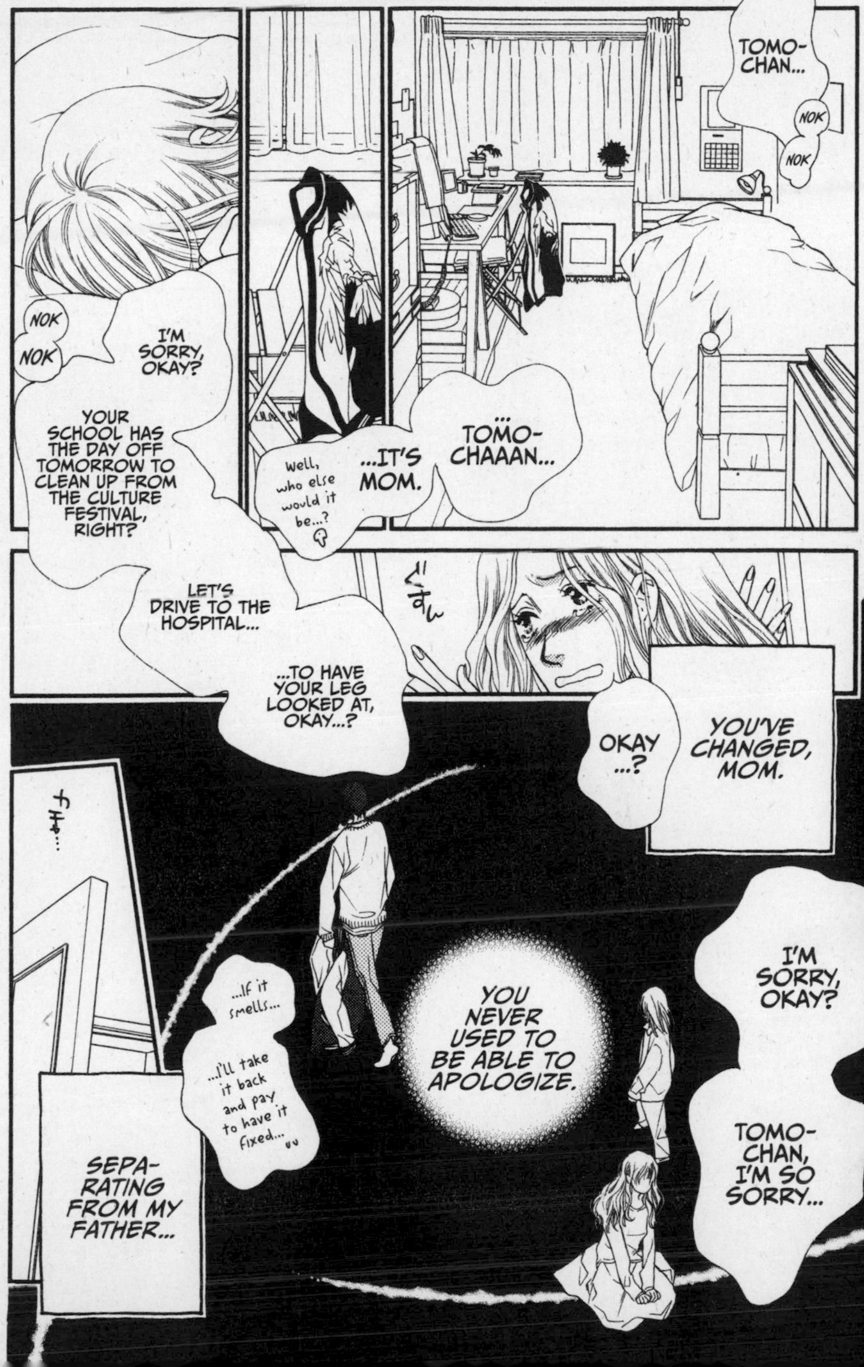
TOMO-CHAN...
NOK
NOK
...TOMO-CHAAAN...
...IT'S MOM.
Well, who else would it be...?
NOK
NOK
I'M SORRY, OKAY?
YOUR SCHOOL HAS THE DAY OFF TOMORROW TO CLEAN UP FROM THE CULTURE FESTIVAL, RIGHT?
LET'S DRIVE TO THE HOSPITAL...
...TO HAVE YOUR LEG LOOKED AT, OKAY...?
ぐすん
OKAY ...?
YOU'VE CHANGED, MOM.
I'M SORRY, OKAY?
TOMO-CHAN, I'M SO SORRY...
YOU NEVER USED TO BE ABLE TO APOLOGIZE.
...If it smells...
...I'll take it back and pay to have it fixed...
SEPA-RATING FROM MY FATHER...

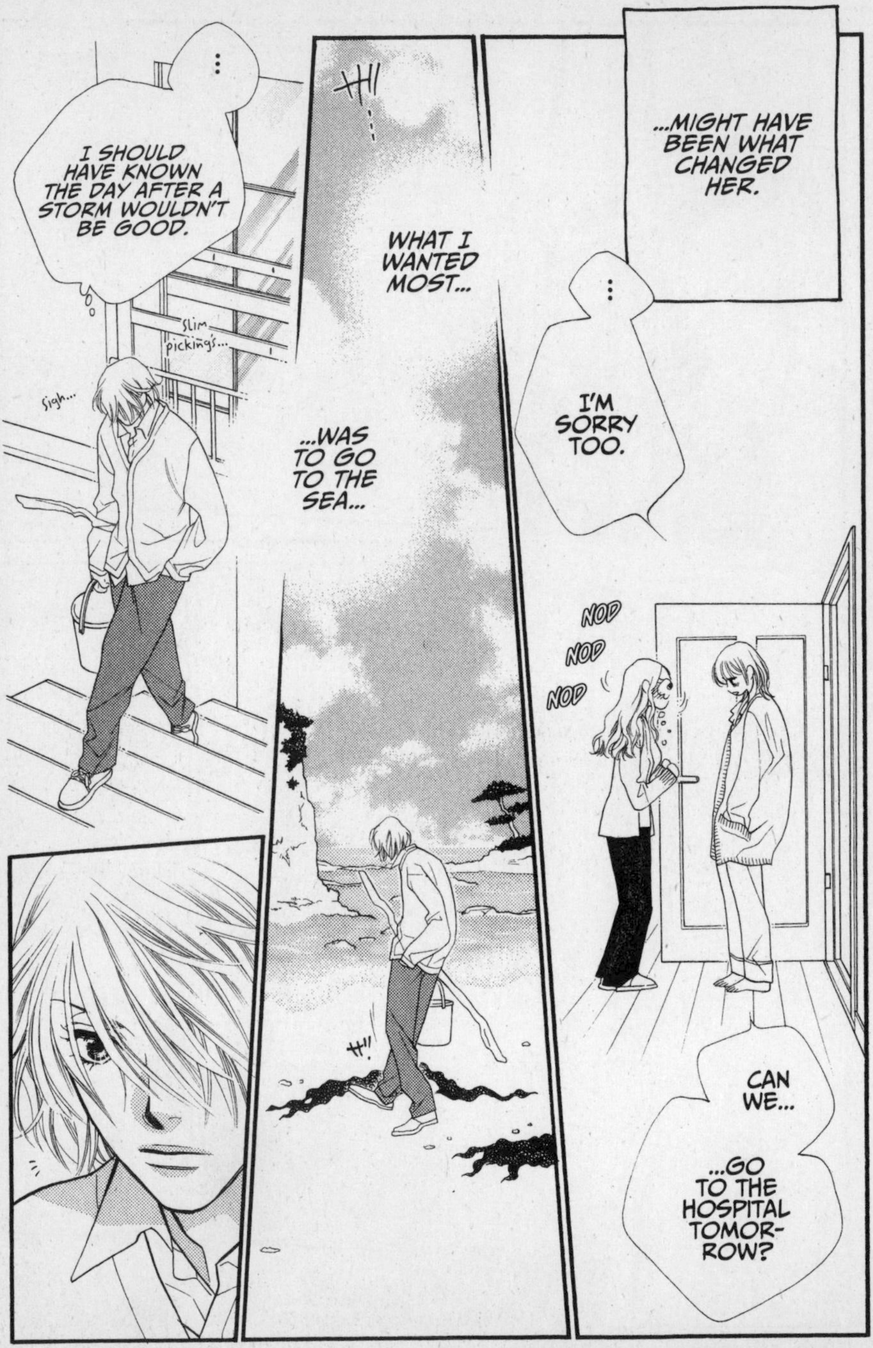
...MIGHT HAVE BEEN WHAT CHANGED HER.
...
I'M SORRY TOO.
NOD
NOD
NOD
CAN WE...
...GO TO THE HOSPITAL TOMOR-ROW?
WHAT I WANTED MOST...
...WAS TO GO TO THE SEA...
...
I SHOULD HAVE KNOWN THE DAY AFTER A STORM WOULDN'T BE GOOD.
Slim picking's...
Sigh...

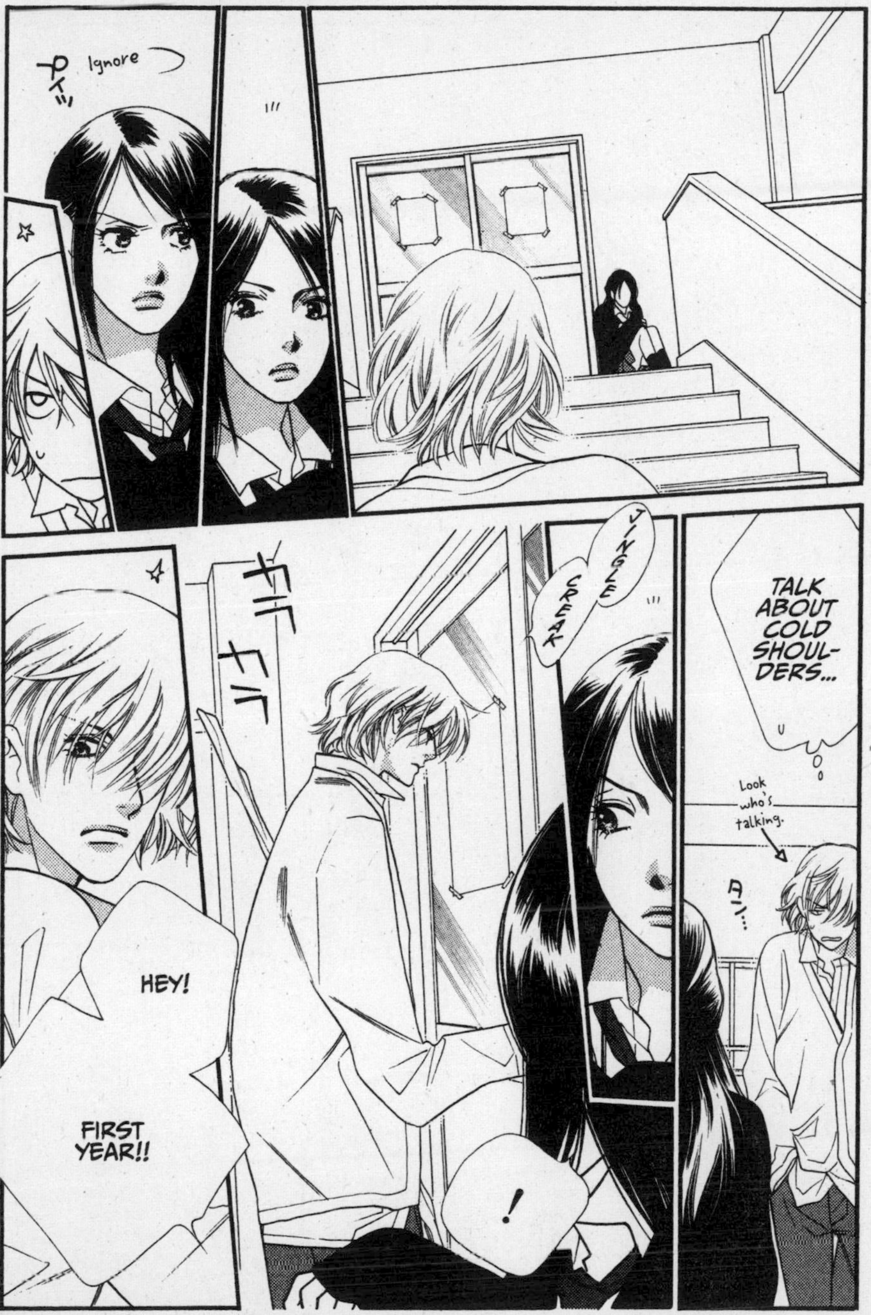

Ignore
TALK ABOUT COLD SHOUL-DERS...
Look who's talking.
JINGLE
CREAK
HEY!
FIRST YEAR!!
!

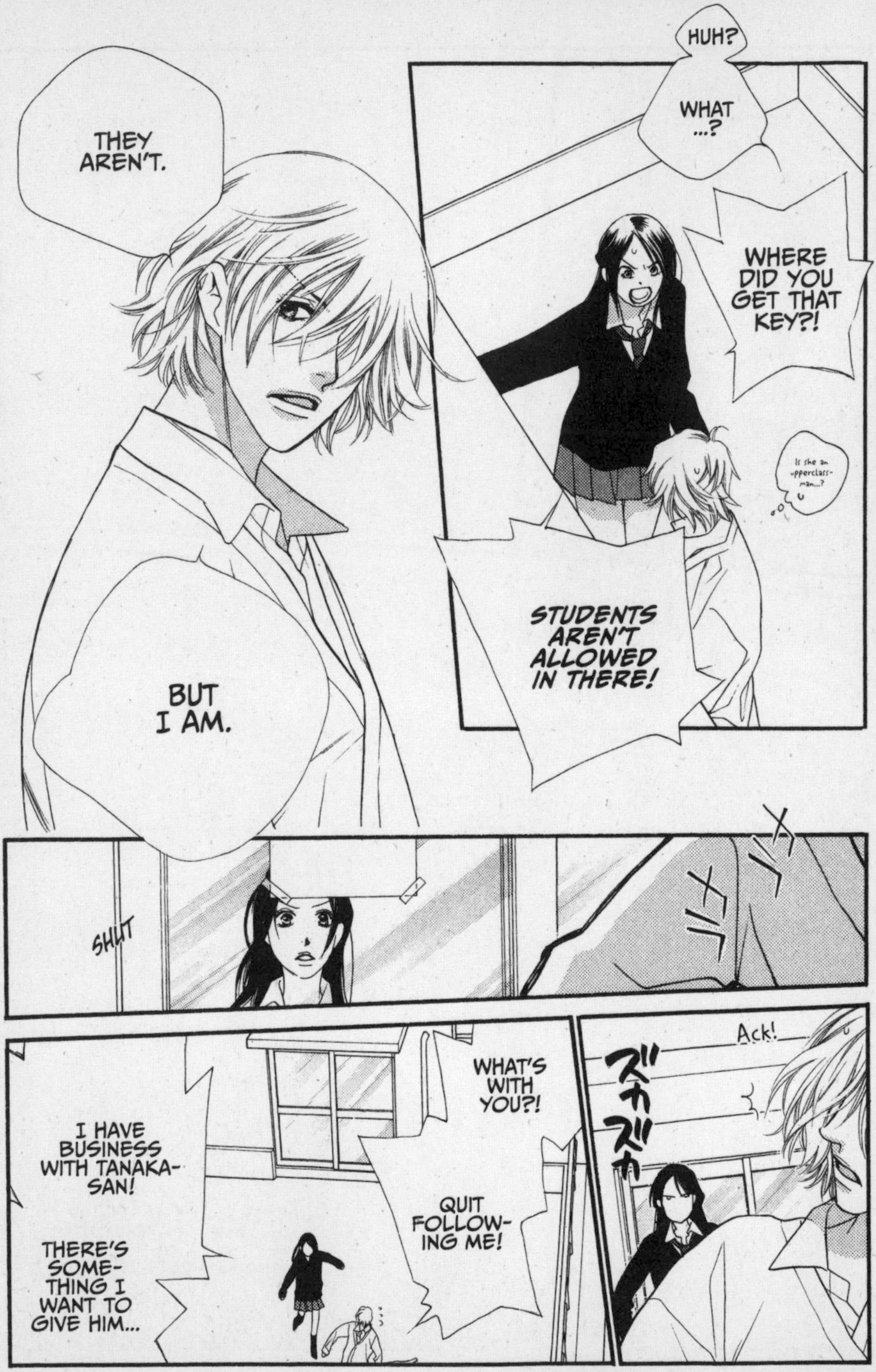
HUH?
WHAT ...?
WHERE DID YOU GET THAT KEY?!
Is she an upperclass-man...?
STUDENTS AREN'T ALLOWED IN THERE!
THEY AREN'T.
BUT I AM.
SHUT
Ack!
ズカズカ
WHAT'S WITH YOU?!
QUIT FOLLOW-ING ME!
I HAVE BUSINESS WITH TANAKA-SAN!
THERE'S SOME-THING I WANT TO GIVE HIM...

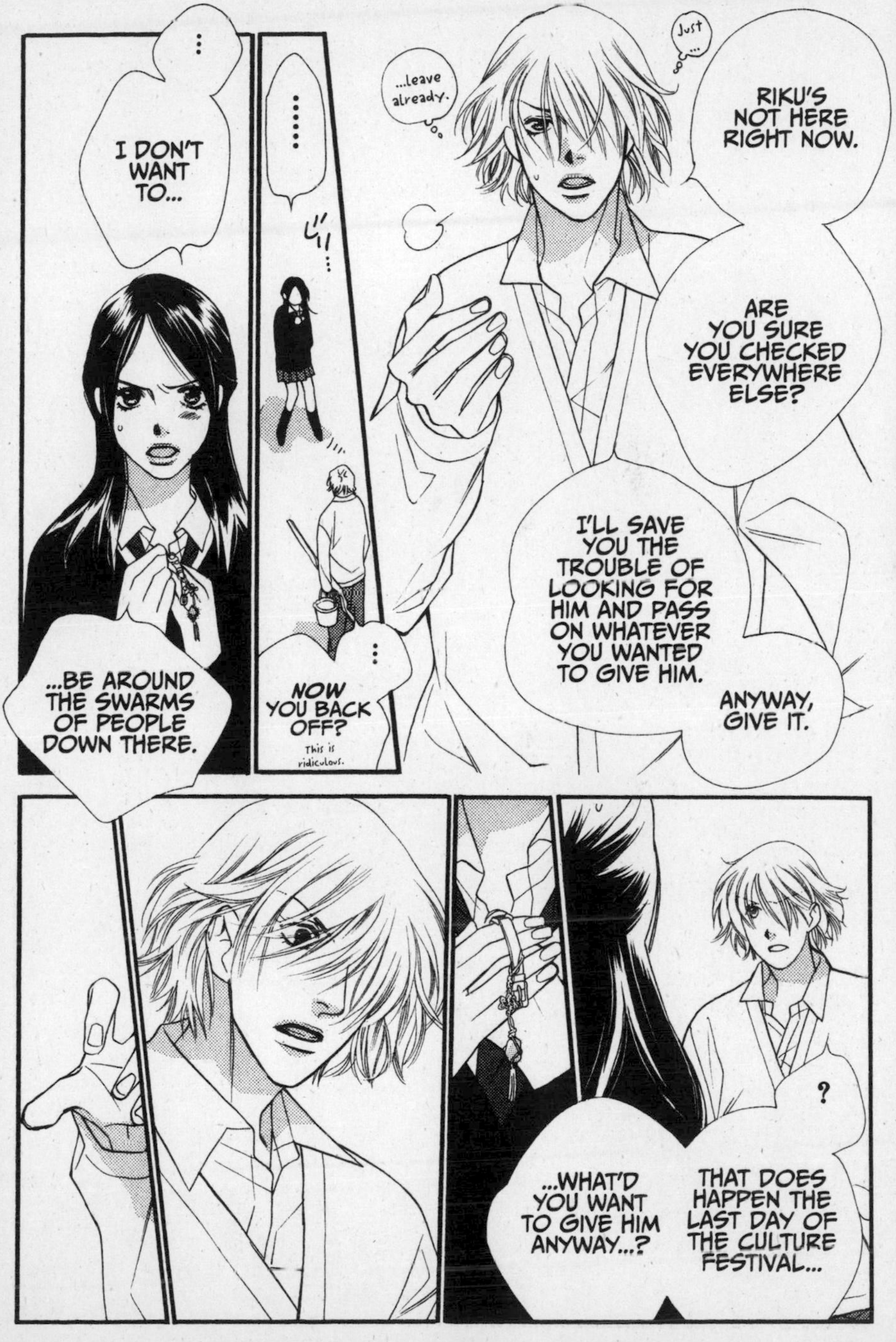
Just ...
RIKU'S NOT HERE RIGHT NOW.
...leave already.
ARE YOU SURE YOU CHECKED EVERYWHERE ELSE?
I'LL SAVE YOU THE TROUBLE OF LOOKING FOR HIM AND PASS ON WHATEVER YOU WANTED TO GIVE HIM.
ANYWAY, GIVE IT.
......
...
NOW YOU BACK OFF?
This is ridiculous.
...
I DON'T WANT TO...
...BE AROUND THE SWARMS OF PEOPLE DOWN THERE.
?
THAT DOES HAPPEN THE LAST DAY OF THE CULTURE FESTIVAL...
...WHAT'D YOU WANT TO GIVE HIM ANYWAY...?

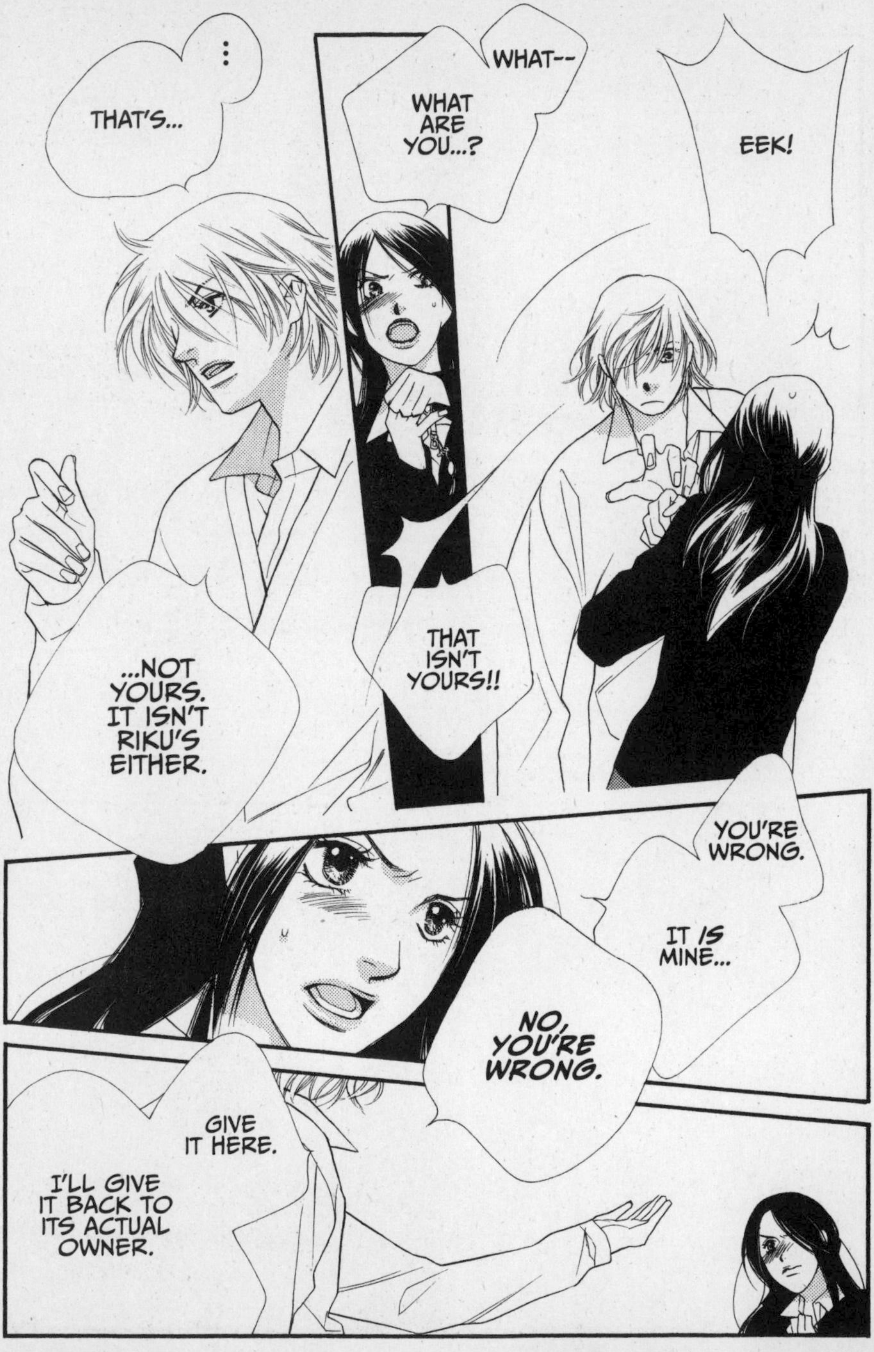
EEK!
WHAT--
WHAT ARE YOU...?
THAT ISN'T YOURS!!
...
THAT'S...
...NOT YOURS. IT ISN'T RIKU'S EITHER.
YOU'RE WRONG.
IT IS MINE...
NO, YOU'RE WRONG.
GIVE IT HERE.
I'LL GIVE IT BACK TO ITS ACTUAL OWNER.

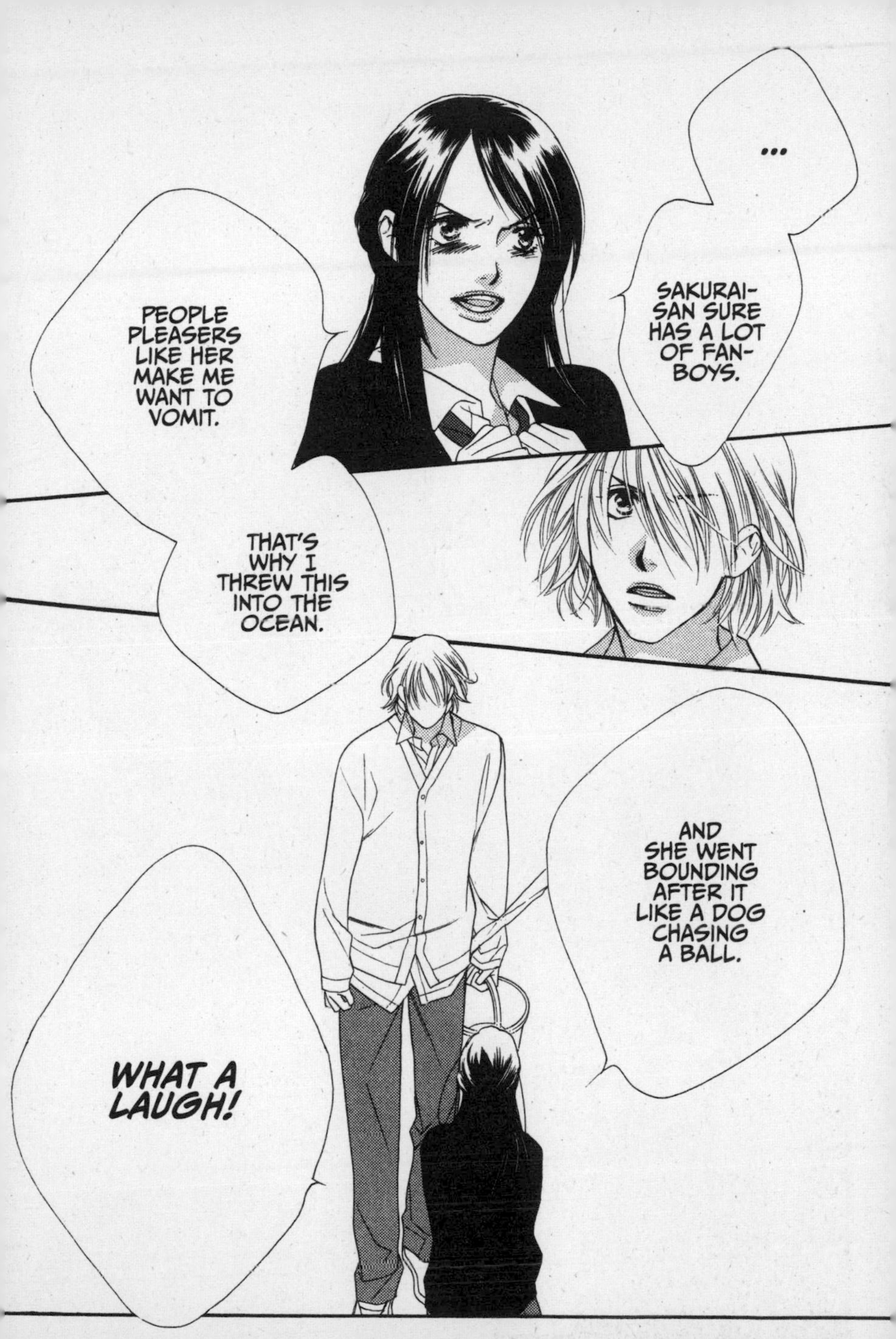
...
SAKURAI-SAN SURE HAS A LOT OF FAN-BOYS.
PEOPLE PLEASERS LIKE HER MAKE ME WANT TO VOMIT.
THAT'S WHY I THREW THIS INTO THE OCEAN.
AND SHE WENT BOUNDING AFTER IT LIKE A DOG CHASING A BALL.
WHAT A LAUGH!

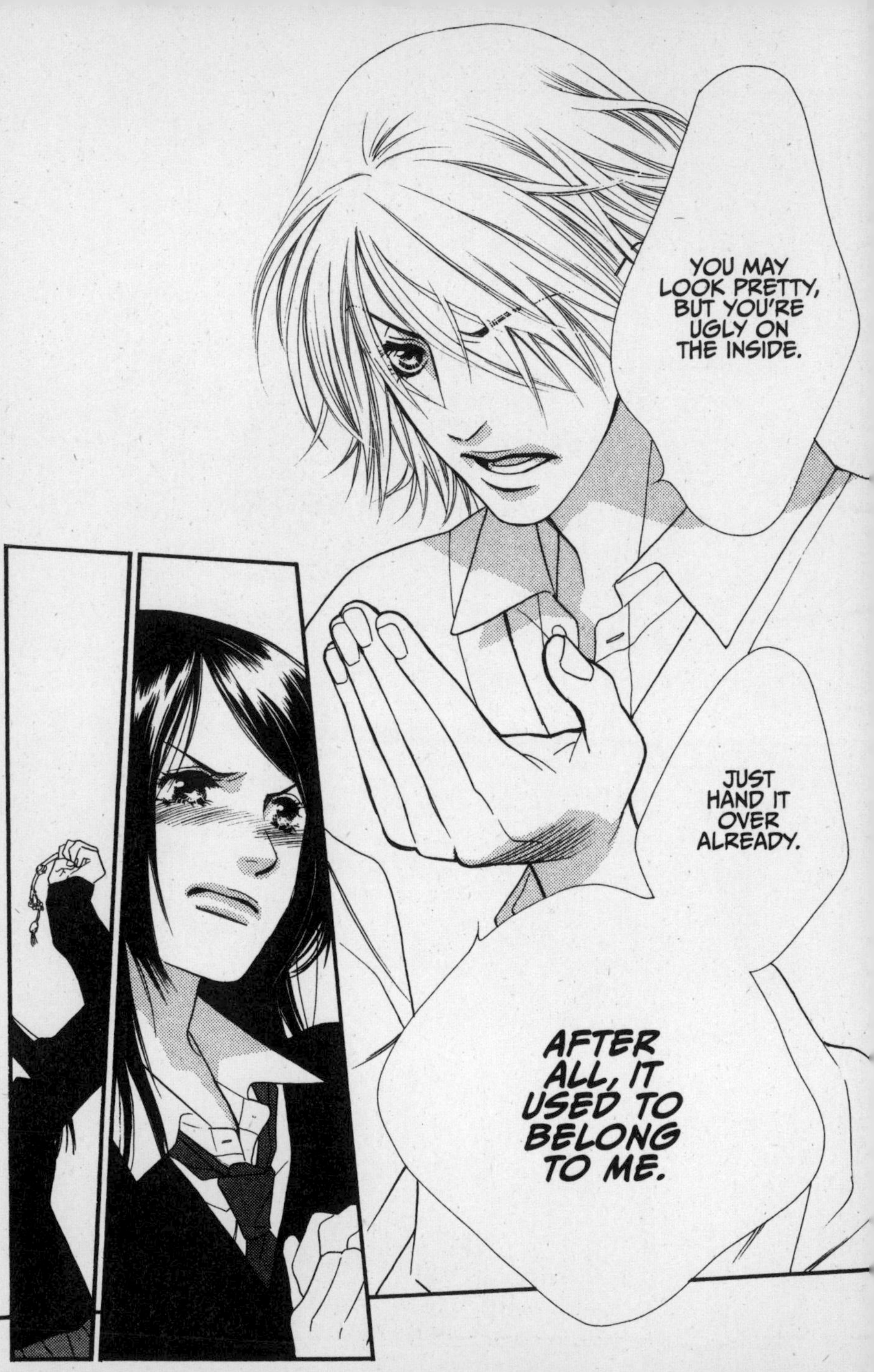
YOU MAY LOOK PRETTY, BUT YOU'RE UGLY ON THE INSIDE.
JUST HAND IT OVER ALREADY.
AFTER ALL, IT USED TO BELONG TO ME.

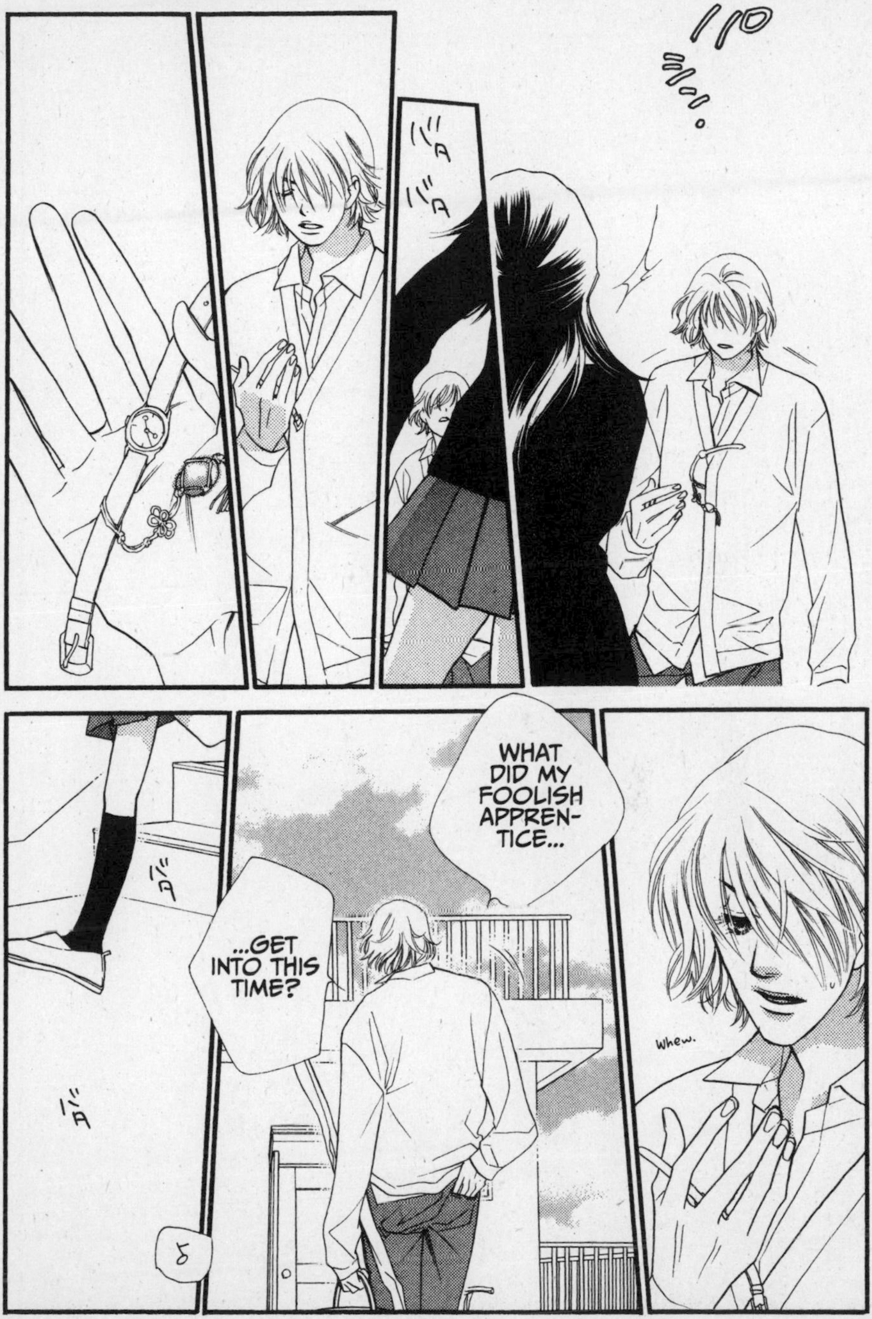
Whew.
WHAT DID MY FOOLISH APPREN- TICE...
...GET INTO THIS TIME?

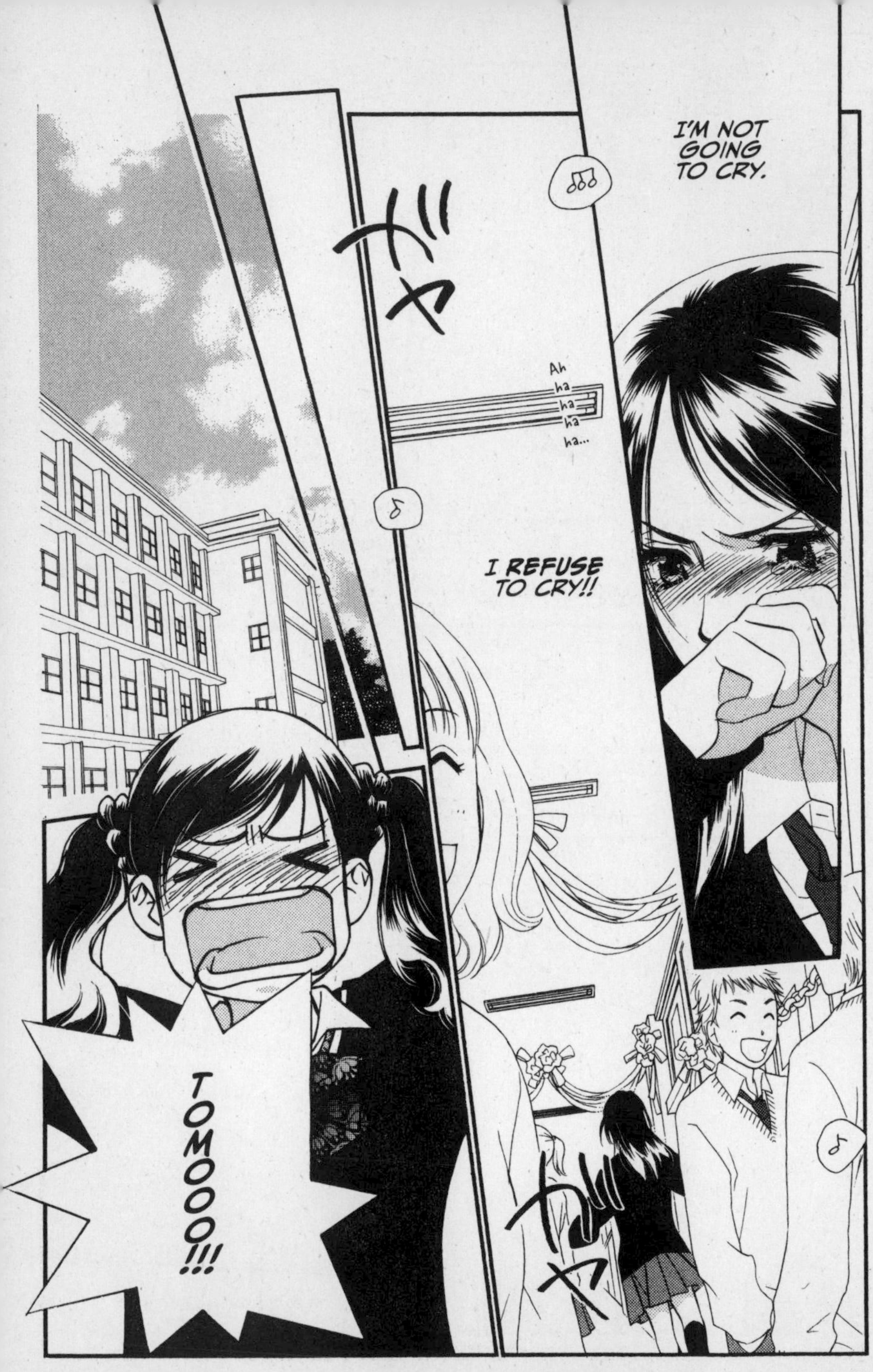
I'M NOT GOING TO CRY.
Ah ha ha ha ha...
I REFUSE TO CRY!!
TOMOOOO!!!

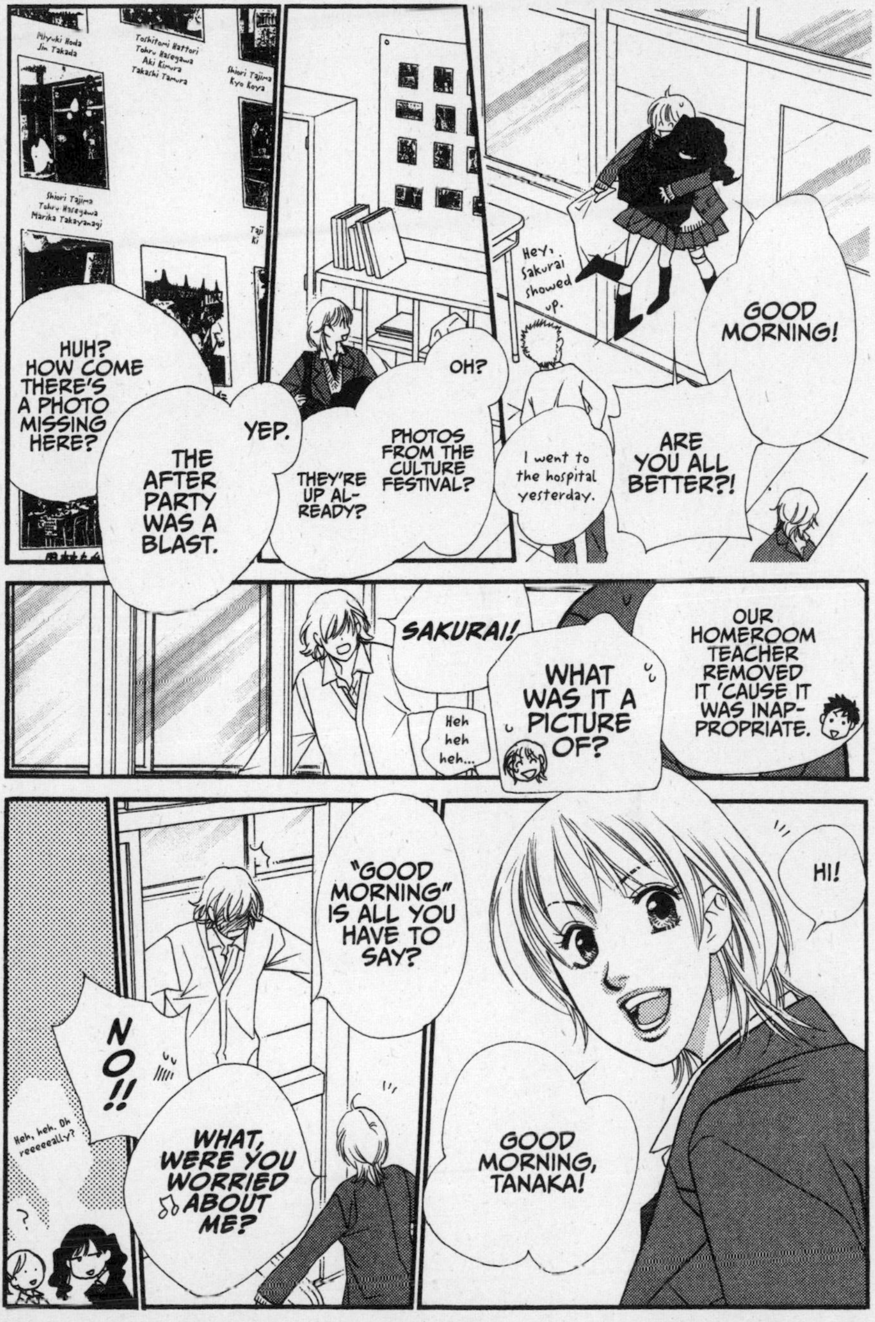
GOOD MORNING!
Hey, Sakurai showed up.
ARE YOU ALL BETTER?!
I went to the hospital yesterday.
OH?
PHOTOS FROM THE CULTURE FESTIVAL?
THEY'RE UP AL-READY?
YEP.
THE AFTER PARTY WAS A BLAST.
Toshitomi Hattori Tohru Hasegawa Aki Kimura Takashi Tamura
Shiori Tajima Kyo Koya
Miyuki Hoda Jim Takada
Shiori Tajima Tohru Hasegawa Marika Takayanagi
HUH? HOW COME THERE'S A PHOTO MISSING HERE?
OUR HOMEROOM TEACHER REMOVED IT 'CAUSE IT WAS INAP-PROPRIATE.
WHAT WAS IT A PICTURE OF?
SAKURAI!
Heh heh heh...
HI!
GOOD MORNING, TANAKA!
"GOOD MORNING" IS ALL YOU HAVE TO SAY?
WHAT, WERE YOU WORRIED ABOUT ME?
NO!!
Heh, heh. Oh reeeeeally?
?

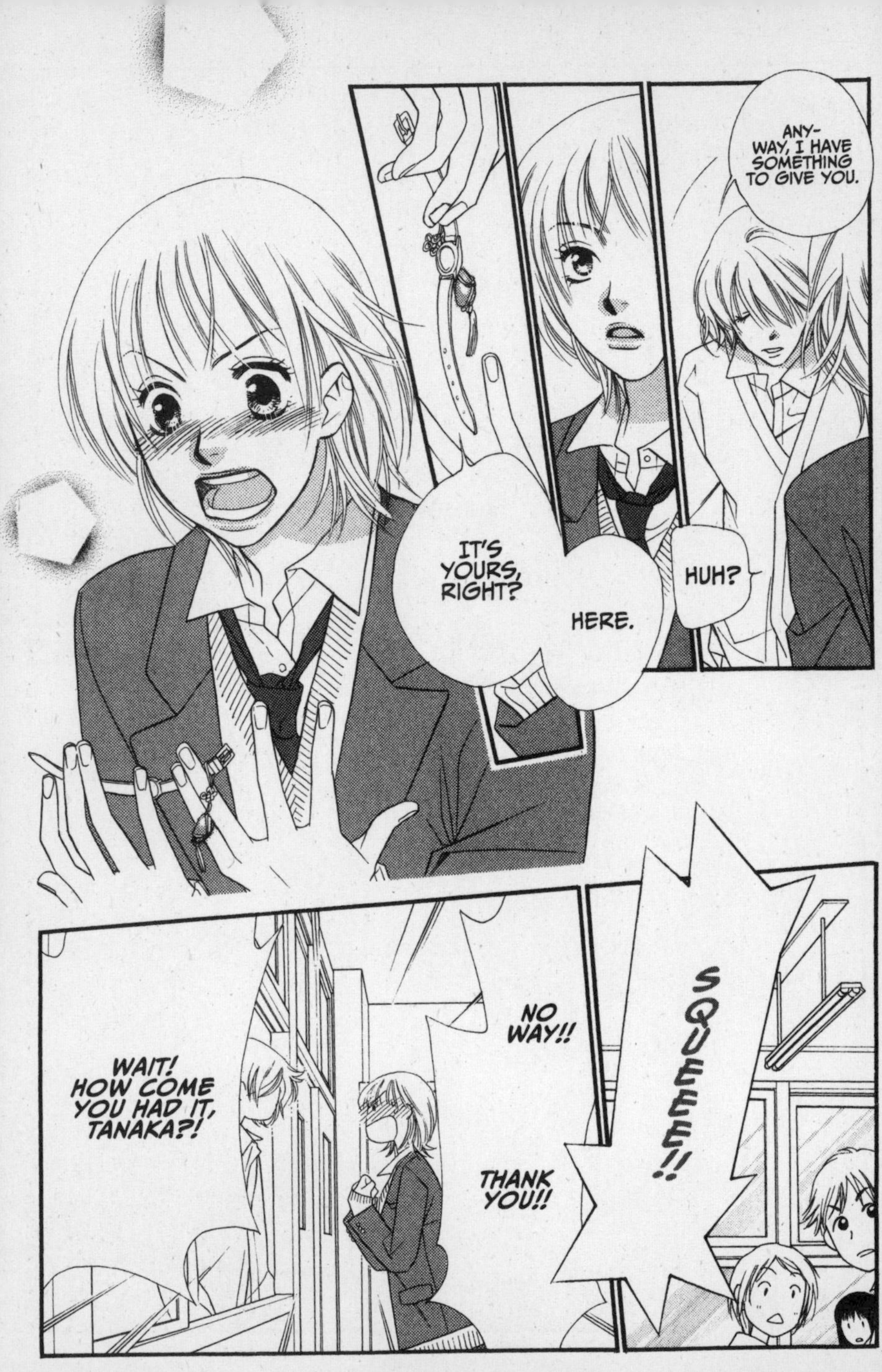
ANY-WAY, I HAVE SOMETHING TO GIVE YOU.
HUH?
HERE.
IT'S YOURS, RIGHT?
SQUEEEE!!
NO WAY!!
THANK YOU!!
WAIT! HOW COME YOU HAD IT, TANAKA?!

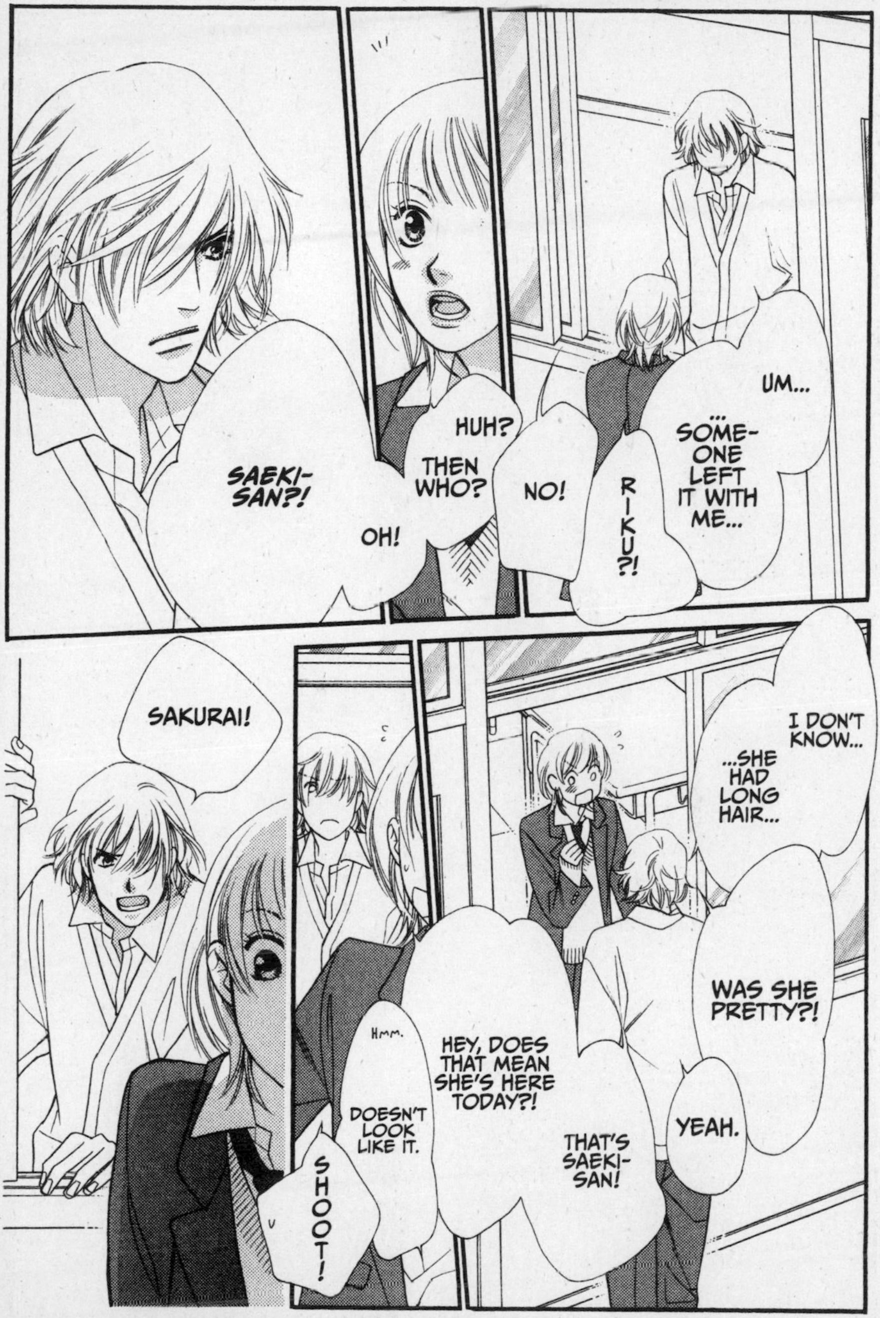
UM...
...SOME-ONE LEFT IT WITH ME...
RIKU?!
NO!
HUH?
THEN WHO?
OH!
SAEKI-SAN?!
I DON'T KNOW...
...SHE HAD LONG HAIR...
WAS SHE PRETTY?!
YEAH.
THAT'S SAEKI-SAN!
HEY, DOES THAT MEAN SHE'S HERE TODAY?!
HMM.
DOESN'T LOOK LIKE IT.
SHOOT!
SAKURAI!

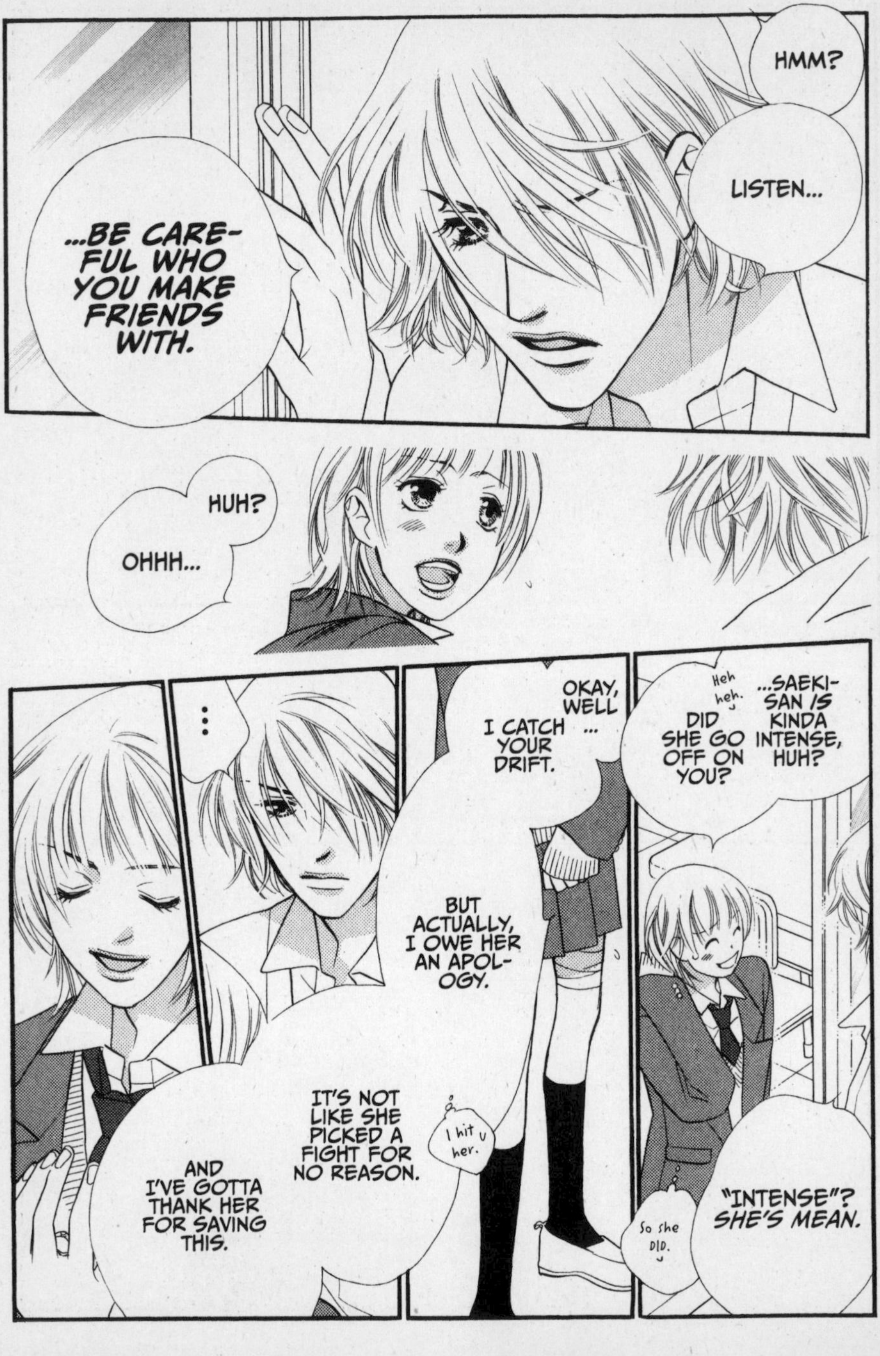
HMM?
LISTEN...
...BE CARE-FUL WHO YOU MAKE FRIENDS WITH.
HUH?
OHHH...
...SAEKI-SAN IS KINDA INTENSE, HUH?
Heh heh.
DID SHE GO OFF ON YOU?
"INTENSE"? SHE'S MEAN.
So she DID.
OKAY, WELL ...
I CATCH YOUR DRIFT.
BUT ACTUALLY, I OWE HER AN APOL-OGY.
I hit her.
IT'S NOT LIKE SHE PICKED A FIGHT FOR NO REASON.
...
AND I'VE GOTTA THANK HER FOR SAVING THIS.

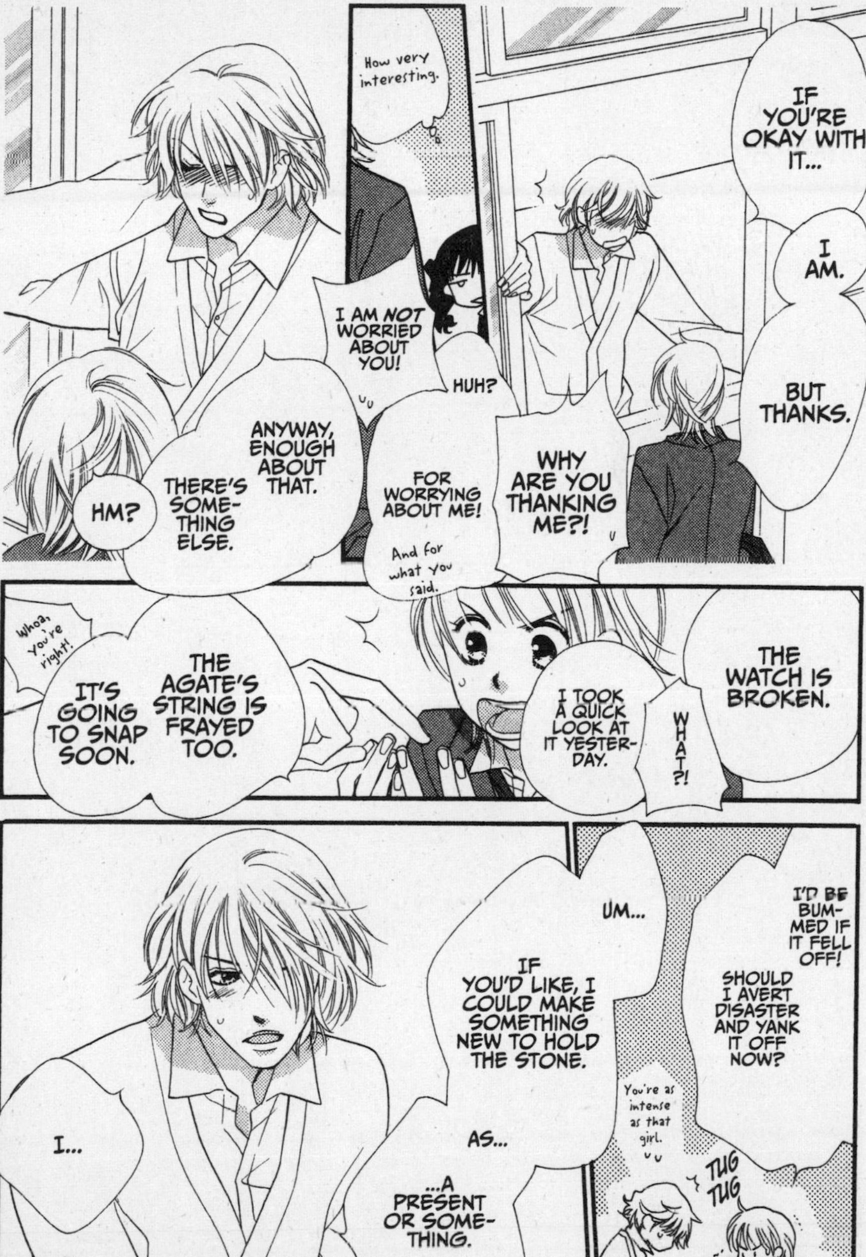
IF YOU'RE OKAY WITH IT...
How very interesting.
I AM.
BUT THANKS.
WHY ARE YOU THANKING ME?!
HUH?
I AM *NOT* WORRIED ABOUT YOU!
FOR WORRYING ABOUT ME!
And for what you said.
ANYWAY, ENOUGH ABOUT THAT.
THERE'S SOME-THING ELSE.
HM?
THE WATCH IS BROKEN.
WHAT?!
I TOOK A QUICK LOOK AT IT YESTER-DAY.
THE AGATE'S STRING IS FRAYED TOO.
IT'S GOING TO SNAP SOON.
Whoa, you're right!
I'D BE BUM-MED IF IT FELL OFF!
SHOULD I AVERT DISASTER AND YANK IT OFF NOW?
You're as intense as that girl.
TUG TUG
UM...
IF YOU'D LIKE, I COULD MAKE SOMETHING NEW TO HOLD THE STONE.
AS...
...A PRESENT OR SOME-THING.
I...

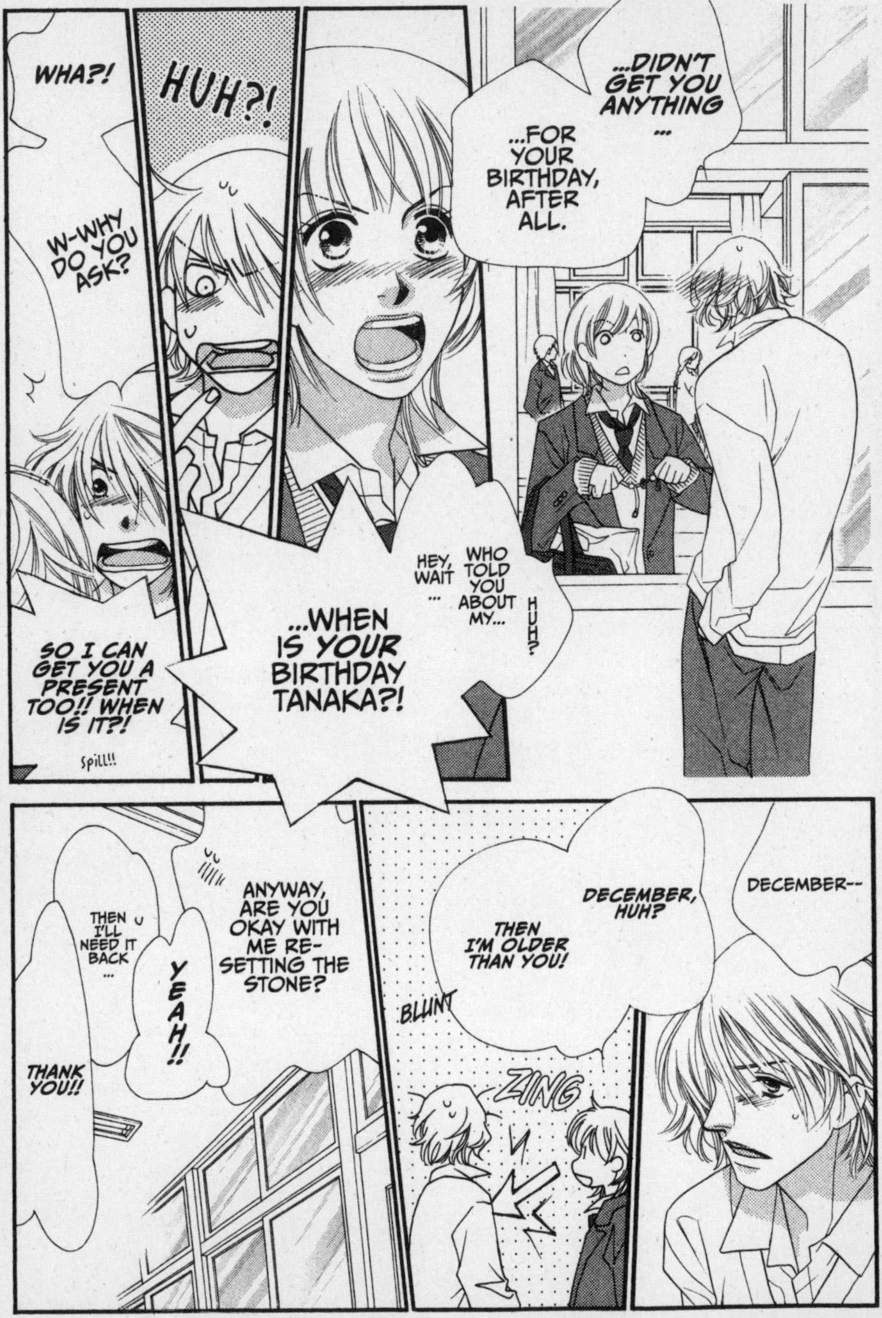

...DIDN'T GET YOU ANYTHING ...
...FOR YOUR BIRTHDAY, AFTER ALL.
HEY, WAIT ...
WHO TOLD YOU ABOUT MY...
HUH?
...WHEN IS YOUR BIRTHDAY TANAKA?!
HUH?!
WHA?!
W-WHY DO YOU ASK?
SO I CAN GET YOU A PRESENT TOO!! WHEN IS IT?!
Spill!!
DECEMBER--
DECEMBER, HUH?
THEN I'M OLDER THAN YOU!
BLUNT
ZING
ANYWAY, ARE YOU OKAY WITH ME RE-SETTING THE STONE?
YEAH!!
THEN I'LL NEED IT BACK ...
THANK YOU!!

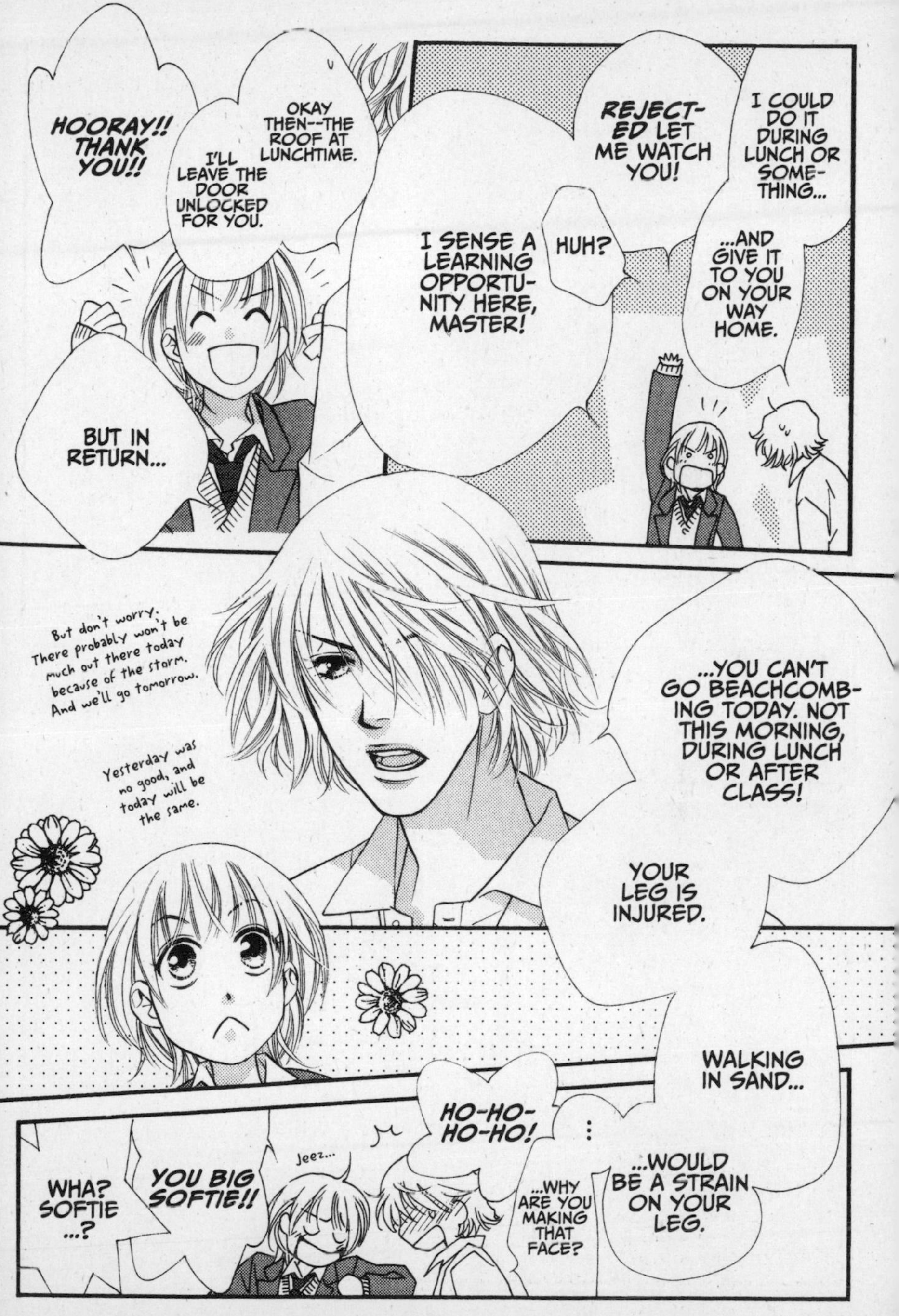
I COULD DO IT DURING LUNCH OR SOME-THING...
...AND GIVE IT TO YOU ON YOUR WAY HOME.
REJECT-ED LET ME WATCH YOU!
HUH?
I SENSE A LEARNING OPPORTU-NITY HERE, MASTER!
OKAY THEN--THE ROOF AT LUNCHTIME.
I'LL LEAVE THE DOOR UNLOCKED FOR YOU.
HOORAY!! THANK YOU!!
BUT IN RETURN...
...YOU CAN'T GO BEACHCOMB-ING TODAY. NOT THIS MORNING, DURING LUNCH OR AFTER CLASS!
YOUR LEG IS INJURED.
WALKING IN SAND...
But don't worry. There probably won't be much out there today because of the storm. And we'll go tomorrow.
Yesterday was no good, and today will be the same.
...WOULD BE A STRAIN ON YOUR LEG.
HO-HO-HO-HO!
...WHY ARE YOU MAKING THAT FACE?
Jeez...
YOU BIG SOFTIE!!
WHA? SOFTIE ...?

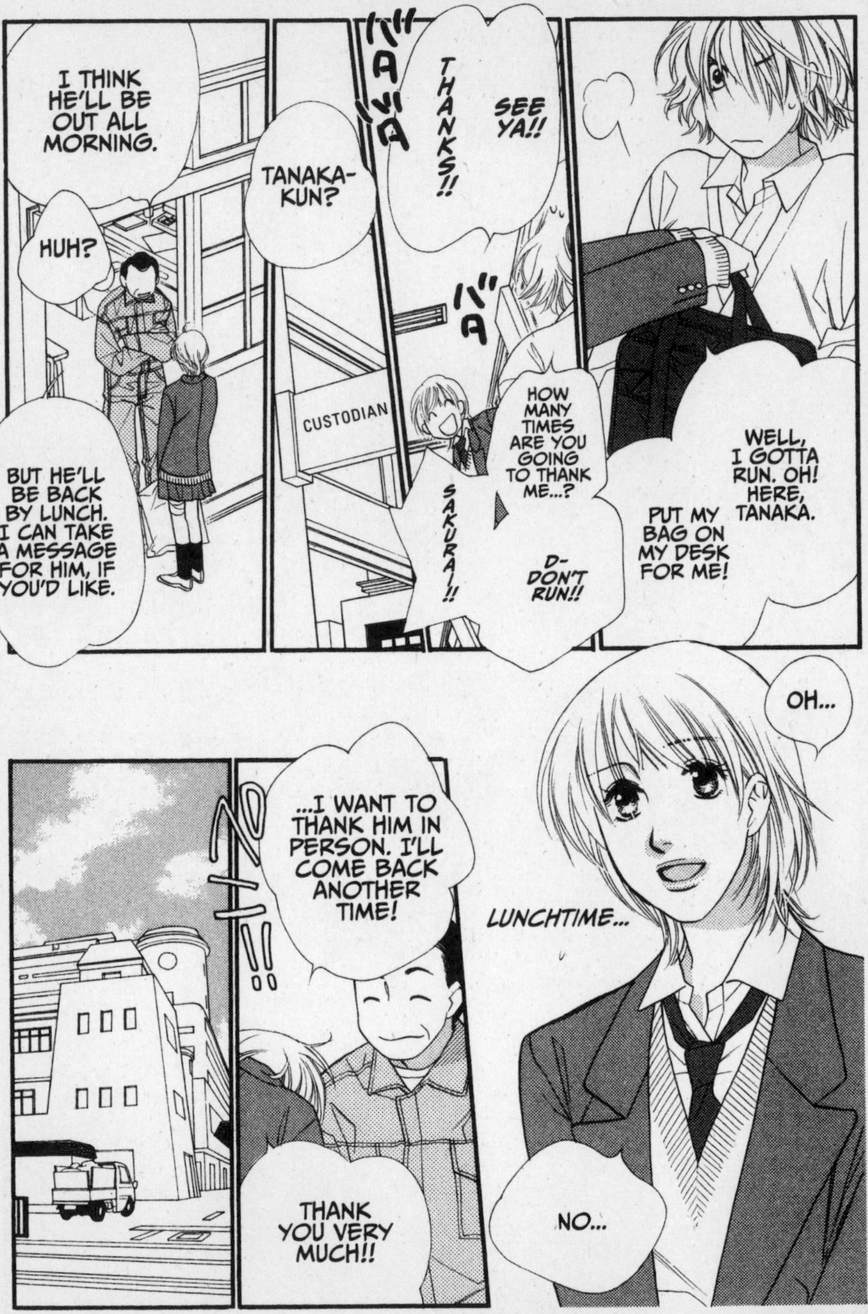
WELL, I GOTTA RUN. OH! HERE, TANAKA.
PUT MY BAG ON MY DESK FOR ME!
SEE YA!!
THANKS!!
バババ
TANAKA-KUN?
HOW MANY TIMES ARE YOU GOING TO THANK ME...?
D-DON'T RUN!!
SAKURAI!!
バタ
I THINK HE'LL BE OUT ALL MORNING.
HUH?
BUT HE'LL BE BACK BY LUNCH. I CAN TAKE A MESSAGE FOR HIM, IF YOU'D LIKE.
OH...
LUNCHTIME...
NO...
...I WANT TO THANK HIM IN PERSON. I'LL COME BACK ANOTHER TIME!
ペコー!!
THANK YOU VERY MUCH!!

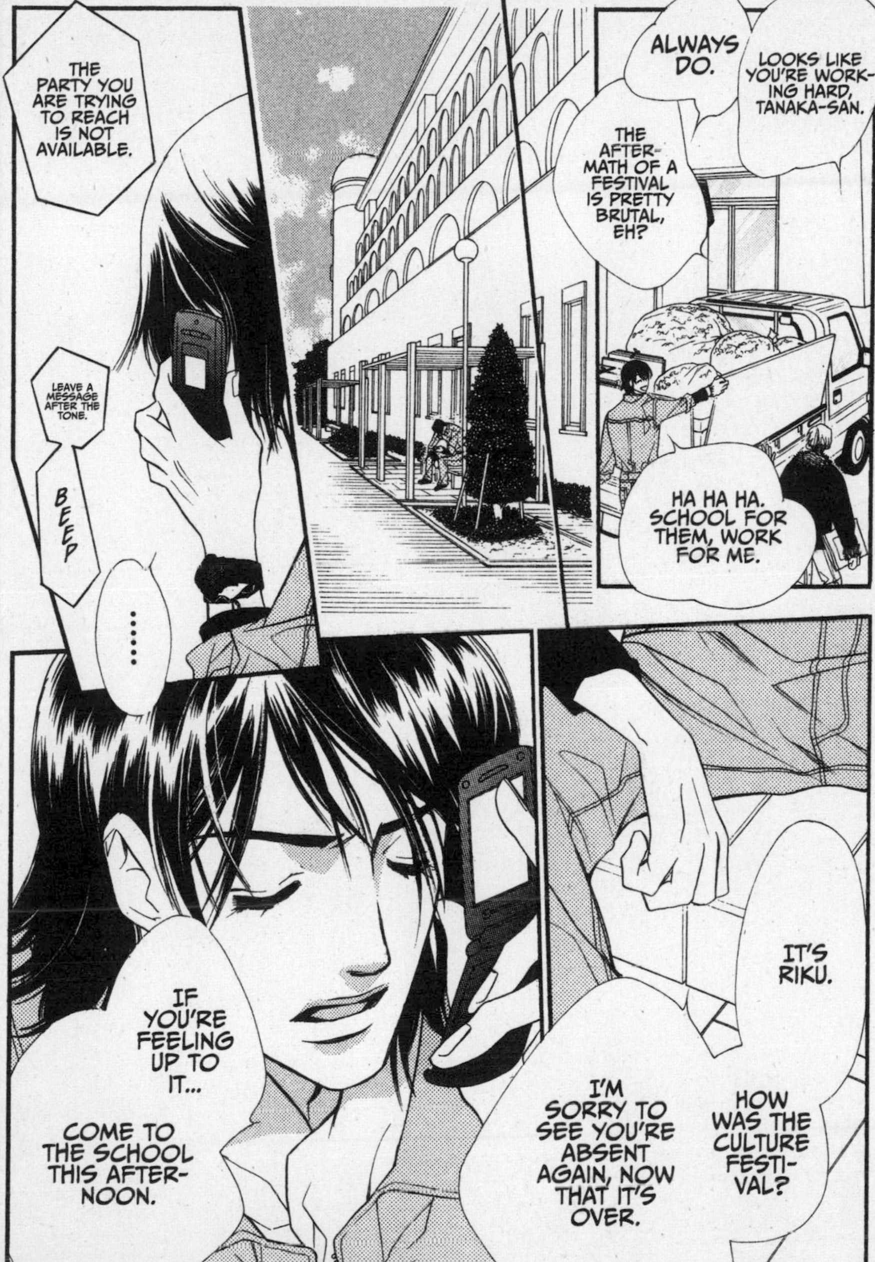
LOOKS LIKE YOU'RE WORKING HARD, TANAKA-SAN.
ALWAYS DO.
THE AFTERMATH OF A FESTIVAL IS PRETTY BRUTAL, EH?
HA HA HA. SCHOOL FOR THEM, WORK FOR ME.
THE PARTY YOU ARE TRYING TO REACH IS NOT AVAILABLE.
LEAVE A MESSAGE AFTER THE TONE.
BEEP
......
IT'S RIKU.
HOW WAS THE CULTURE FESTIVAL?
I'M SORRY TO SEE YOU'RE ABSENT AGAIN, NOW THAT IT'S OVER.
IF YOU'RE FEELING UP TO IT...
COME TO THE SCHOOL THIS AFTERNOON.

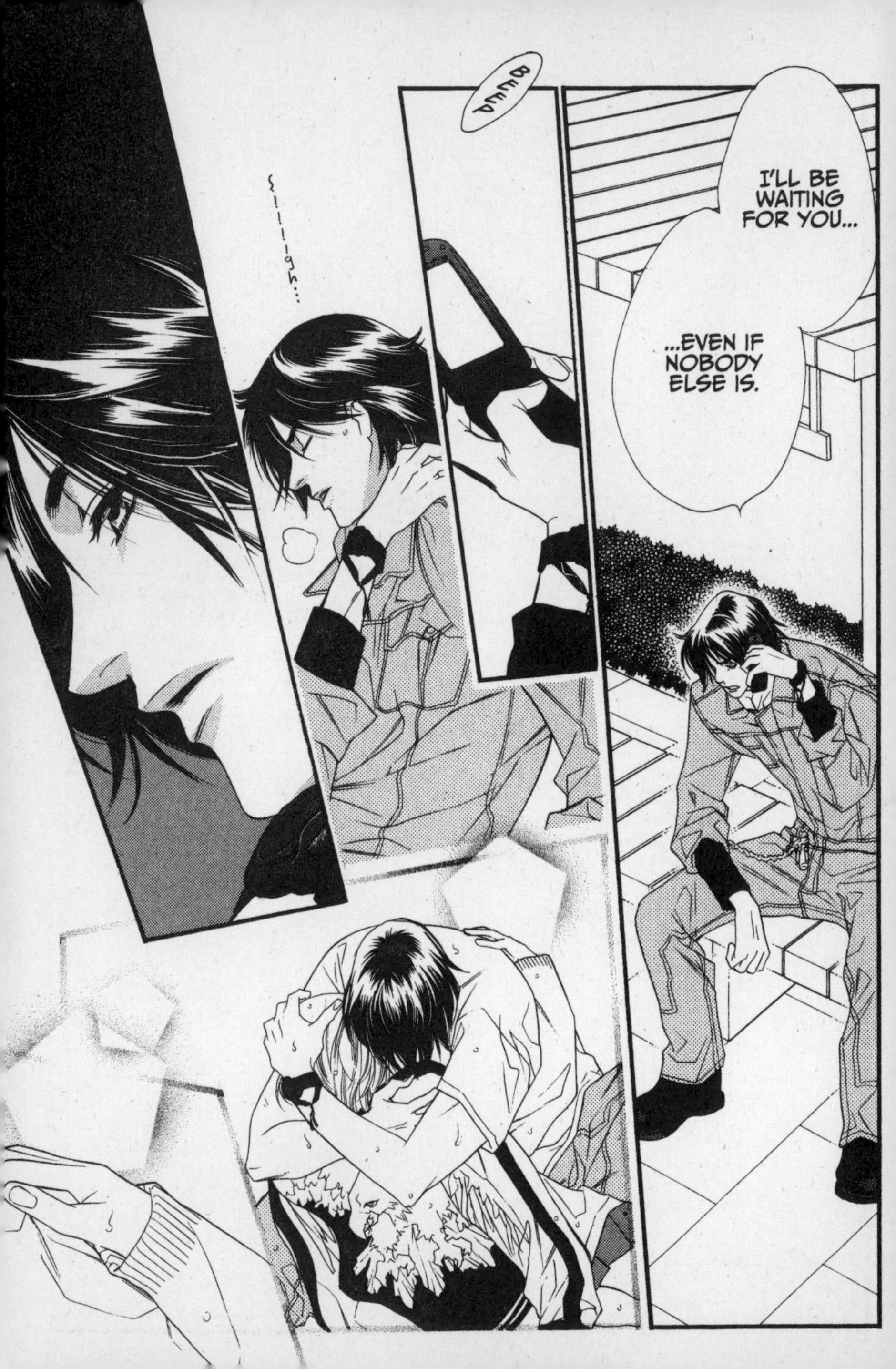
I'LL BE WAITING FOR YOU...
...EVEN IF NOBODY ELSE IS.
BEEP
si...igh...

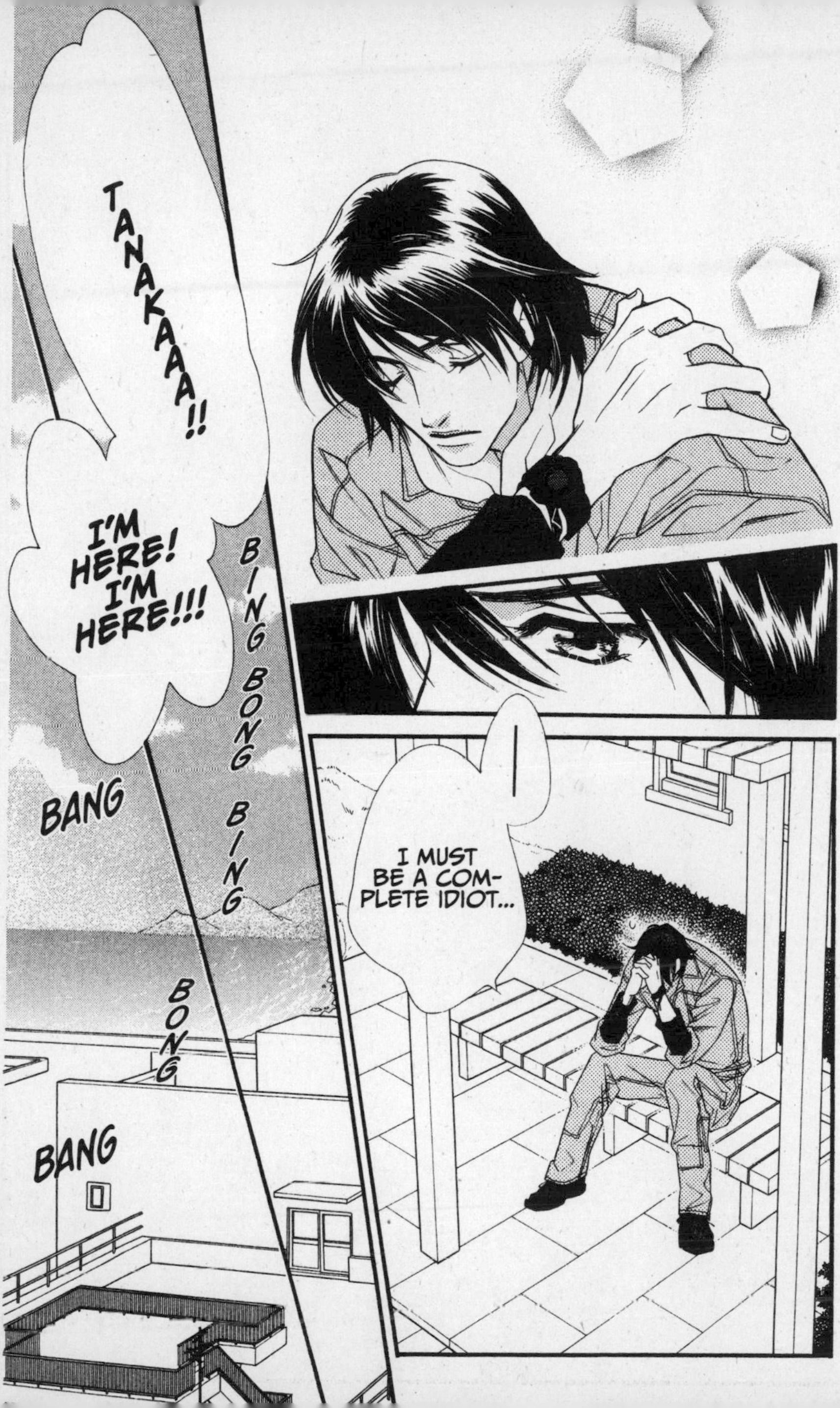
!
I MUST BE A COMPLETE IDIOT...
TANAKAAAA!!
I'M HERE! I'M HERE!!!
BING BONG BING BONG
BANG
BANG

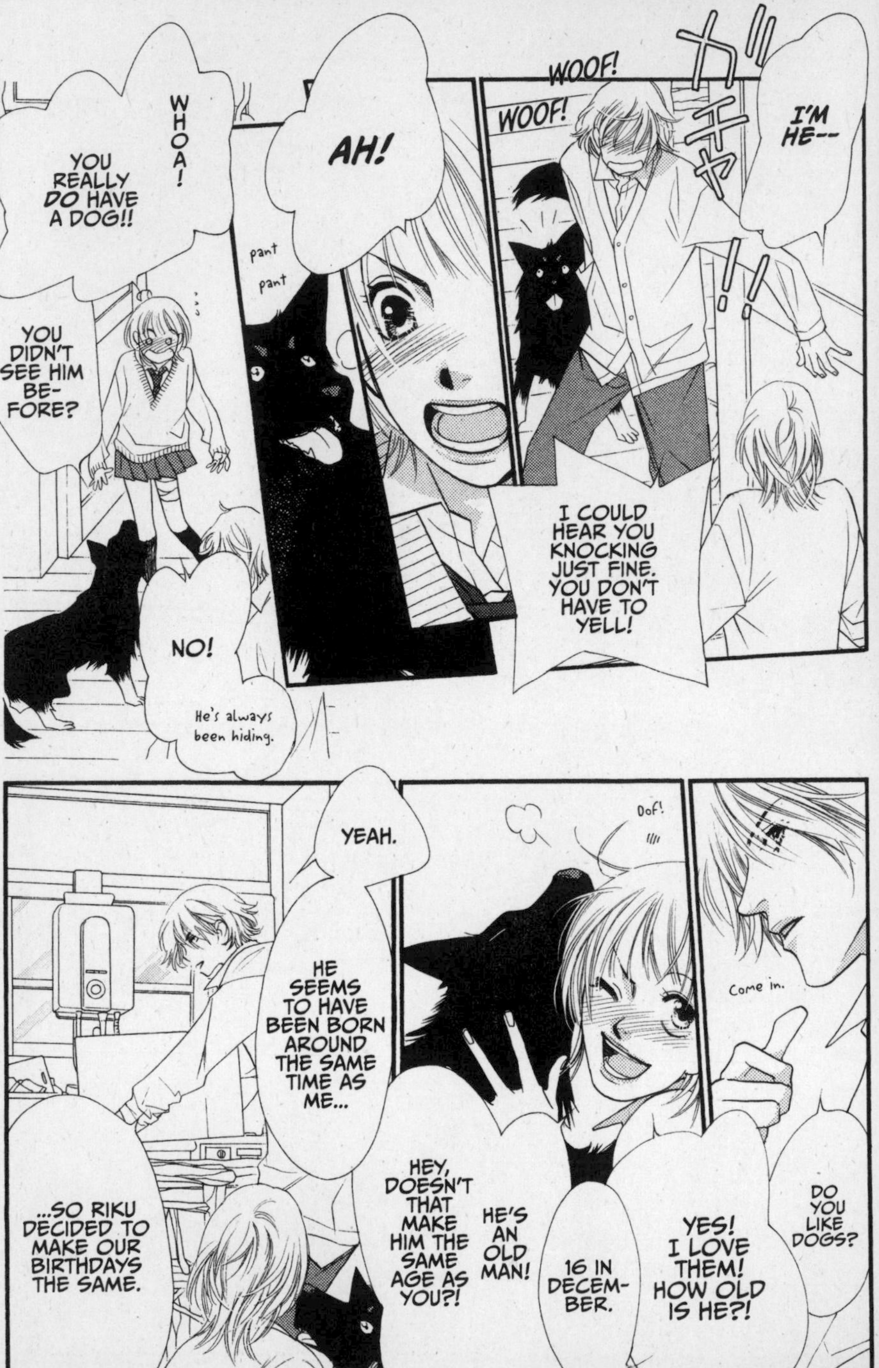

ガチャ!!
I'M HE--
WOOF!
WOOF!
I COULD HEAR YOU KNOCKING JUST FINE. YOU DON'T HAVE TO YELL!
AH!
pant
pant
WHOA!
YOU REALLY DO HAVE A DOG!!
YOU DIDN'T SEE HIM BEFORE?
NO!
He's always been hiding.
Come in.
DO YOU LIKE DOGS?
YES! I LOVE THEM! HOW OLD IS HE?!
Oof!
16 IN DECEMBER.
HE'S AN OLD MAN!
HEY, DOESN'T THAT MAKE HIM THE SAME AGE AS YOU?!
YEAH.
HE SEEMS TO HAVE BEEN BORN AROUND THE SAME TIME AS ME...
...SO RIKU DECIDED TO MAKE OUR BIRTHDAYS THE SAME.

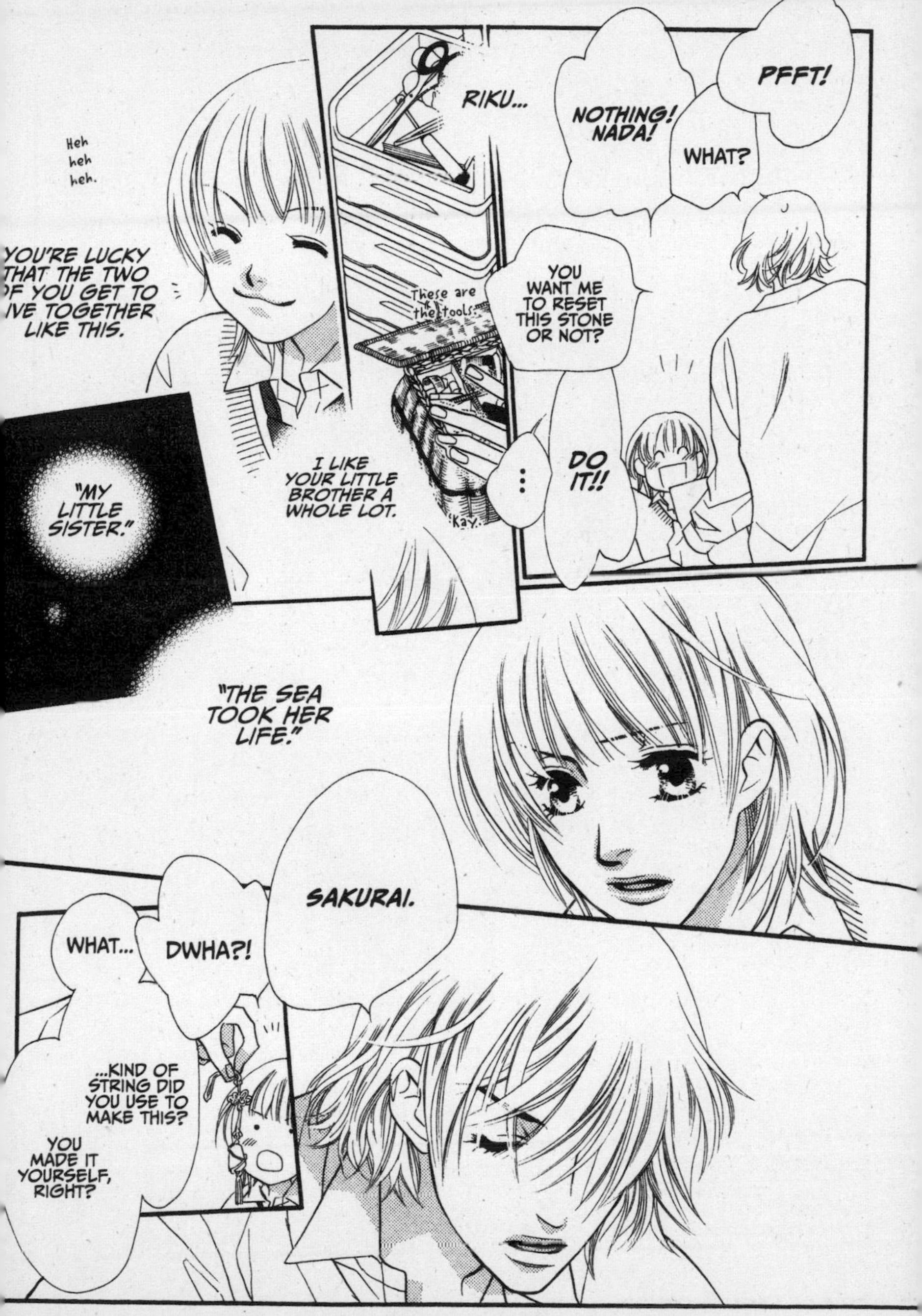
PFFT!
WHAT?
NOTHING! NADA!
YOU WANT ME TO RESET THIS STONE OR NOT?
DO IT!!
...
RIKU...
These are the tools.
'Kay.
I LIKE YOUR LITTLE BROTHER A WHOLE LOT.
Heh heh heh.
YOU'RE LUCKY THAT THE TWO F YOU GET TO IVE TOGETHER LIKE THIS.
"MY LITTLE SISTER."
"THE SEA TOOK HER LIFE."
SAKURAI.
DWHA?!
WHAT...
...KIND OF STRING DID YOU USE TO MAKE THIS?
YOU MADE IT YOURSELF, RIGHT?

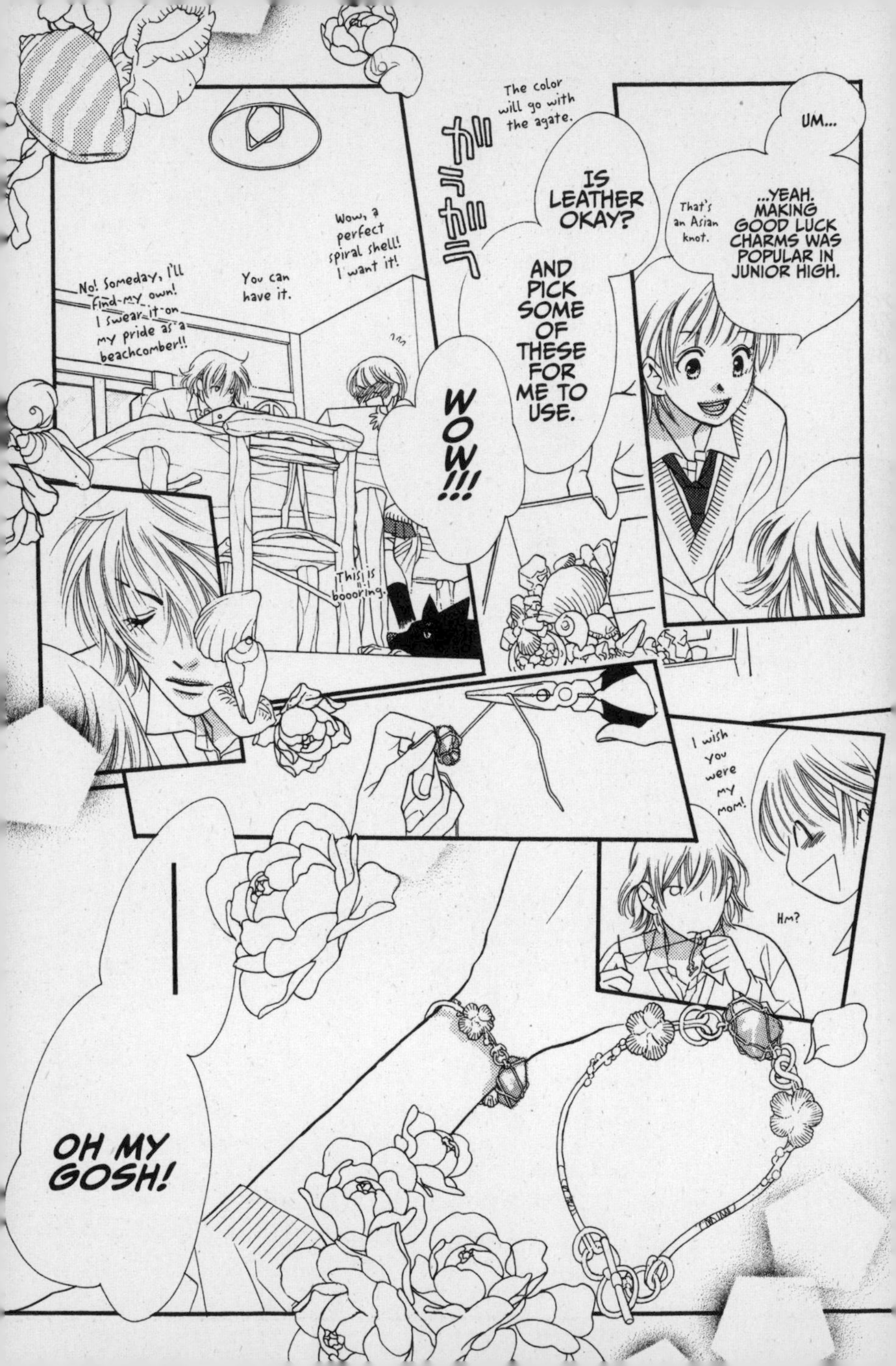
UM...
...YEAH. MAKING GOOD LUCK CHARMS WAS POPULAR IN JUNIOR HIGH.
That's an Asian knot.
The color will go with the agate.
IS LEATHER OKAY?
AND PICK SOME OF THESE FOR ME TO USE.
WOW!!!
Wow, a perfect spiral shell! I want it!
You can have it.
No! Someday, I'll find my own! I swear it on my pride as a beachcomber!!
This is booooring.
I wish you were my mom!
Hm?
OH MY GOSH!

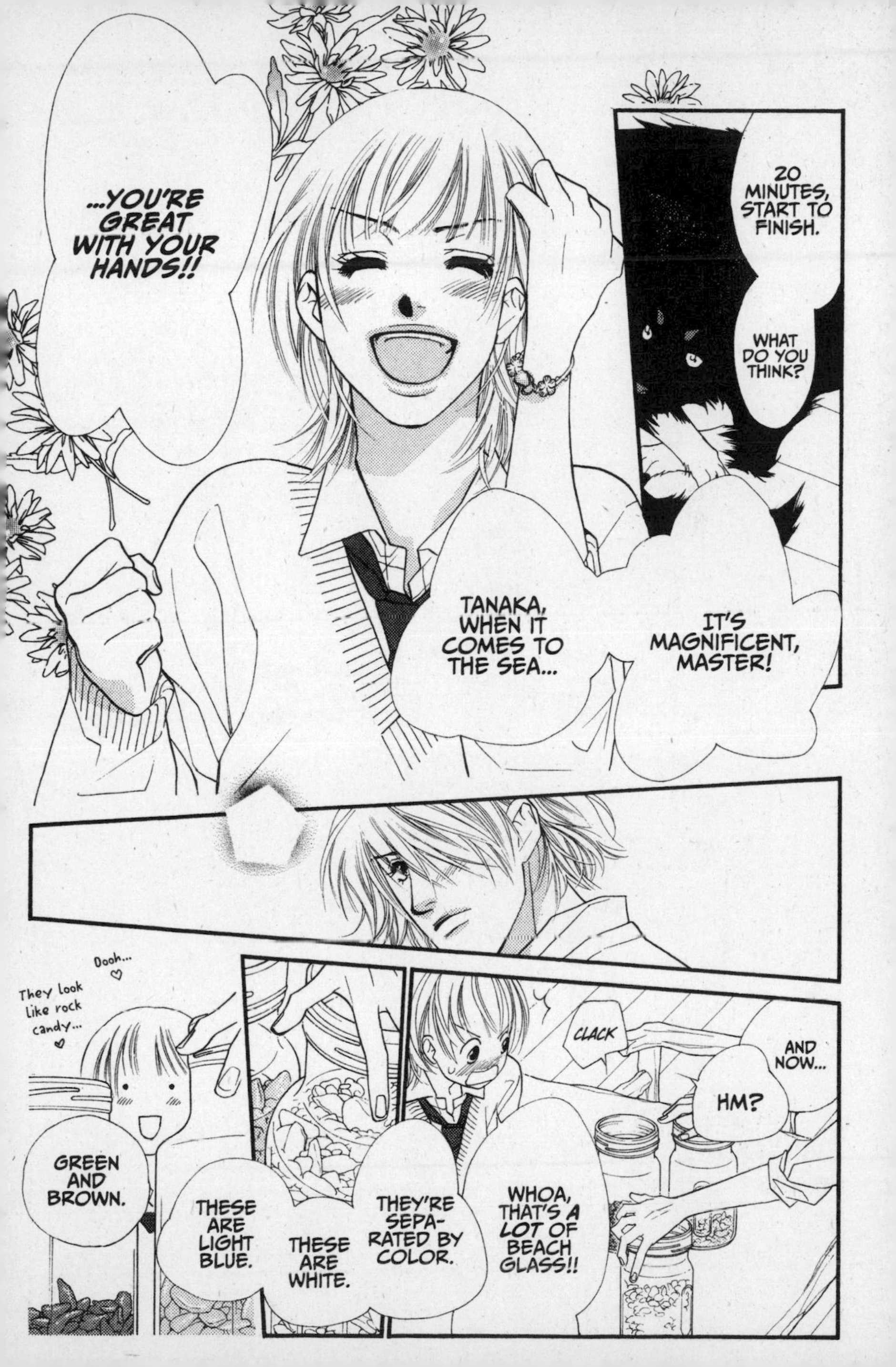
20 MINUTES, START TO FINISH.
WHAT DO YOU THINK?
IT'S MAGNIFICENT, MASTER!
TANAKA, WHEN IT COMES TO THE SEA...
...YOU'RE GREAT WITH YOUR HANDS!!
AND NOW...
HM?
CLACK
WHOA, THAT'S A *LOT* OF BEACH GLASS!!
THEY'RE SEPA-RATED BY COLOR.
THESE ARE WHITE.
THESE ARE LIGHT BLUE.
GREEN AND BROWN.
Oooh... ♡
They look like rock candy... ♡

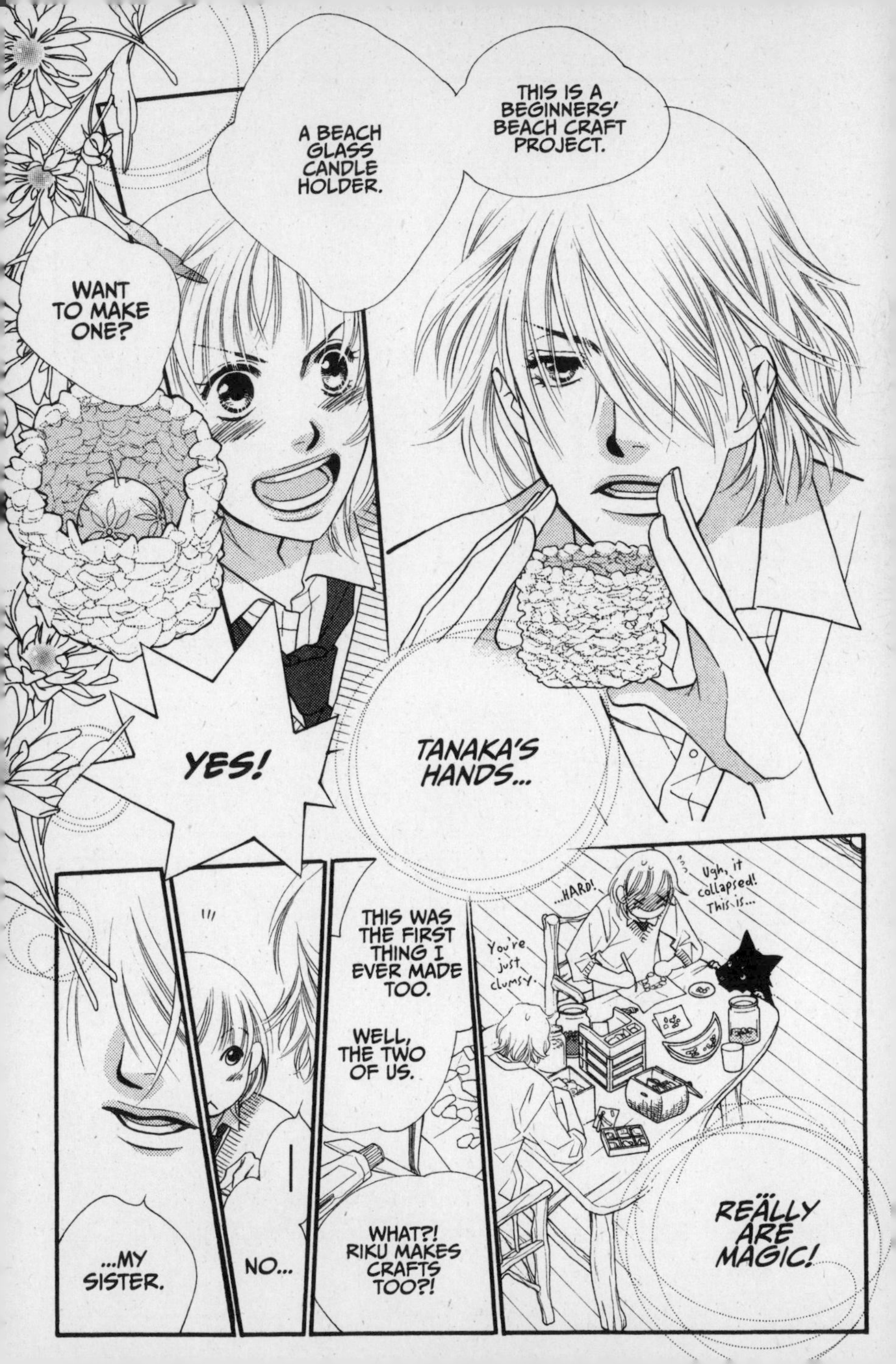

THIS IS A BEGINNERS' BEACH CRAFT PROJECT.
A BEACH GLASS CANDLE HOLDER.
WANT TO MAKE ONE?
YES!
TANAKA'S HANDS...
Ugh, it collapsed! This is...
...HARD!
You're just clumsy.
...REALLY ARE MAGIC!
THIS WAS THE FIRST THING I EVER MADE TOO.
WELL, THE TWO OF US.
WHAT?! RIKU MAKES CRAFTS TOO?!
NO...
...MY SISTER.

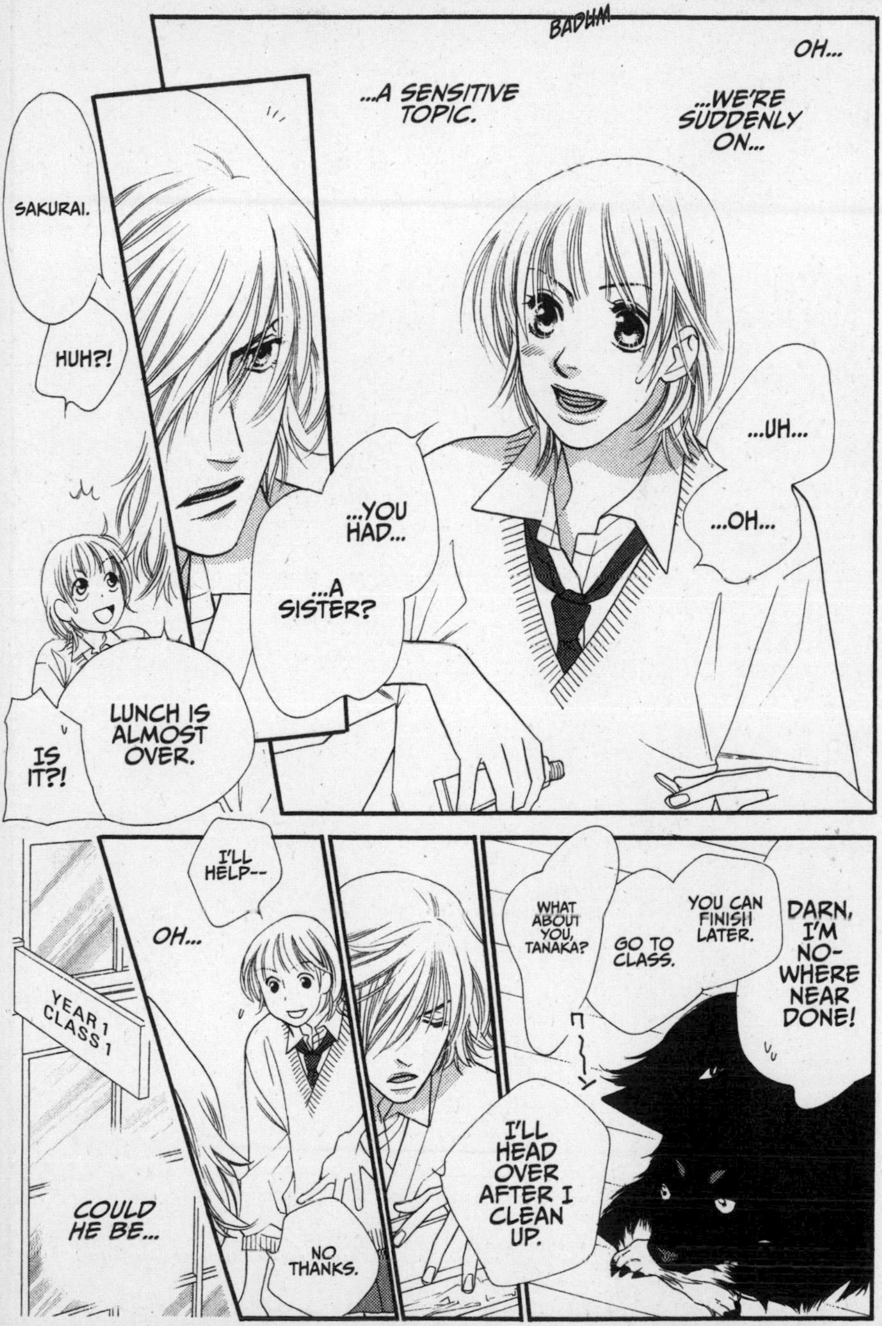
BADUM
OH...
...WE'RE SUDDENLY ON...
...A SENSITIVE TOPIC.
...UH...
...OH...
...YOU HAD...
...A SISTER?
SAKURAI.
HUH?!
LUNCH IS ALMOST OVER.
IS IT?!
DARN, I'M NO-WHERE NEAR DONE!
YOU CAN FINISH LATER.
GO TO CLASS.
WHAT ABOUT YOU, TANAKA?
I'LL HEAD OVER AFTER I CLEAN UP.
I'LL HELP--
OH...
YEAR 1 CLASS 1
COULD HE BE...
NO THANKS.

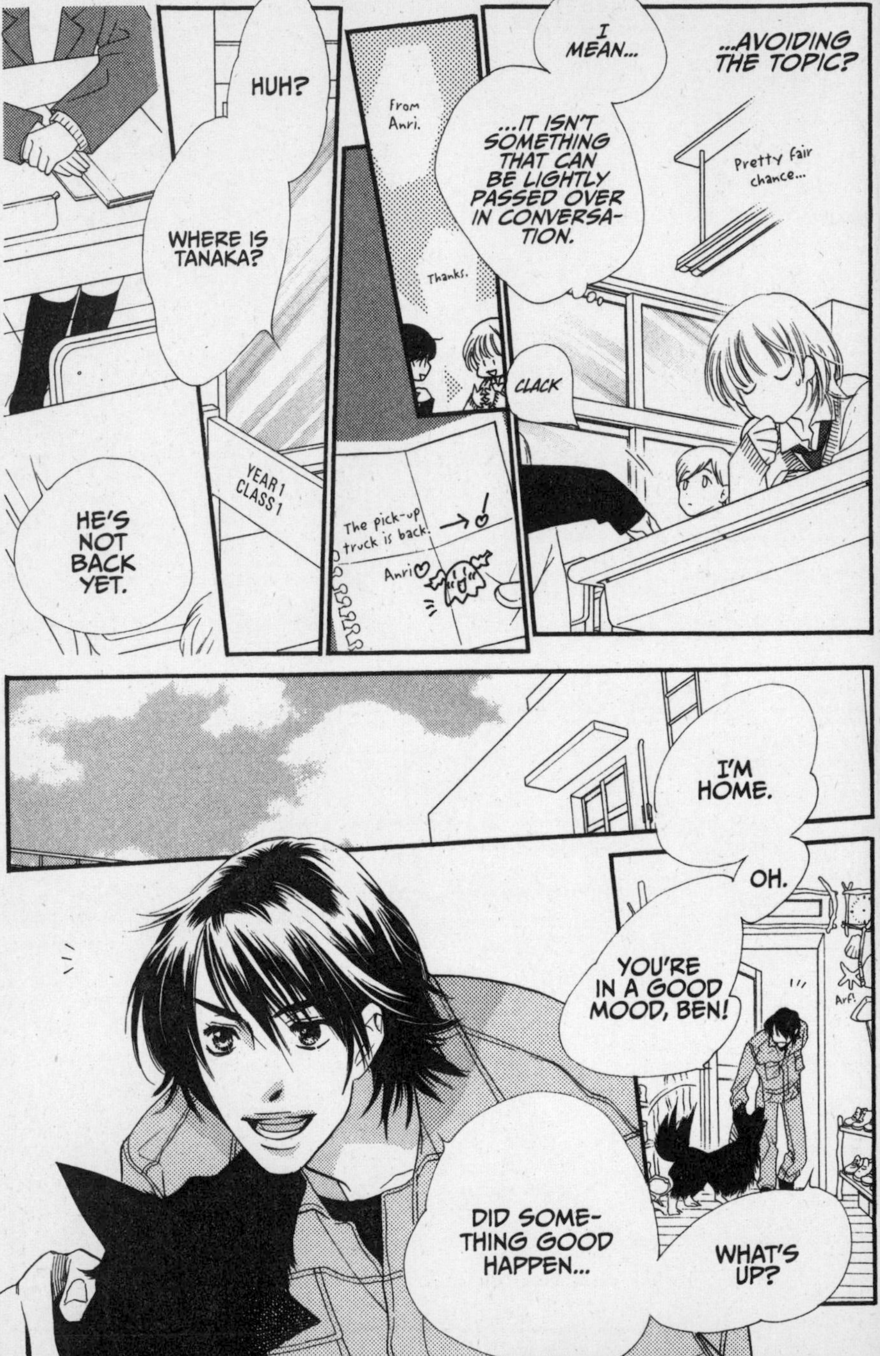
...AVOIDING THE TOPIC?
I MEAN...
...IT ISN'T SOMETHING THAT CAN BE LIGHTLY PASSED OVER IN CONVERSATION.
Pretty fair chance...
CLACK
From Anri.
Thanks.
The pick-up truck is back.
Anri
YEAR 1 CLASS 1
HUH?
WHERE IS TANAKA?
HE'S NOT BACK YET.
I'M HOME.
OH.
YOU'RE IN A GOOD MOOD, BEN!
Arf!
WHAT'S UP?
DID SOMETHING GOOD HAPPEN...

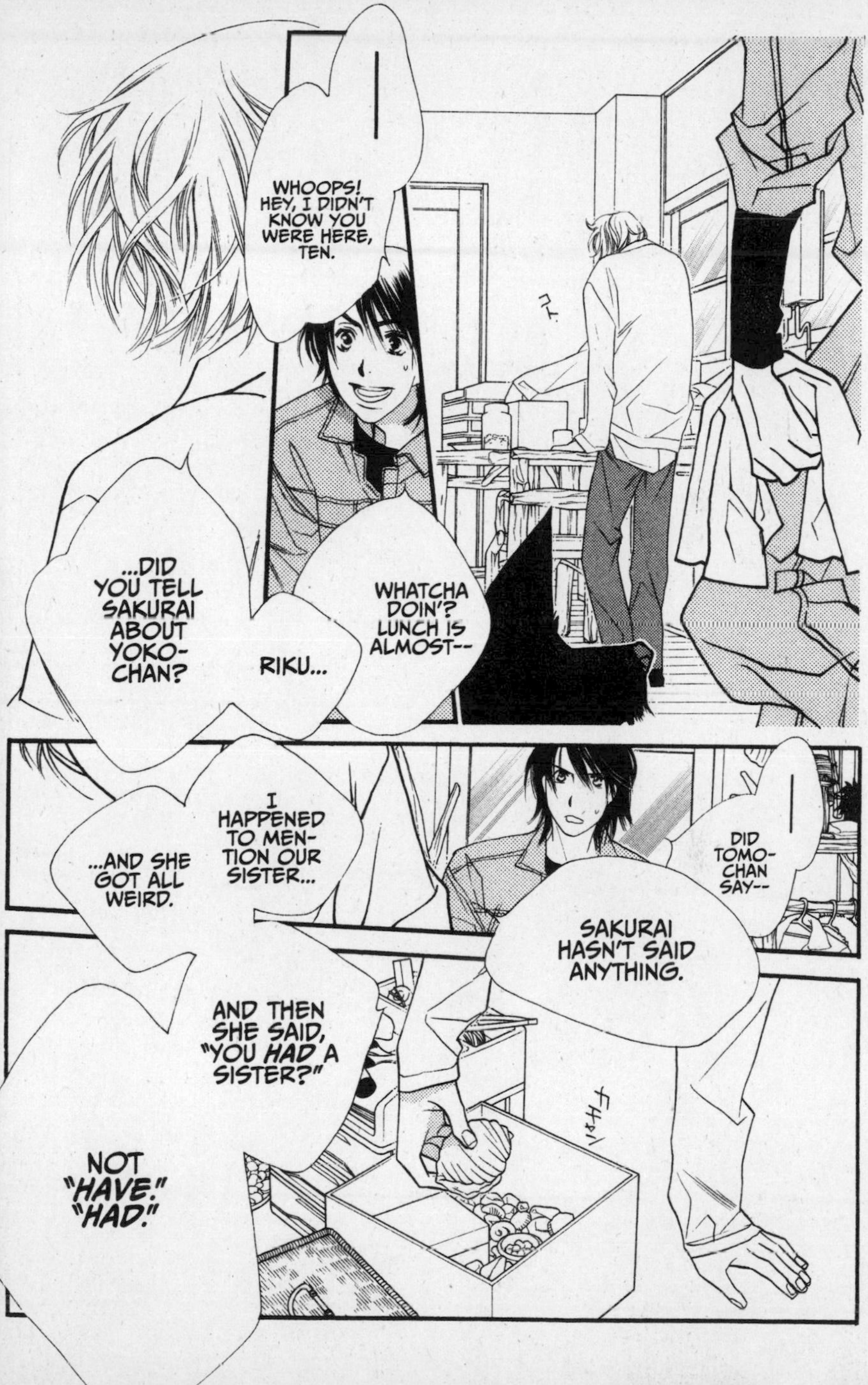
WHOOPS! HEY, I DIDN'T KNOW YOU WERE HERE, TEN.
WHATCHA DOIN'? LUNCH IS ALMOST--
RIKU...
...DID YOU TELL SAKURAI ABOUT YOKO-CHAN?
DID TOMO-CHAN SAY--
SAKURAI HASN'T SAID ANYTHING.
I HAPPENED TO MENTION OUR SISTER...
...AND SHE GOT ALL WEIRD.
AND THEN SHE SAID, "YOU *HAD* A SISTER?"
NOT "*HAVE.*" "*HAD.*"

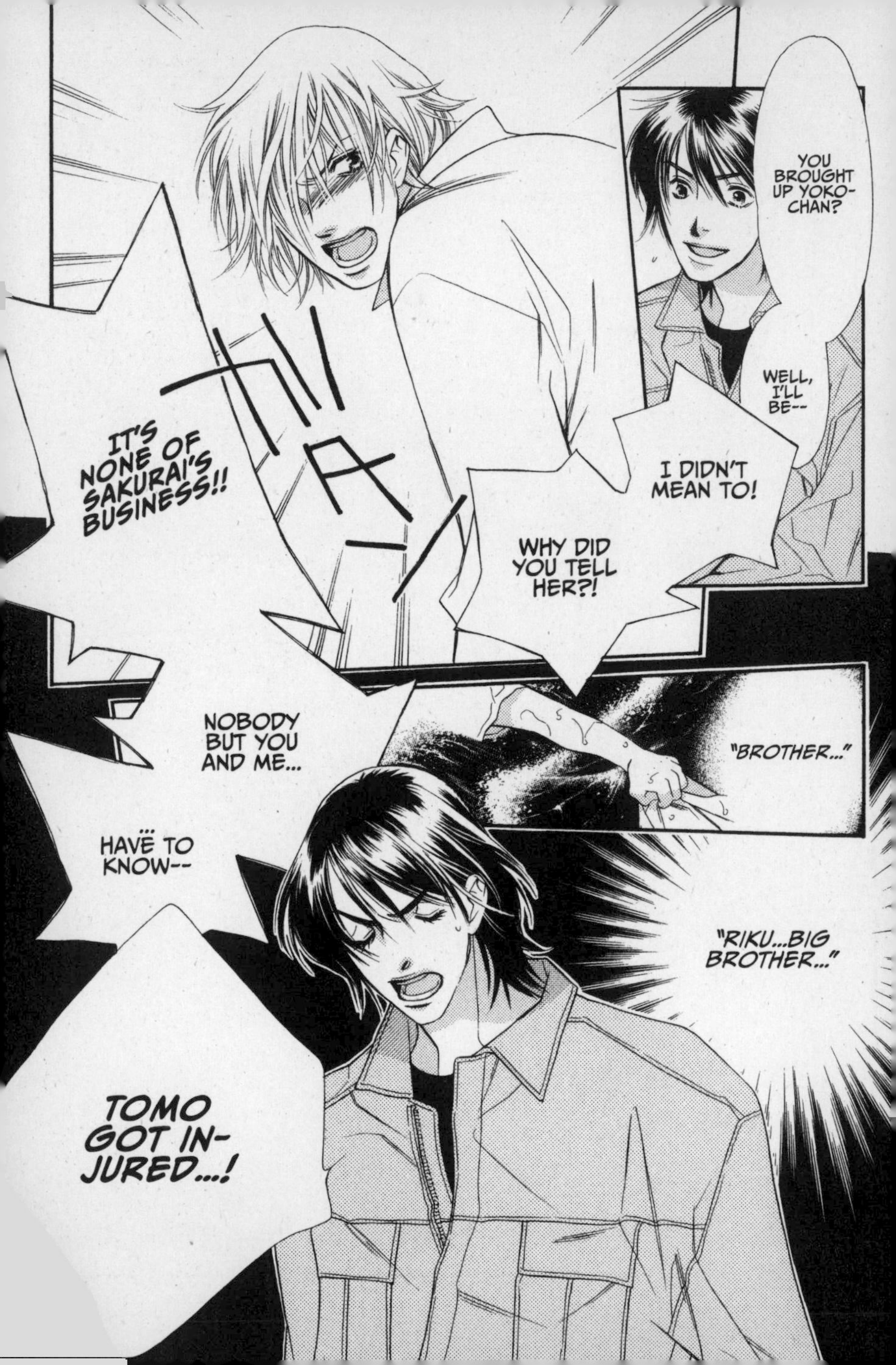
YOU BROUGHT UP YOKO-CHAN?
WELL, I'LL BE--
I DIDN'T MEAN TO!
WHY DID YOU TELL HER?!
IT'S NONE OF SAKURAI'S BUSINESS!!
"BROTHER..."
NOBODY BUT YOU AND ME...
HAVE TO KNOW--
"RIKU...BIG BROTHER..."
TOMO GOT IN-JURED...!

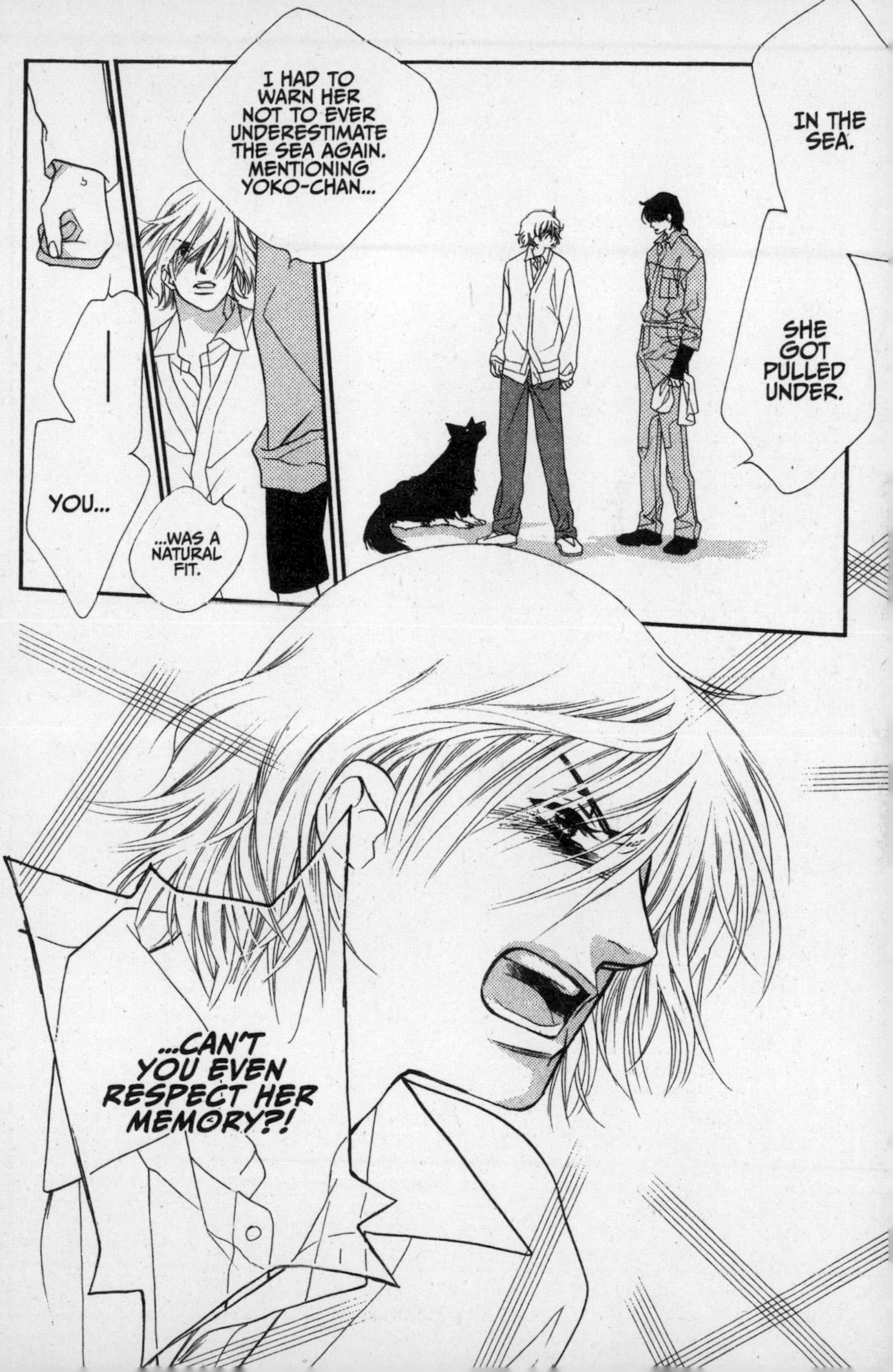
IN THE SEA.
SHE GOT PULLED UNDER.
I HAD TO WARN HER NOT TO EVER UNDERESTIMATE THE SEA AGAIN. MENTIONING YOKO-CHAN...
YOU...
...WAS A NATURAL FIT.
...CAN'T YOU EVEN RESPECT HER MEMORY?!

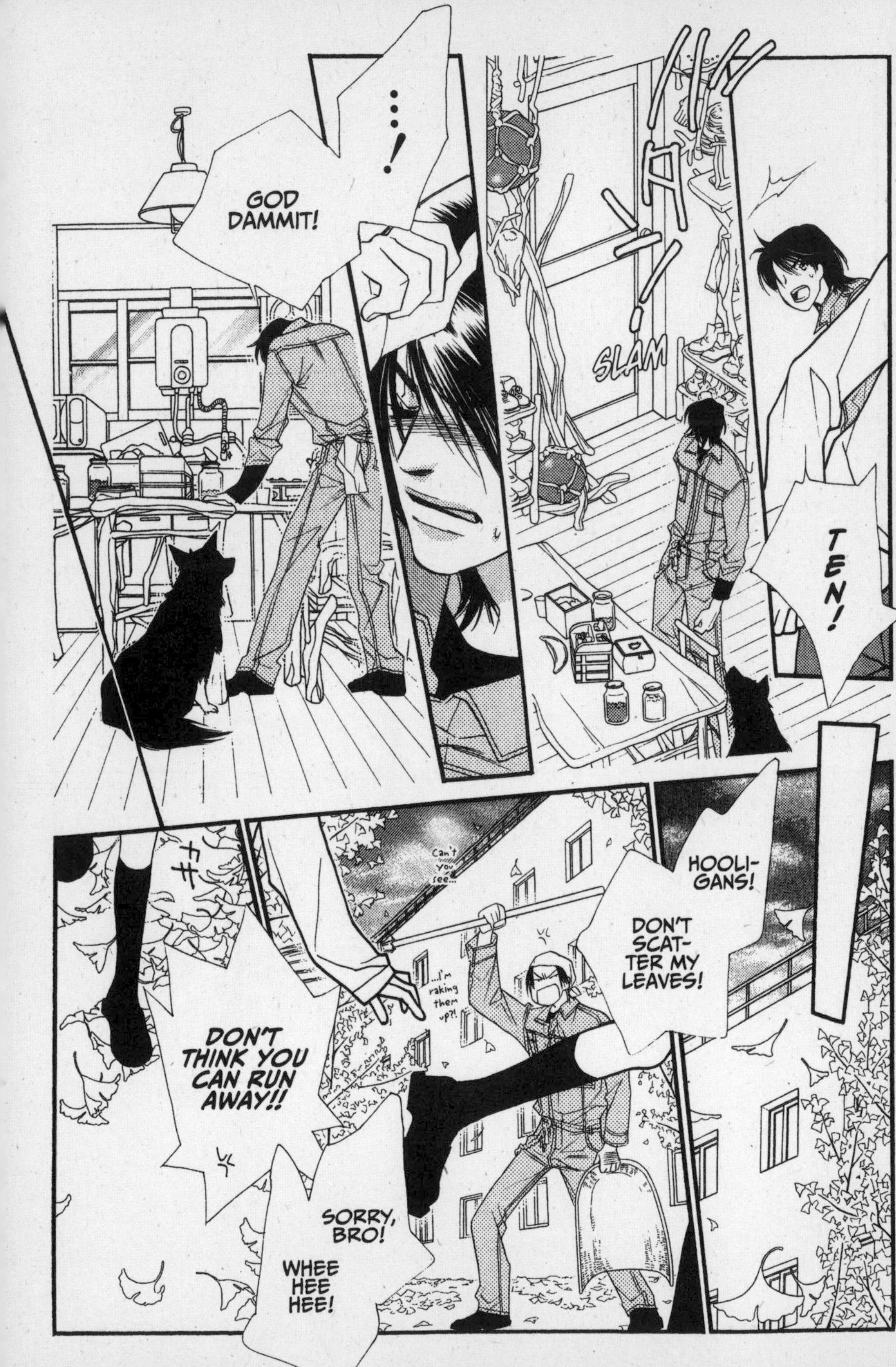
TEN!
SLAM
...!
GOD DAMMIT!
HOOLI-GANS!
DON'T SCAT-TER MY LEAVES!
Can't you see...
...I'm raking them up?!
SORRY, BRO!
WHEE HEE HEE!
DON'T THINK YOU CAN RUN AWAY!!

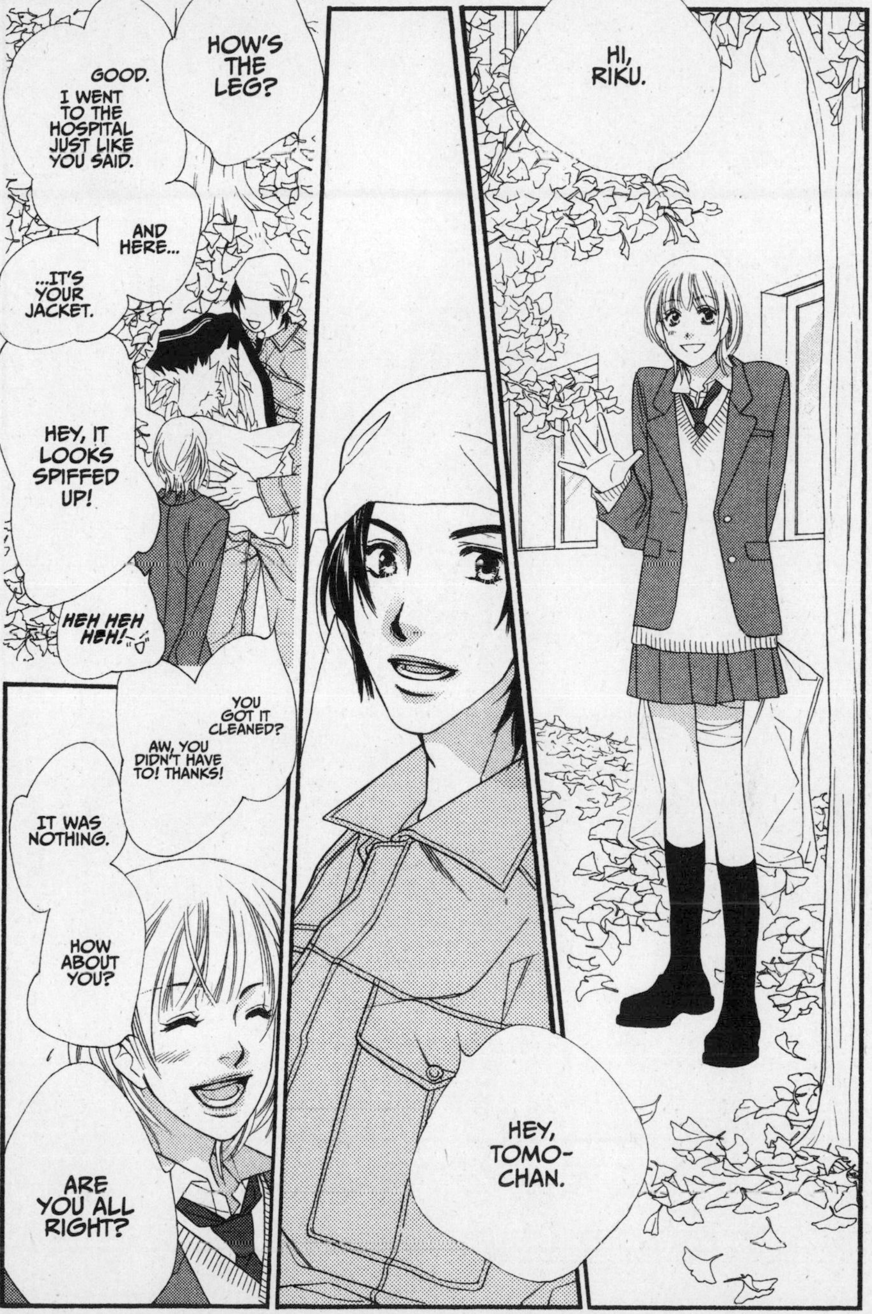
HI, RIKU.
HEY, TOMO-CHAN.
HOW'S THE LEG?
GOOD. I WENT TO THE HOSPITAL JUST LIKE YOU SAID.
AND HERE...
...IT'S YOUR JACKET.
HEY, IT LOOKS SPIFFED UP!
HEH HEH HEH!
YOU GOT IT CLEANED?
AW, YOU DIDN'T HAVE TO! THANKS!
IT WAS NOTHING.
HOW ABOUT YOU?
ARE YOU ALL RIGHT?

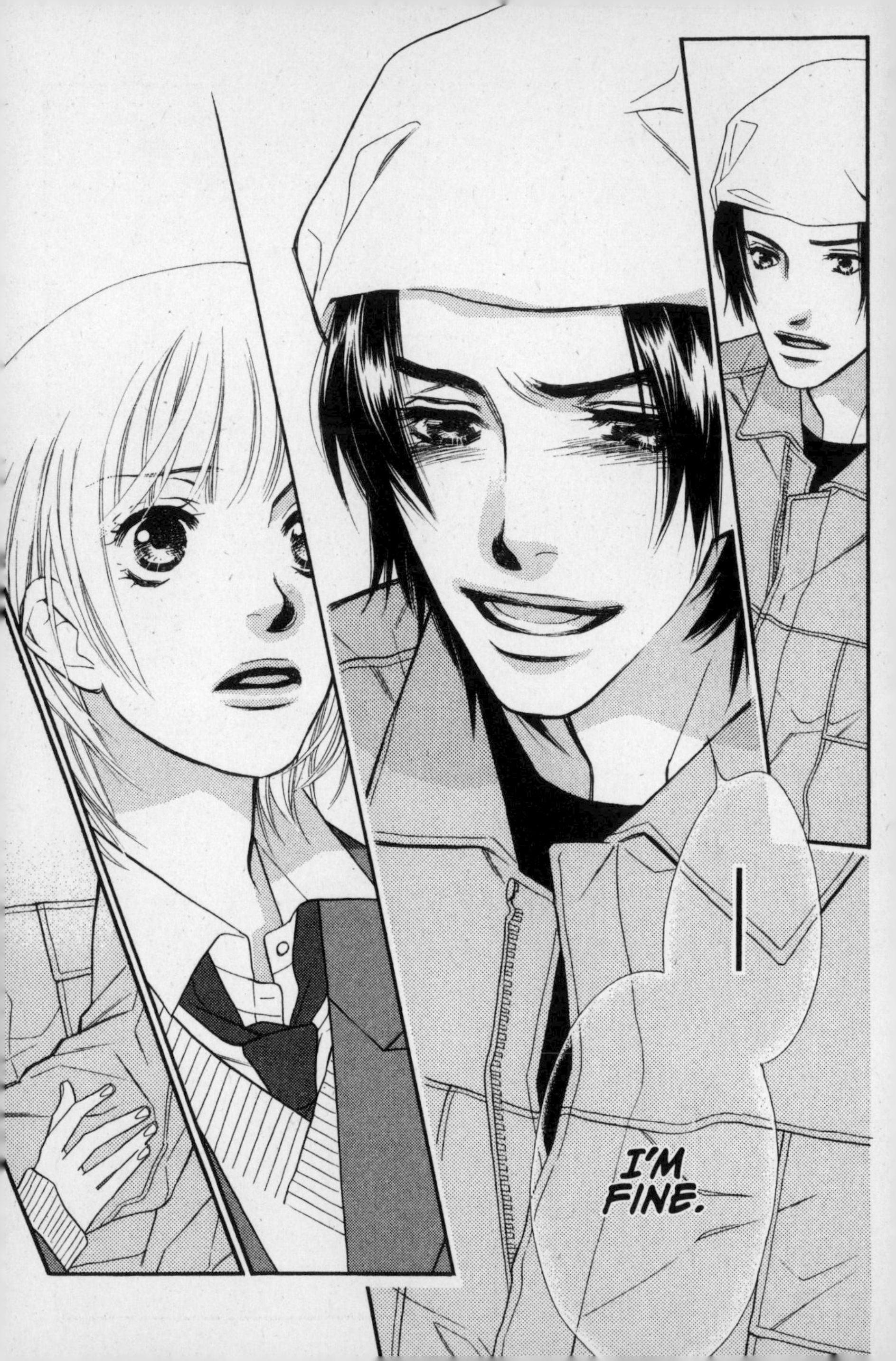
I'M FINE.

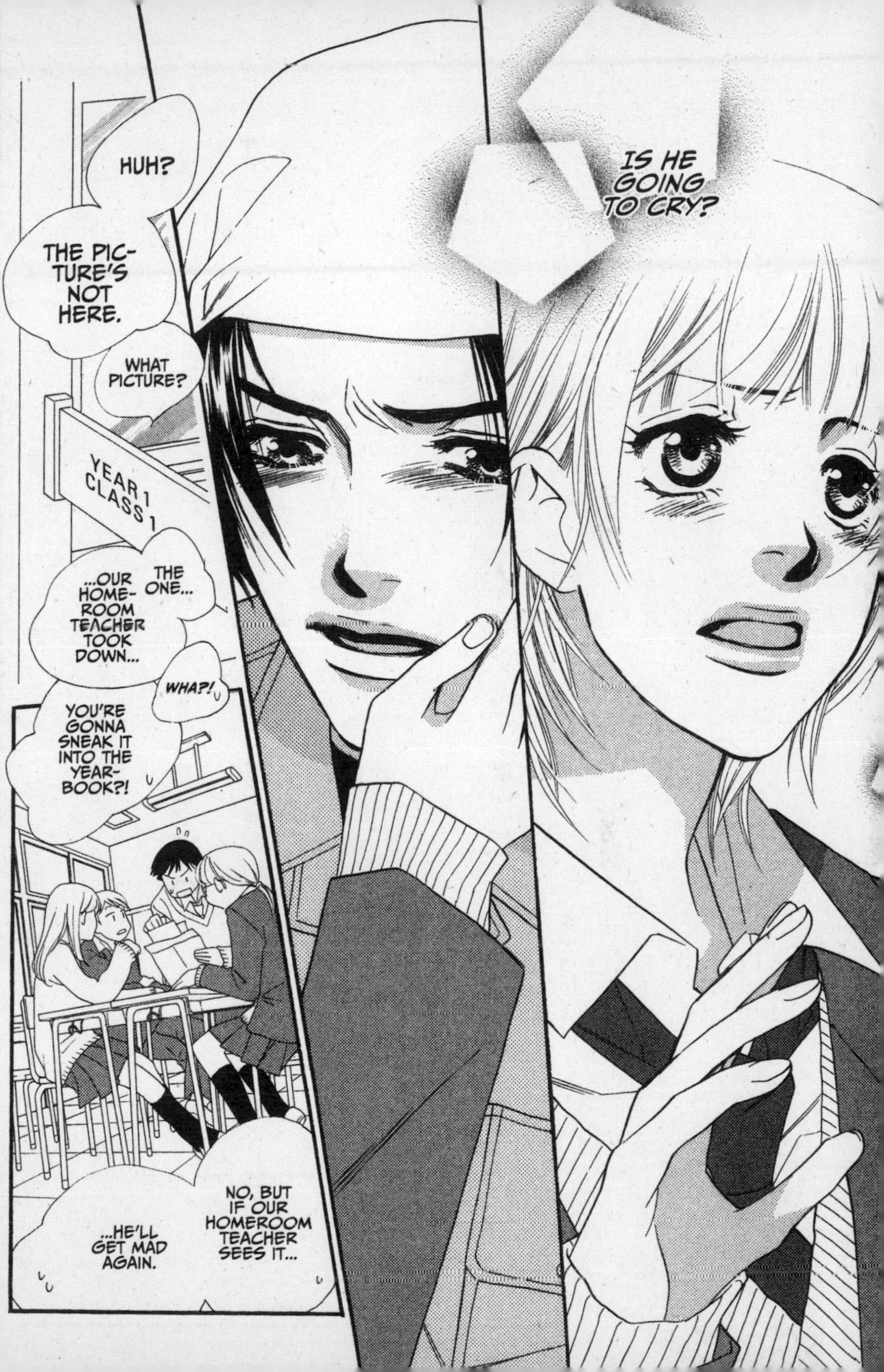
IS HE GOING TO CRY?
HUH?
THE PIC-TURE'S NOT HERE.
WHAT PICTURE?
YEAR 1 CLASS 1
THE ONE...
...OUR HOME-ROOM TEACHER TOOK DOWN...
WHA?!
YOU'RE GONNA SNEAK IT INTO THE YEAR-BOOK?!
NO, BUT IF OUR HOMEROOM TEACHER SEES IT...
...HE'LL GET MAD AGAIN.

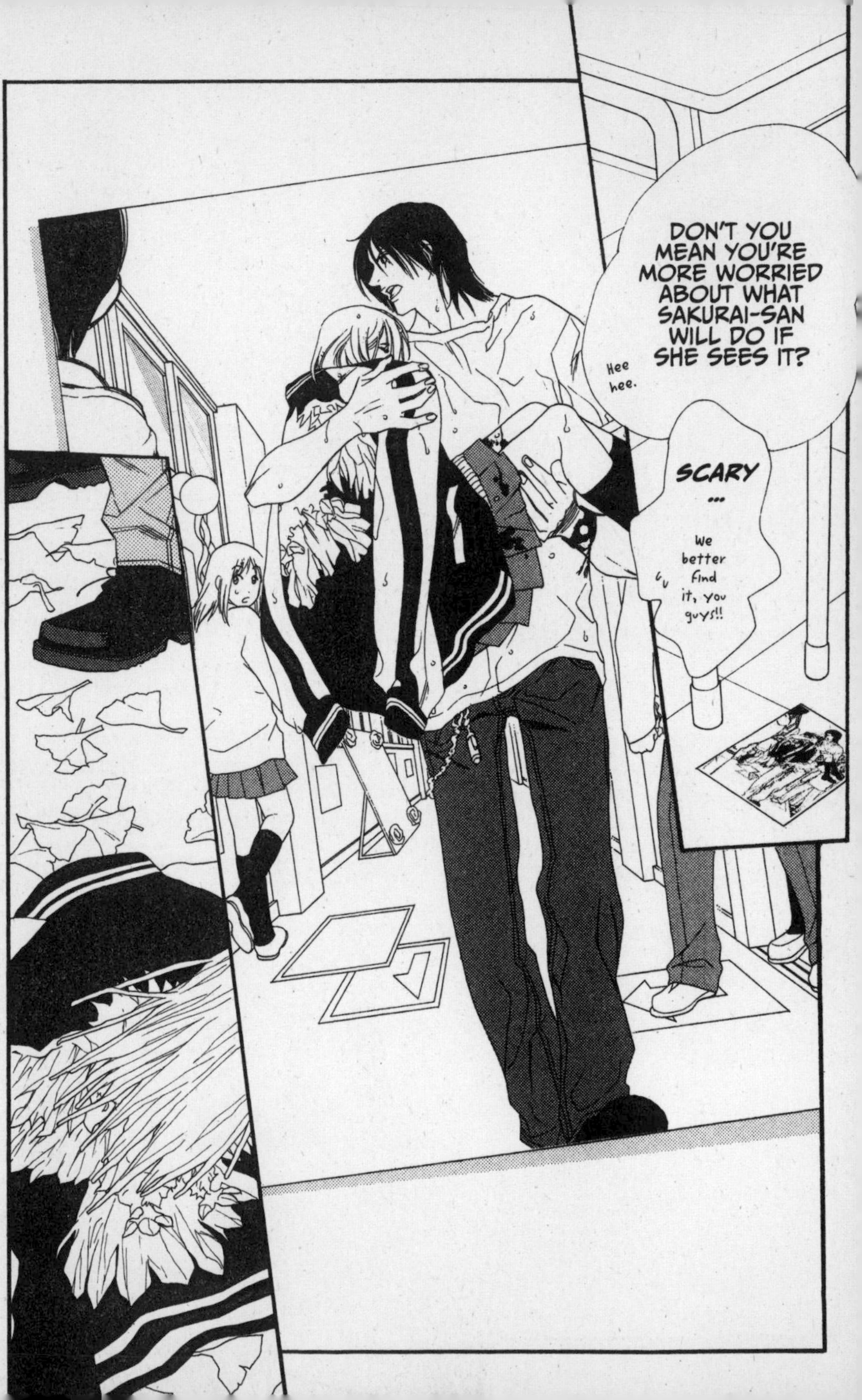
DON'T YOU MEAN YOU'RE MORE WORRIED ABOUT WHAT SAKURAI-SAN WILL DO IF SHE SEES IT?
Hee hee.
SCARY ...
We better find it, you guys!!

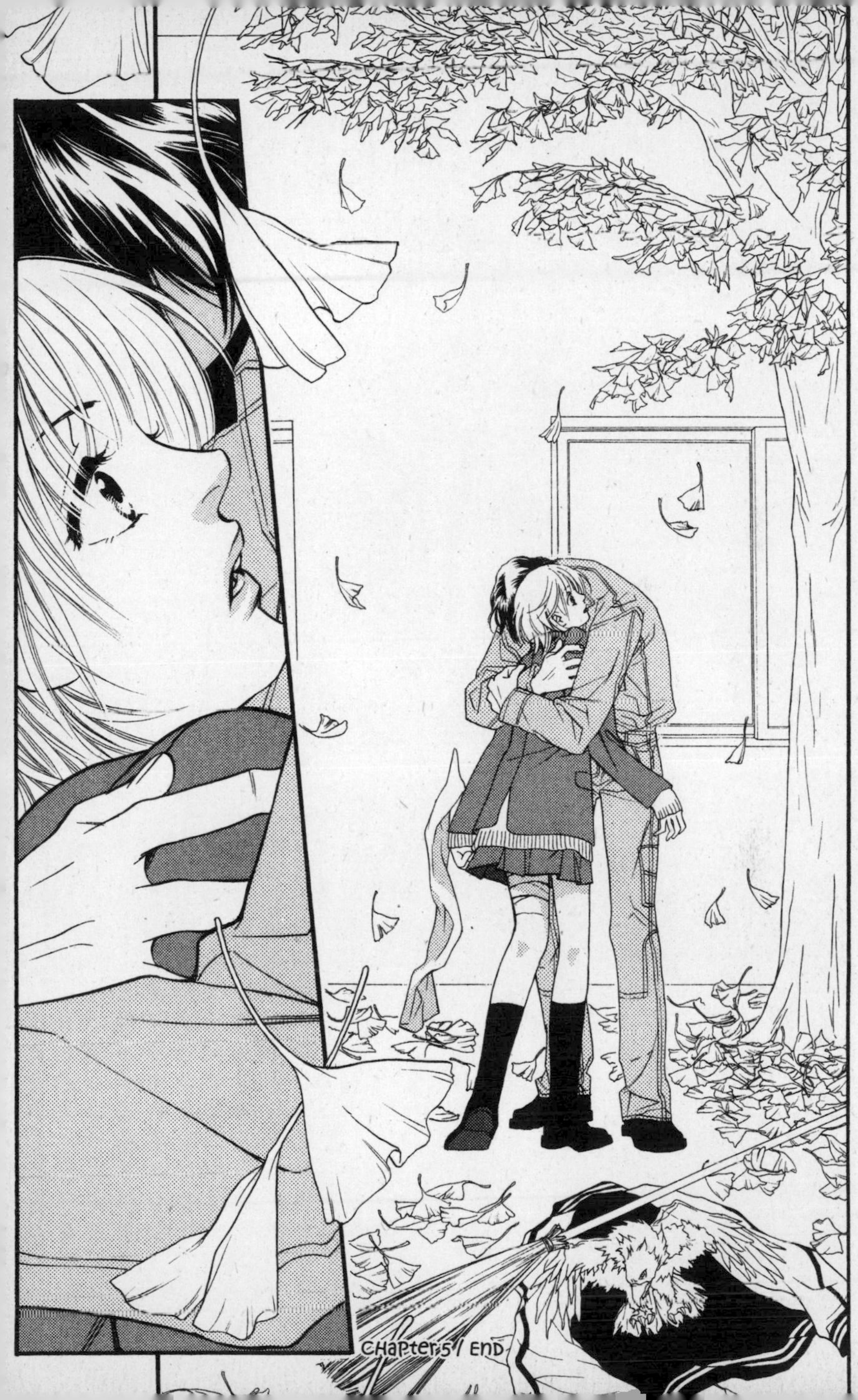
Chapter 5 / End

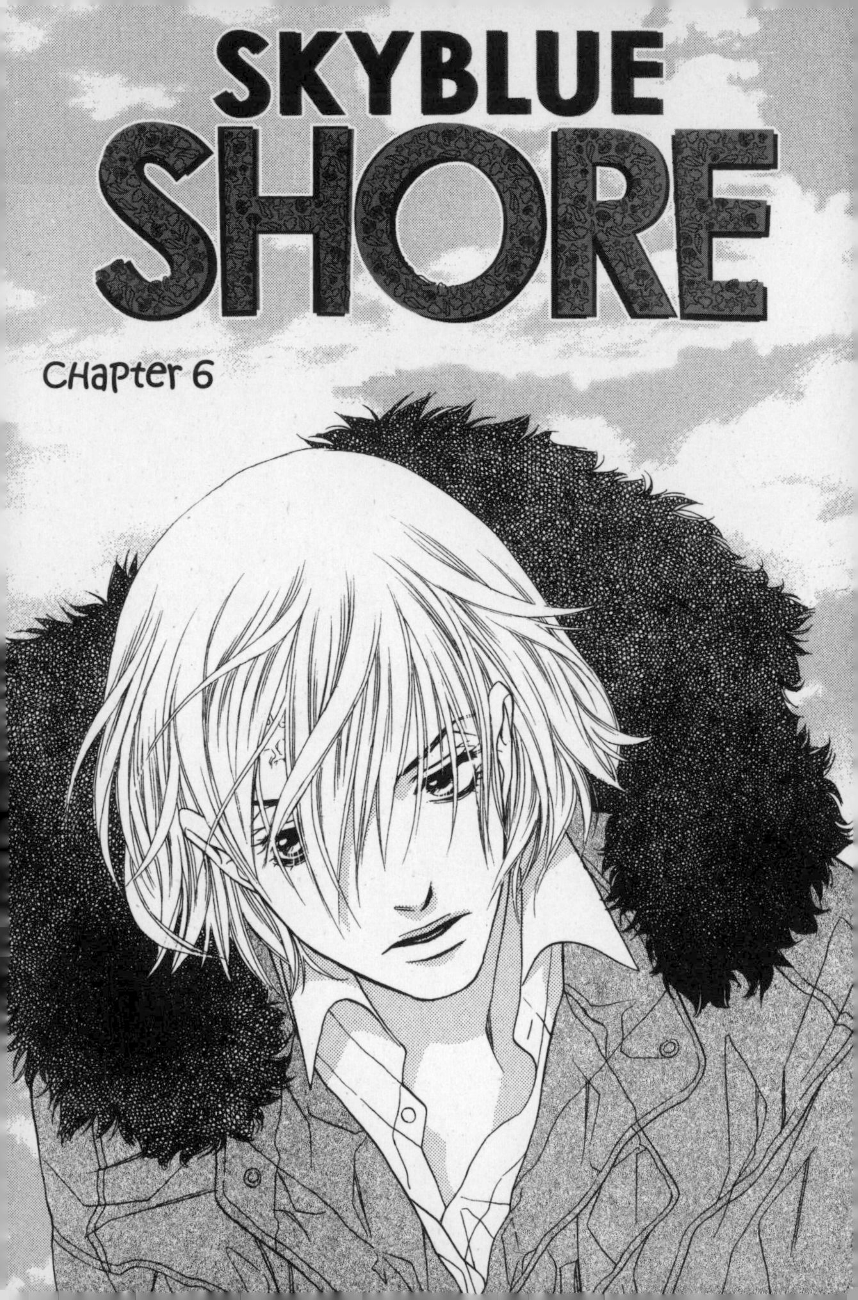
SKYBLUE
SHORE
Chapter 6

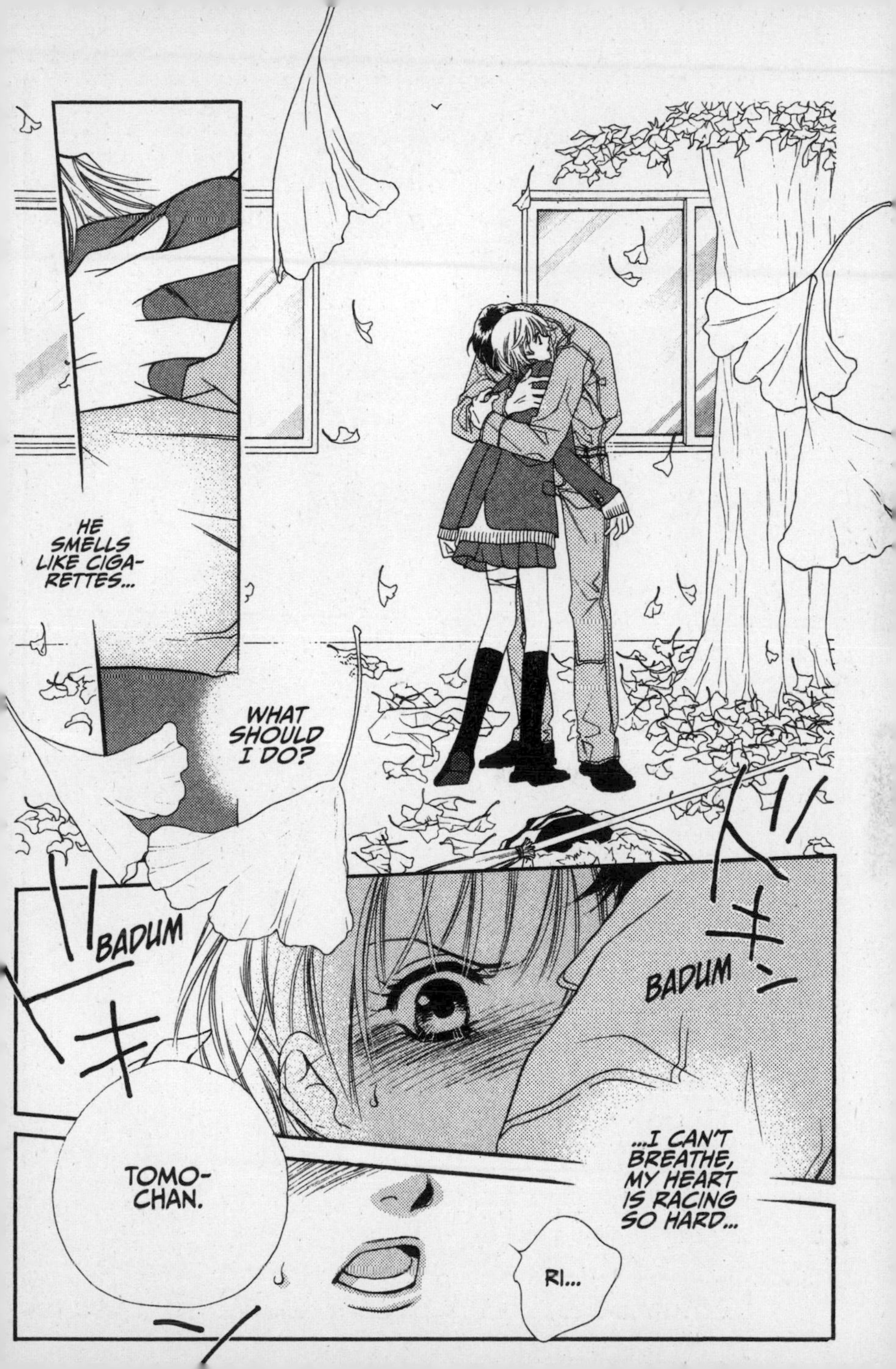
HE SMELLS LIKE CIGARETTES...
WHAT SHOULD I DO?
BADUM
...I CAN'T BREATHE, MY HEART IS RACING SO HARD...
BADUM
RI...
TOMO-CHAN.

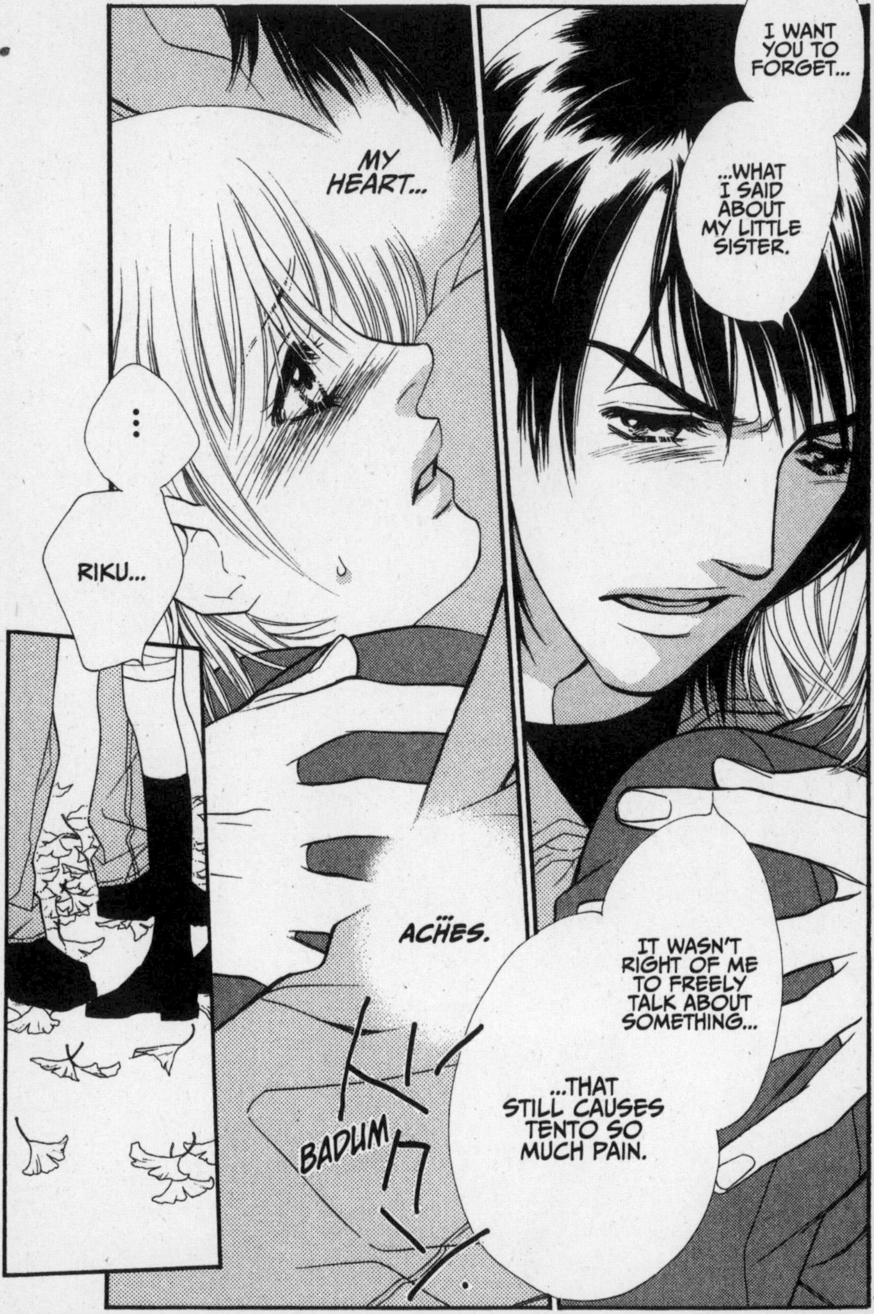
I WANT YOU TO FORGET...
...WHAT I SAID ABOUT MY LITTLE SISTER.
IT WASN'T RIGHT OF ME TO FREELY TALK ABOUT SOMETHING...
...THAT STILL CAUSES TENTO SO MUCH PAIN.
MY HEART...
...
RIKU...
ACHES.
BADUM

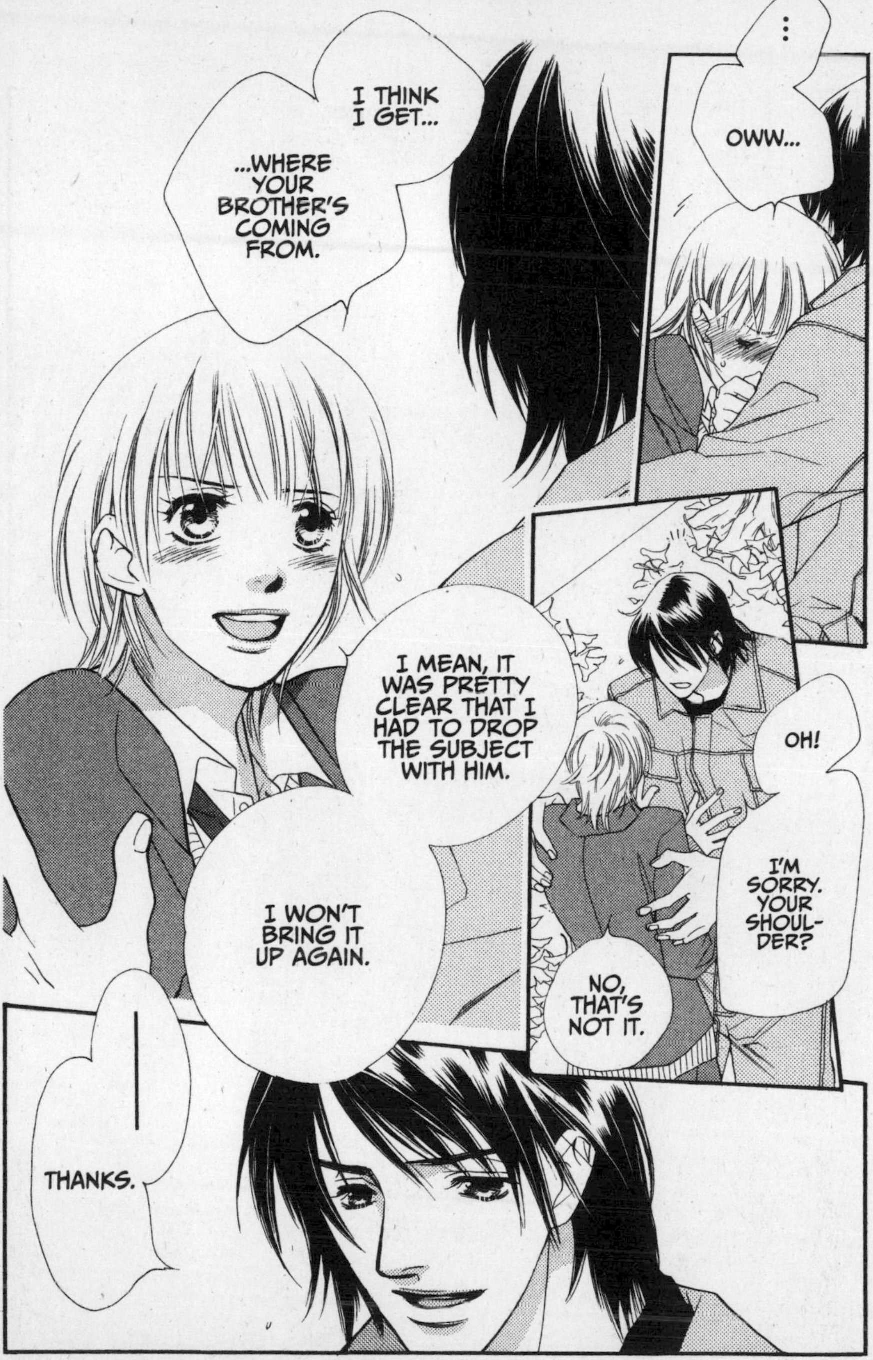
...
OWW...
OH!
I'M SORRY. YOUR SHOULDER?
NO, THAT'S NOT IT.
I THINK I GET...
...WHERE YOUR BROTHER'S COMING FROM.
I MEAN, IT WAS PRETTY CLEAR THAT I HAD TO DROP THE SUBJECT WITH HIM.
I WON'T BRING IT UP AGAIN.
—
THANKS.

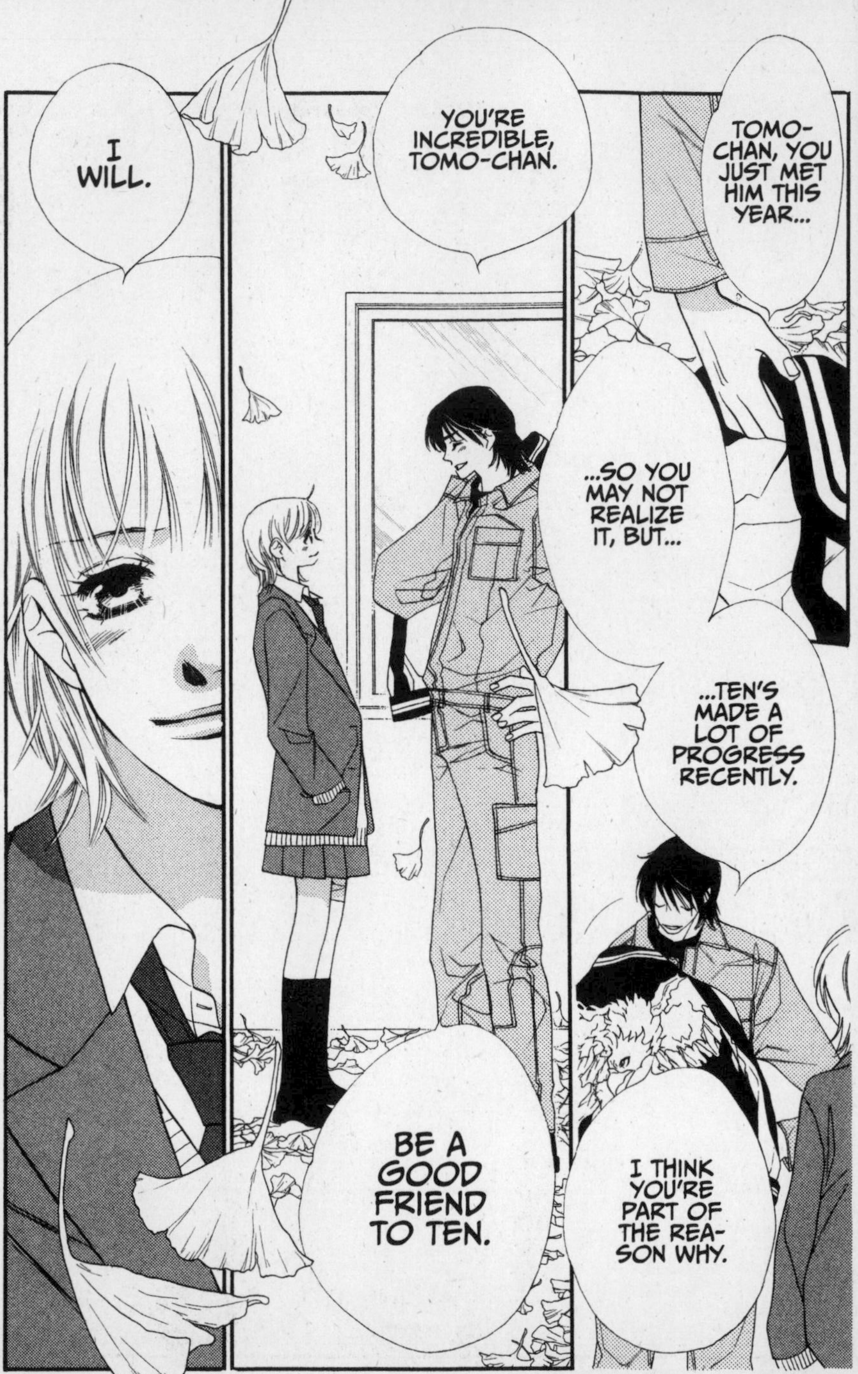
TOMO-CHAN, YOU JUST MET HIM THIS YEAR...
...SO YOU MAY NOT REALIZE IT, BUT...
...TEN'S MADE A LOT OF PROGRESS RECENTLY.
I THINK YOU'RE PART OF THE REA-SON WHY.
YOU'RE INCREDIBLE, TOMO-CHAN.
BE A GOOD FRIEND TO TEN.
I WILL.

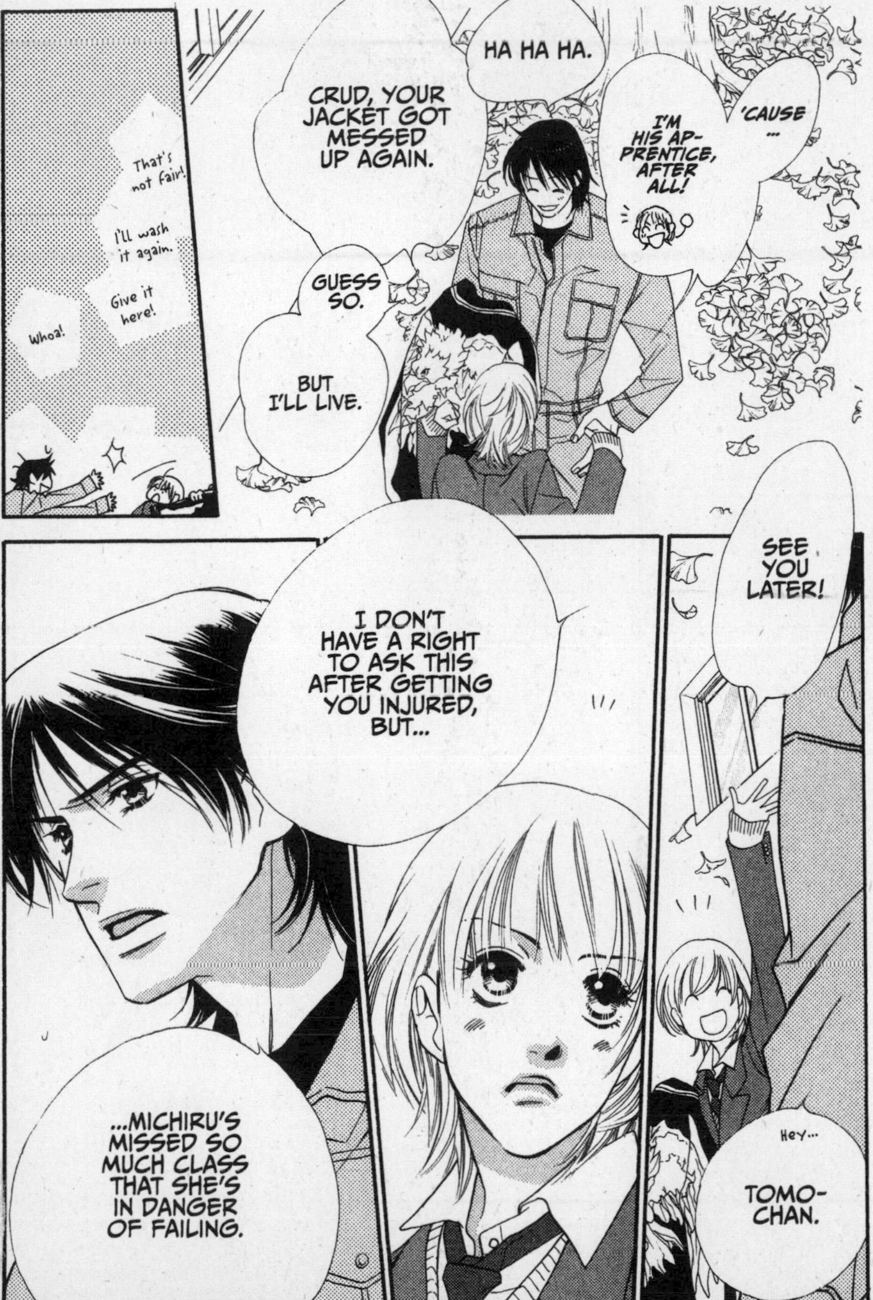

HA HA HA.
'CAUSE ...
I'M HIS AP-PRENTICE, AFTER ALL!
CRUD, YOUR JACKET GOT MESSED UP AGAIN.
GUESS SO.
BUT I'LL LIVE.
That's not fair!
I'll wash it again.
Give it here!
Whoa!
SEE YOU LATER!
Hey...
TOMO-CHAN.
I DON'T HAVE A RIGHT TO ASK THIS AFTER GETTING YOU INJURED, BUT...
...MICHIRU'S MISSED SO MUCH CLASS THAT SHE'S IN DANGER OF FAILING.

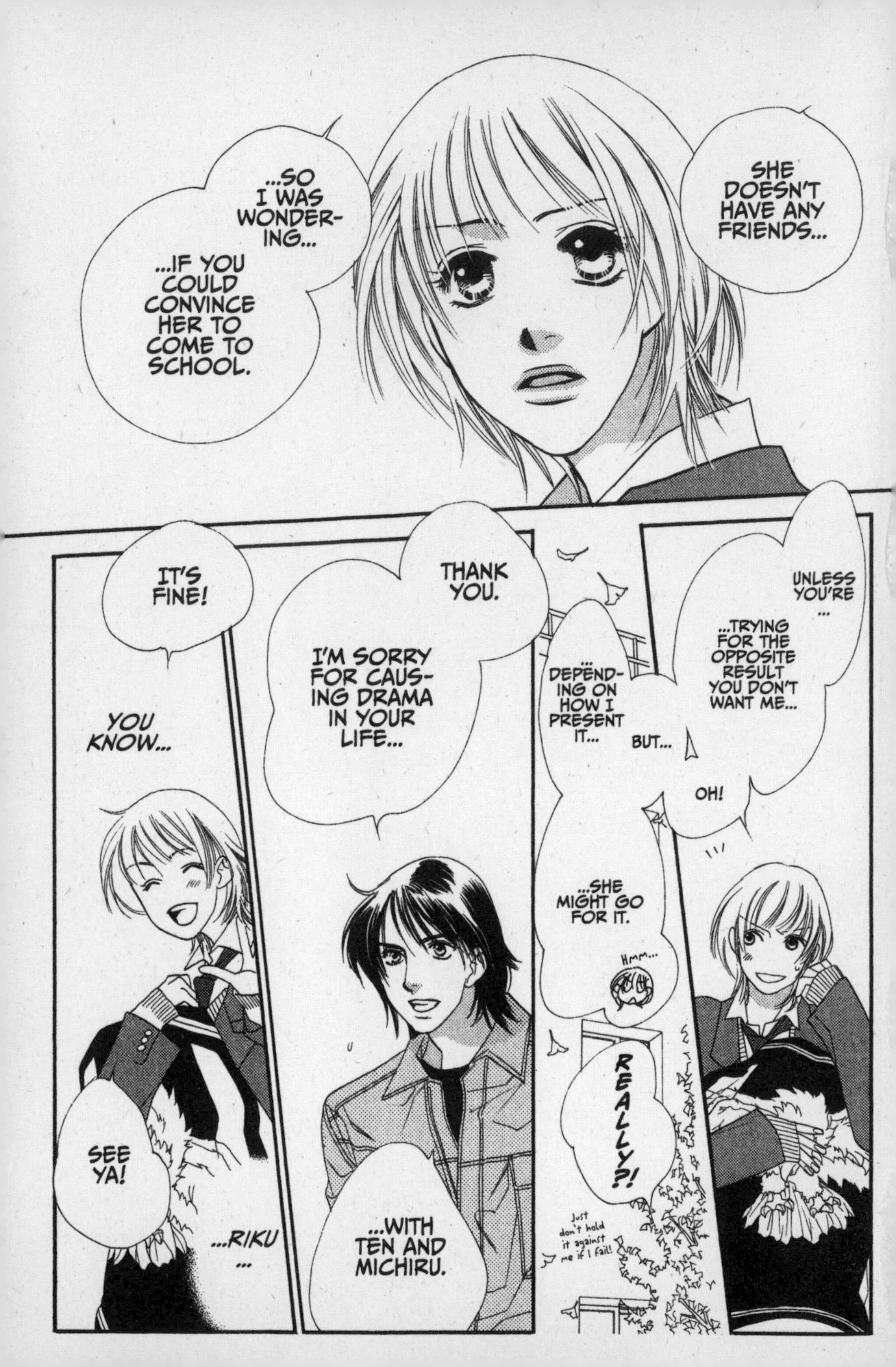
SHE DOESN'T HAVE ANY FRIENDS...
...SO I WAS WONDERING-ING...
...IF YOU COULD CONVINCE HER TO COME TO SCHOOL.
UNLESS YOU'RE ...
...TRYING FOR THE OPPOSITE RESULT YOU DON'T WANT ME...
OH!
...DEPENDING ON HOW I PRESENT IT...
BUT...
...SHE MIGHT GO FOR IT.
Hmm...
REALLY?!
Just don't hold it against me if I fail!
THANK YOU.
I'M SORRY FOR CAUS-ING DRAMA IN YOUR LIFE...
...WITH TEN AND MICHIRU.
IT'S FINE!
YOU KNOW...
SEE YA!
...RIKU ...

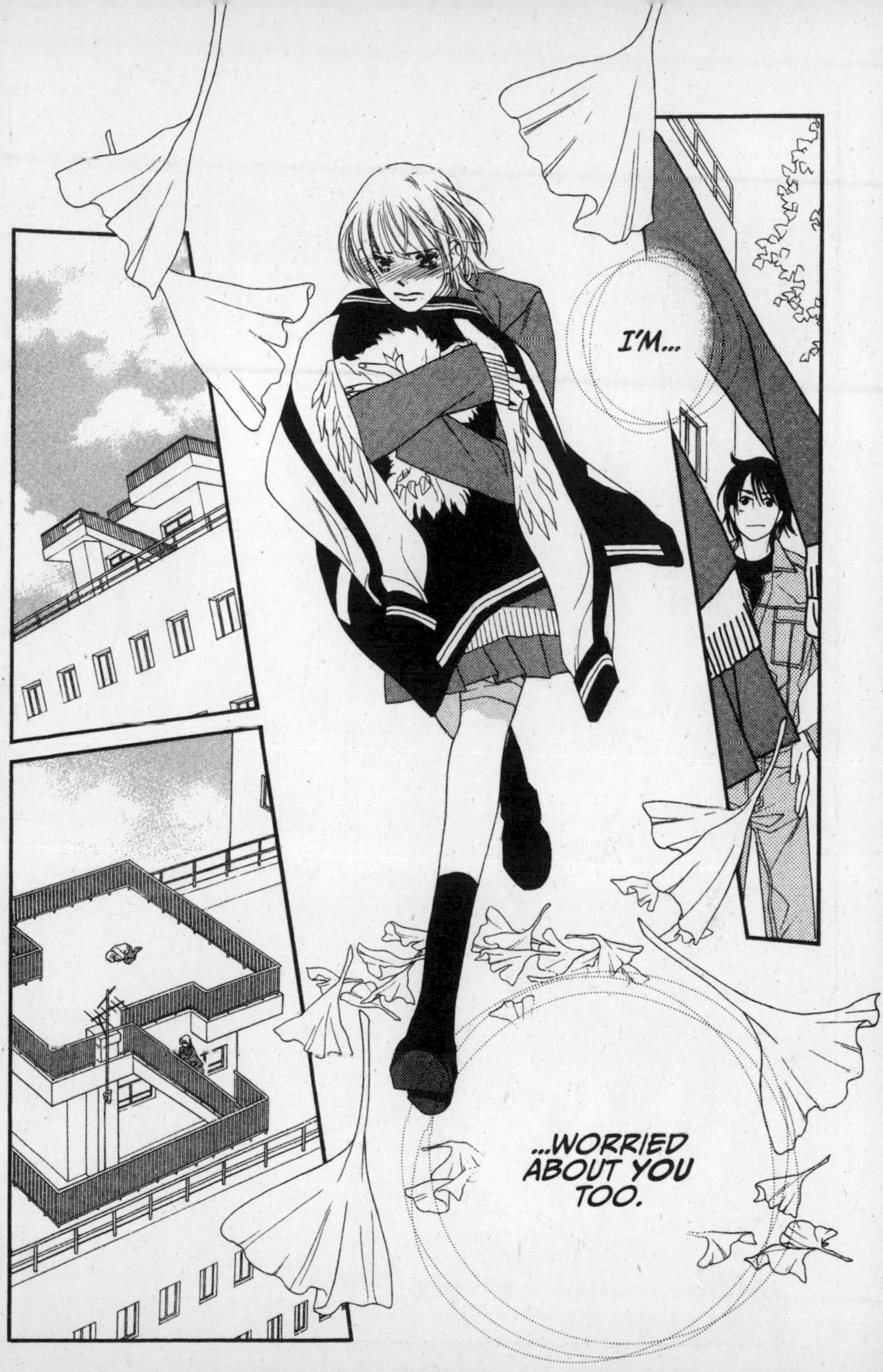
I'M...
...WORRIED ABOUT YOU TOO.

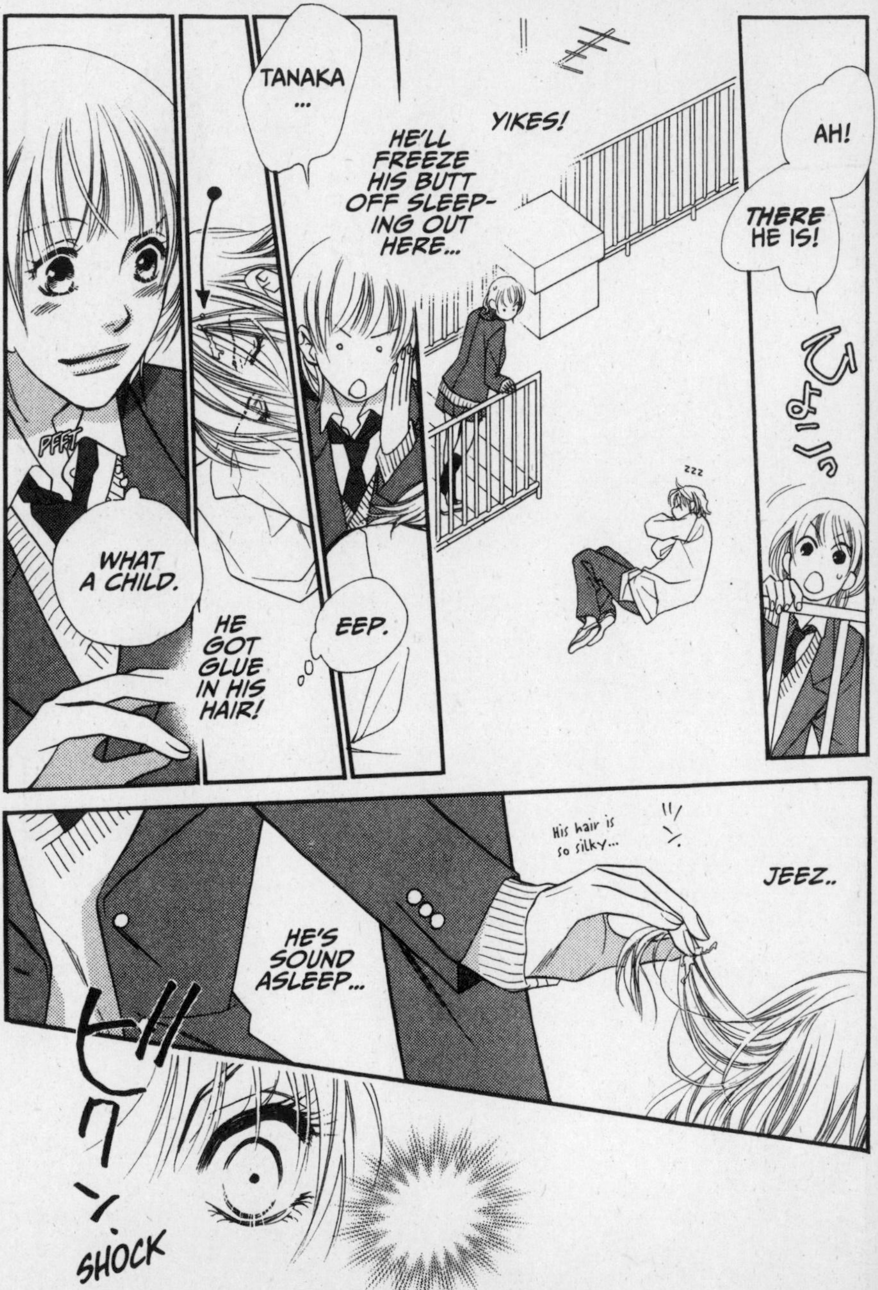
AH!
THERE HE IS!
YIKES!
HE'LL FREEZE HIS BUTT OFF SLEEP-ING OUT HERE...
zzz
TANAKA ...
EEP.
HE GOT GLUE IN HIS HAIR!
PFFT
WHAT A CHILD.
JEEZ..
His hair is so silky...
HE'S SOUND ASLEEP...
SHOCK

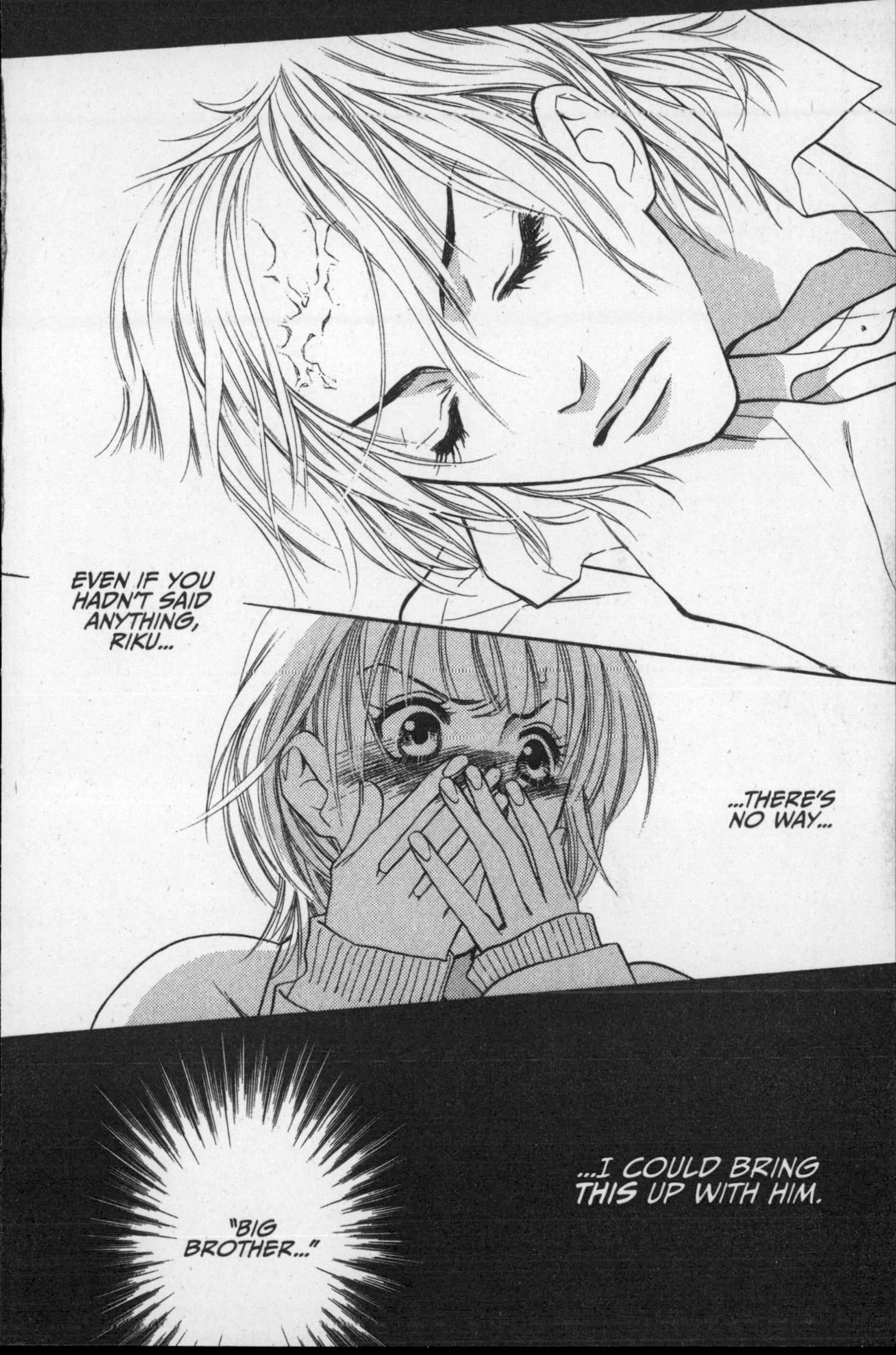
EVEN IF YOU HADN'T SAID ANYTHING, RIKU...
...THERE'S NO WAY...
...I COULD BRING THIS UP WITH HIM.
"BIG BROTHER..."

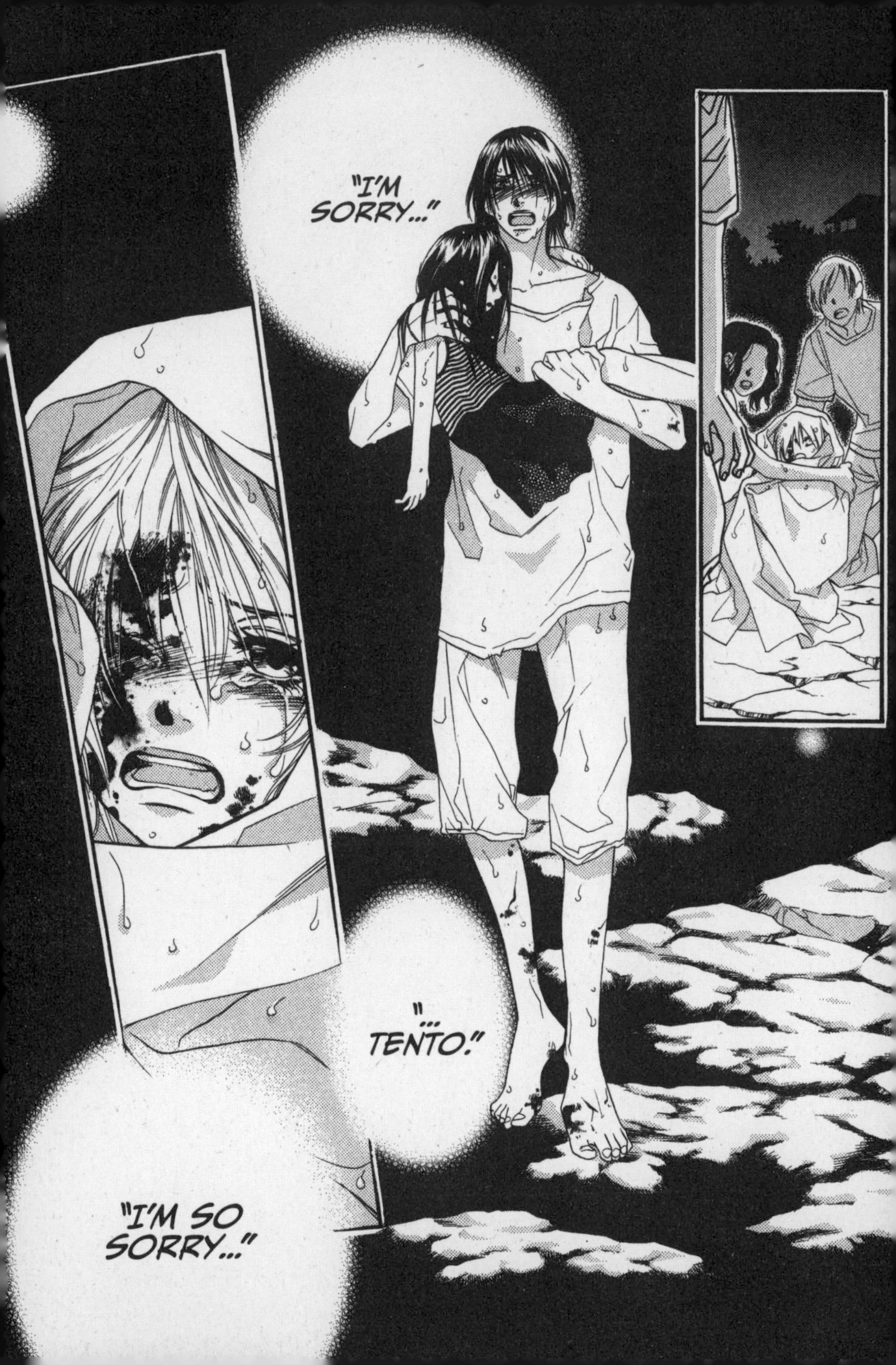
"I'M SORRY..."
"...TENTO."
"I'M SO SORRY..."

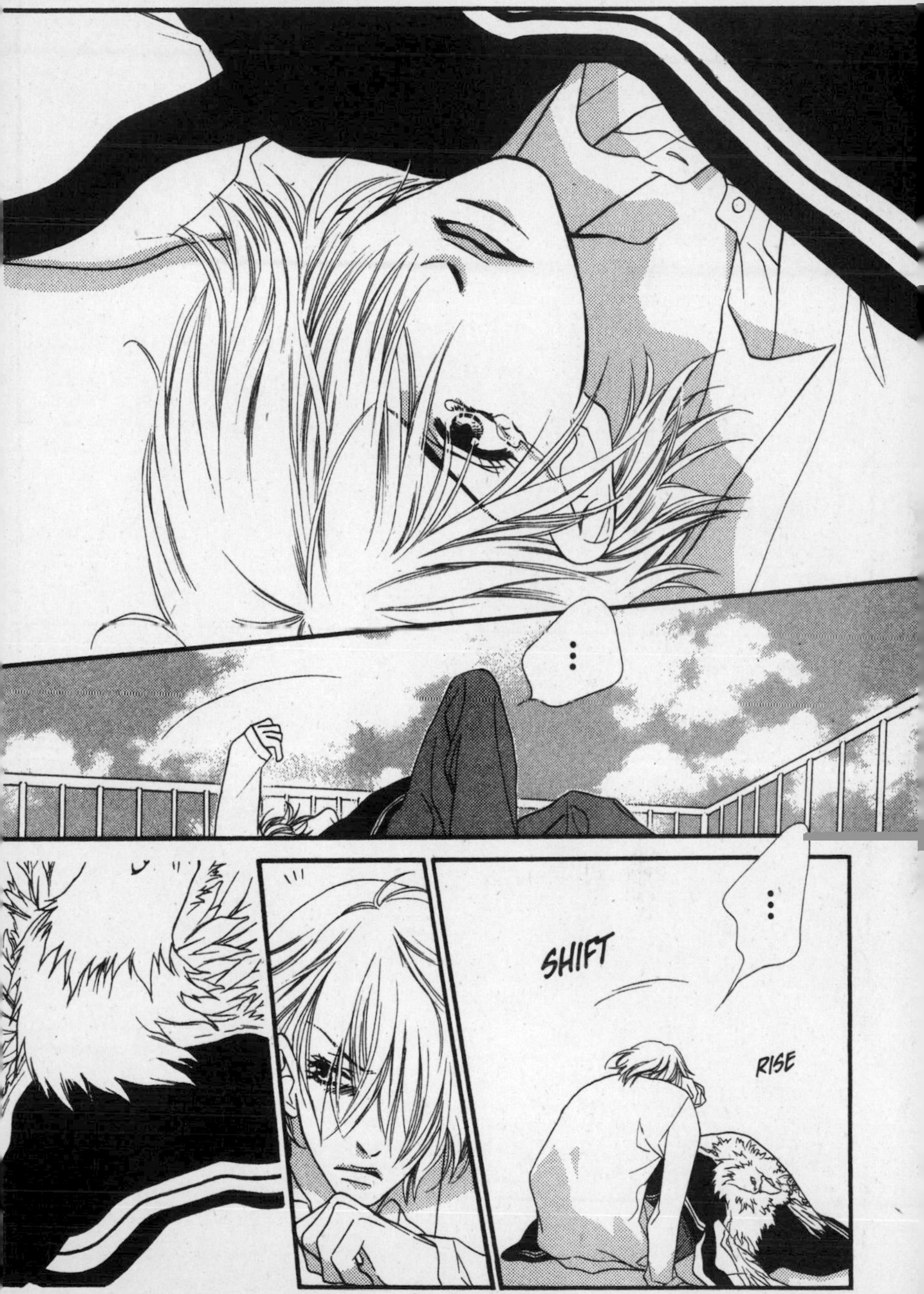
...
...
SHIFT
RISE

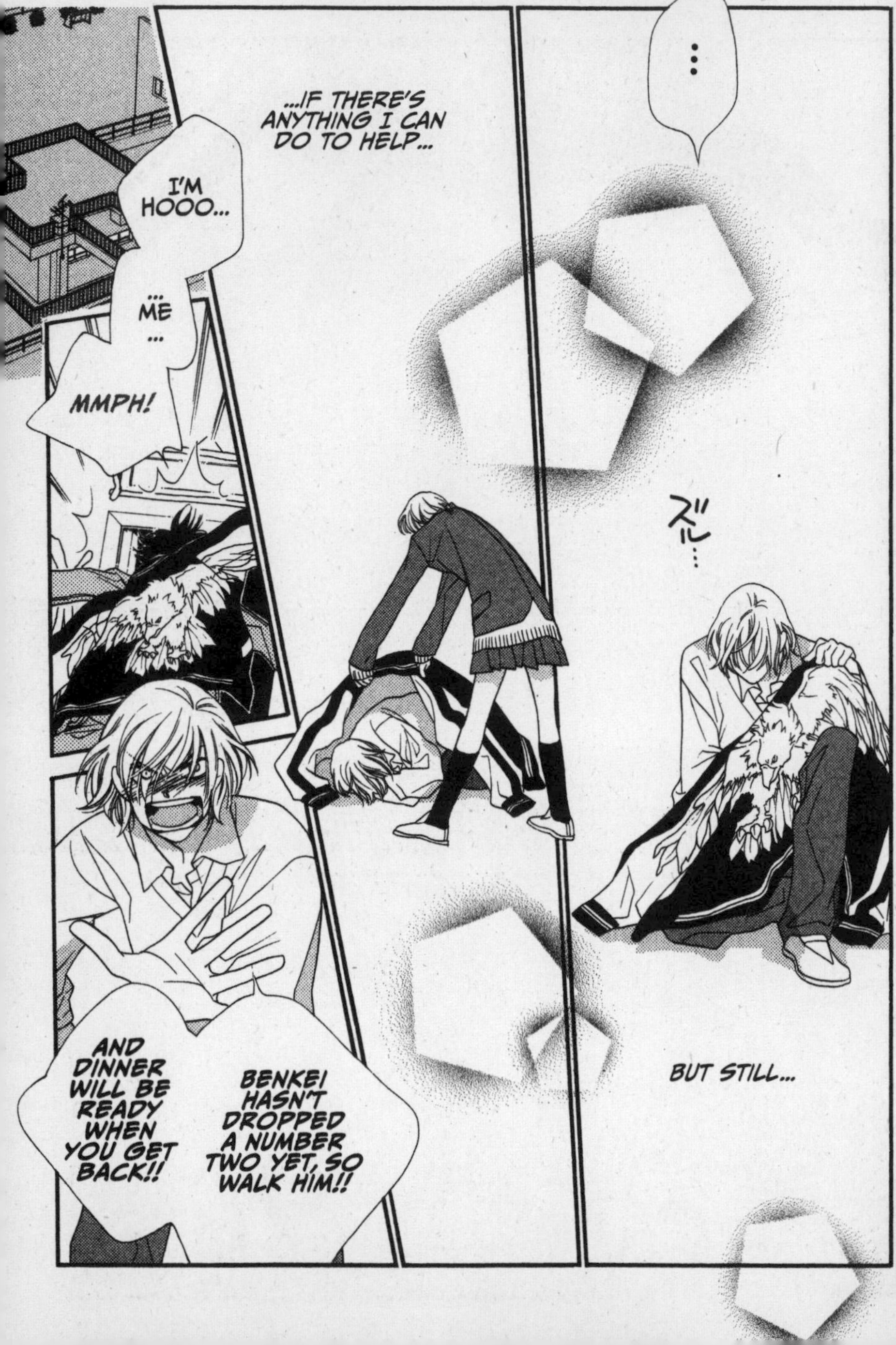

...
ズル...
BUT STILL...
...IF THERE'S ANYTHING I CAN DO TO HELP...
I'M HOOO...
... ME ...
MMPH!
BENKEI HASN'T DROPPED A NUMBER TWO YET, SO WALK HIM!!
AND DINNER WILL BE READY WHEN YOU GET BACK!!

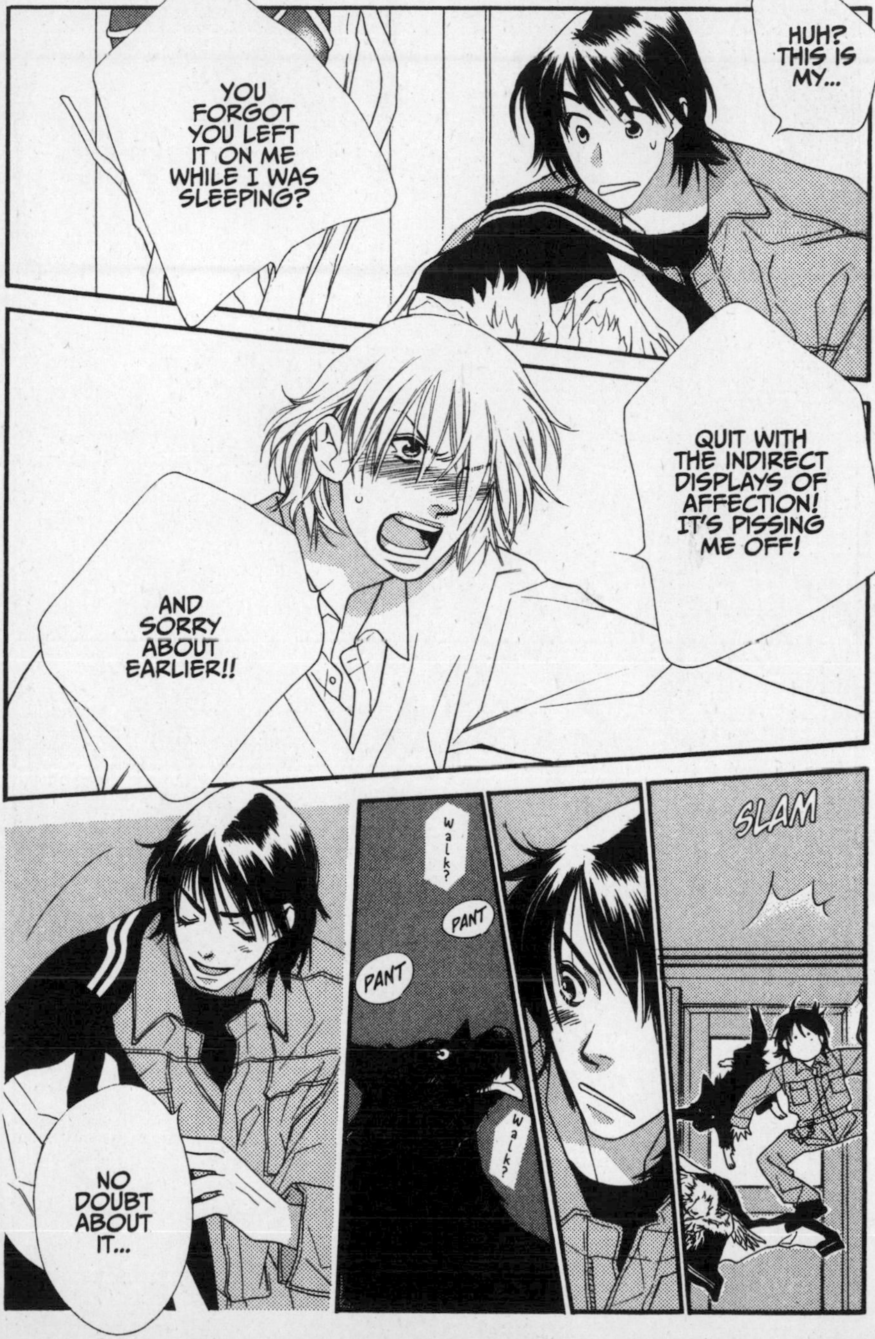
HUH? THIS IS MY...
YOU FORGOT YOU LEFT IT ON ME WHILE I WAS SLEEPING?
QUIT WITH THE INDIRECT DISPLAYS OF AFFECTION! IT'S PISSING ME OFF!
AND SORRY ABOUT EARLIER!!
SLAM
walk?
PANT
PANT
walk?
NO DOUBT ABOUT IT...

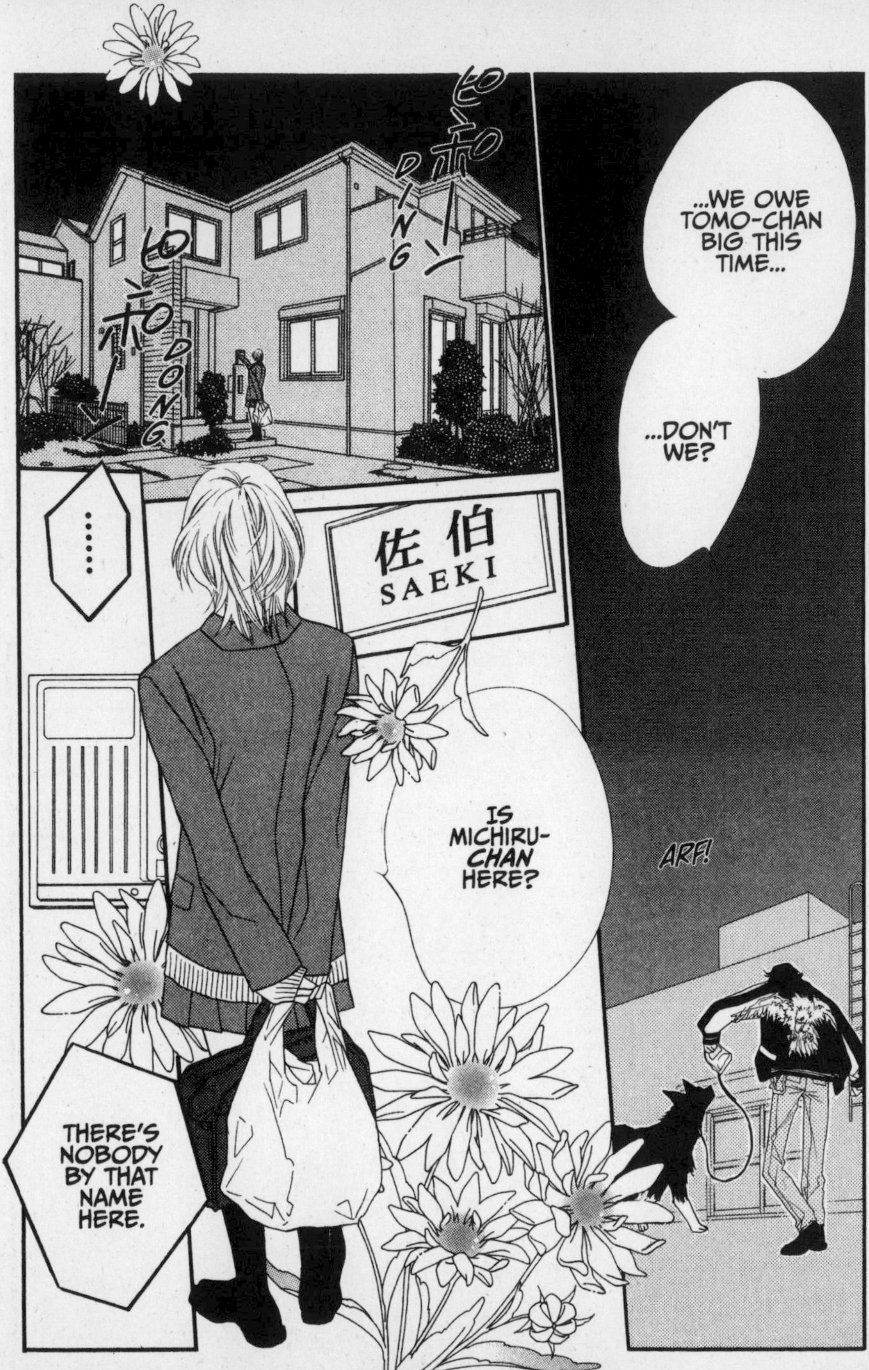
...WE OWE TOMO-CHAN BIG THIS TIME...
...DON'T WE?
ARF!
ピンポーン
DING
ピンポーン
DONG
......
佐伯
SAEKI
IS MICHIRU-CHAN HERE?
THERE'S NOBODY BY THAT NAME HERE.

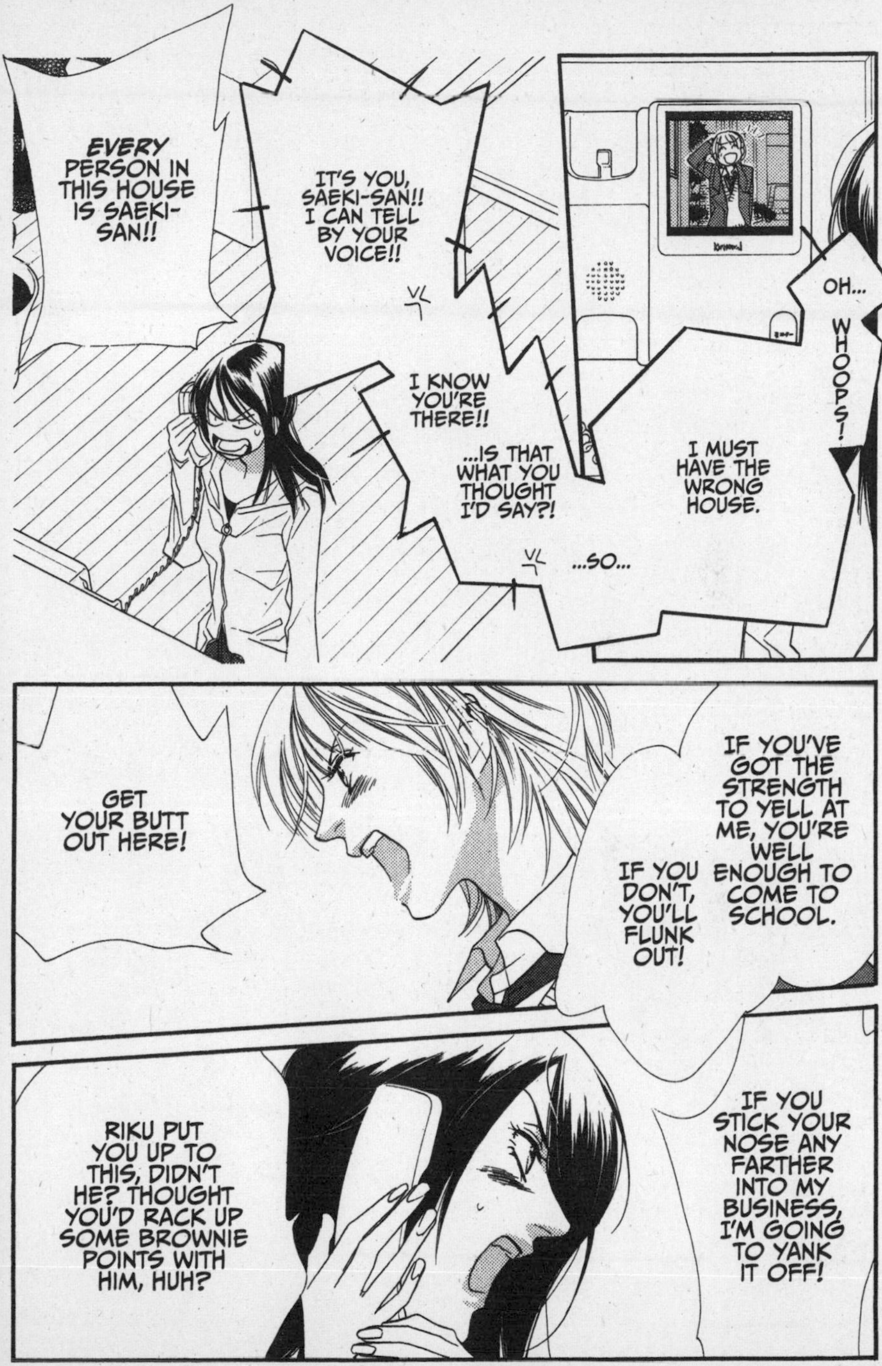
OH... WHOOPS!
I MUST HAVE THE WRONG HOUSE.
...SO...
IT'S YOU, SAEKI-SAN!! I CAN TELL BY YOUR VOICE!!
I KNOW YOU'RE THERE!!
...IS THAT WHAT YOU THOUGHT I'D SAY?!
EVERY PERSON IN THIS HOUSE IS SAEKI-SAN!!
IF YOU'VE GOT THE STRENGTH TO YELL AT ME, YOU'RE WELL ENOUGH TO COME TO SCHOOL.
IF YOU DON'T, YOU'LL FLUNK OUT!
GET YOUR BUTT OUT HERE!
IF YOU STICK YOUR NOSE ANY FARTHER INTO MY BUSINESS, I'M GOING TO YANK IT OFF!
RIKU PUT YOU UP TO THIS, DIDN'T HE? THOUGHT YOU'D RACK UP SOME BROWNIE POINTS WITH HIM, HUH?

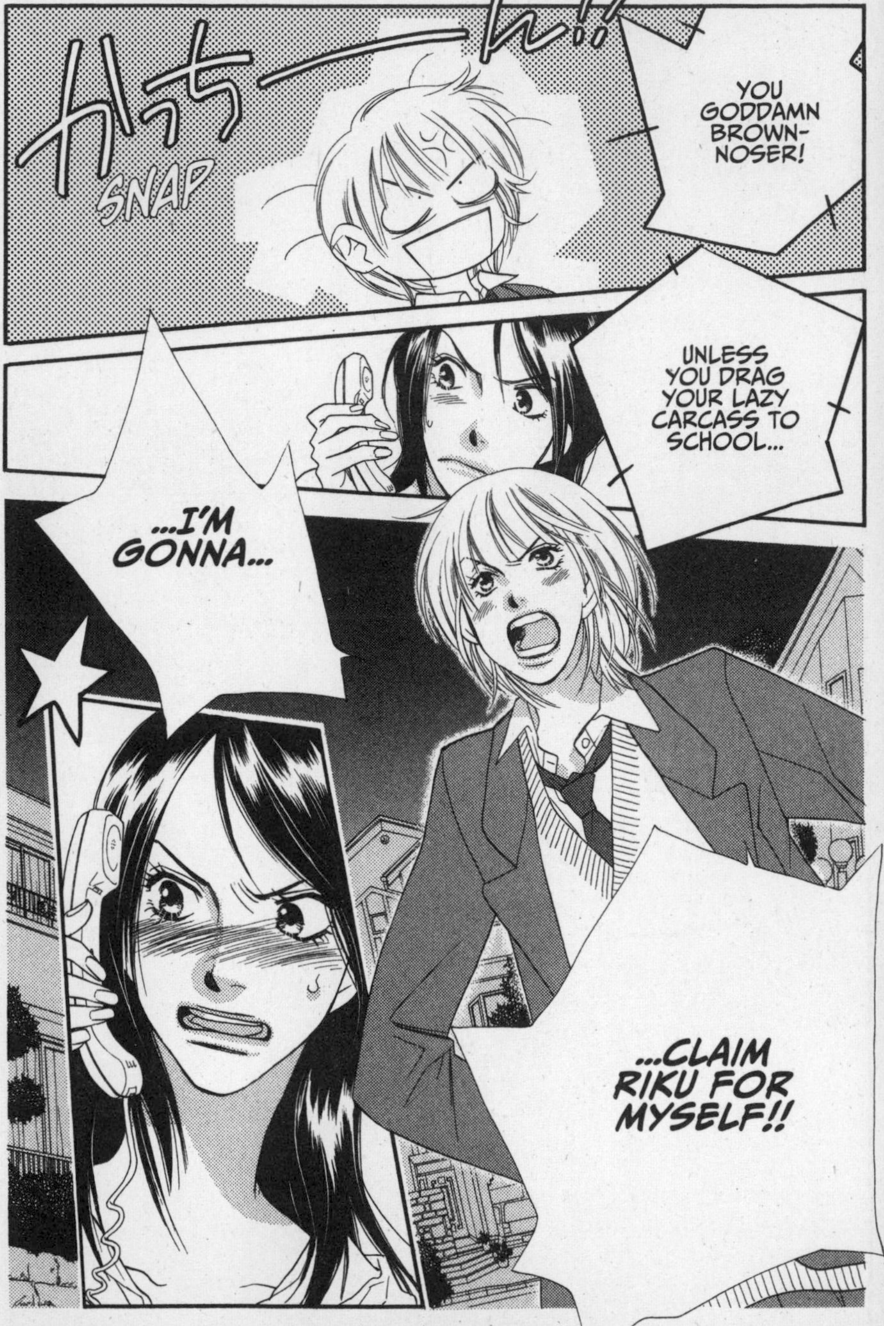
YOU GODDAMN BROWN-NOSER!
カっちーん!!
SNAP
UNLESS YOU DRAG YOUR LAZY CARCASS TO SCHOOL...
...I'M GONNA...
...CLAIM RIKU FOR MYSELF!!

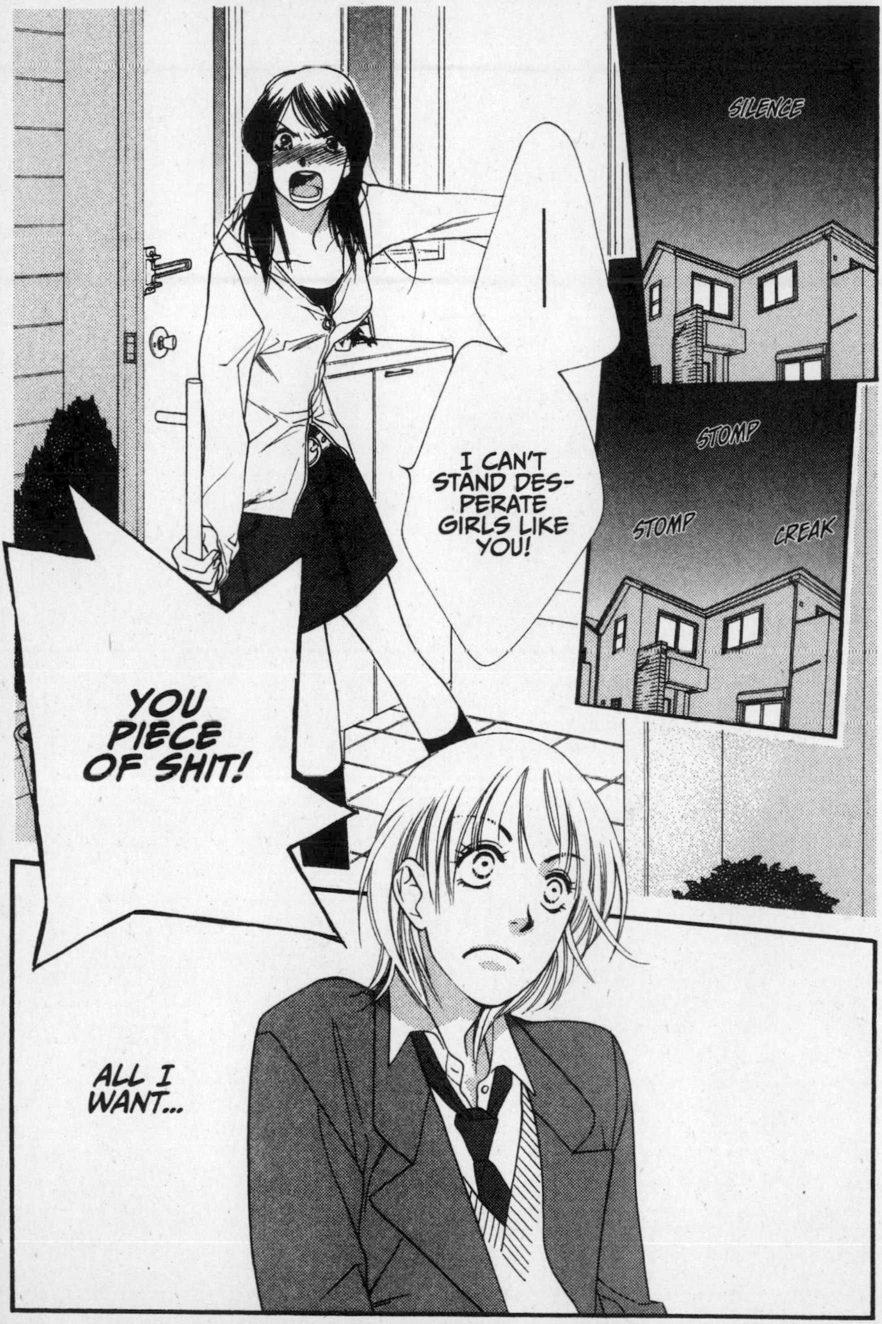
SILENCE
STOMP
STOMP
CREAK
I CAN'T STAND DES-PERATE GIRLS LIKE YOU!
YOU PIECE OF SHIT!
ALL I WANT...

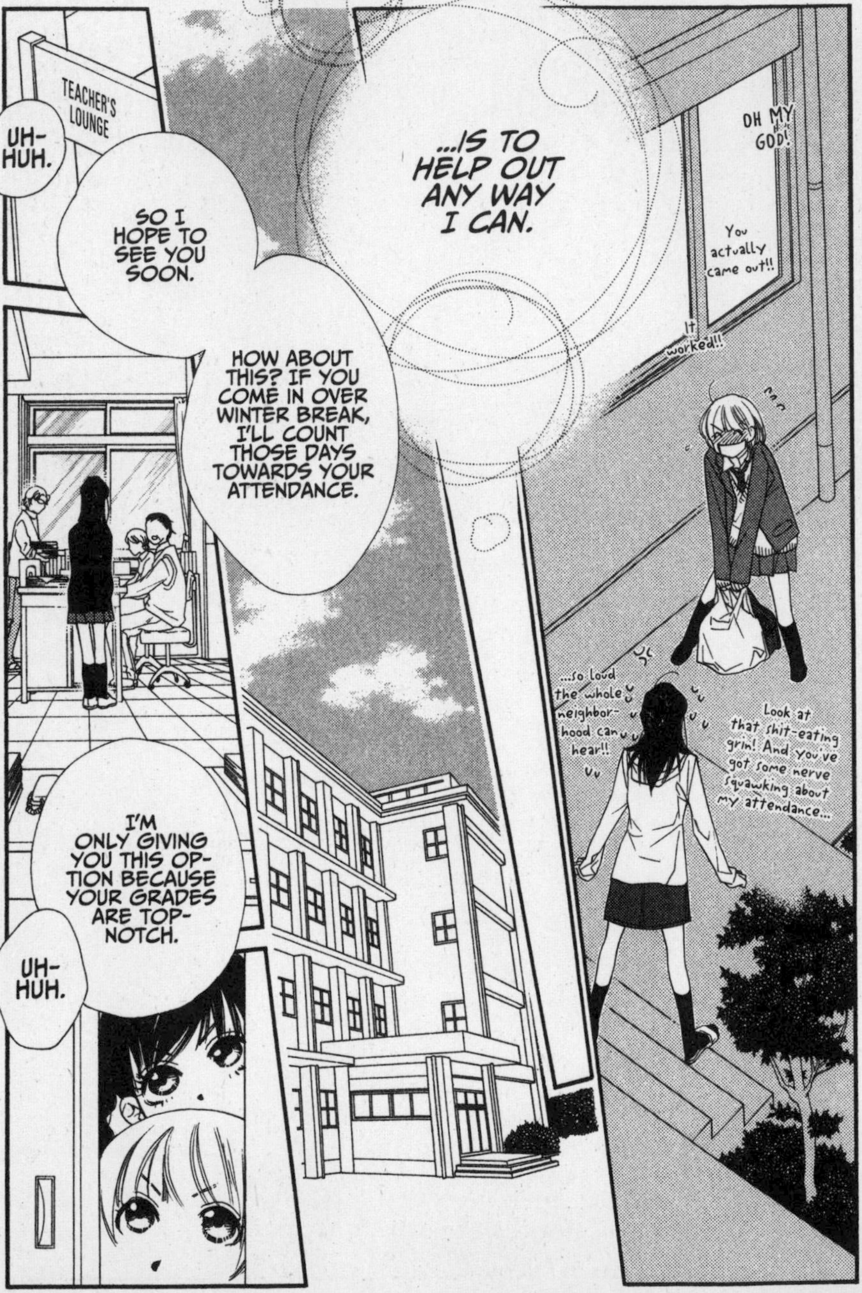
OH MY GOD!
You actually came out!!
It worked!!
Look at that shit-eating grin! And you've got some nerve squawking about my attendance...
...so loud the whole neighbor-hood can hear!!
...IS TO HELP OUT ANY WAY I CAN.
TEACHER'S LOUNGE
UH-HUH.
SO I HOPE TO SEE YOU SOON.
HOW ABOUT THIS? IF YOU COME IN OVER WINTER BREAK, I'LL COUNT THOSE DAYS TOWARDS YOUR ATTENDANCE.
I'M ONLY GIVING YOU THIS OP-TION BECAUSE YOUR GRADES ARE TOP-NOTCH.
UH-HUH.

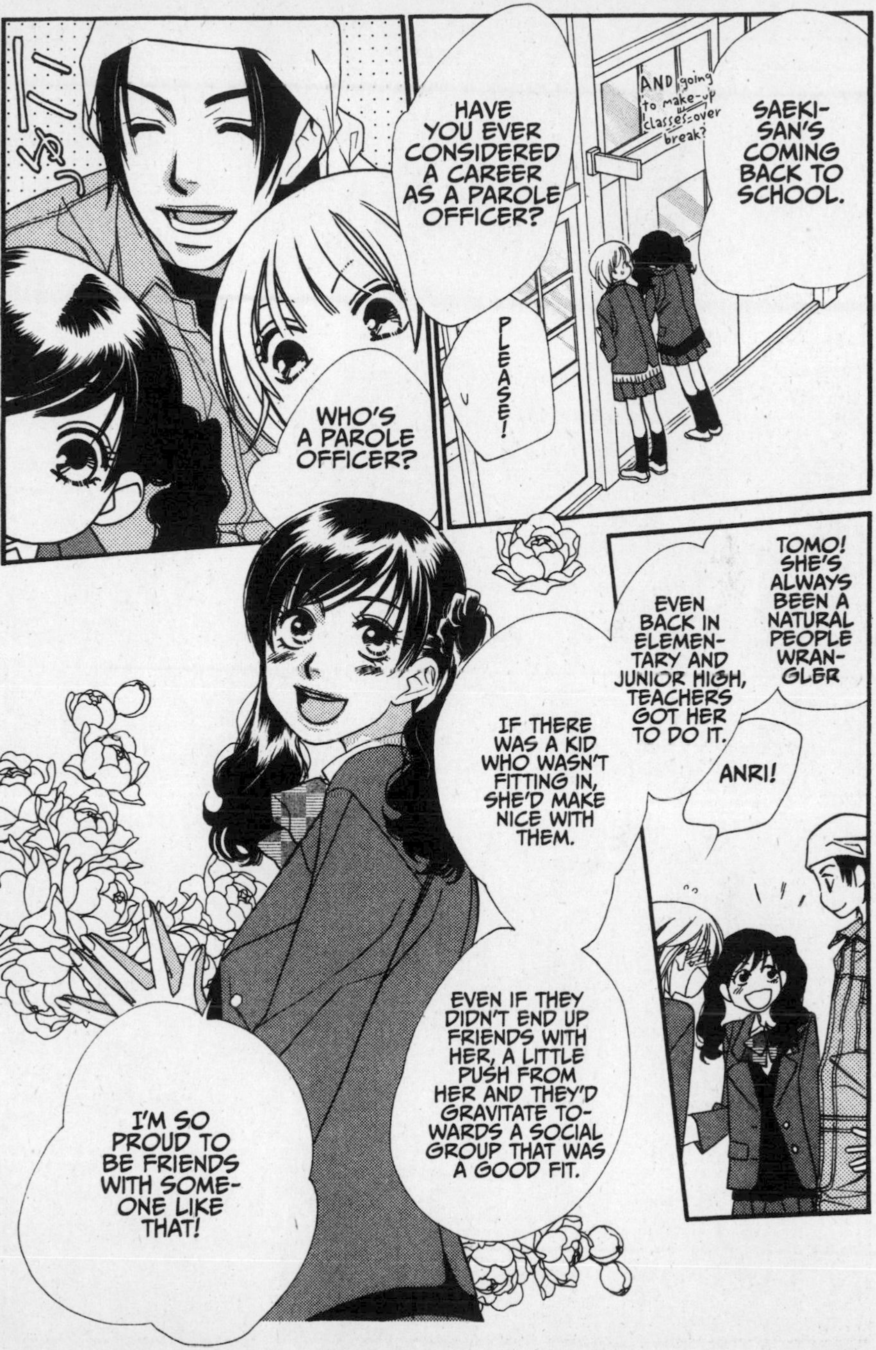
SAEKI-SAN'S COMING BACK TO SCHOOL.
AND going to make-up classes over break?
HAVE YOU EVER CONSIDERED A CAREER AS A PAROLE OFFICER?
PLEASE!
WHO'S A PAROLE OFFICER?
TOMO! SHE'S ALWAYS BEEN A NATURAL PEOPLE WRANGLER
EVEN BACK IN ELEMENTARY AND JUNIOR HIGH, TEACHERS GOT HER TO DO IT.
ANRI!
IF THERE WAS A KID WHO WASN'T FITTING IN, SHE'D MAKE NICE WITH THEM.
EVEN IF THEY DIDN'T END UP FRIENDS WITH HER, A LITTLE PUSH FROM HER AND THEY'D GRAVITATE TOWARDS A SOCIAL GROUP THAT WAS A GOOD FIT.
I'M SO PROUD TO BE FRIENDS WITH SOMEONE LIKE THAT!

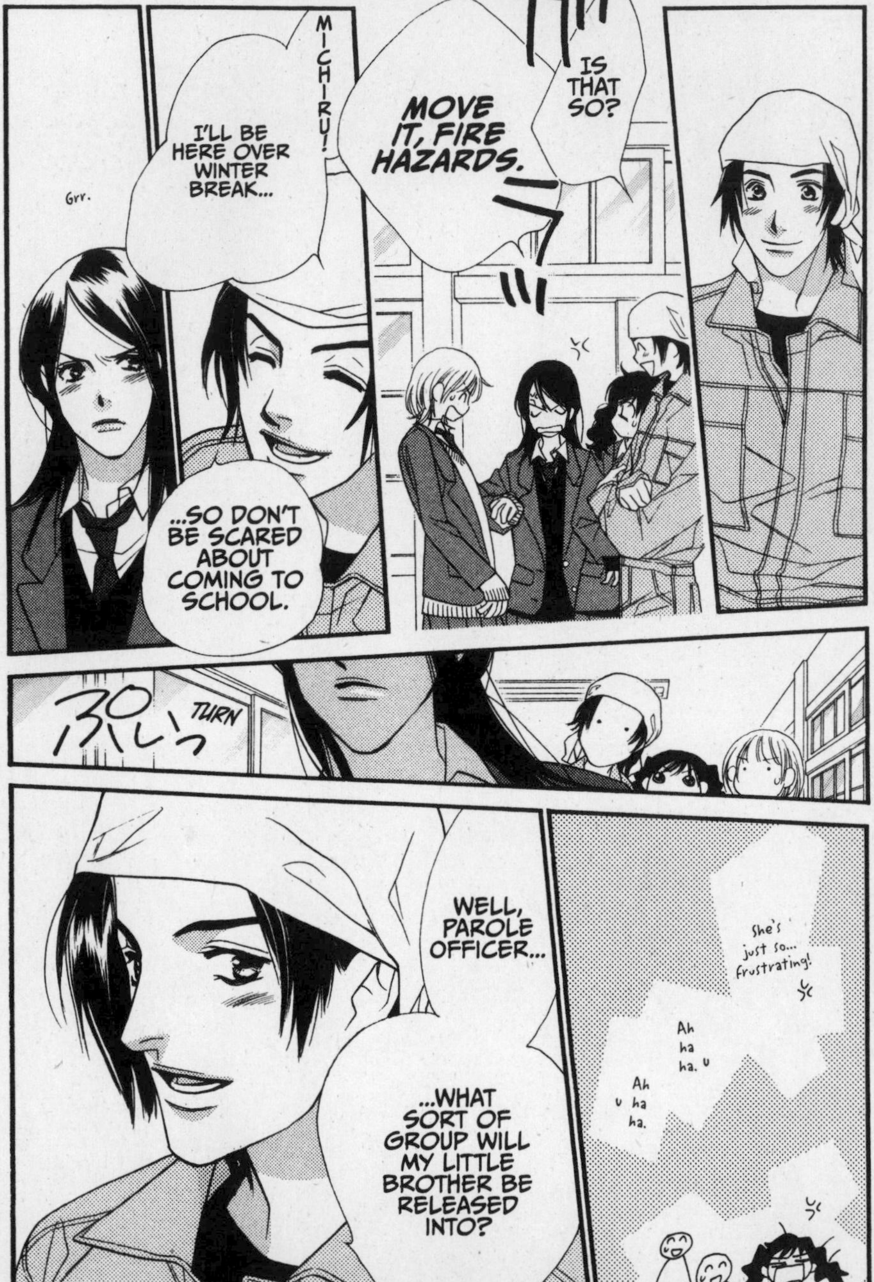
IS THAT SO?
MOVE IT, FIRE HAZARDS.
MICHIRU!
I'LL BE HERE OVER WINTER BREAK...
...SO DON'T BE SCARED ABOUT COMING TO SCHOOL.
Grr.
ぷいっ
TURN
She's just so... frustrating!
Ah ha ha.
Ah ha ha.
WELL, PAROLE OFFICER...
...WHAT SORT OF GROUP WILL MY LITTLE BROTHER BE RELEASED INTO?

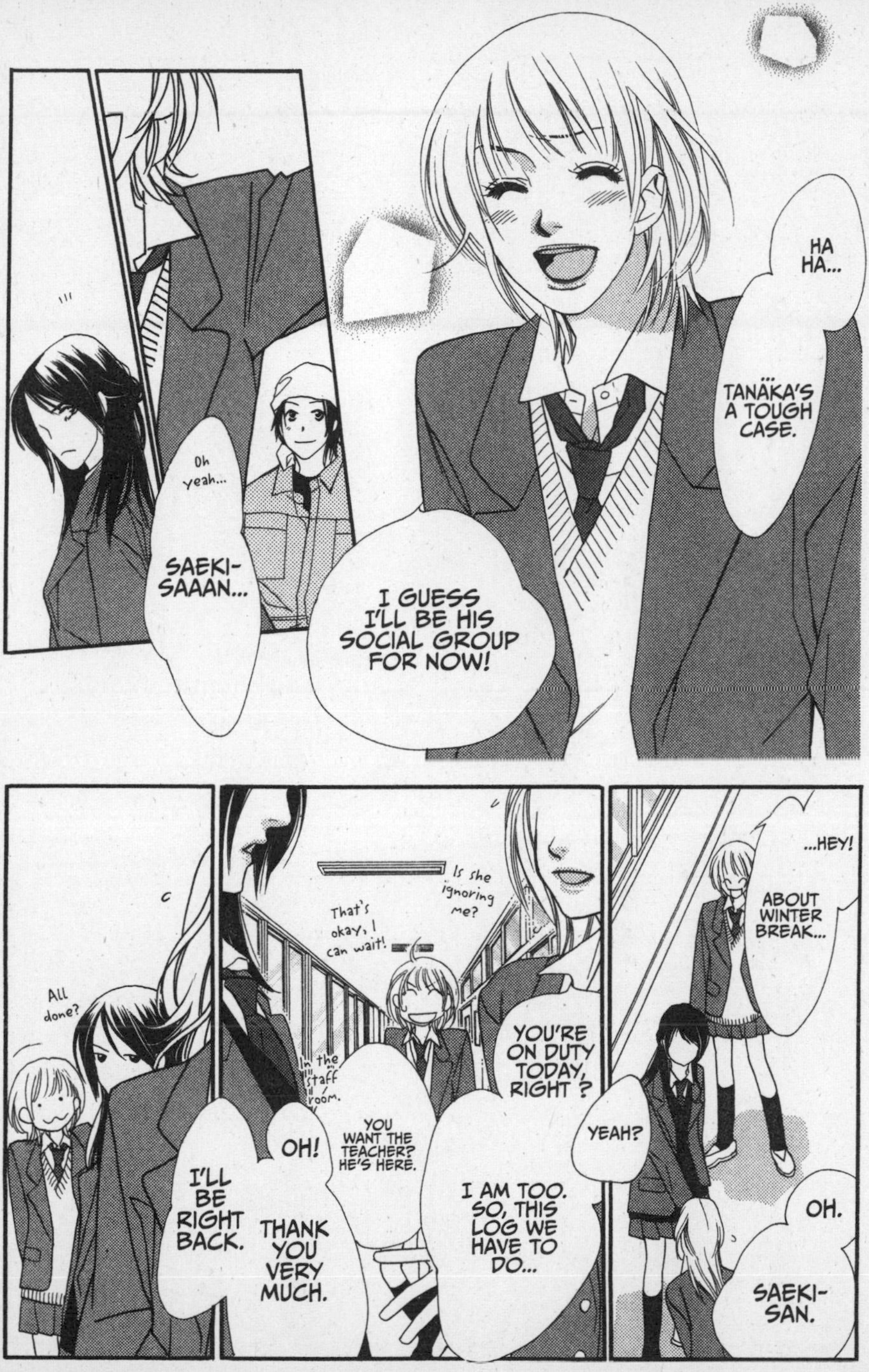
HA HA...
...TANAKA'S A TOUGH CASE.
I GUESS I'LL BE HIS SOCIAL GROUP FOR NOW!
Oh yeah...
SAEKI-SAAAN...
...HEY!
ABOUT WINTER BREAK...
OH.
SAEKI-SAN.
YEAH?
YOU'RE ON DUTY TODAY, RIGHT?
I AM TOO. SO, THIS LOG WE HAVE TO DO...
Is she ignoring me?
That's okay, I can wait!
YOU WANT THE TEACHER? HE'S HERE.
In the staff room.
OH!
THANK YOU VERY MUCH.
All done?
I'LL BE RIGHT BACK.

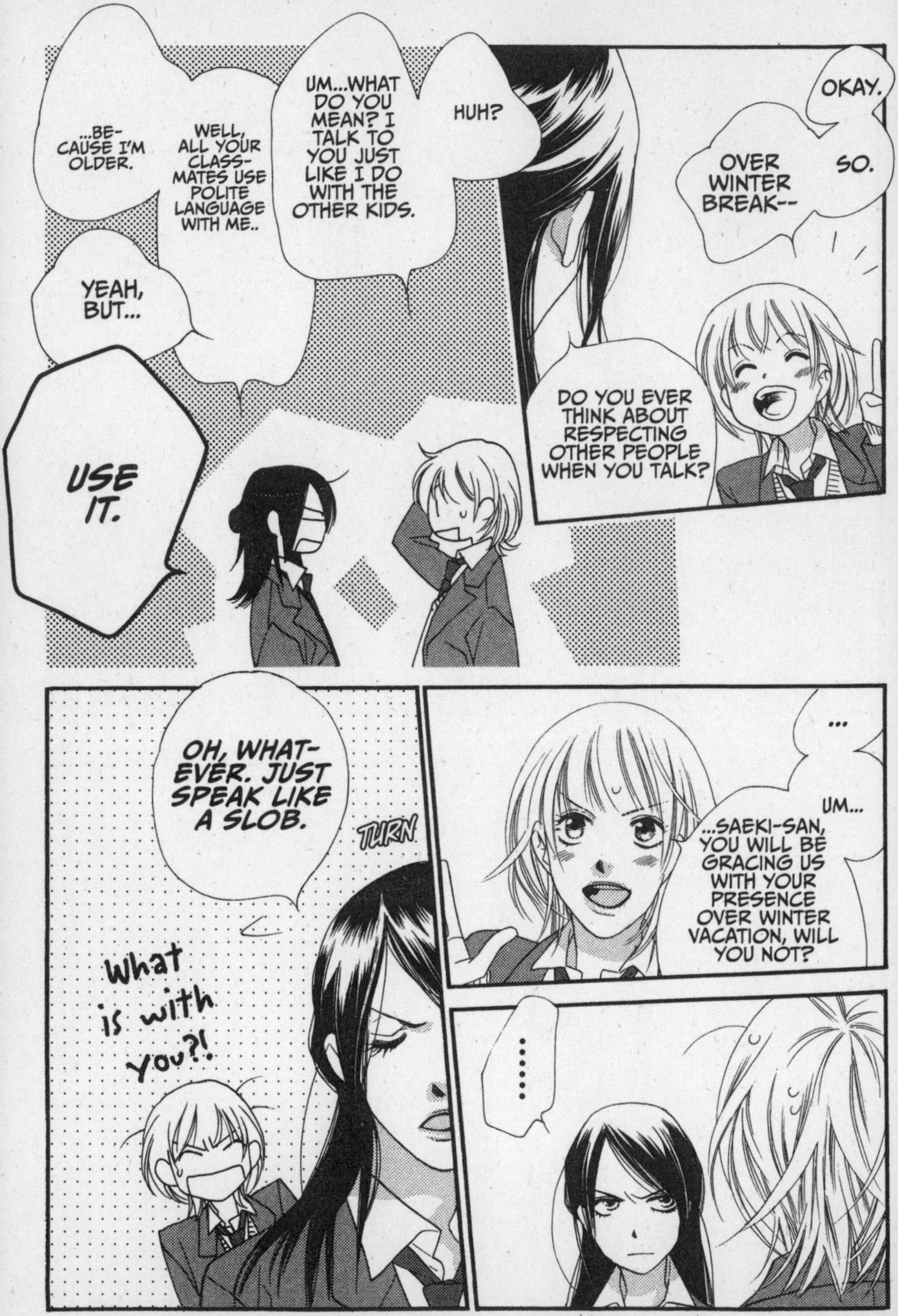
OKAY.
SO.
OVER WINTER BREAK--
DO YOU EVER THINK ABOUT RESPECTING OTHER PEOPLE WHEN YOU TALK?
HUH?
UM...WHAT DO YOU MEAN? I TALK TO YOU JUST LIKE I DO WITH THE OTHER KIDS.
WELL, ALL YOUR CLASS-MATES USE POLITE LANGUAGE WITH ME..
...BE-CAUSE I'M OLDER.
YEAH, BUT...
USE IT.
...
UM...
...SAEKI-SAN, YOU WILL BE GRACING US WITH YOUR PRESENCE OVER WINTER VACATION, WILL YOU NOT?
......
OH, WHAT-EVER. JUST SPEAK LIKE A SLOB.
TURN
What is with you?!

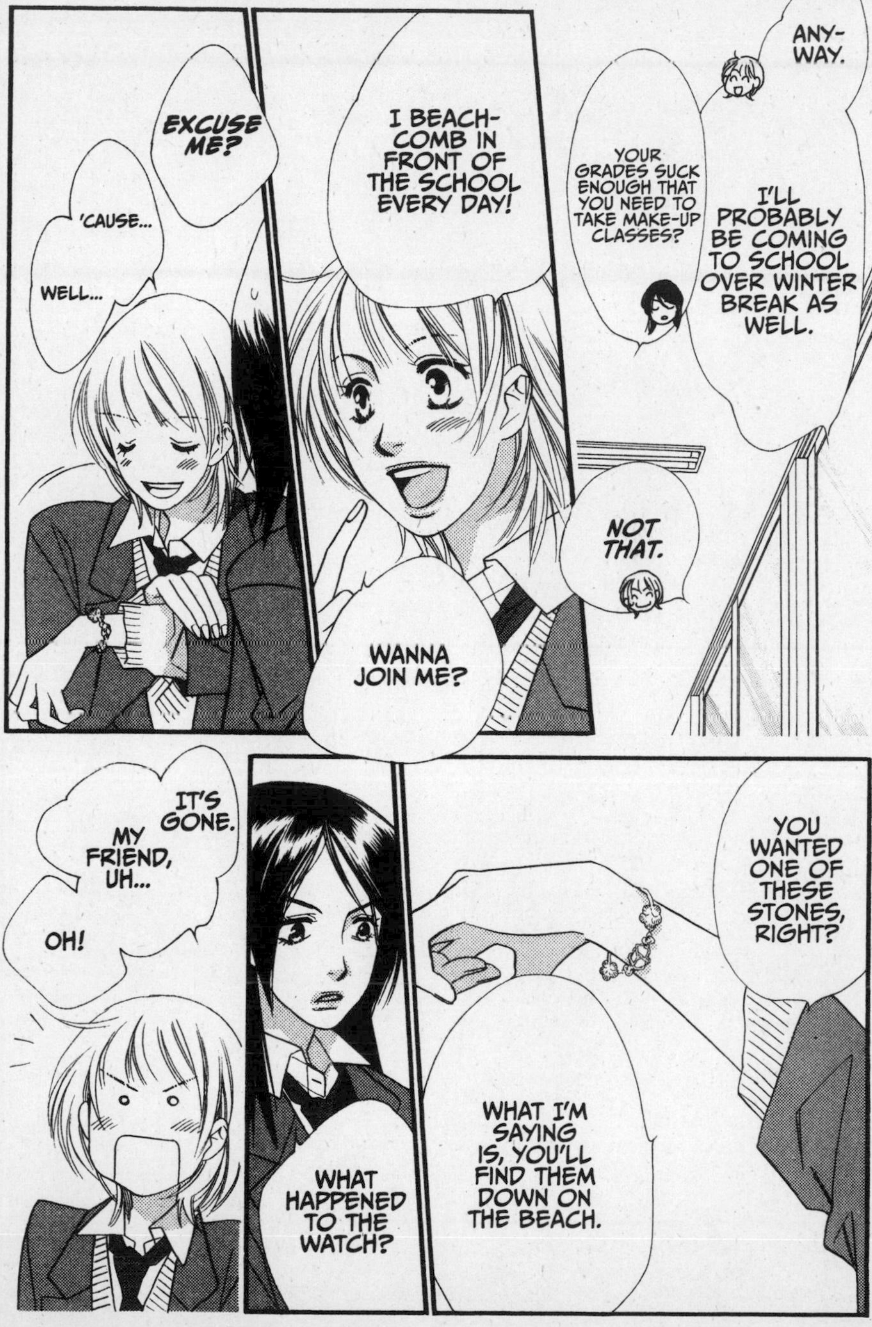
ANY-WAY.
I'LL PROBABLY BE COMING TO SCHOOL OVER WINTER BREAK AS WELL.
YOUR GRADES SUCK ENOUGH THAT YOU NEED TO TAKE MAKE-UP CLASSES?
NOT THAT.
I BEACH-COMB IN FRONT OF THE SCHOOL EVERY DAY!
WANNA JOIN ME?
EXCUSE ME?
'CAUSE...
WELL...
YOU WANTED ONE OF THESE STONES, RIGHT?
WHAT I'M SAYING IS, YOU'LL FIND THEM DOWN ON THE BEACH.
WHAT HAPPENED TO THE WATCH?
IT'S GONE.
MY FRIEND, UH...
OH!

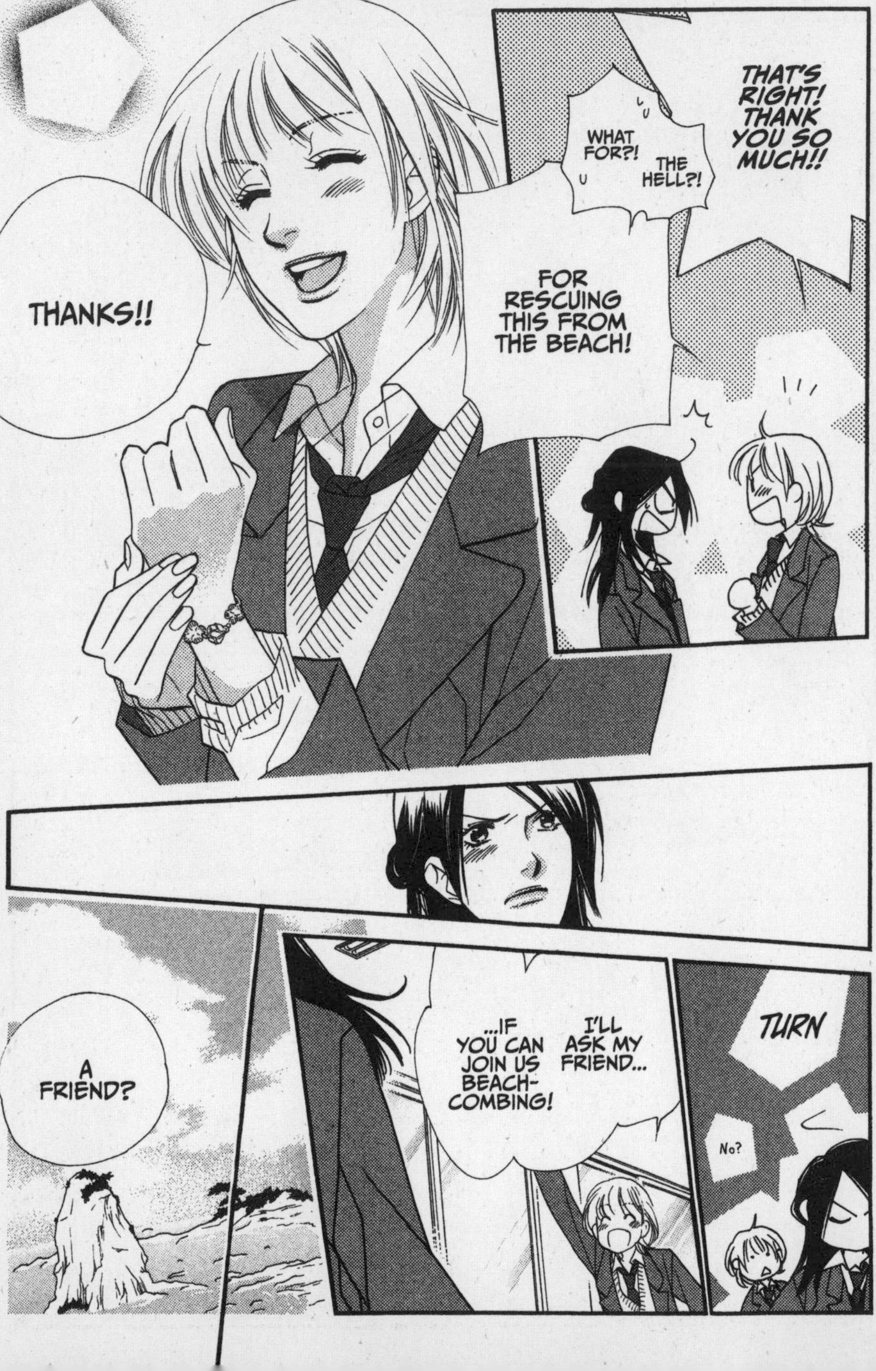
THAT'S RIGHT! THANK YOU SO MUCH!!
WHAT FOR?! THE HELL?!
FOR RESCUING THIS FROM THE BEACH!
THANKS!!
TURN
No?
I'LL ASK MY FRIEND... ...IF YOU CAN JOIN US BEACH-COMBING!
A FRIEND?

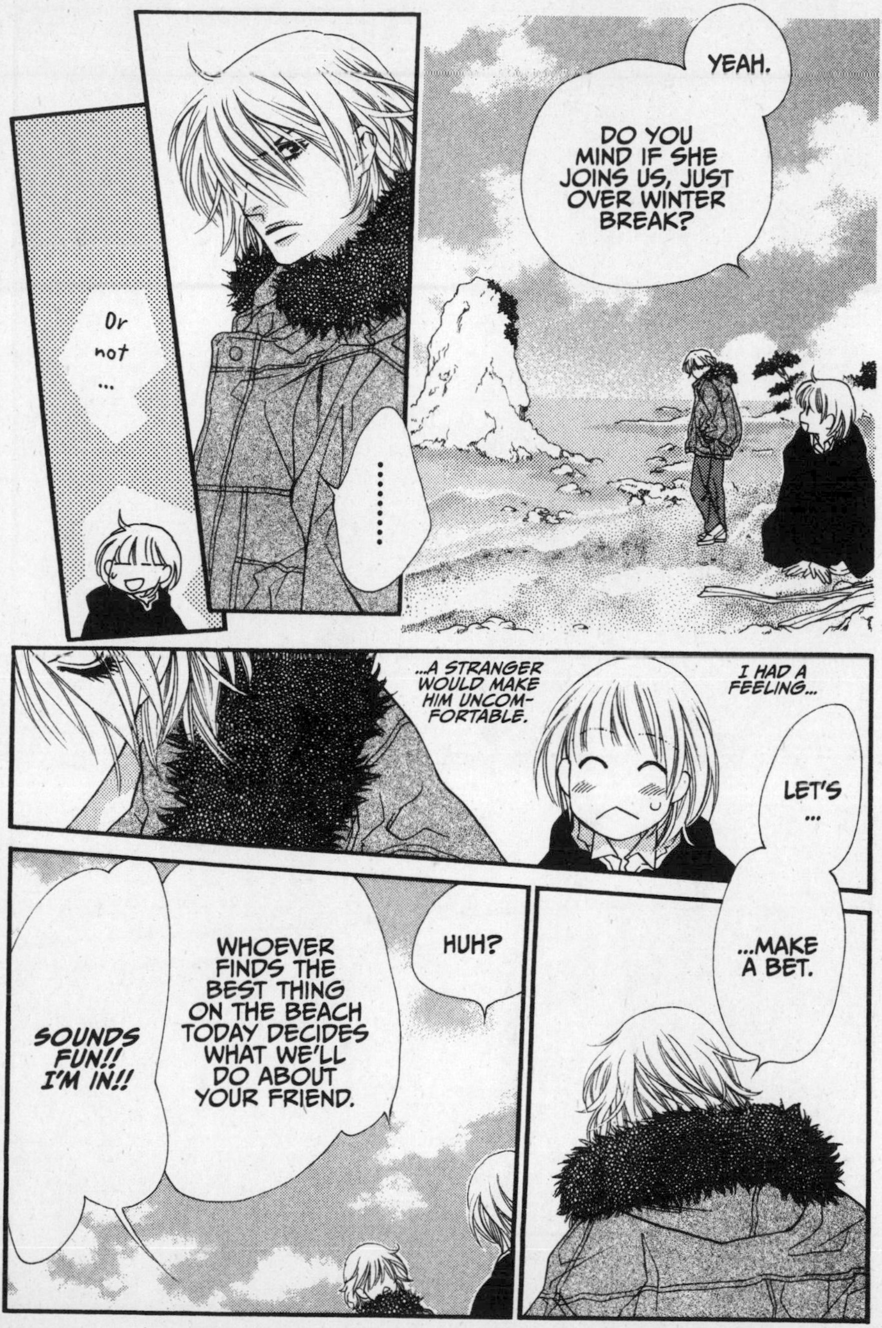

YEAH.
DO YOU MIND IF SHE JOINS US, JUST OVER WINTER BREAK?
....
Or not ...
I HAD A FEELING...
...A STRANGER WOULD MAKE HIM UNCOMFORTABLE.
LET'S ...
...MAKE A BET.
HUH?
WHOEVER FINDS THE BEST THING ON THE BEACH TODAY DECIDES WHAT WE'LL DO ABOUT YOUR FRIEND.
SOUNDS FUN!! I'M IN!!

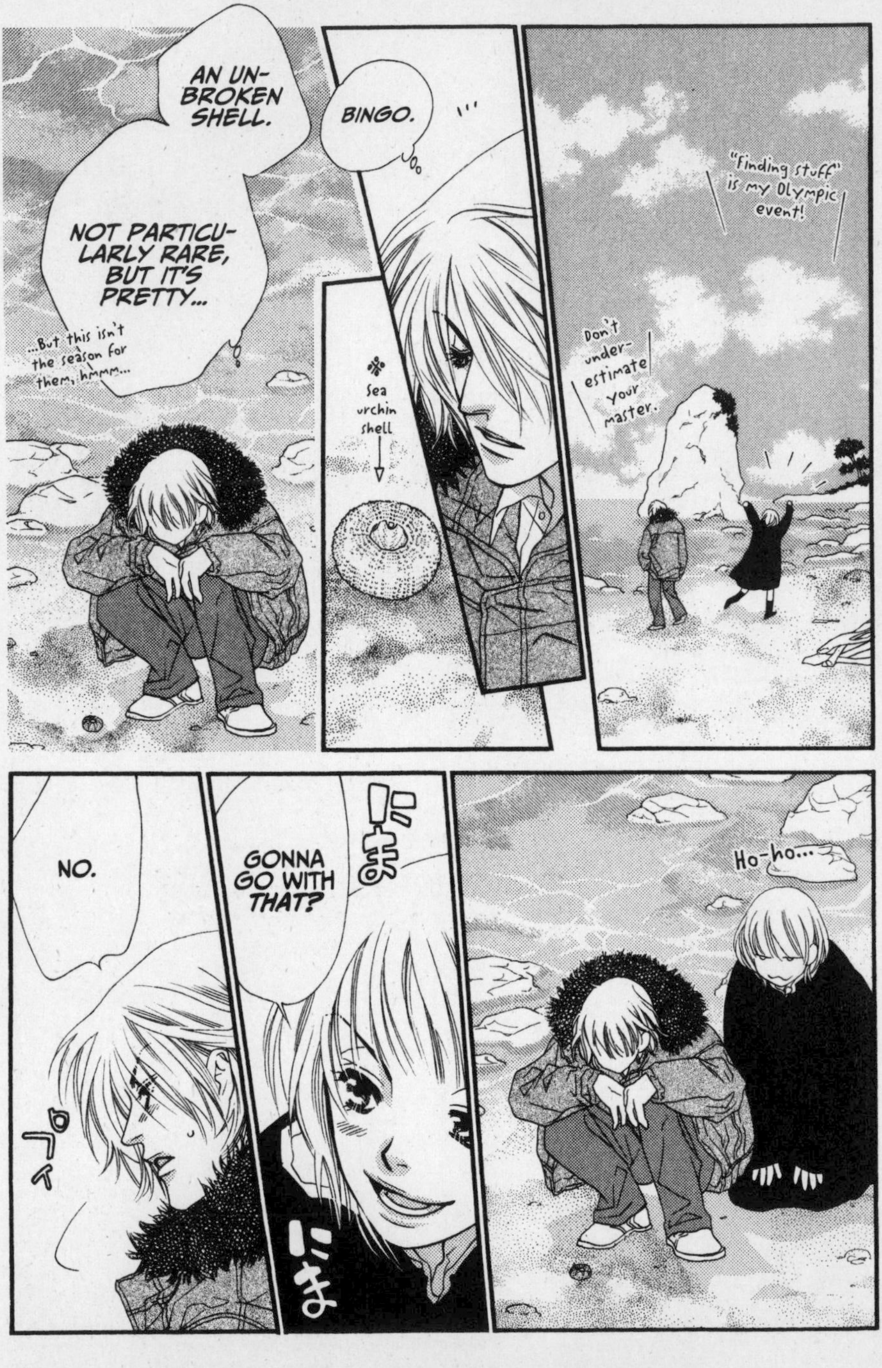
"Finding stuff" is my Olympic event!
Don't under-estimate your master.
BINGO.
...
Sea urchin shell
AN UN-BROKEN SHELL.
NOT PARTICU-LARLY RARE, BUT IT'S PRETTY...
...But this isn't the season for them, hmmm...
Ho-ho...
にま
GONNA GO WITH THAT?
にま
NO.
プイ

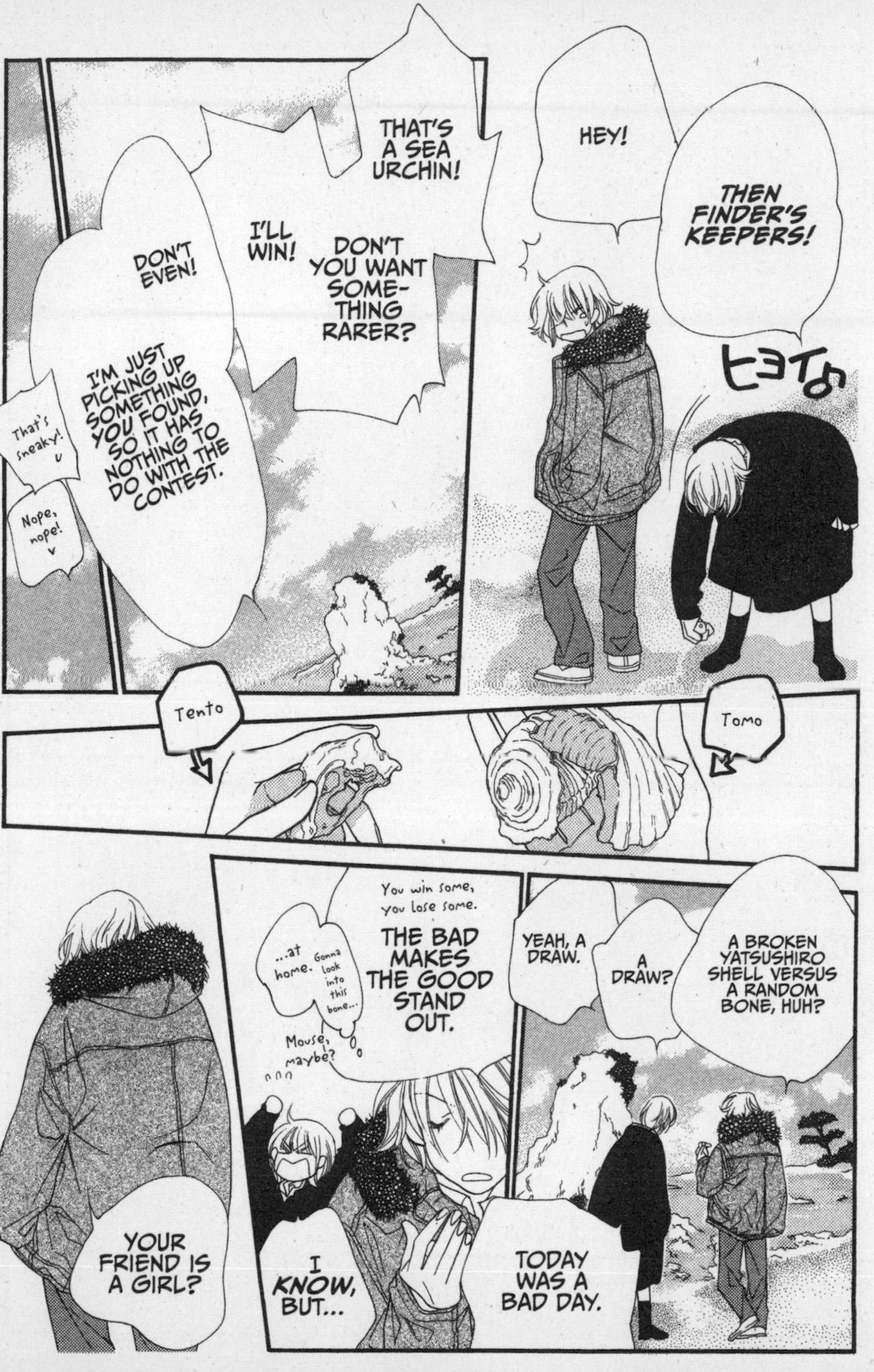
HEY!
THEN FINDER'S KEEPERS!
THAT'S A SEA URCHIN!
DON'T YOU WANT SOMETHING RARER?
I'LL WIN!
DON'T EVEN!
I'M JUST PICKING UP SOMETHING *YOU* FOUND, SO IT HAS NOTHING TO DO WITH THE CONTEST.
That's sneaky!
Nope, nope!
Tomo
Tento
A BROKEN YATSUSHIRO SHELL VERSUS A RANDOM BONE, HUH?
A DRAW?
YEAH, A DRAW.
You win some, you lose some.
THE BAD MAKES THE GOOD STAND OUT.
...at home. Gonna look into this bone...
Mouse, maybe?
TODAY WAS A BAD DAY.
I *KNOW*, BUT...
YOUR FRIEND IS A GIRL?

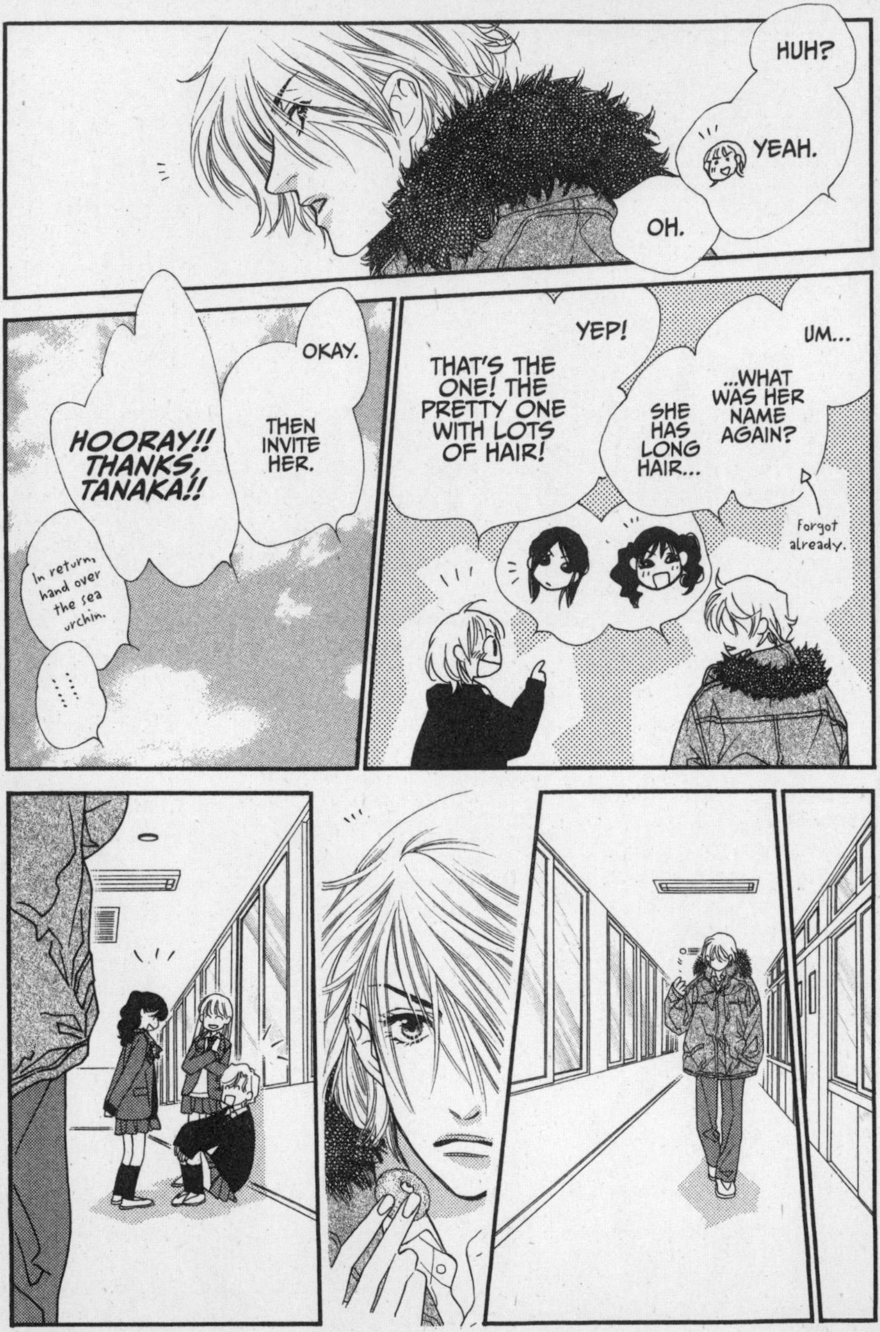
HUH?
YEAH.
OH.
UM...
...WHAT WAS HER NAME AGAIN?
Forgot already.
SHE HAS LONG HAIR...
YEP!
THAT'S THE ONE! THE PRETTY ONE WITH LOTS OF HAIR!
OKAY.
THEN INVITE HER.
HOORAY!! THANKS, TANAKA!!
In return, hand over the sea urchin.
......

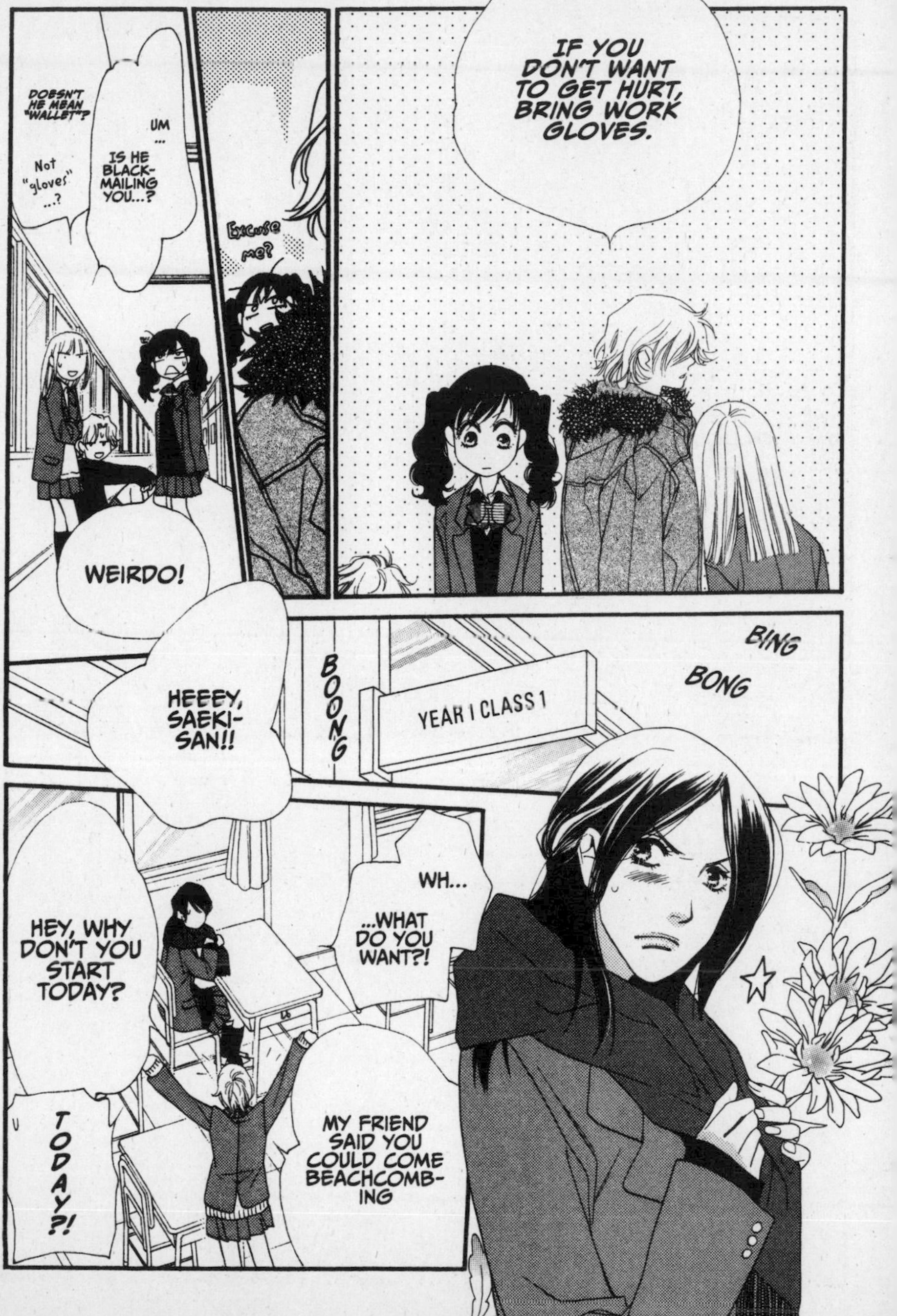
IF YOU DON'T WANT TO GET HURT, BRING WORK GLOVES.
Excuse me?
UM ...
IS HE BLACK-MAILING YOU...?
Not "gloves" ...?
DOESN'T HE MEAN "WALLET"?
WEIRDO!
BING
BONG
YEAR 1 CLASS 1
BOONG
HEEEY, SAEKI-SAN!!
WH...
...WHAT DO YOU WANT?!
MY FRIEND SAID YOU COULD COME BEACHCOMB-ING
HEY, WHY DON'T YOU START TODAY?
TODAY?!

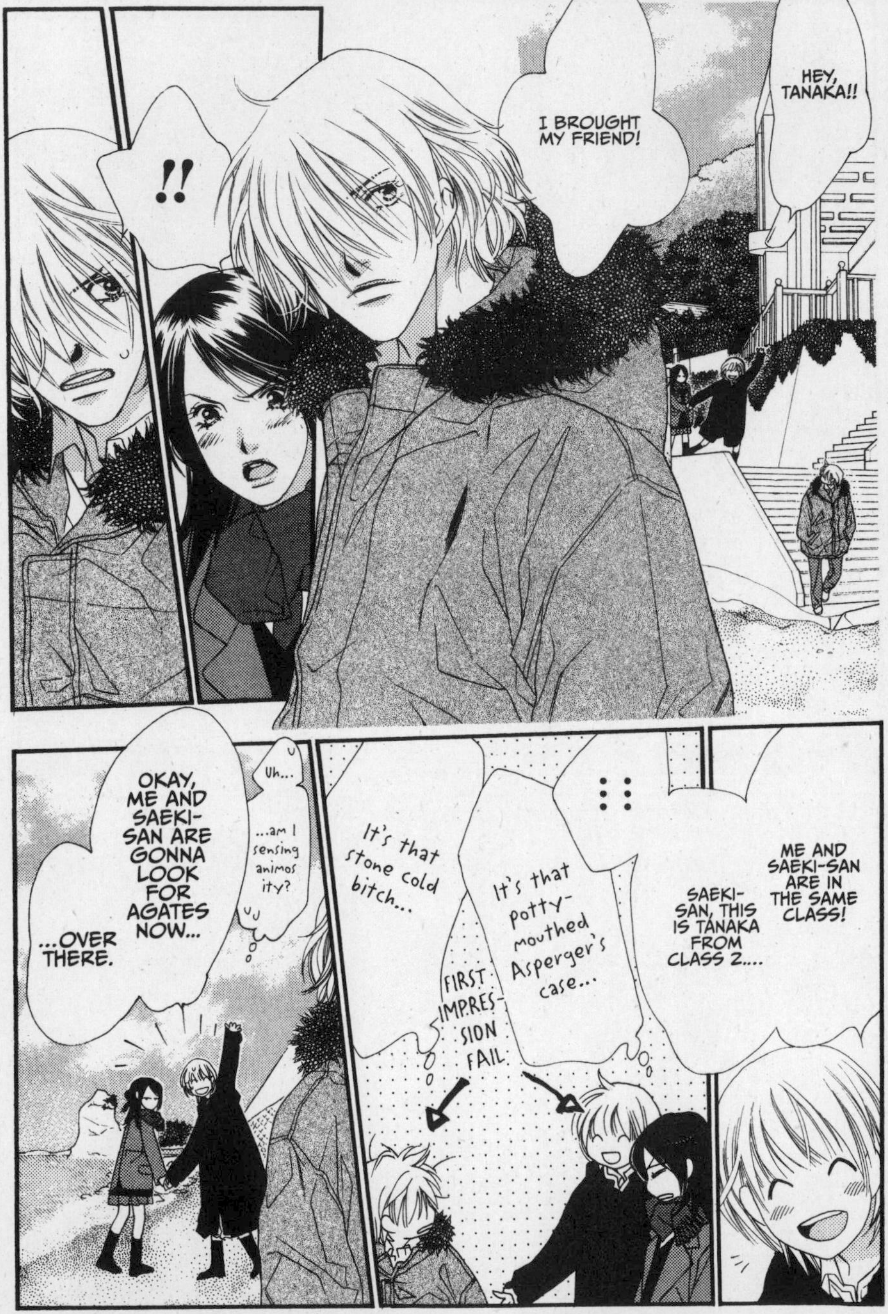
HEY, TANAKA!!
I BROUGHT MY FRIEND!
!!
ME AND SAEKI-SAN ARE IN THE SAME CLASS!
SAEKI-SAN, THIS IS TANAKA FROM CLASS 2....
:: ::
It's that potty-mouthed Asperger's case...
It's that stone cold bitch...
FIRST IMPRES-SION FAIL
Uh...
...am I sensing animos ity?
OKAY, ME AND SAEKI-SAN ARE GONNA LOOK FOR AGATES NOW...
...OVER THERE.

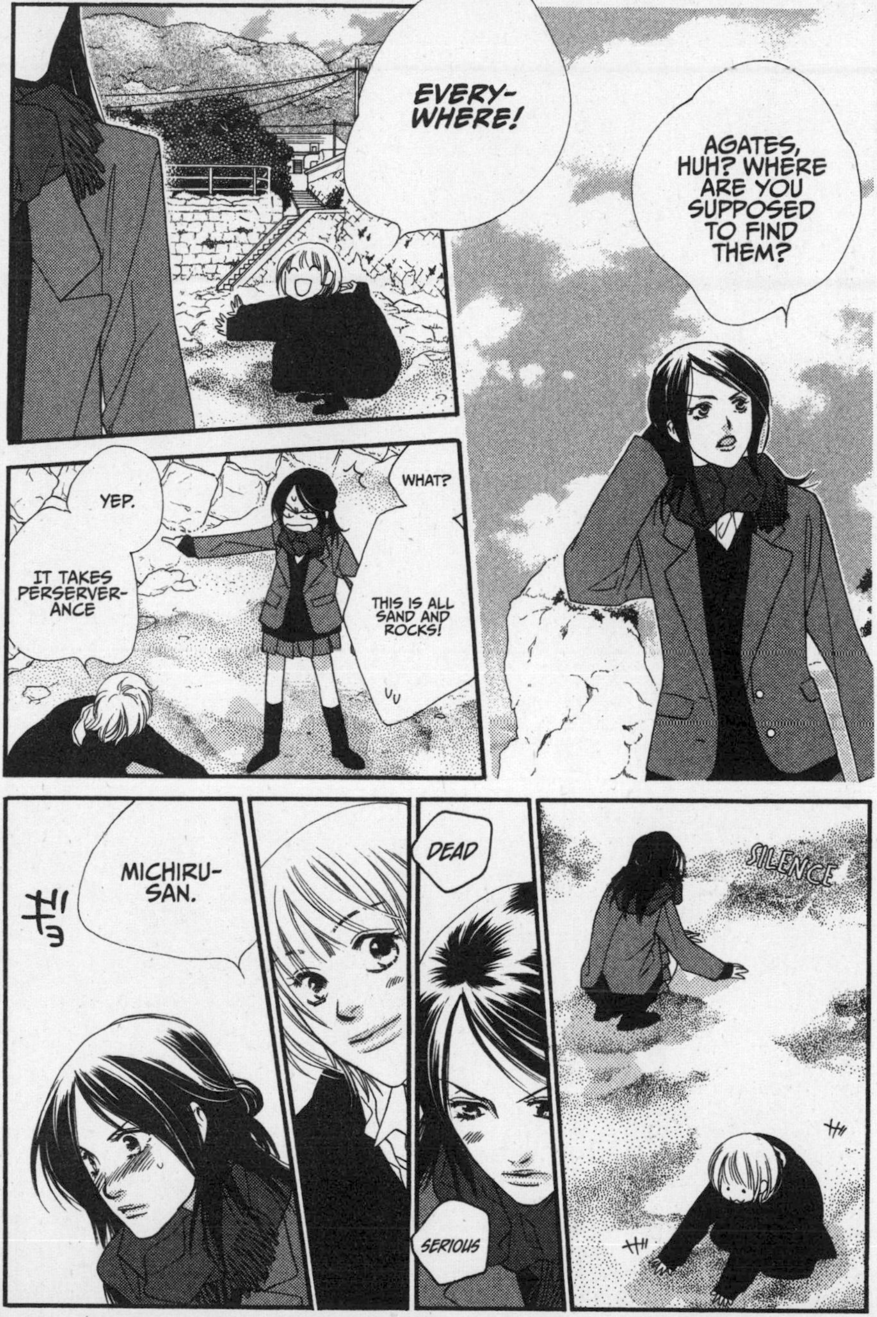
AGATES, HUH? WHERE ARE YOU SUPPOSED TO FIND THEM?
EVERY-WHERE!
WHAT?
THIS IS ALL SAND AND ROCKS!
YEP.
IT TAKES PERSERVER-ANCE
SILENCE
DEAD
SERIOUS
MICHIRU-SAN.

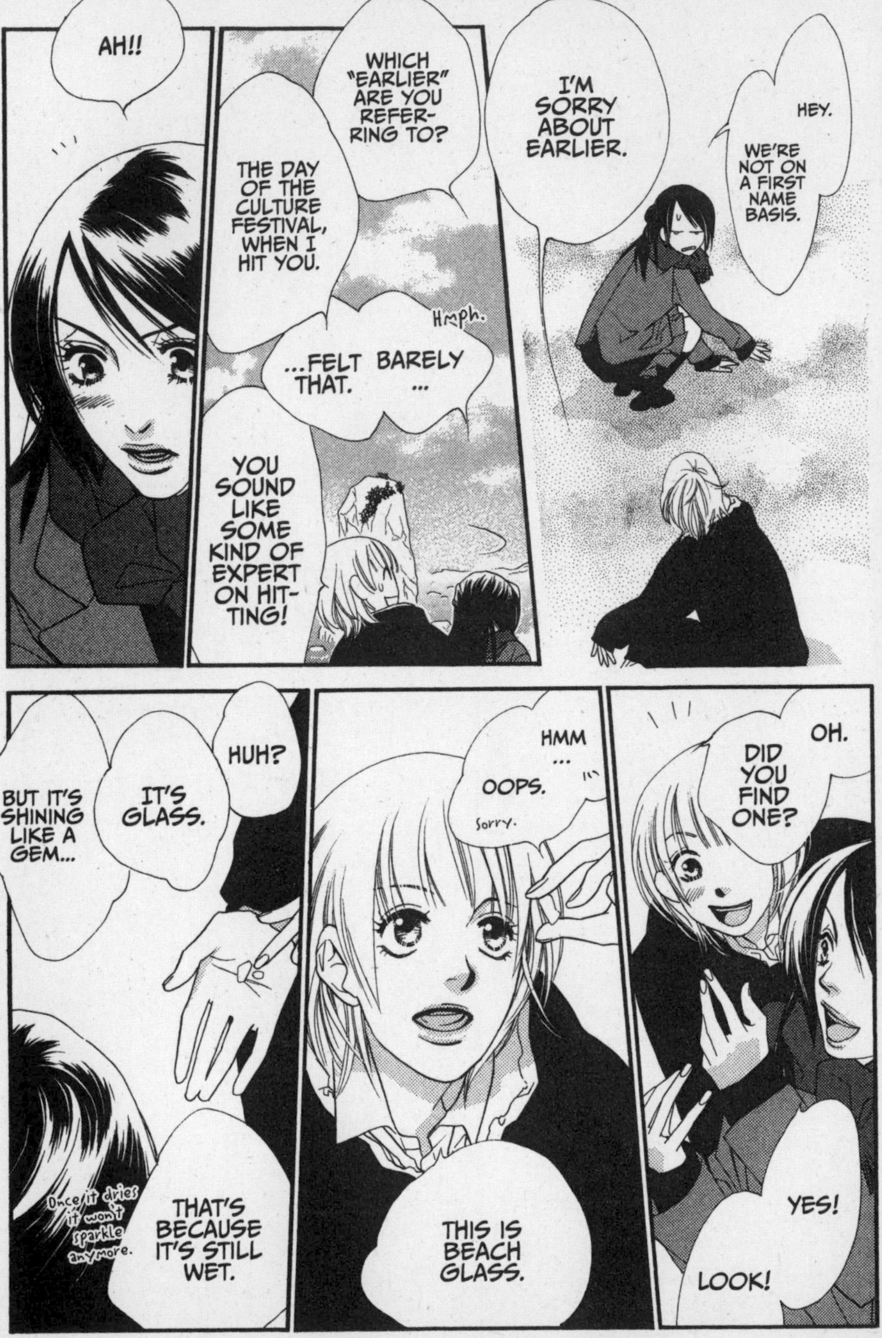
HEY.
WE'RE NOT ON A FIRST NAME BASIS.
I'M SORRY ABOUT EARLIER.
WHICH "EARLIER" ARE YOU REFER-RING TO?
THE DAY OF THE CULTURE FESTIVAL, WHEN I HIT YOU.
Hmph.
...FELT BARELY THAT. ...
YOU SOUND LIKE SOME KIND OF EXPERT ON HIT-TING!
AH!!
OH.
DID YOU FIND ONE?
YES!
LOOK!
HMM ...
OOPS.
Sorry.
THIS IS BEACH GLASS.
HUH?
IT'S GLASS.
BUT IT'S SHINING LIKE A GEM...
THAT'S BECAUSE IT'S STILL WET.
Once it dries it won't sparkle anymore.

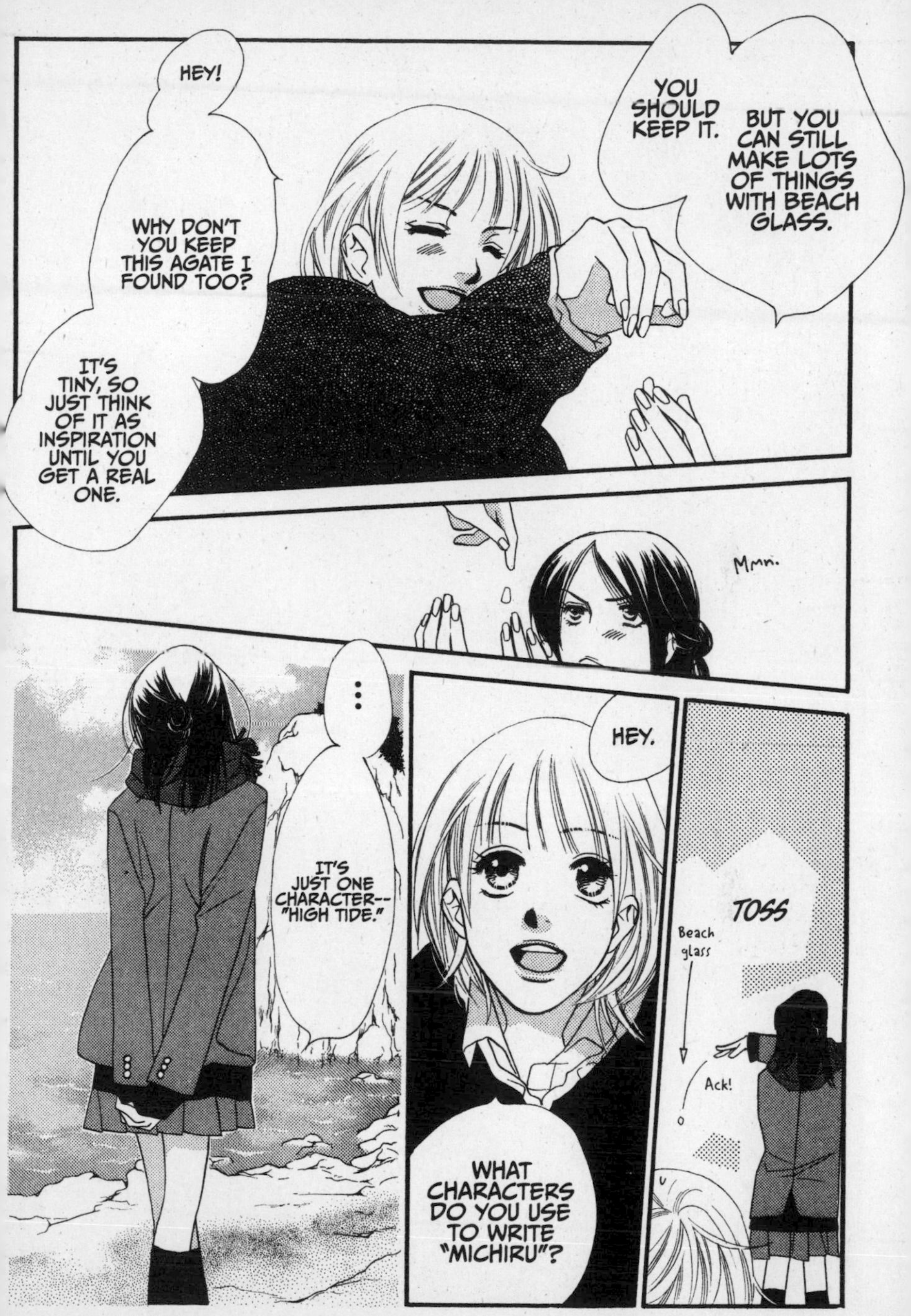
BUT YOU CAN STILL MAKE LOTS OF THINGS WITH BEACH GLASS.
YOU SHOULD KEEP IT.
HEY!
WHY DON'T YOU KEEP THIS AGATE I FOUND TOO?
IT'S TINY, SO JUST THINK OF IT AS INSPIRATION UNTIL YOU GET A REAL ONE.
Mmn.
TOSS
Beach glass
Ack!
HEY.
WHAT CHARACTERS DO YOU USE TO WRITE "MICHIRU"?
...
IT'S JUST ONE CHARACTER-- "HIGH TIDE."

......
A TIDE BIG ENOUGH TO OVERWHELM A PERSON.
SMACK
WELL, "TOMO" ...
...I'M LIKE THE MORNING LIGHT THAT SHINES UPON THAT SPECIAL SOMEONE--
...IS WRITTEN USING THE CHARACTER FOR "MORNING," SO...

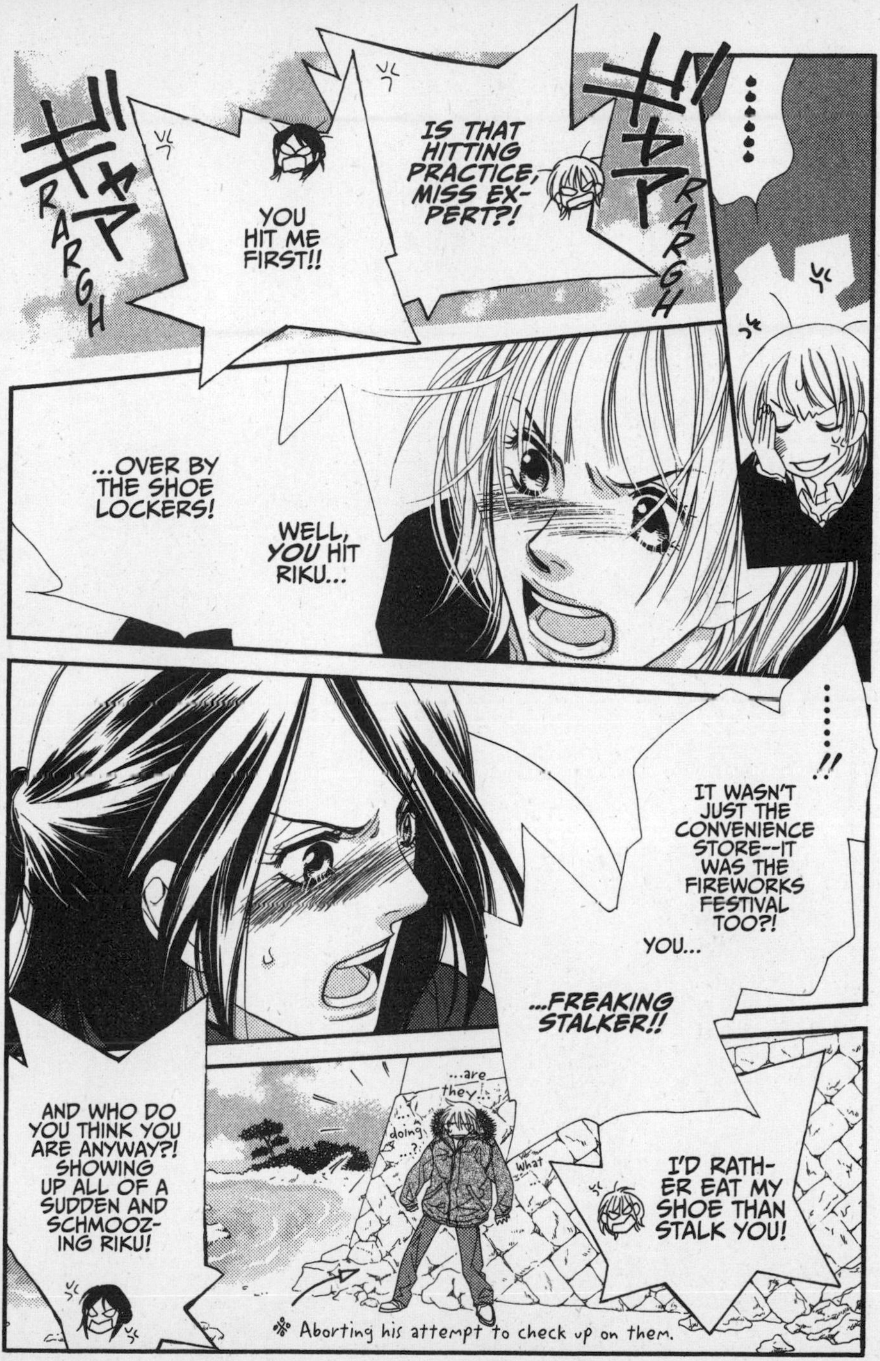
......
RARGH
IS THAT HITTING PRACTICE, MISS EXPERT?!
YOU HIT ME FIRST!!
RARGH
WELL, *YOU* HIT RIKU...
...OVER BY THE SHOE LOCKERS!
......!!
IT WASN'T JUST THE CONVENIENCE STORE--IT WAS THE FIREWORKS FESTIVAL TOO?!
YOU...
...FREAKING STALKER!!
I'D RATHER EAT MY SHOE THAN STALK YOU!
What...
...are they...
doing...?
AND WHO DO YOU THINK YOU ARE ANYWAY?! SHOWING UP ALL OF A SUDDEN AND SCHMOOZING RIKU!
※ Aborting his attempt to check up on them.

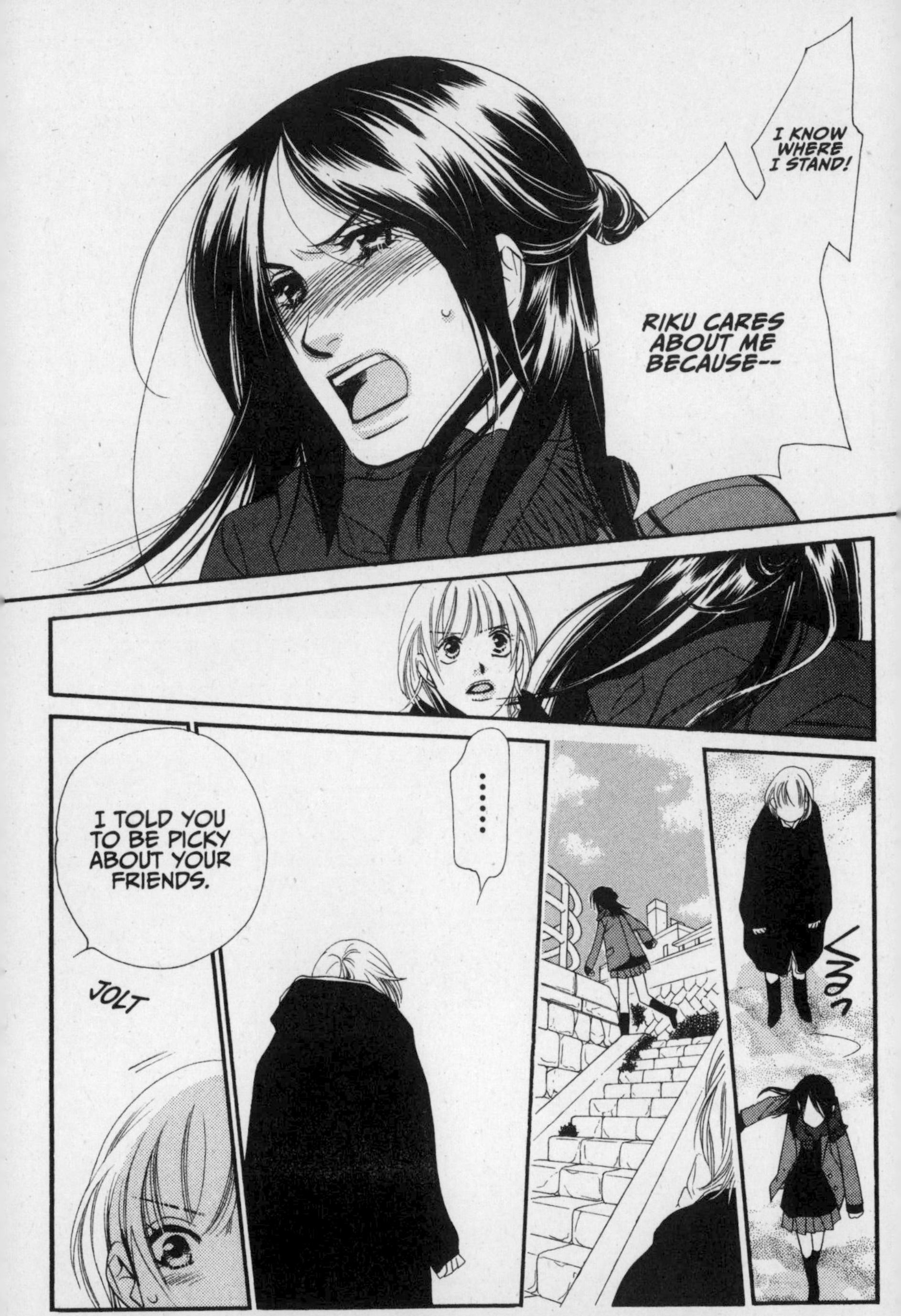

I KNOW WHERE I STAND!
RIKU CARES ABOUT ME BECAUSE--
......
I TOLD YOU TO BE PICKY ABOUT YOUR FRIENDS.
JOLT

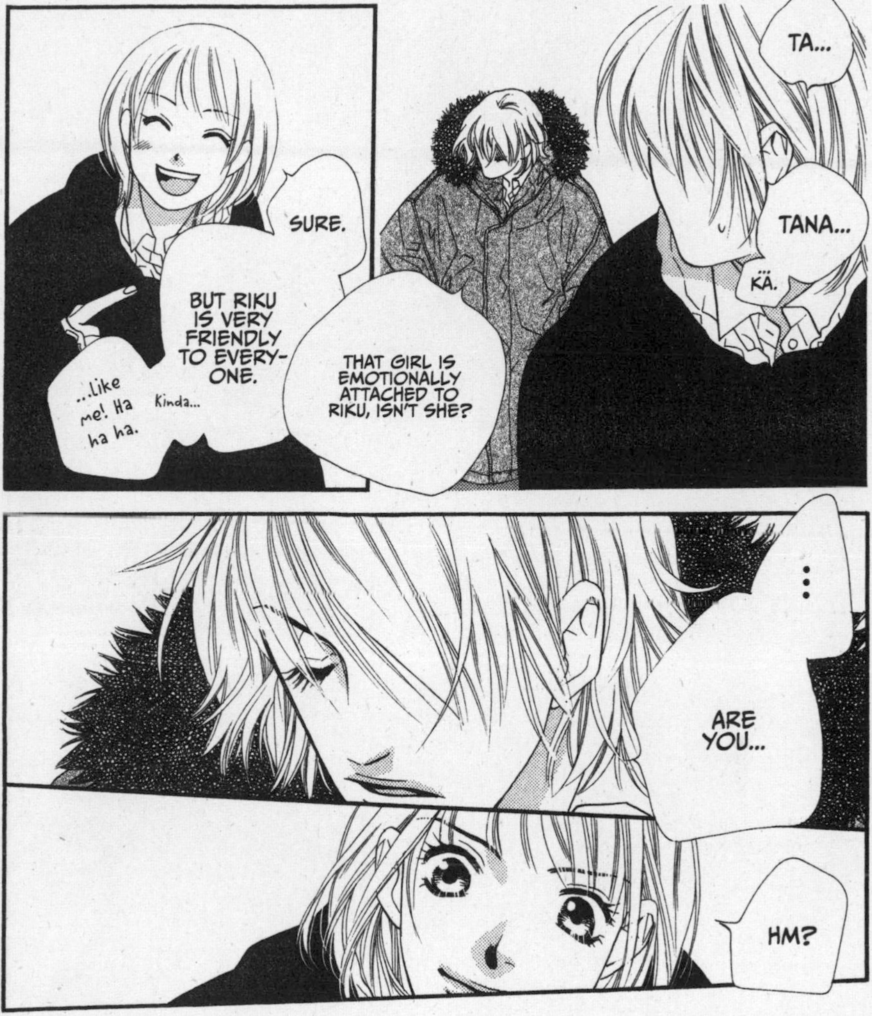
TA...
TANA...
...KÄ.
THAT GIRL IS EMOTIONALLY ATTACHED TO RIKU, ISN'T SHE?
SURE.
BUT RIKU IS VERY FRIENDLY TO EVERY-ONE.
Kinda...
...like me! Ha ha ha.
...
ARE YOU...
HM?

"ARE YOU OKAY WITH THAT?"

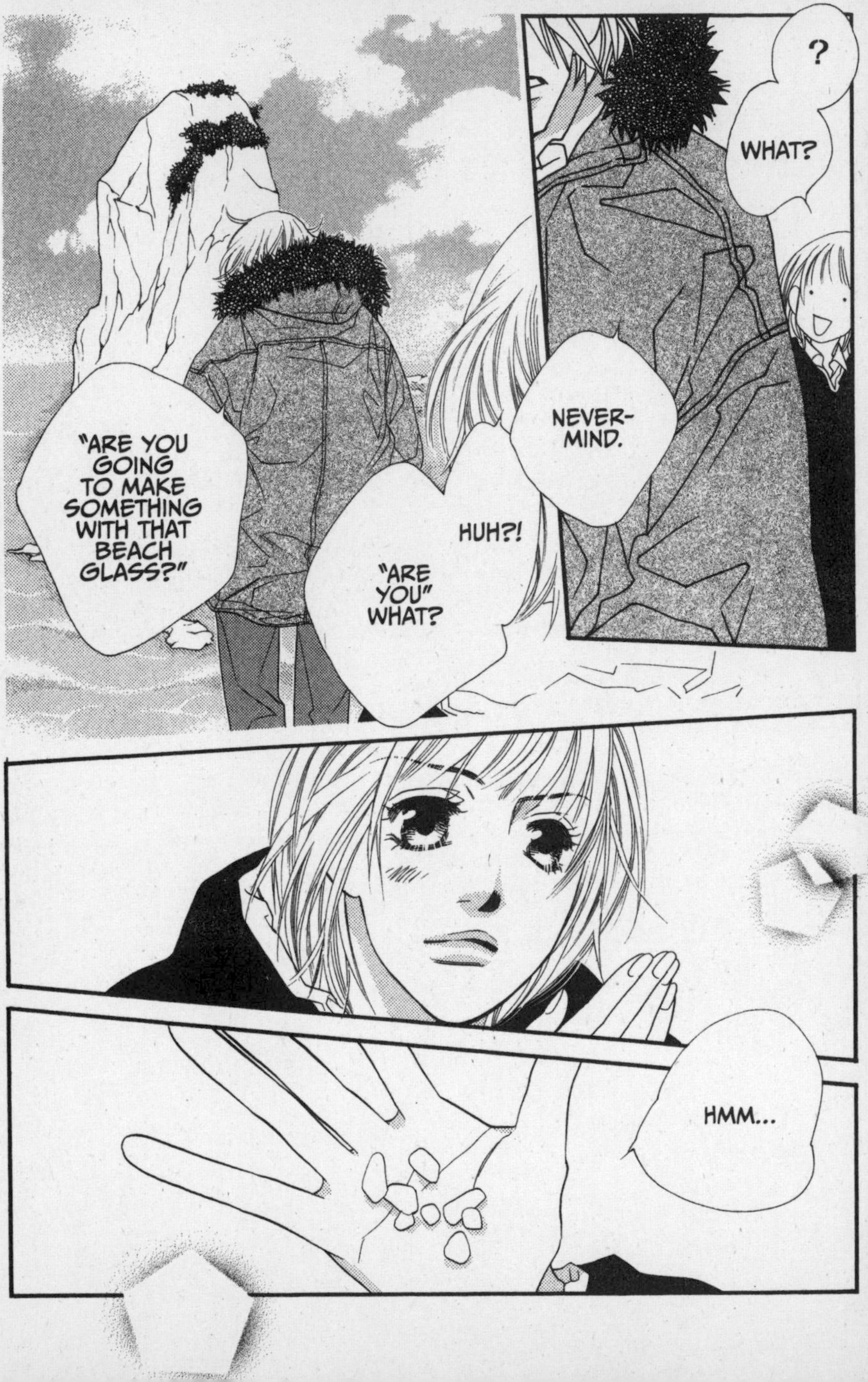
?
WHAT?
NEVER-MIND.
HUH?!
"ARE YOU" WHAT?
"ARE YOU GOING TO MAKE SOMETHING WITH THAT BEACH GLASS?"
HMM...

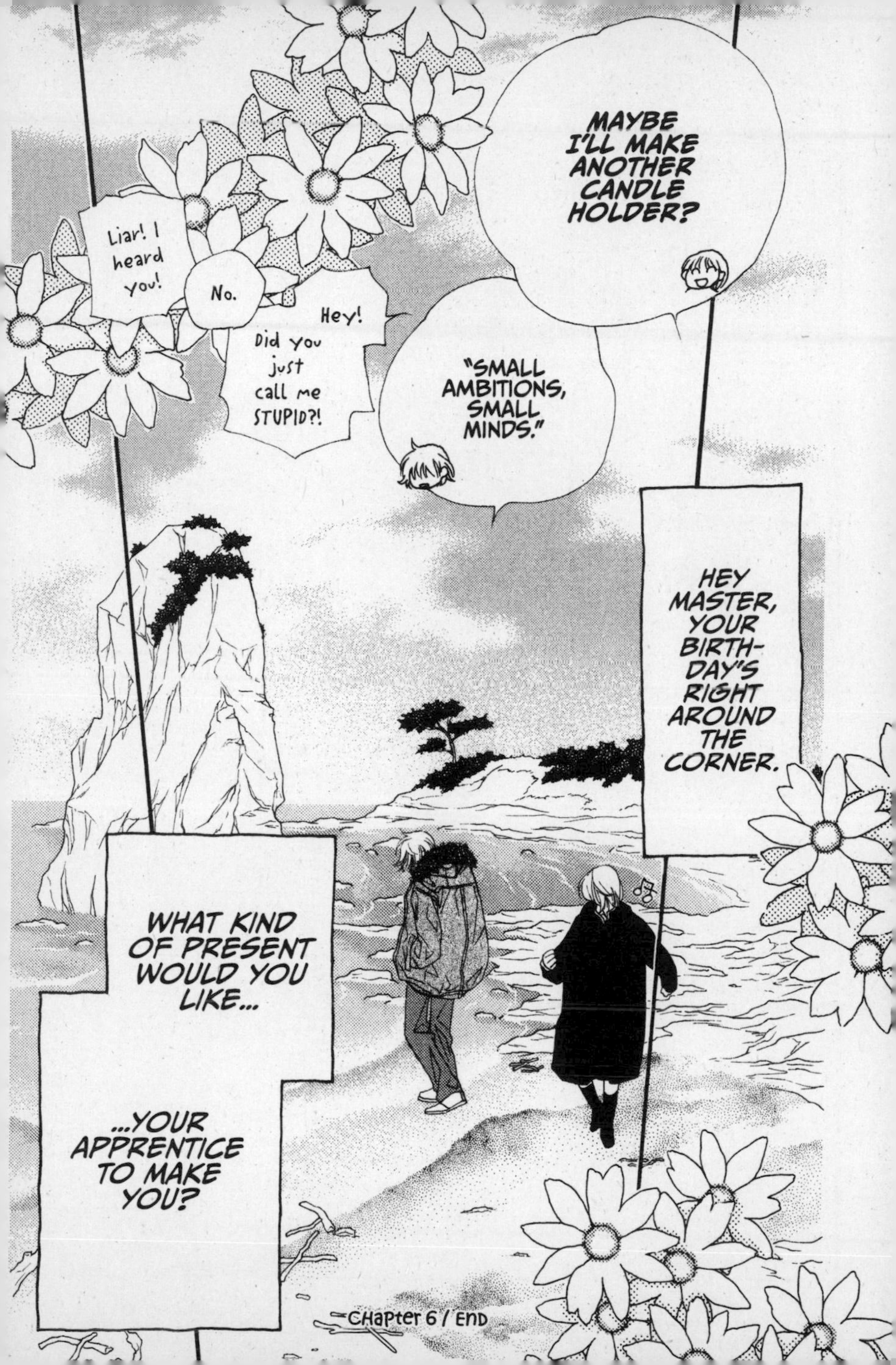
MAYBE I'LL MAKE ANOTHER CANDLE HOLDER?
"SMALL AMBITIONS, SMALL MINDS."
Hey! Did you just call me STUPID?!
No.
Liar! I heard you!
HEY MASTER, YOUR BIRTH-DAY'S RIGHT AROUND THE CORNER.
WHAT KIND OF PRESENT WOULD YOU LIKE...
...YOUR APPRENTICE TO MAKE YOU?
Chapter 6 / END

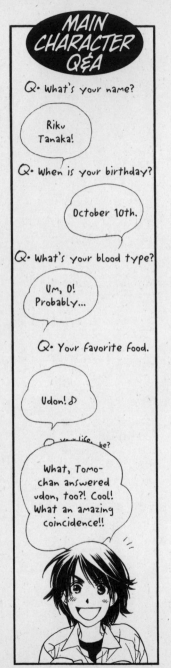

MAIN CHARACTER Q&A

Q. What's your name?

Riku Tanaka!

Q. When is your birthday?

October 10th.

Q. What's your blood type?

Um, O! Probably...

Q. Your favorite food.

Udon! ♪

...your life be?

What, Tomo-chan answered udon, too?! Cool! What an amazing coincidence!!

Yeah...it went something like that.

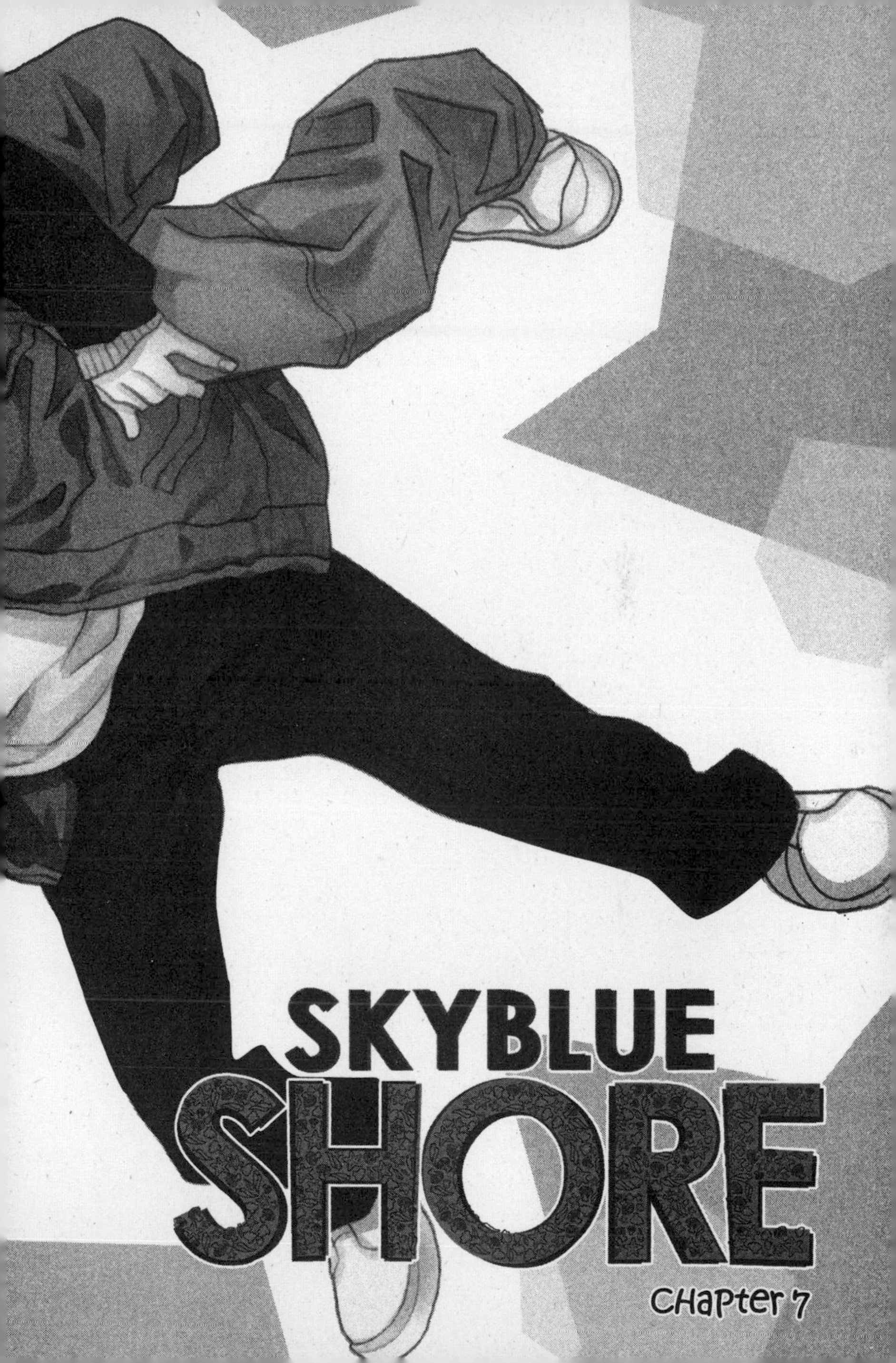
SKYBLUE
SHORE
Chapter 7

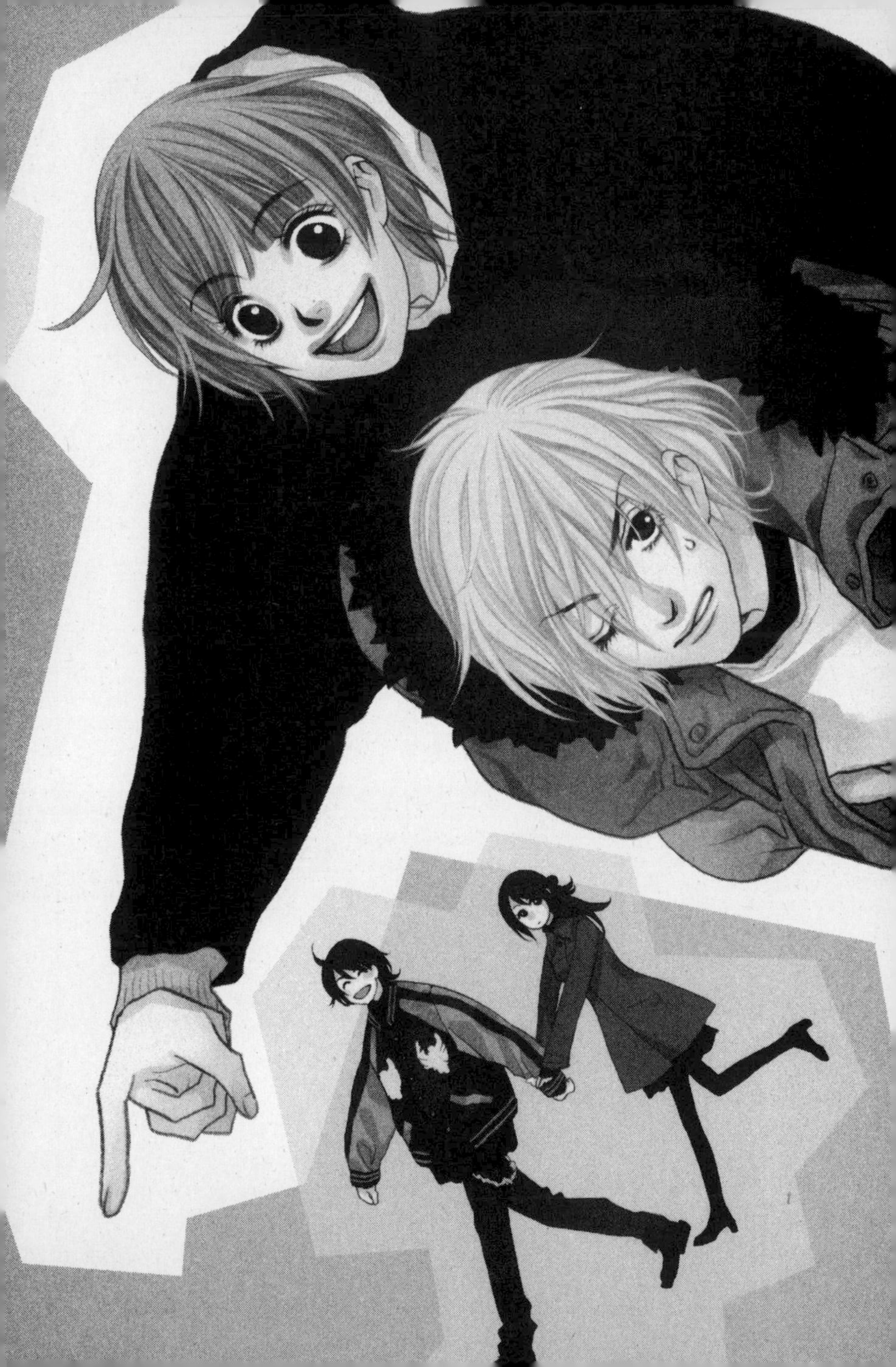

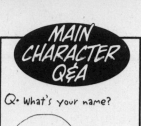

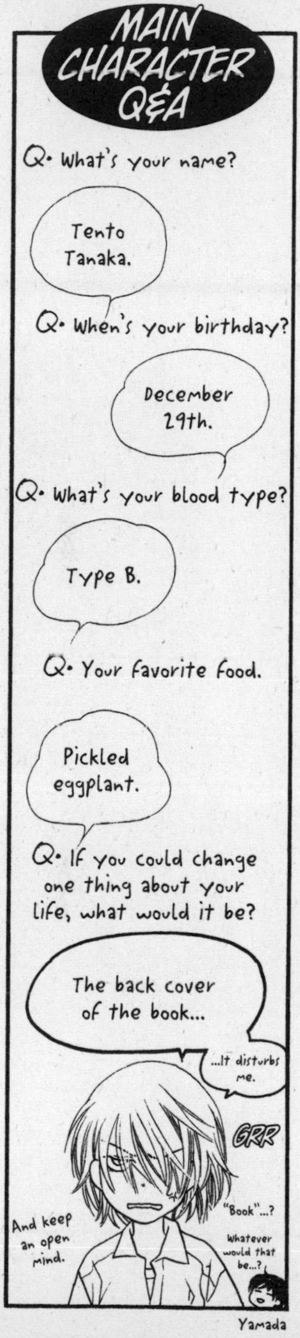

MAIN CHARACTER Q&A
Q. What's your name?
Tento Tanaka.
Q. When's your birthday?
December 29th.
Q. What's your blood type?
Type B.
Q. Your favorite food.
Pickled eggplant.
Q. If you could change one thing about your life, what would it be?
The back cover of the book...
...It disturbs me.
GRR
"Book"...?
Whatever would that be...?
And keep an open mind.

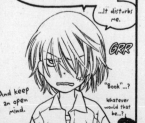

Yamada

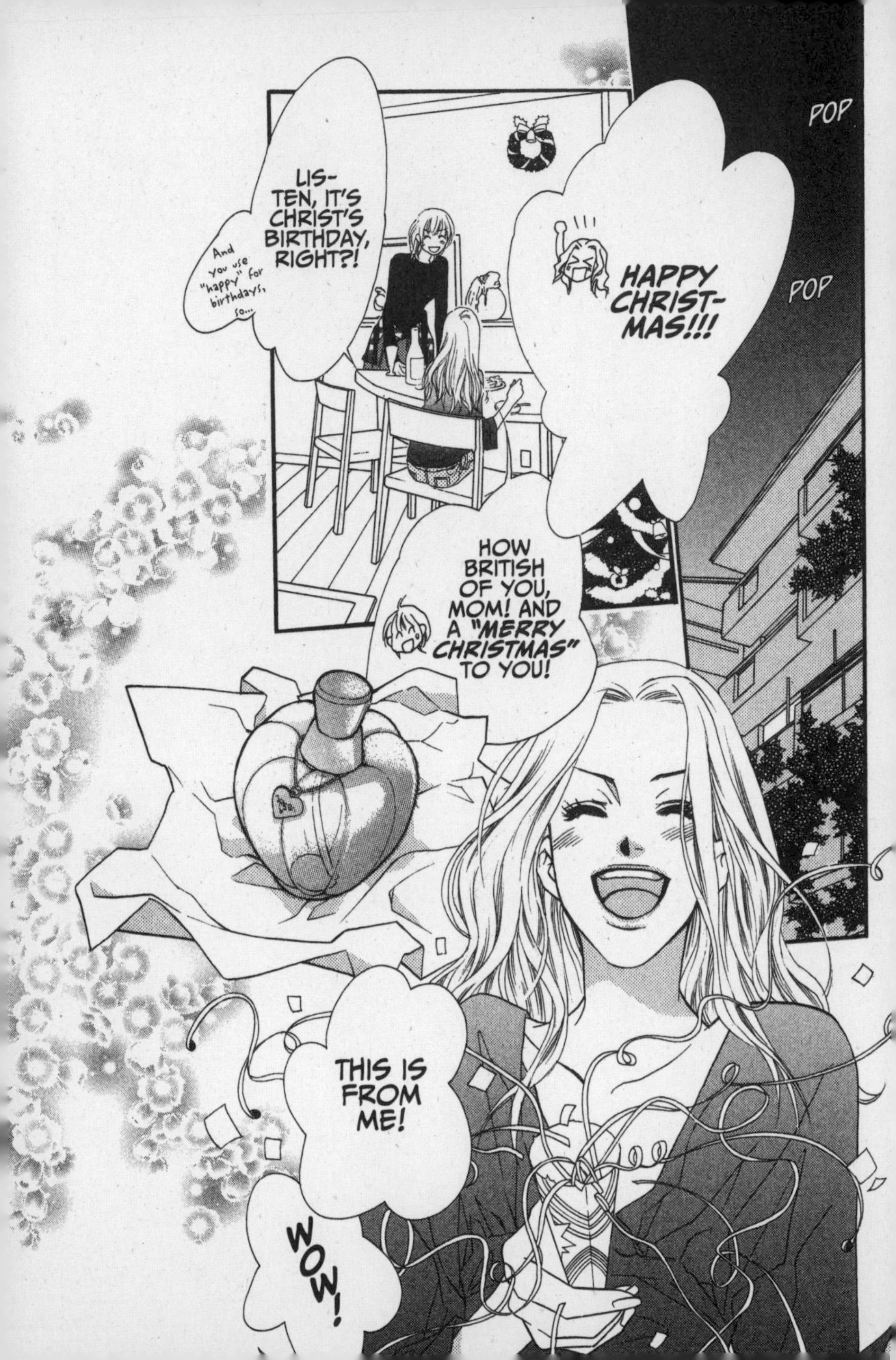
POP
POP
HAPPY CHRISTMAS!!!
LISTEN, IT'S CHRIST'S BIRTHDAY, RIGHT?!
And you use "happy" for birthdays, so...
HOW BRITISH OF YOU, MOM! AND A "MERRY CHRISTMAS" TO YOU!
THIS IS FROM ME!
WOW!

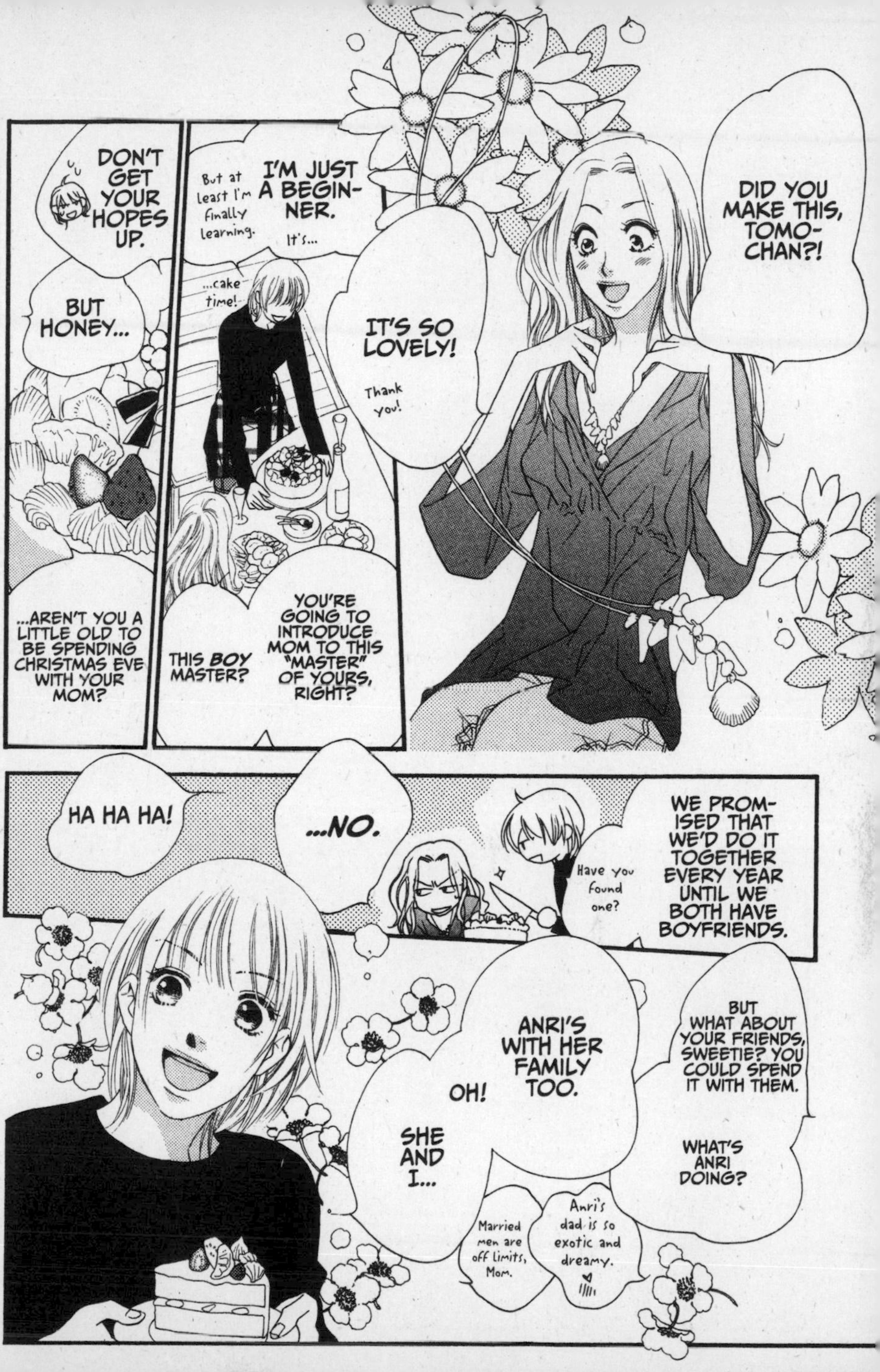
DID YOU MAKE THIS, TOMO-CHAN?!
IT'S SO LOVELY!
Thank you!
I'M JUST A BEGINNER.
But at least I'm finally learning.
It's...
...cake time!
YOU'RE GOING TO INTRODUCE MOM TO THIS "MASTER" OF YOURS, RIGHT?
THIS BOY MASTER?
DON'T GET YOUR HOPES UP.
BUT HONEY...
...AREN'T YOU A LITTLE OLD TO BE SPENDING CHRISTMAS EVE WITH YOUR MOM?
WE PROMISED THAT WE'D DO IT TOGETHER EVERY YEAR UNTIL WE BOTH HAVE BOYFRIENDS.
Have you found one?
...NO.
HA HA HA!
BUT WHAT ABOUT YOUR FRIENDS, SWEETIE? YOU COULD SPEND IT WITH THEM.
WHAT'S ANRI DOING?
ANRI'S WITH HER FAMILY TOO.
OH!
SHE AND I...
Anri's dad is so exotic and dreamy.
Married men are off limits, Mom.

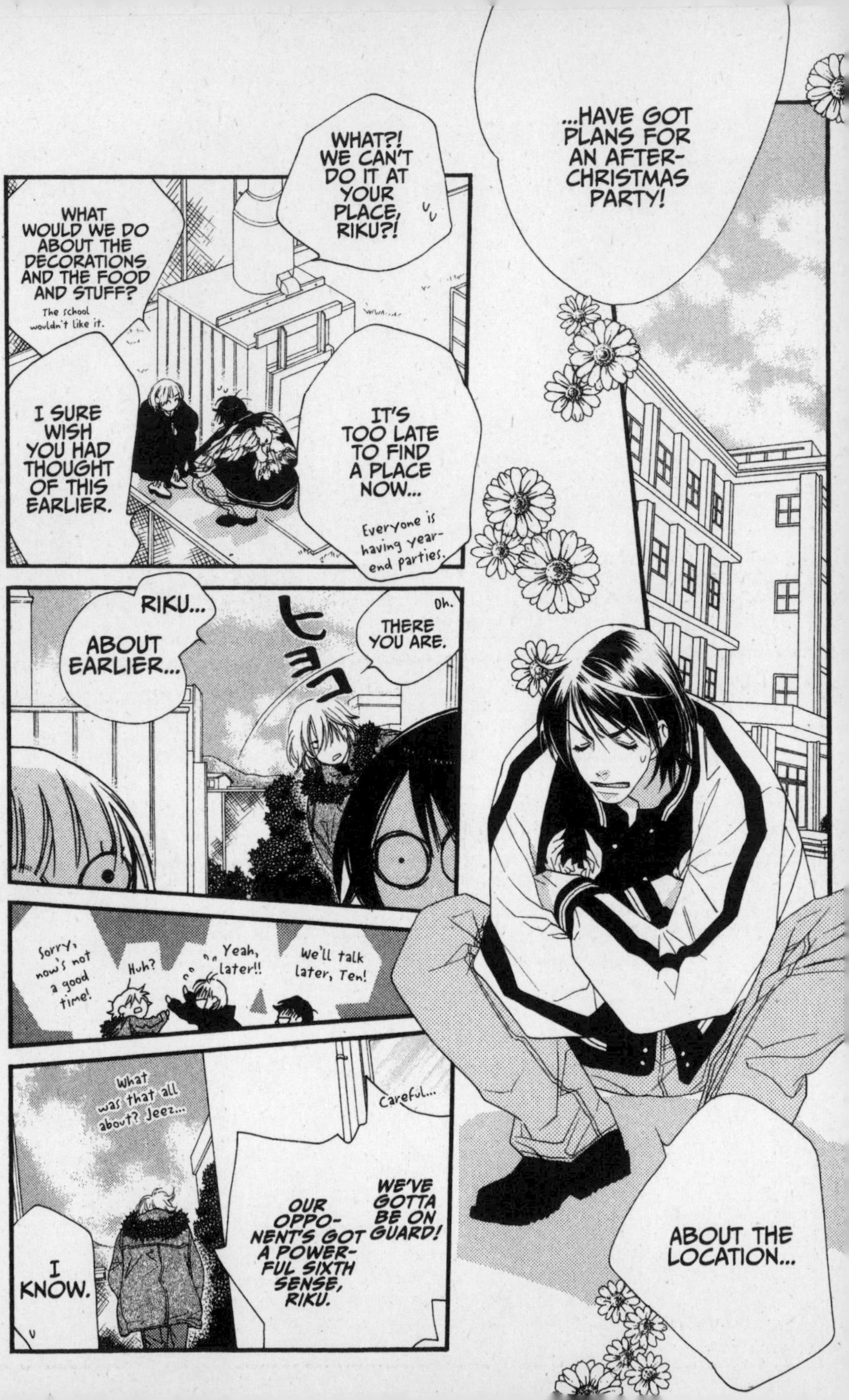
...HAVE GOT PLANS FOR AN AFTER-CHRISTMAS PARTY!
ABOUT THE LOCATION...
WHAT?! WE CAN'T DO IT AT YOUR PLACE, RIKU?!
WHAT WOULD WE DO ABOUT THE DECORATIONS AND THE FOOD AND STUFF?
The school wouldn't like it.
IT'S TOO LATE TO FIND A PLACE NOW...
Everyone is having year-end parties.
I SURE WISH YOU HAD THOUGHT OF THIS EARLIER.
Oh.
THERE YOU ARE.
ヒョコ
RIKU...
ABOUT EARLIER...
We'll talk later, Ten!
Yeah, later!!
Huh?
Sorry, now's not a good time!
Careful...
WE'VE GOTTA BE ON GUARD!
OUR OPPONENT'S GOT A POWERFUL SIXTH SENSE, RIKU.
What was that all about? Jeez...
I KNOW.

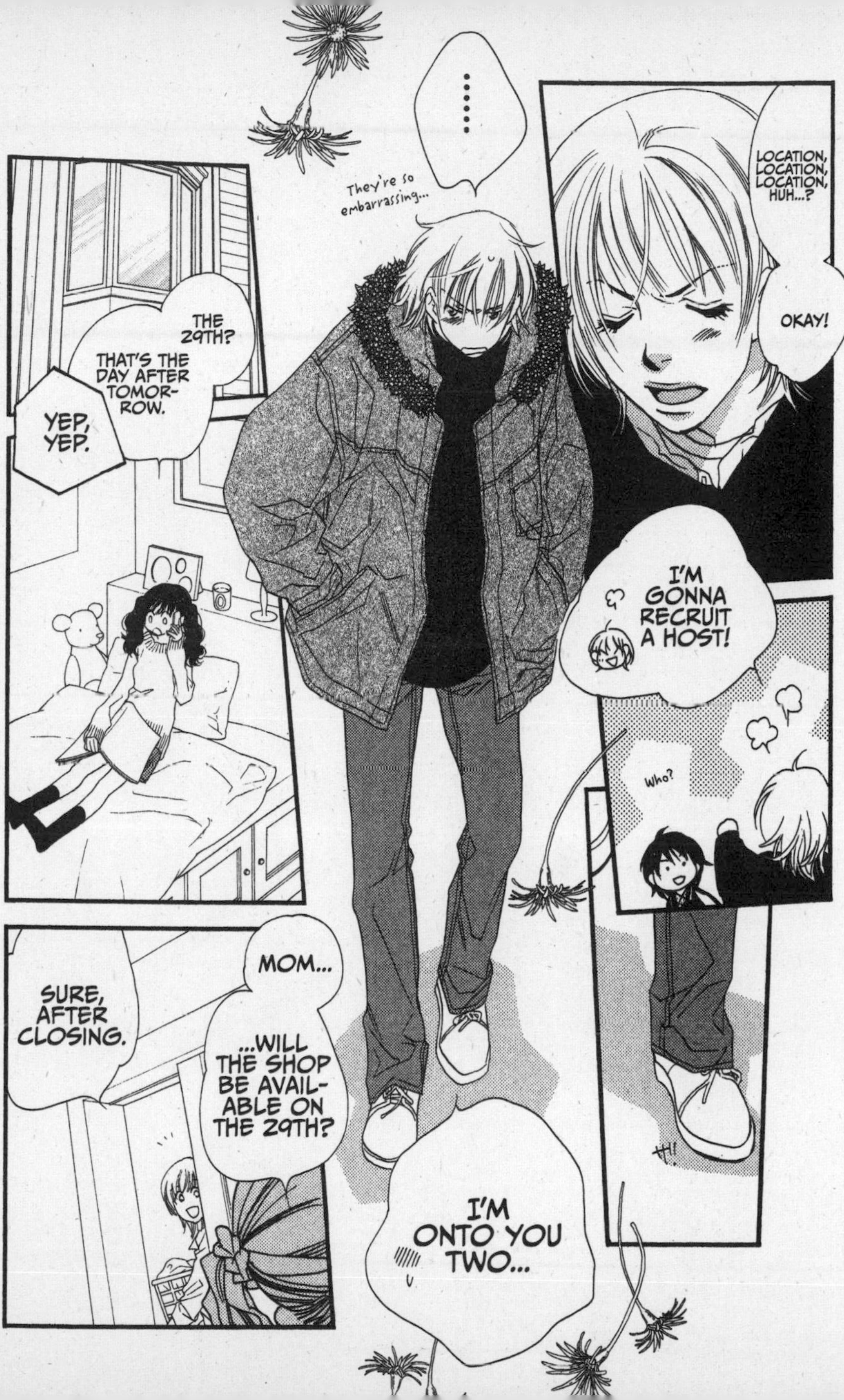
LOCATION, LOCATION, LOCATION, HUH...?
OKAY!
I'M GONNA RECRUIT A HOST!
Who?
......
They're so embarrassing...
I'M ONTO YOU TWO...
THE 29TH?
THAT'S THE DAY AFTER TOMORROW.
YEP, YEP.
MOM...
...WILL THE SHOP BE AVAILABLE ON THE 29TH?
SURE, AFTER CLOSING.

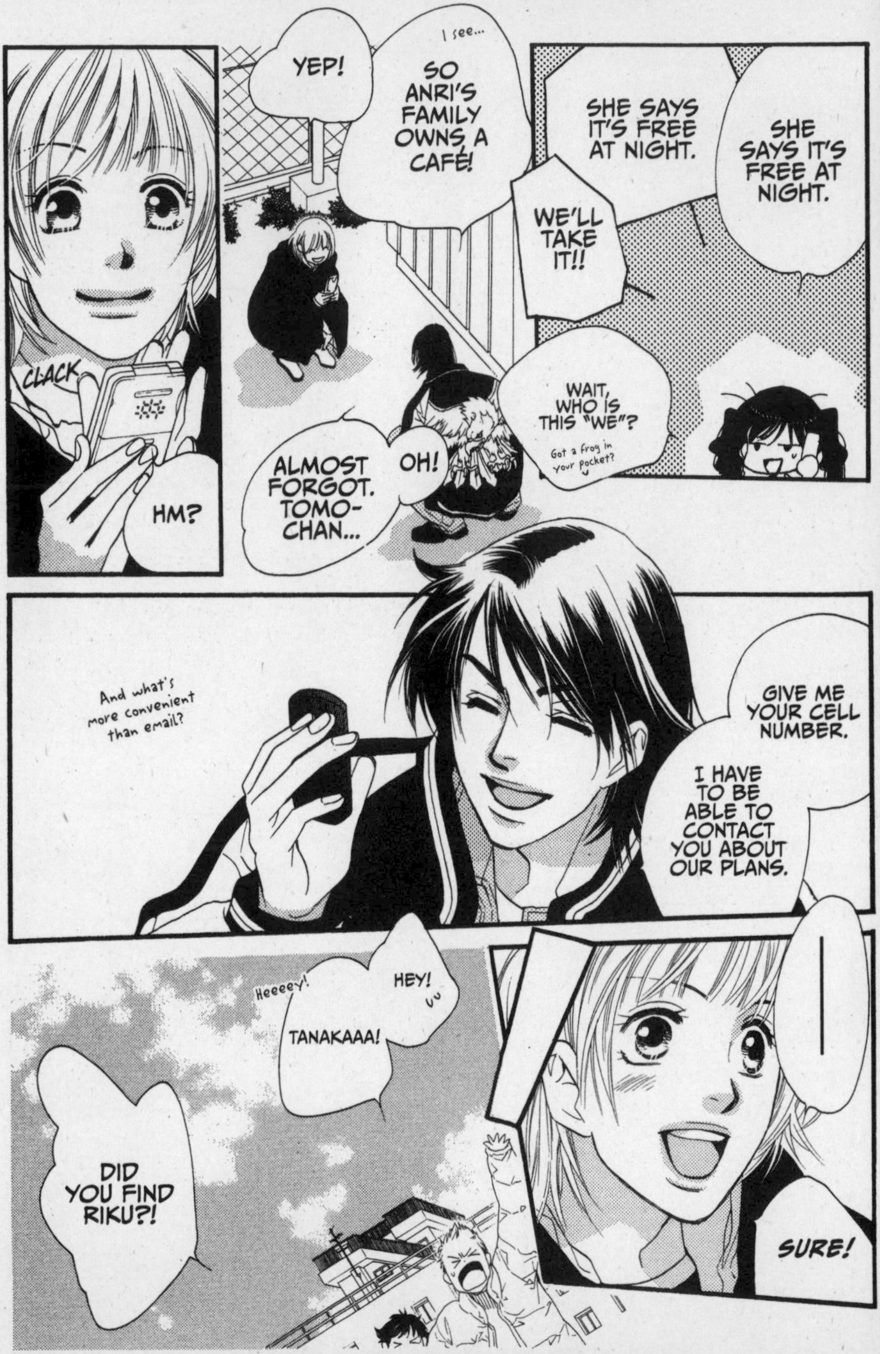
SHE SAYS IT'S FREE AT NIGHT.
SHE SAYS IT'S FREE AT NIGHT.
WE'LL TAKE IT!!
WAIT, WHO IS THIS "WE"?
Got a frog in your pocket?
I see...
SO ANRI'S FAMILY OWNS A CAFÉ!
YEP!
OH!
ALMOST FORGOT. TOMO-CHAN...
CLACK
HM?
GIVE ME YOUR CELL NUMBER.
I HAVE TO BE ABLE TO CONTACT YOU ABOUT OUR PLANS.
And what's more convenient than email?
SURE!
HEY!
Heeeey!
TANAKAAA!
DID YOU FIND RIKU?!

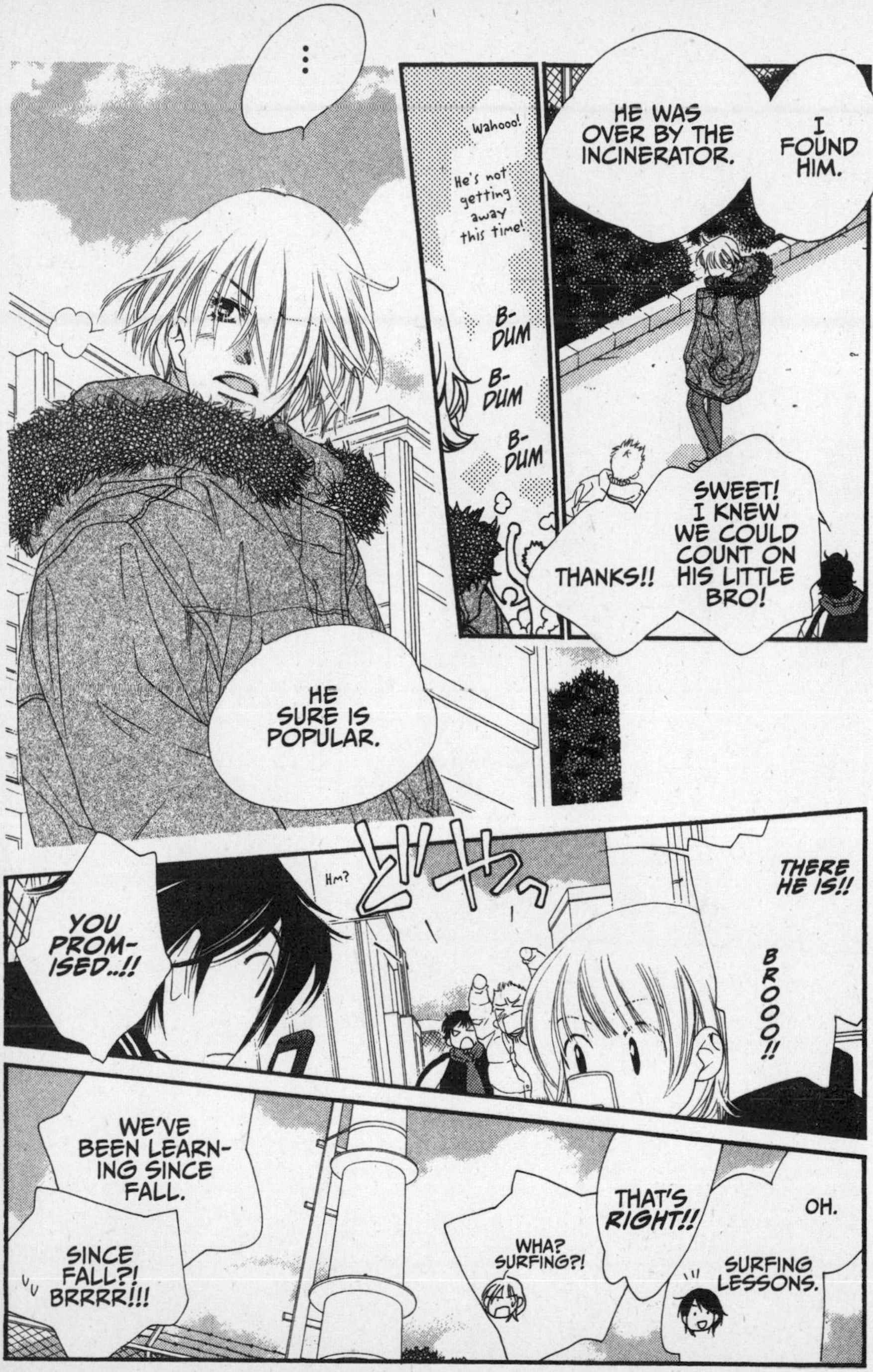
I FOUND HIM.
HE WAS OVER BY THE INCINERATOR.
SWEET! I KNEW WE COULD COUNT ON HIS LITTLE BRO!
THANKS!!
Wahooo!
He's not getting away this time!
B-DUM
B-DUM
B-DUM
...
HE SURE IS POPULAR.
THERE HE IS!!
BROOOO!!
Hm?
YOU PROMISED..!!
OH.
SURFING LESSONS.
THAT'S RIGHT!!
WHA? SURFING?!
WE'VE BEEN LEARNING SINCE FALL.
SINCE FALL?! BRRRR!!!

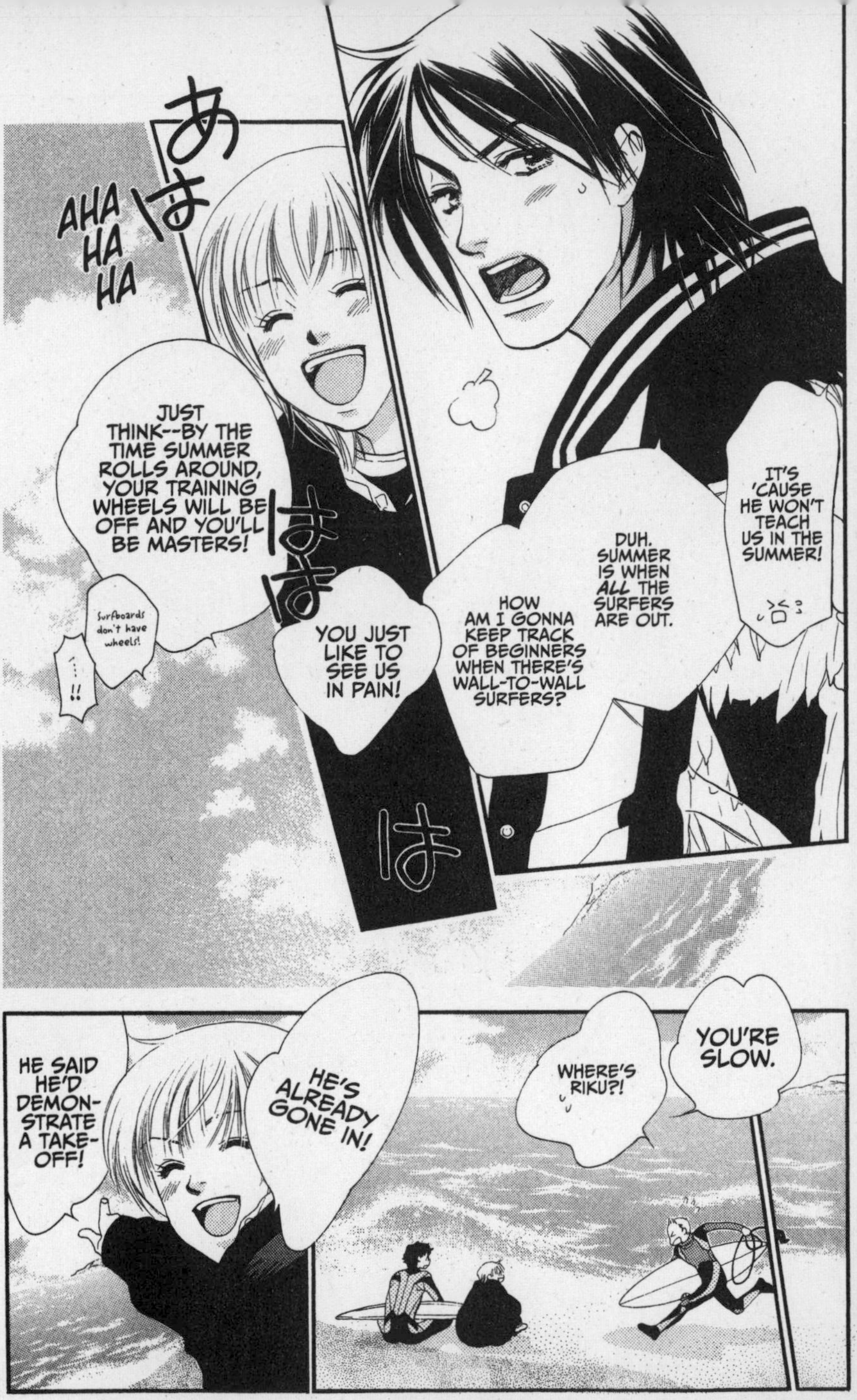
IT'S 'CAUSE HE WON'T TEACH US IN THE SUMMER!
DUH. SUMMER IS WHEN ALL THE SURFERS ARE OUT.
HOW AM I GONNA KEEP TRACK OF BEGINNERS WHEN THERE'S WALL-TO-WALL SURFERS?
YOU JUST LIKE TO SEE US IN PAIN!
あははははは
AHA HA HA
JUST THINK--BY THE TIME SUMMER ROLLS AROUND, YOUR TRAINING WHEELS WILL BE OFF AND YOU'LL BE MASTERS!
Surfboards don't have wheels!
…!!
YOU'RE SLOW.
WHERE'S RIKU?!
HE'S ALREADY GONE IN!
HE SAID HE'D DEMONSTRATE A TAKE-OFF!

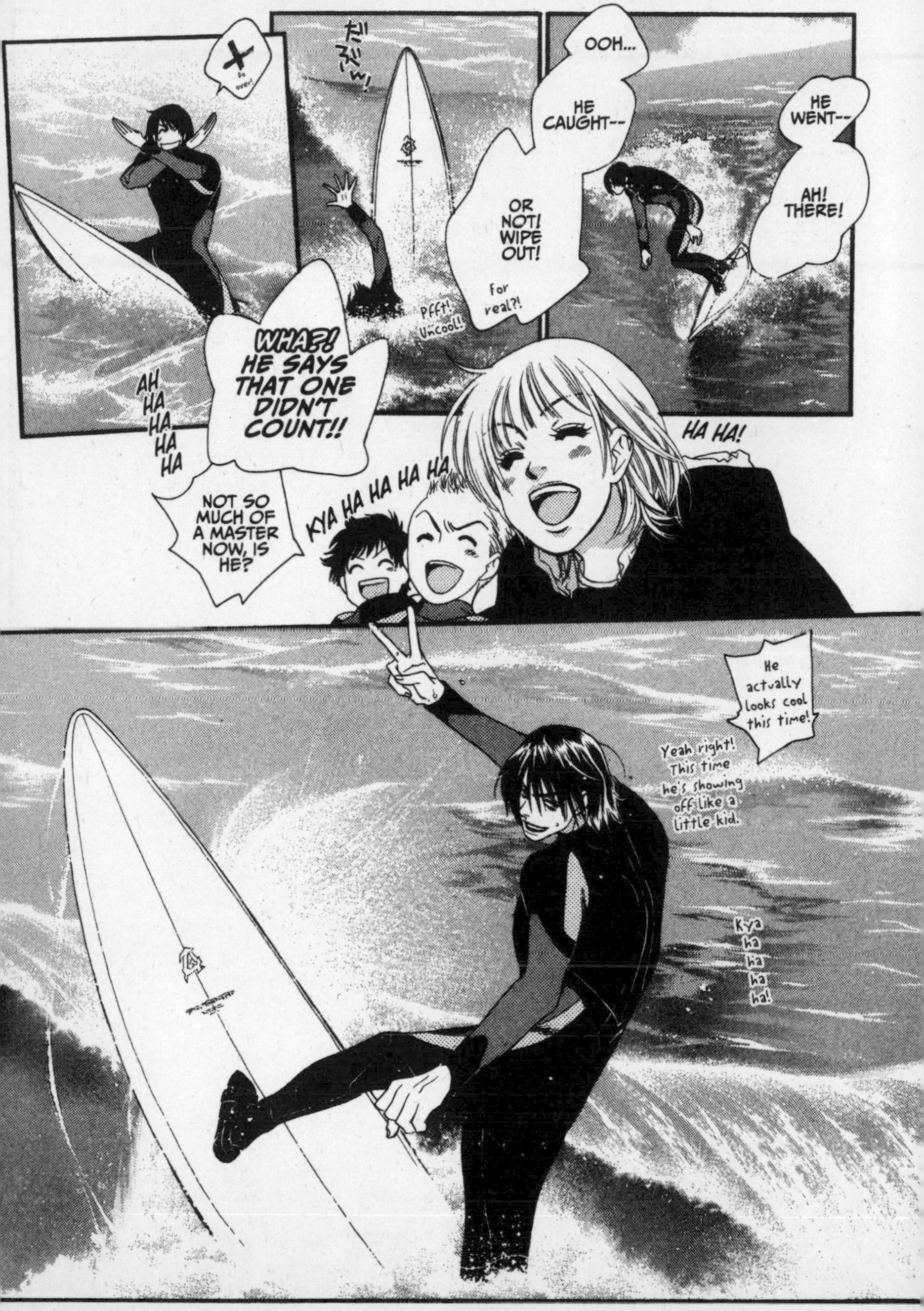

HE WENT--
AH! THERE!
OOH...
HE CAUGHT--
だぶーん!
OR NOT! WIPE OUT!
For real?!
Pfft! Uncool!
Do over!
WHA?! HE SAYS THAT ONE DIDN'T COUNT!!
AH HA HA HA HA HA
HA HA!
KYA HA HA HA HA
NOT SO MUCH OF A MASTER NOW, IS HE?
He actually looks cool this time!
Yeah right! This time he's showing off like a little kid.
Kya ha ha ha ha!

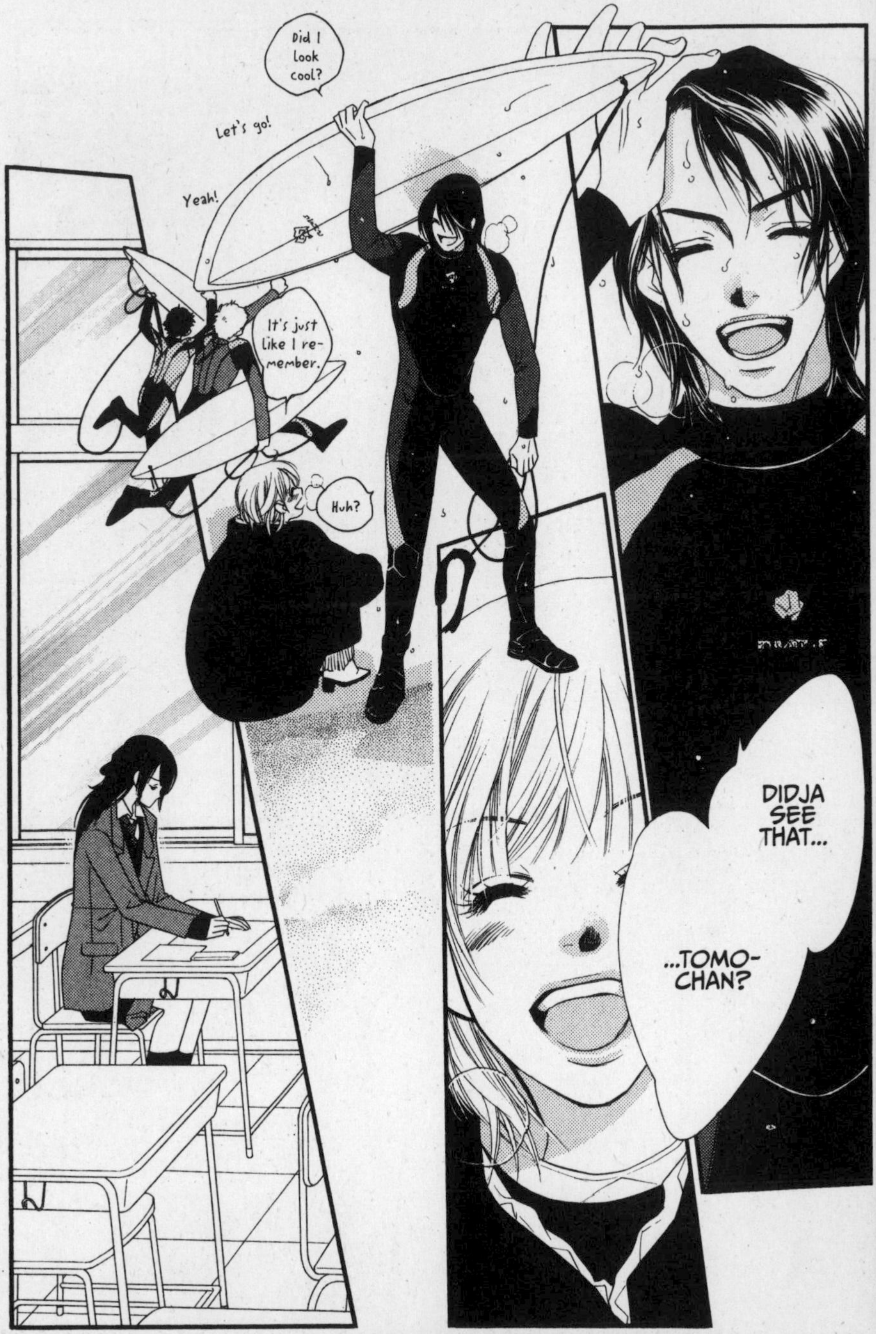
DIDJA SEE THAT...
...TOMO-CHAN?
Did I look cool?
Let's go!
Yeah!
It's just like I re-member.
Huh?

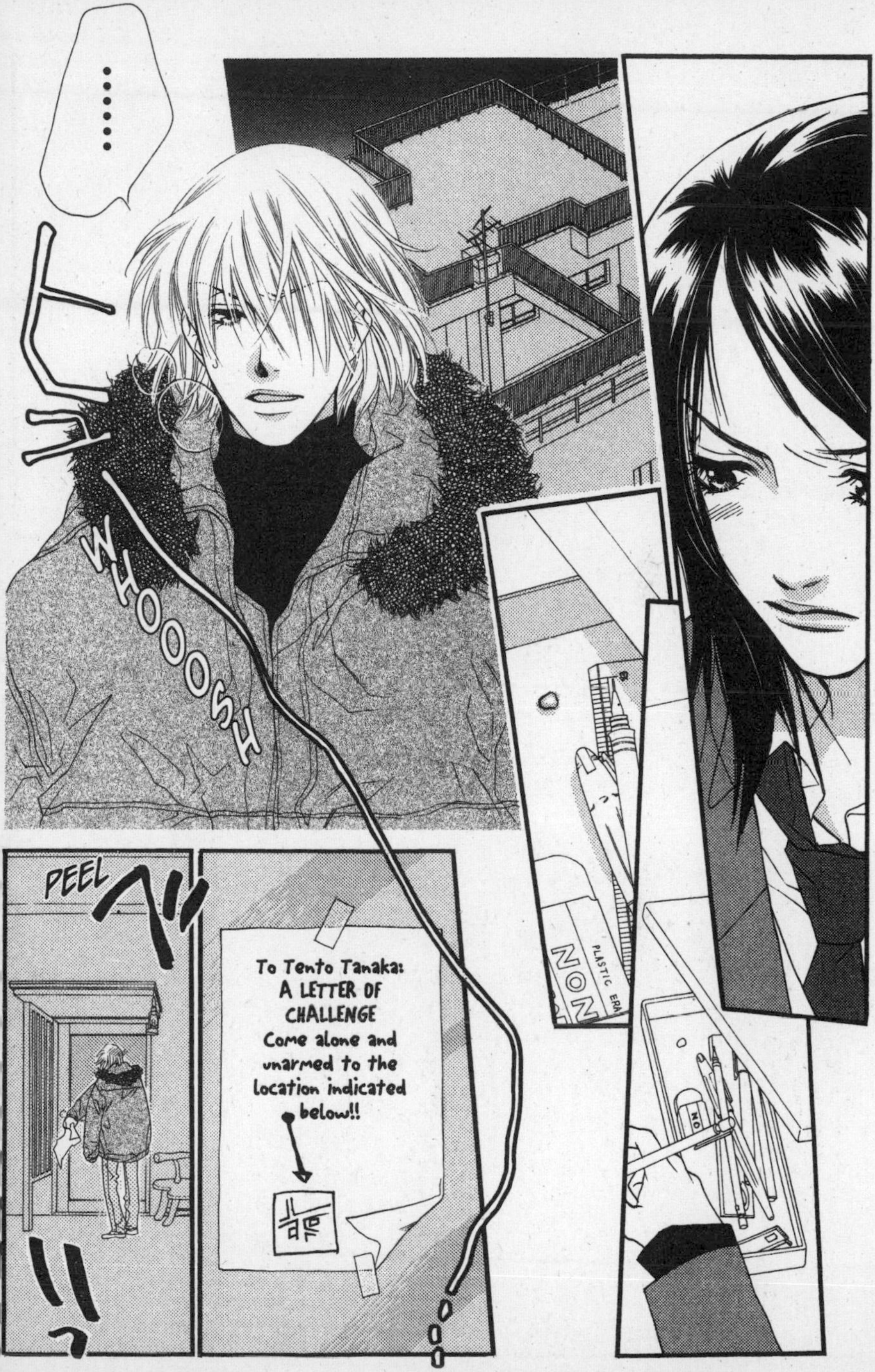
......
WHOOSH
To Tento Tanaka:
A LETTER OF CHALLENGE
Come alone and unarmed to the location indicated below!!
PEEL

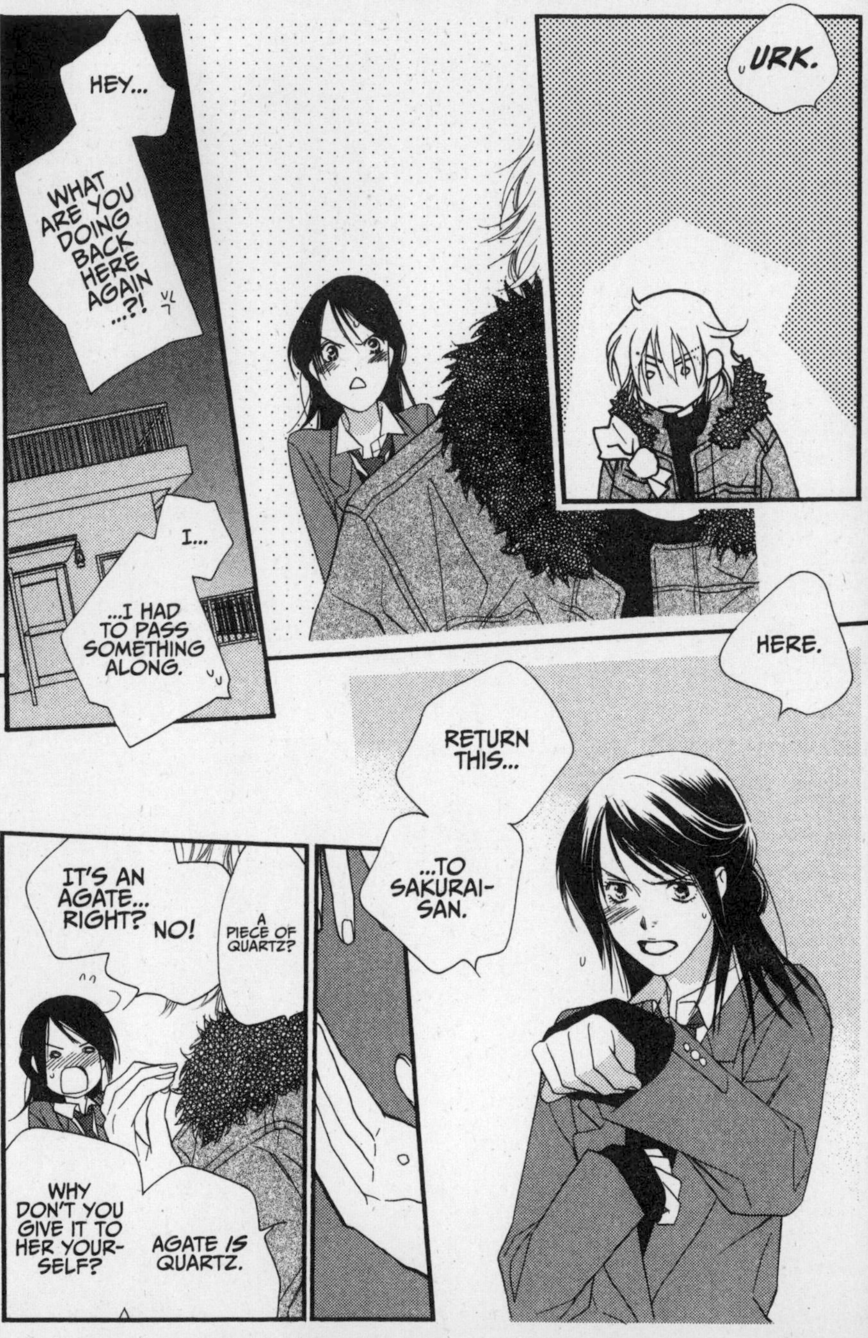
URK.
HEY...
WHAT ARE YOU DOING BACK HERE AGAIN ...?!
I...
...I HAD TO PASS SOMETHING ALONG.
HERE.
RETURN THIS...
...TO SAKURAI-SAN.
A PIECE OF QUARTZ?
IT'S AN AGATE... RIGHT?
NO!
AGATE *IS* QUARTZ.
WHY DON'T YOU GIVE IT TO HER YOUR-SELF?

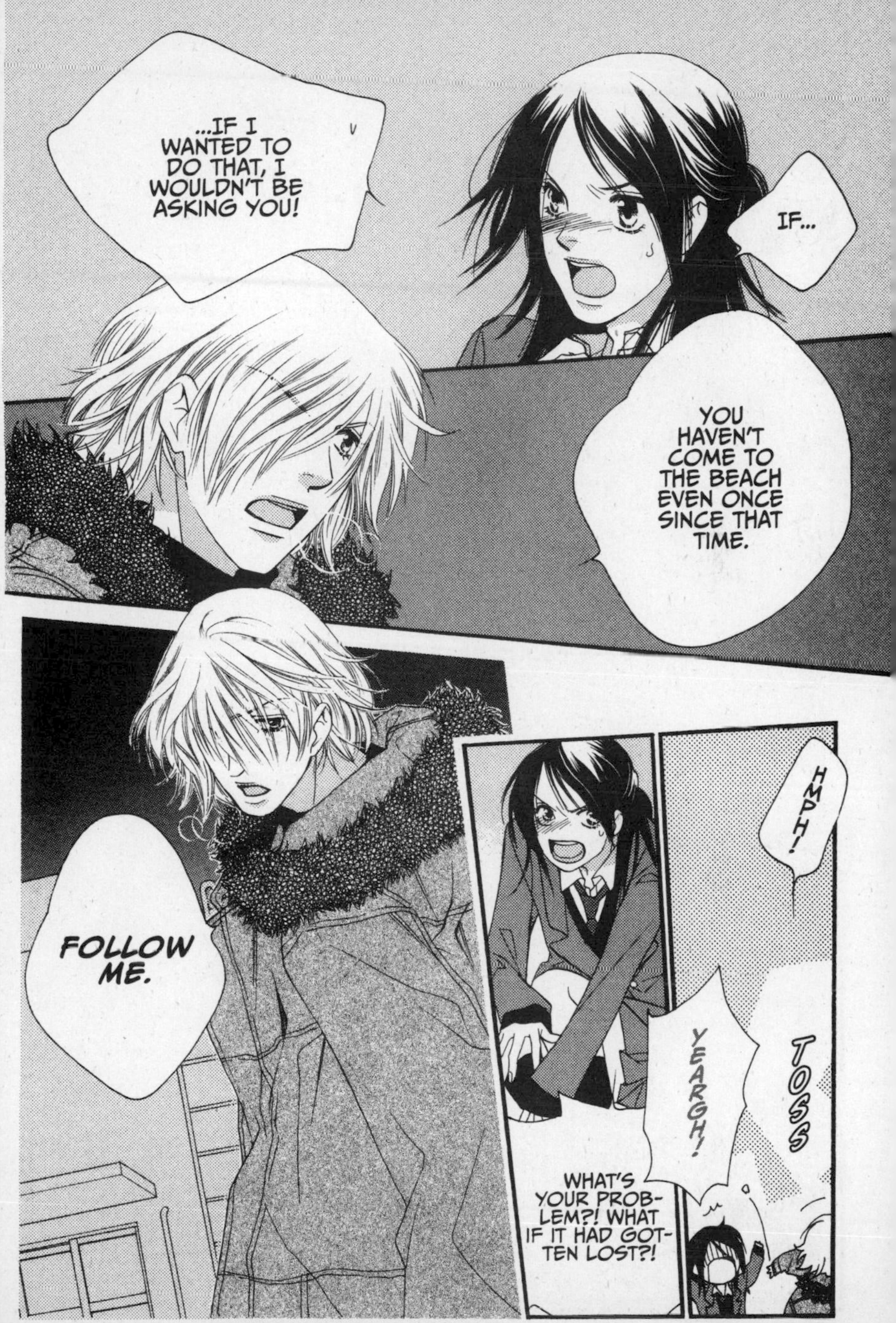
IF...
...IF I WANTED TO DO THAT, I WOULDN'T BE ASKING YOU!
YOU HAVEN'T COME TO THE BEACH EVEN ONCE SINCE THAT TIME.
HMPH!
TOSS
YEARGH!
WHAT'S YOUR PROB-LEM?! WHAT IF IT HAD GOT-TEN LOST?!
FOLLOW ME.

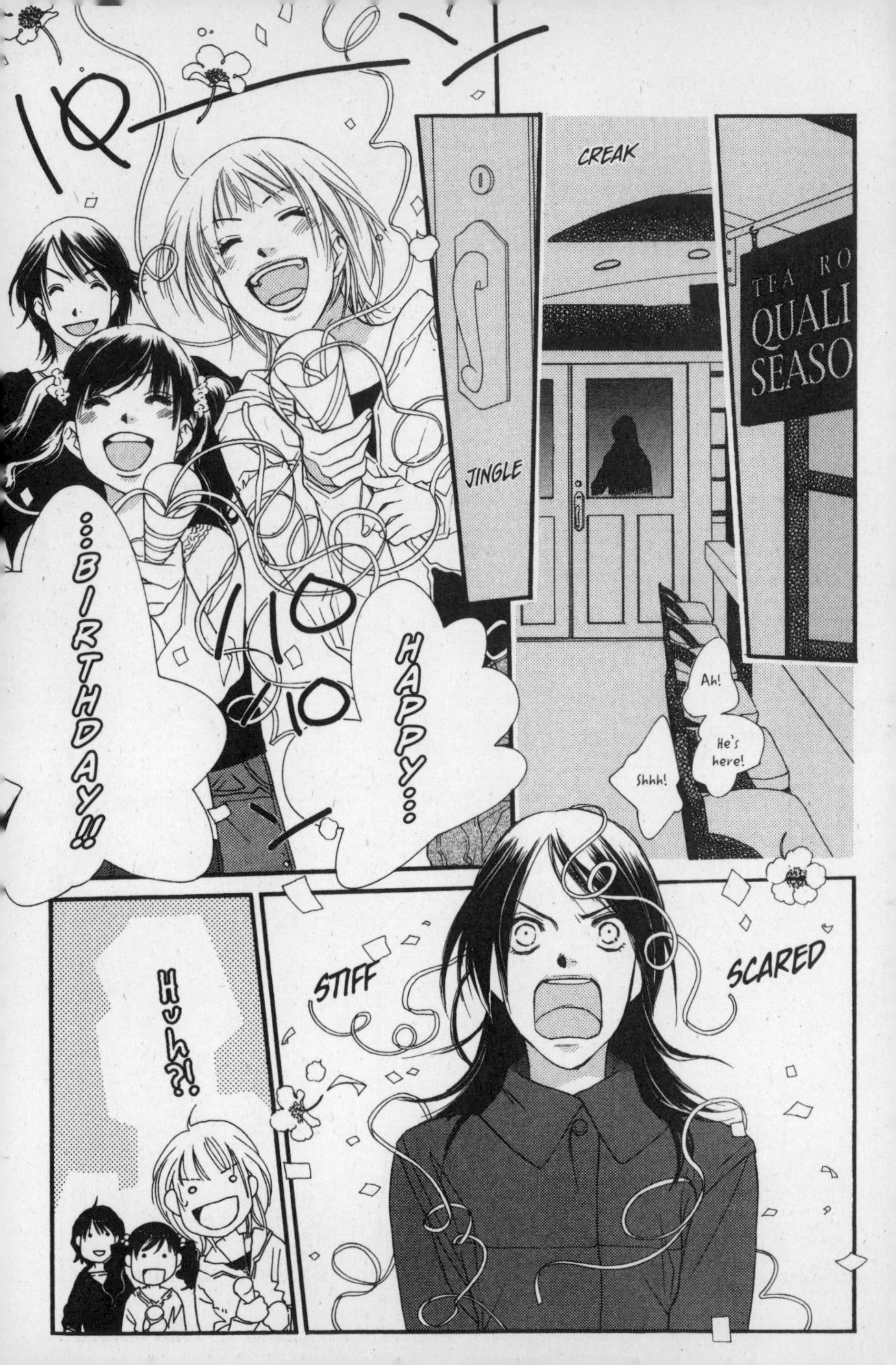
TEA RO
QUALI
SEASO
CREAK
JINGLE
Ah!
He's here!
Shhh!
HAPPY...
...BIRTHDAY!!
SCARED
STIFF
Huh?!

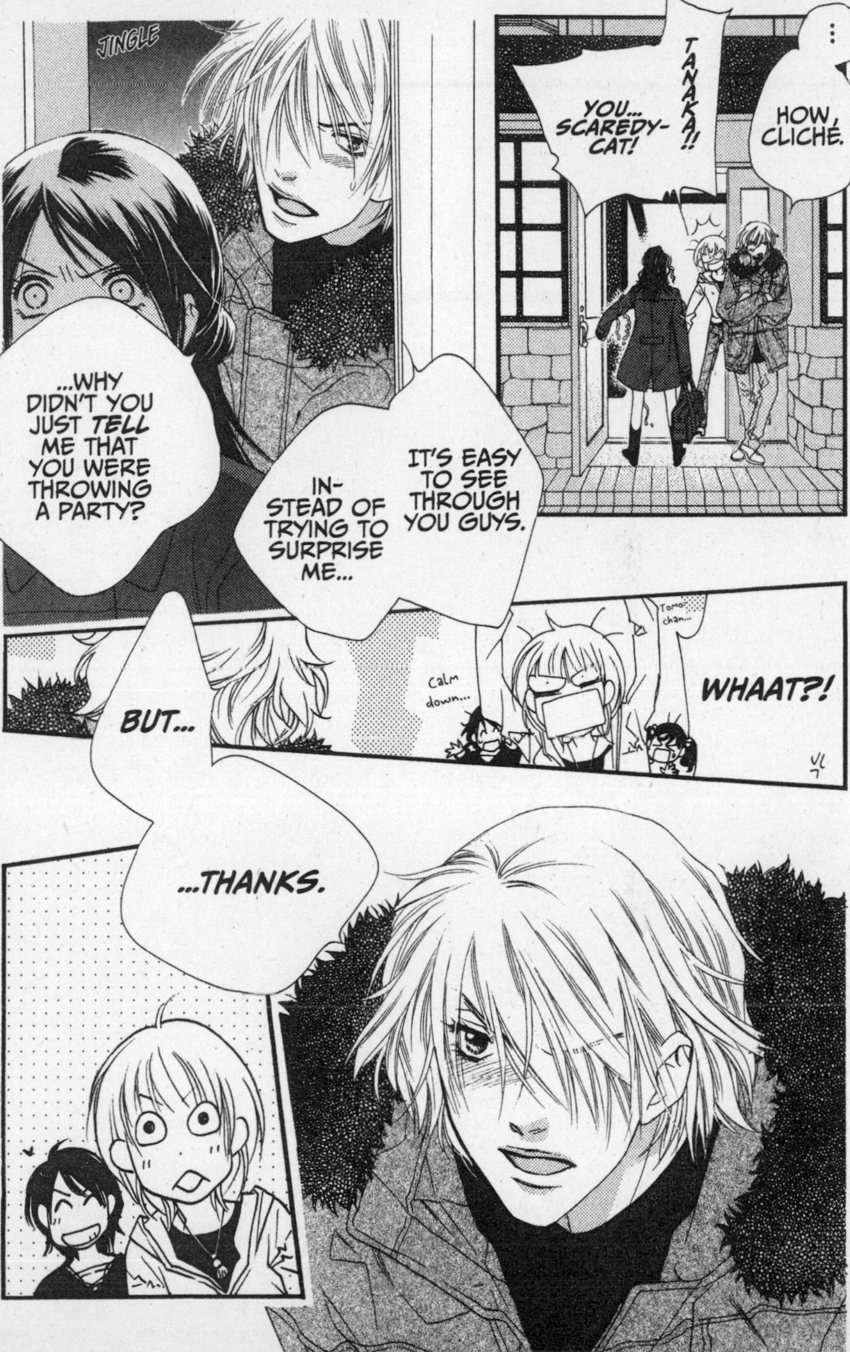

...
HOW, CLICHÉ.
TANAKA!!
YOU... SCAREDY-CAT!
JINGLE
IT'S EASY TO SEE THROUGH YOU GUYS.
IN-STEAD OF TRYING TO SURPRISE ME...
...WHY DIDN'T YOU JUST *TELL* ME THAT YOU WERE THROWING A PARTY?
WHAAT?!
Tomo-chan...
Calm down...
BUT...
...THANKS.

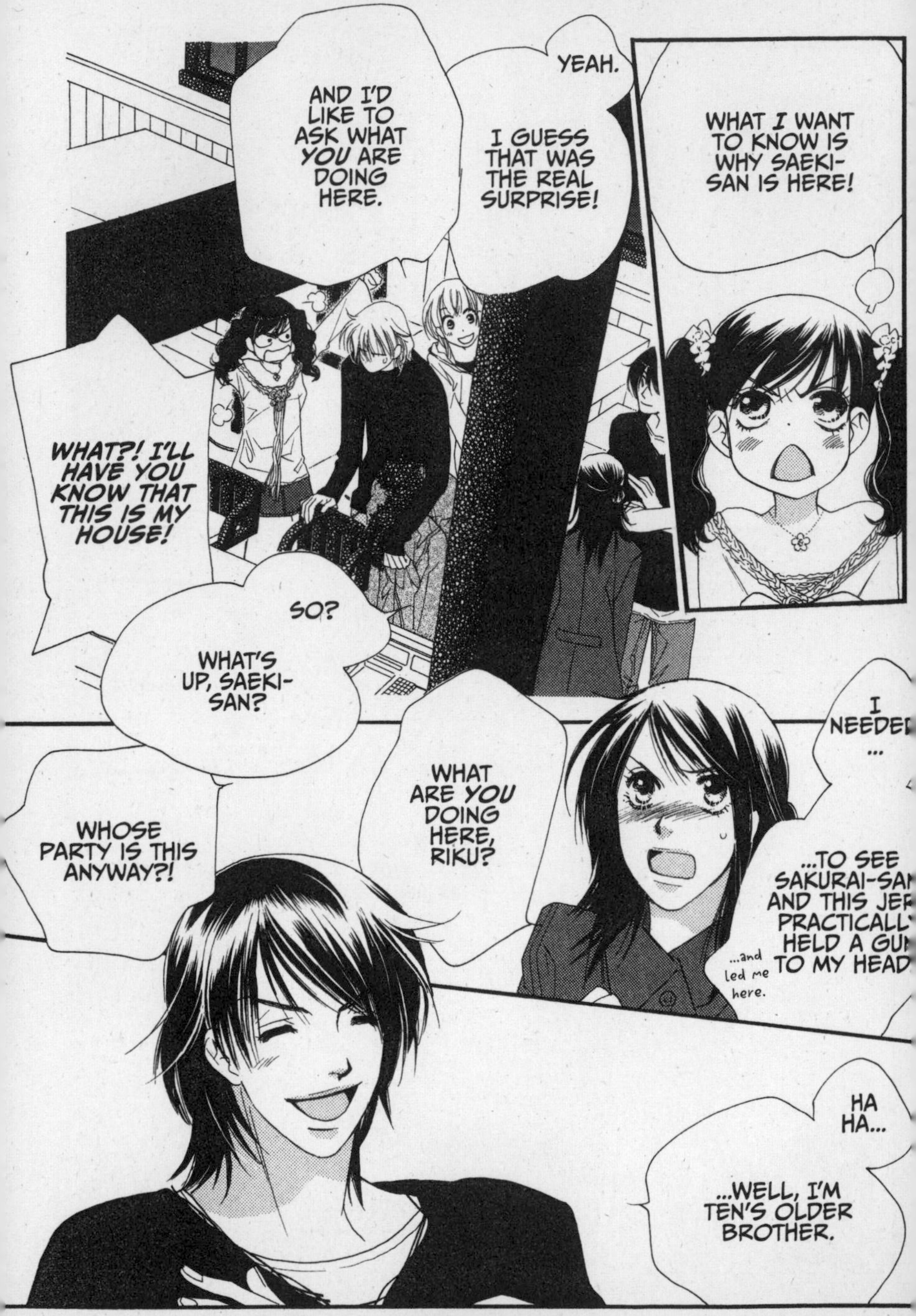
WHAT I WANT TO KNOW IS WHY SAEKI-SAN IS HERE!
YEAH.
I GUESS THAT WAS THE REAL SURPRISE!
AND I'D LIKE TO ASK WHAT YOU ARE DOING HERE.
WHAT?! I'LL HAVE YOU KNOW THAT THIS IS MY HOUSE!
SO?
WHAT'S UP, SAEKI-SAN?
I NEEDED ...
...TO SEE SAKURAI-SAN AND THIS JERK PRACTICALLY HELD A GUN TO MY HEAD
...and led me here.
WHAT ARE YOU DOING HERE, RIKU?
WHOSE PARTY IS THIS ANYWAY?!
HA HA...
...WELL, I'M TEN'S OLDER BROTHER.

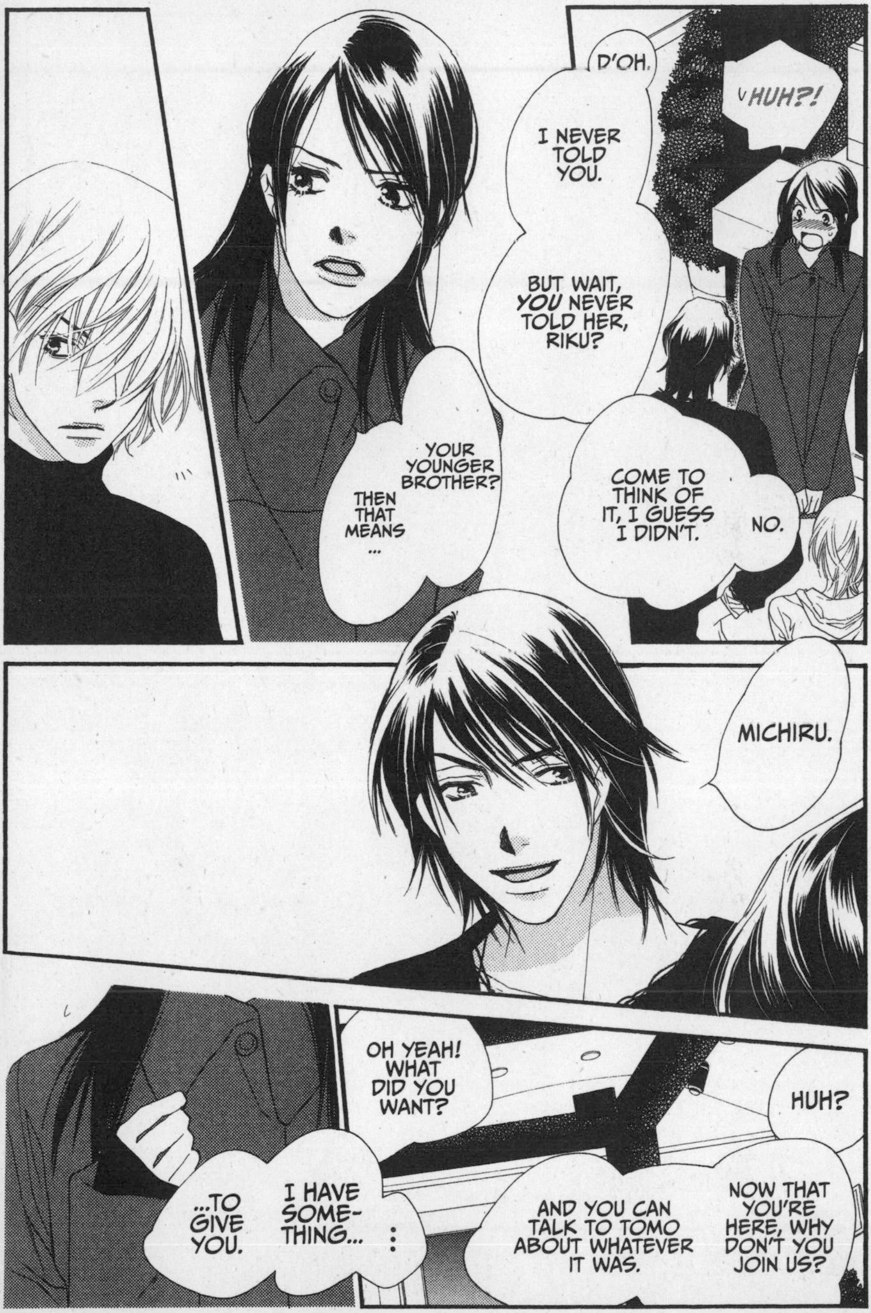
HUH?!
D'OH.
I NEVER TOLD YOU.
BUT WAIT, *YOU* NEVER TOLD HER, RIKU?
NO.
COME TO THINK OF IT, I GUESS I DIDN'T.
YOUR YOUNGER BROTHER?
THEN THAT MEANS...
MICHIRU.
HUH?
NOW THAT YOU'RE HERE, WHY DON'T YOU JOIN US?
AND YOU CAN TALK TO TOMO ABOUT WHATEVER IT WAS.
OH YEAH! WHAT DID YOU WANT?
...
I HAVE SOME-THING...
...TO GIVE YOU.

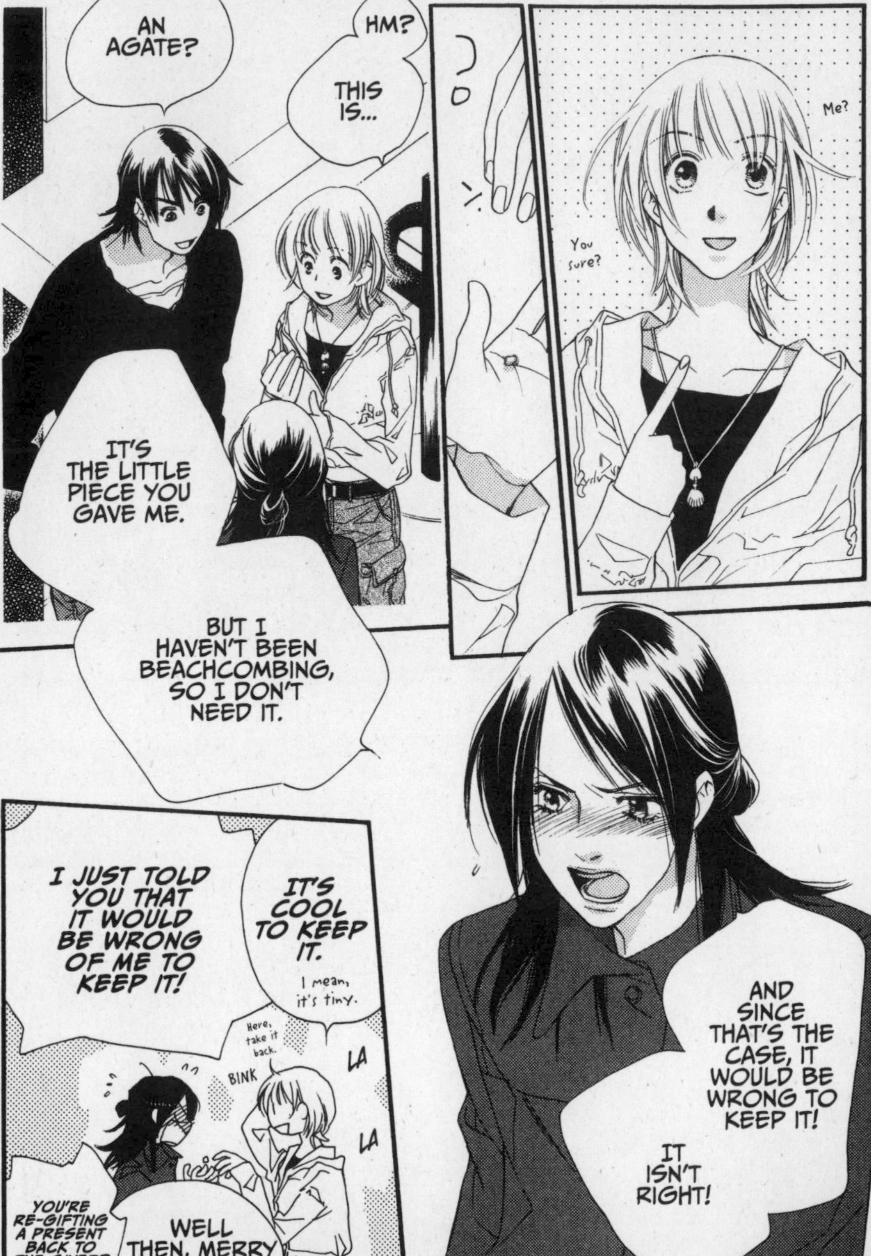
Me?
You sure?
HM?
THIS IS...
AN AGATE?
IT'S THE LITTLE PIECE YOU GAVE ME.
BUT I HAVEN'T BEEN BEACHCOMBING, SO I DON'T NEED IT.
AND SINCE THAT'S THE CASE, IT WOULD BE WRONG TO KEEP IT!
IT ISN'T RIGHT!
IT'S COOL TO KEEP IT.
I mean, it's tiny.
I JUST TOLD YOU THAT IT WOULD BE WRONG OF ME TO KEEP IT!
Here, take it back.
LA
LA
BINK
WELL THEN, MERRY CHRISTMAS.
YOU'RE RE-GIFTING A PRESENT BACK TO THE GIVER?

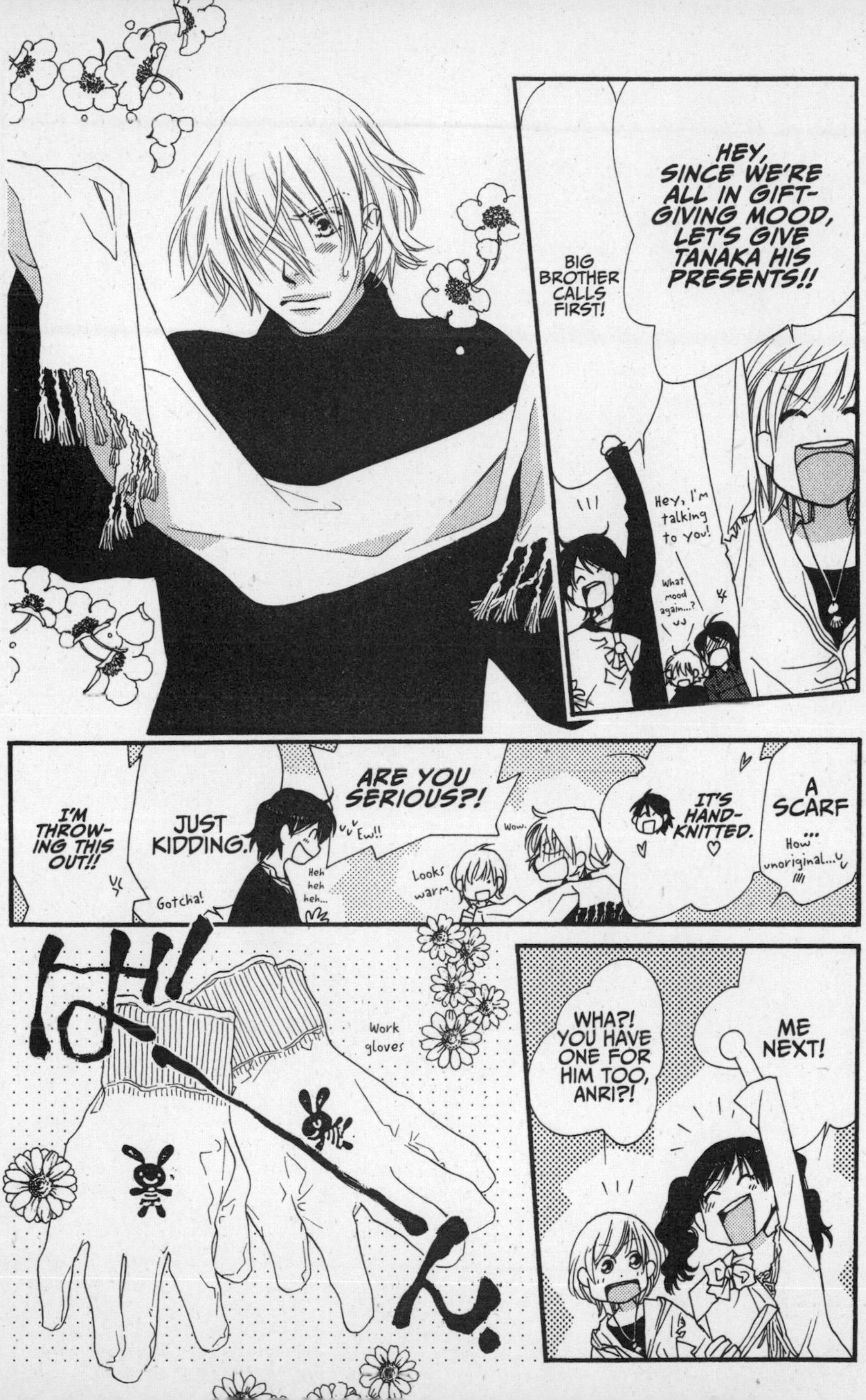

HEY, SINCE WE'RE ALL IN GIFT-GIVING MOOD, LET'S GIVE TANAKA HIS PRESENTS!!
BIG BROTHER CALLS FIRST!
Hey, I'm talking to you!
What mood again...?
A SCARF
How... unoriginal...
IT'S HAND-KNITTED.
Wow.
Looks warm.
ARE YOU SERIOUS?!
Ew!!
Heh heh heh...
JUST KIDDING.
I'M THROWING THIS OUT!!
Gotcha!
ME NEXT!
WHA?! YOU HAVE ONE FOR HIM TOO, ANRI?!
Work gloves

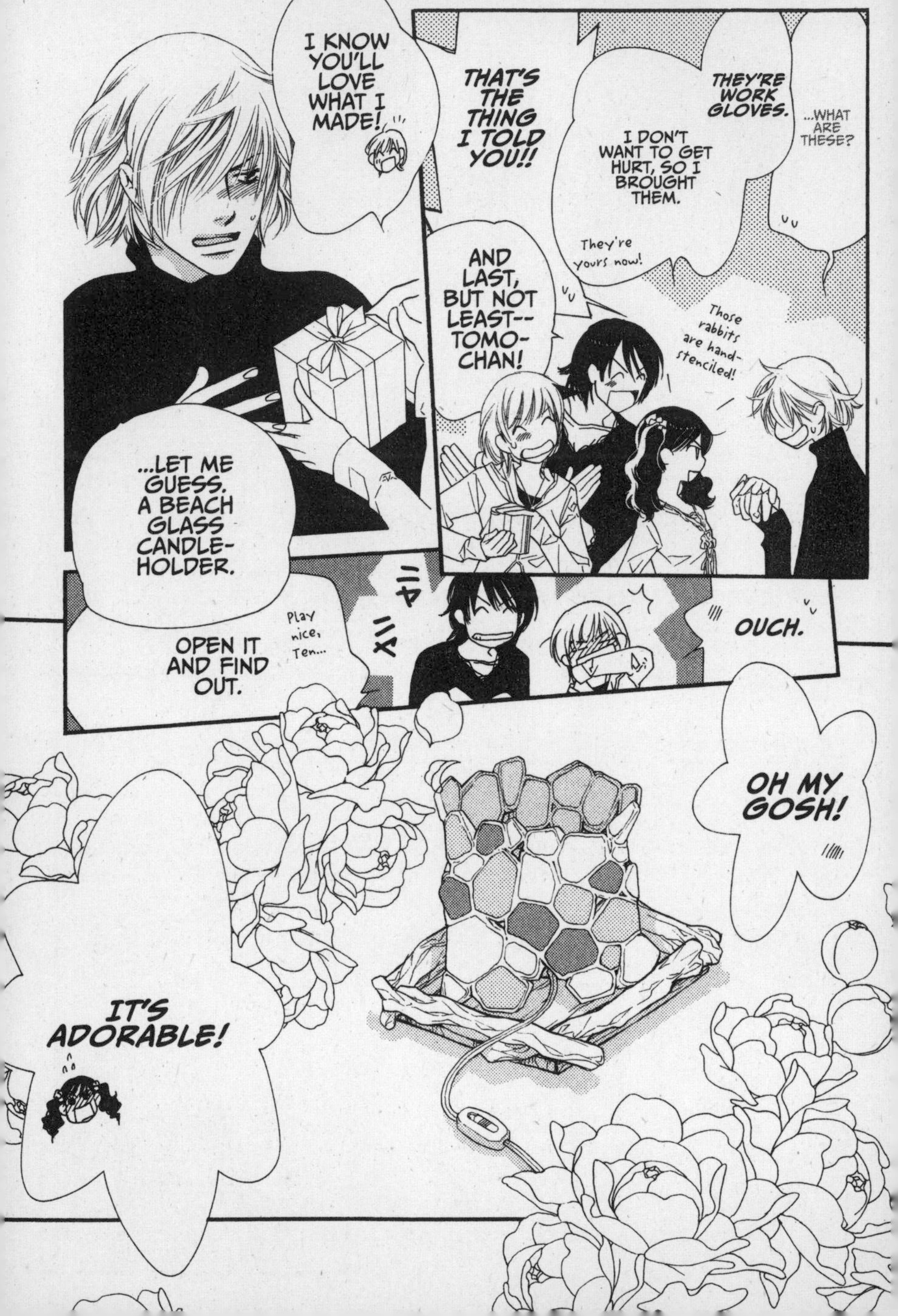
...WHAT ARE THESE?
THEY'RE WORK GLOVES.
I DON'T WANT TO GET HURT, SO I BROUGHT THEM.
They're yours now!
THAT'S THE THING I TOLD YOU!!
Those rabbits are hand-stenciled!
AND LAST, BUT NOT LEAST-- TOMO-CHAN!
I KNOW YOU'LL LOVE WHAT I MADE!
...LET ME GUESS. A BEACH GLASS CANDLE-HOLDER.
OUCH.
ニヤ ニヤ
Play nice, Ten...
OPEN IT AND FIND OUT.
OH MY GOSH!
IT'S ADORABLE!

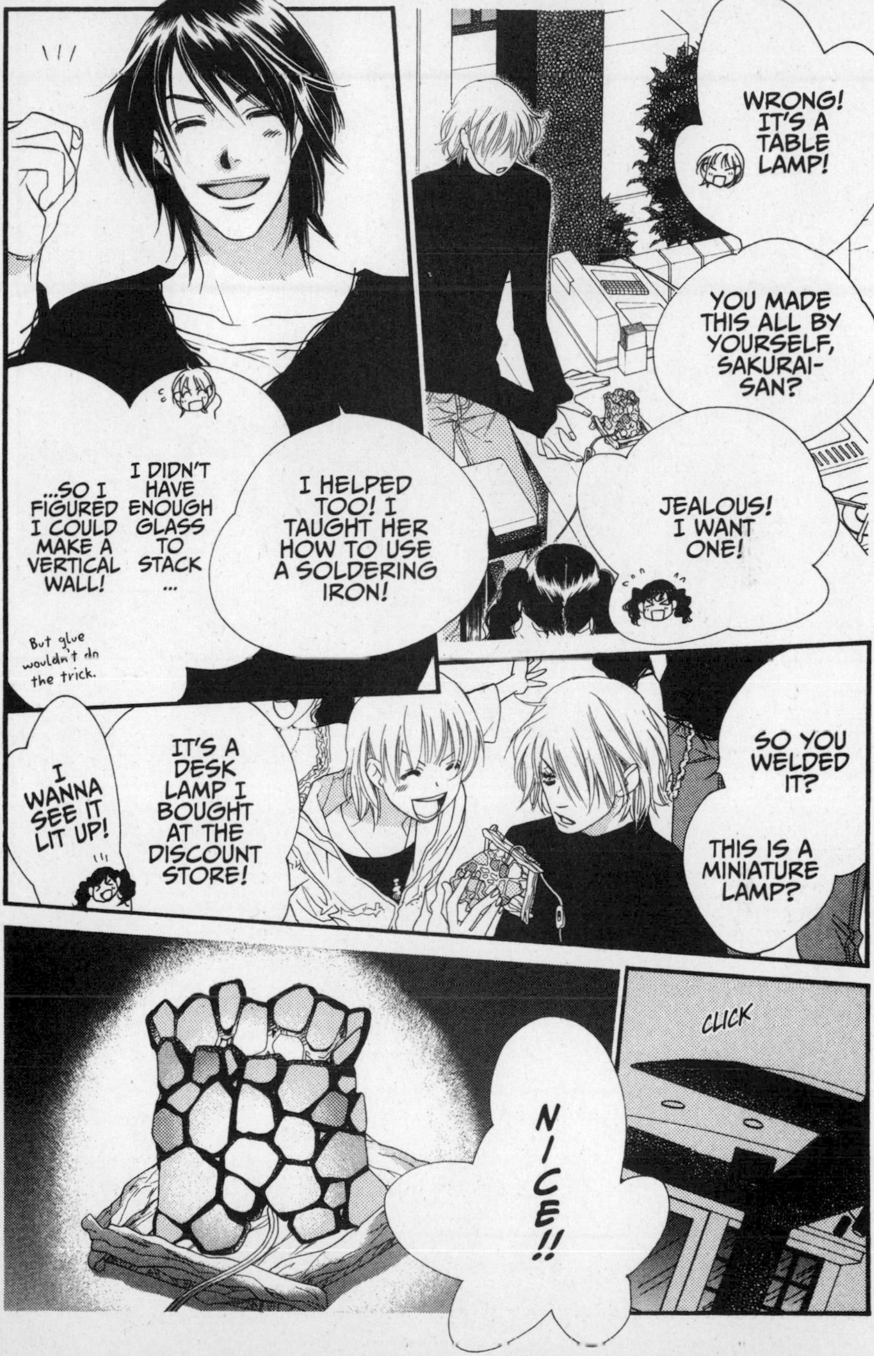
WRONG! IT'S A TABLE LAMP!
YOU MADE THIS ALL BY YOURSELF, SAKURAI-SAN?
JEALOUS! I WANT ONE!
I HELPED TOO! I TAUGHT HER HOW TO USE A SOLDERING IRON!
I DIDN'T HAVE ENOUGH GLASS TO STACK...
...SO I FIGURED I COULD MAKE A VERTICAL WALL!
But glue wouldn't do the trick.
SO YOU WELDED IT?
THIS IS A MINIATURE LAMP?
IT'S A DESK LAMP I BOUGHT AT THE DISCOUNT STORE!
I WANNA SEE IT LIT UP!
CLICK
NICE!!

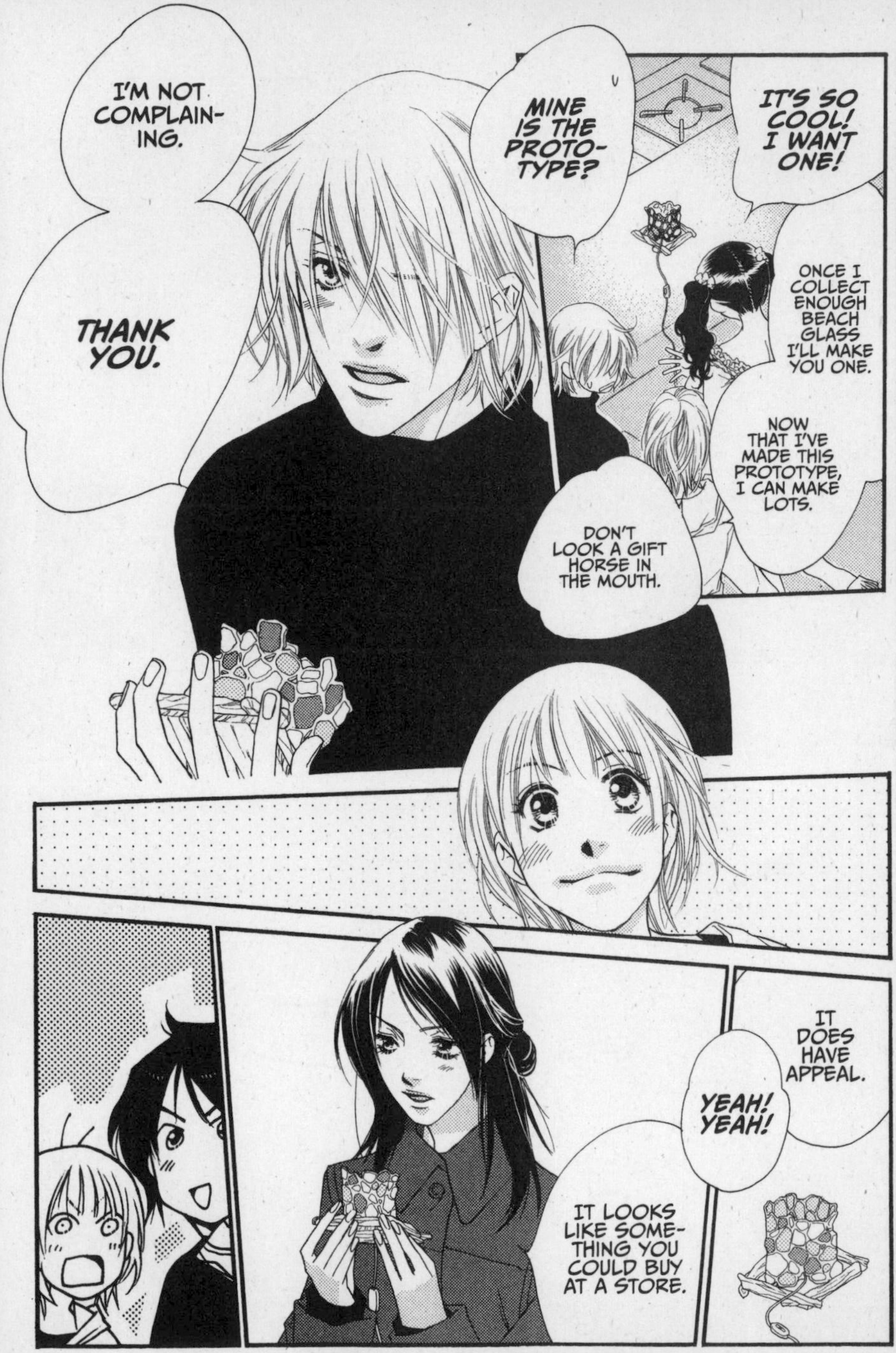
IT'S SO COOL! I WANT ONE!
ONCE I COLLECT ENOUGH BEACH GLASS I'LL MAKE YOU ONE.
NOW THAT I'VE MADE THIS PROTOTYPE, I CAN MAKE LOTS.
MINE IS THE PROTOTYPE?
DON'T LOOK A GIFT HORSE IN THE MOUTH.
I'M NOT COMPLAINING.
THANK YOU.
IT DOES HAVE APPEAL.
IT LOOKS LIKE SOMETHING YOU COULD BUY AT A STORE.
YEAH! YEAH!

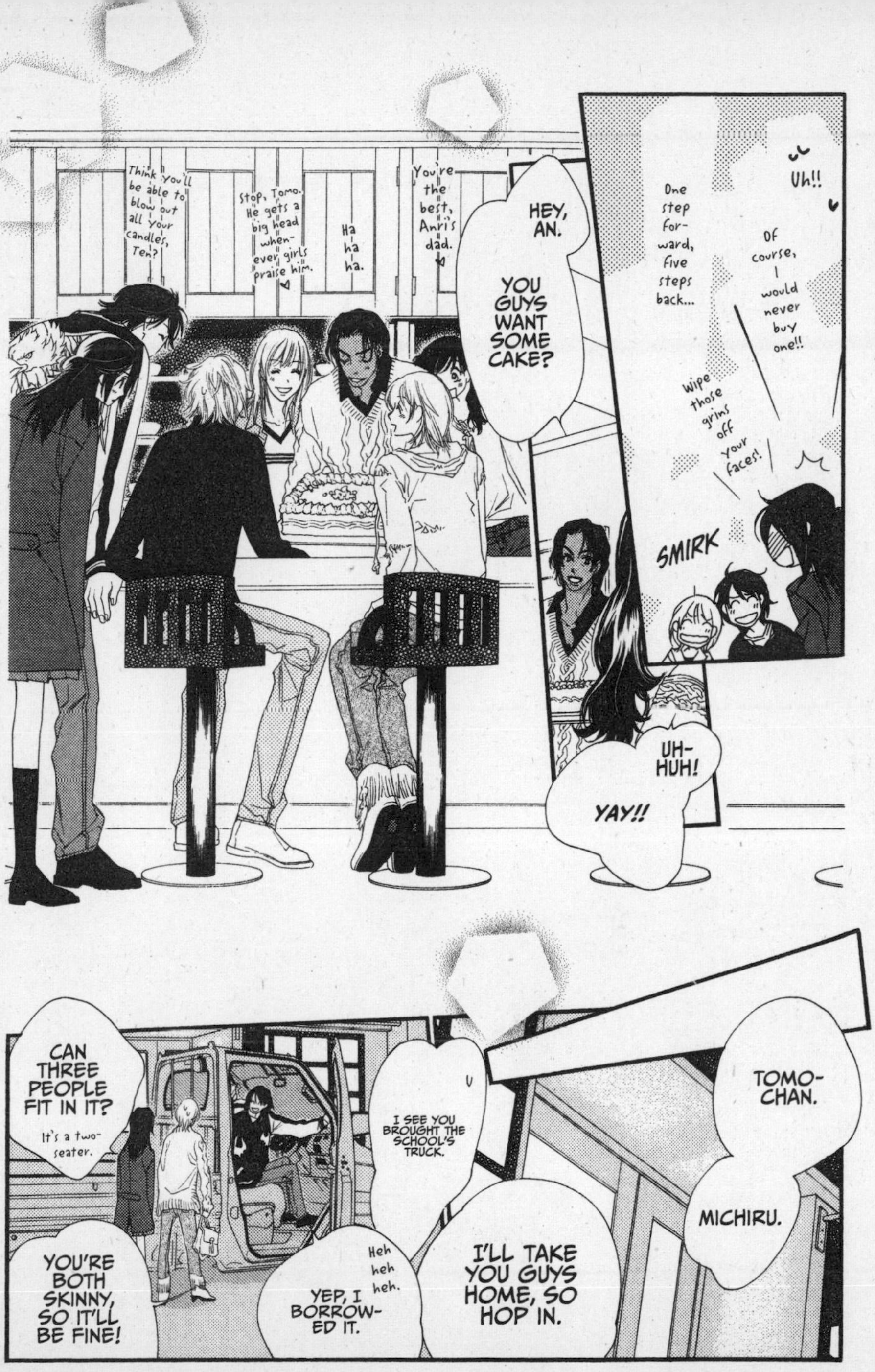

One step forward, five steps back...
Uh!!
Of course, I would never buy one!!
Wipe those grins off your faces!
SMIRK
HEY, AN. YOU GUYS WANT SOME CAKE?
UH-HUH!
YAY!!
You're the best, Anri's dad.
Ha ha ha.
Stop, Tomo. He gets a big head whenever girls praise him.
Think you'll be able to blow out all your candles, Ten?
TOMO-CHAN.
MICHIRU.
I SEE YOU BROUGHT THE SCHOOL'S TRUCK.
I'LL TAKE YOU GUYS HOME, SO HOP IN.
Heh heh heh.
YEP, I BORROWED IT.
CAN THREE PEOPLE FIT IN IT?
It's a two-seater.
YOU'RE BOTH SKINNY, SO IT'LL BE FINE!

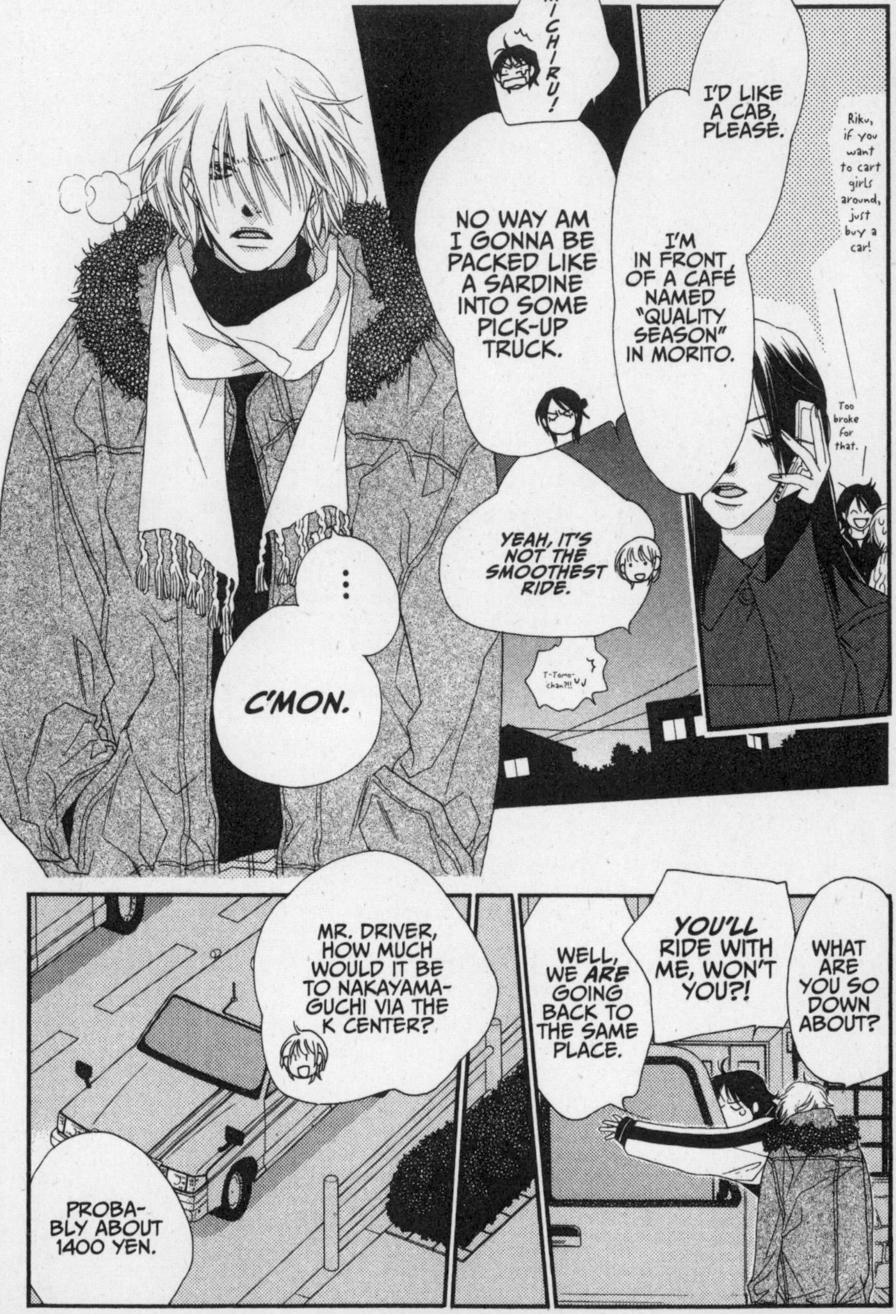
I'D LIKE A CAB, PLEASE.
I'M IN FRONT OF A CAFÉ NAMED "QUALITY SEASON" IN MORITO.
Riku, if you want to cart girls around, just buy a car!
Too broke for that.
MICHIRU!
NO WAY AM I GONNA BE PACKED LIKE A SARDINE INTO SOME PICK-UP TRUCK.
YEAH, IT'S NOT THE SMOOTHEST RIDE.
T-Tomo-chan?!!
...
C'MON.
WHAT ARE YOU SO DOWN ABOUT?
YOU'LL RIDE WITH ME, WON'T YOU?!
WELL, WE ARE GOING BACK TO THE SAME PLACE.
MR. DRIVER, HOW MUCH WOULD IT BE TO NAKAYAMA-GUCHI VIA THE K CENTER?
PROBA-BLY ABOUT 1400 YEN.

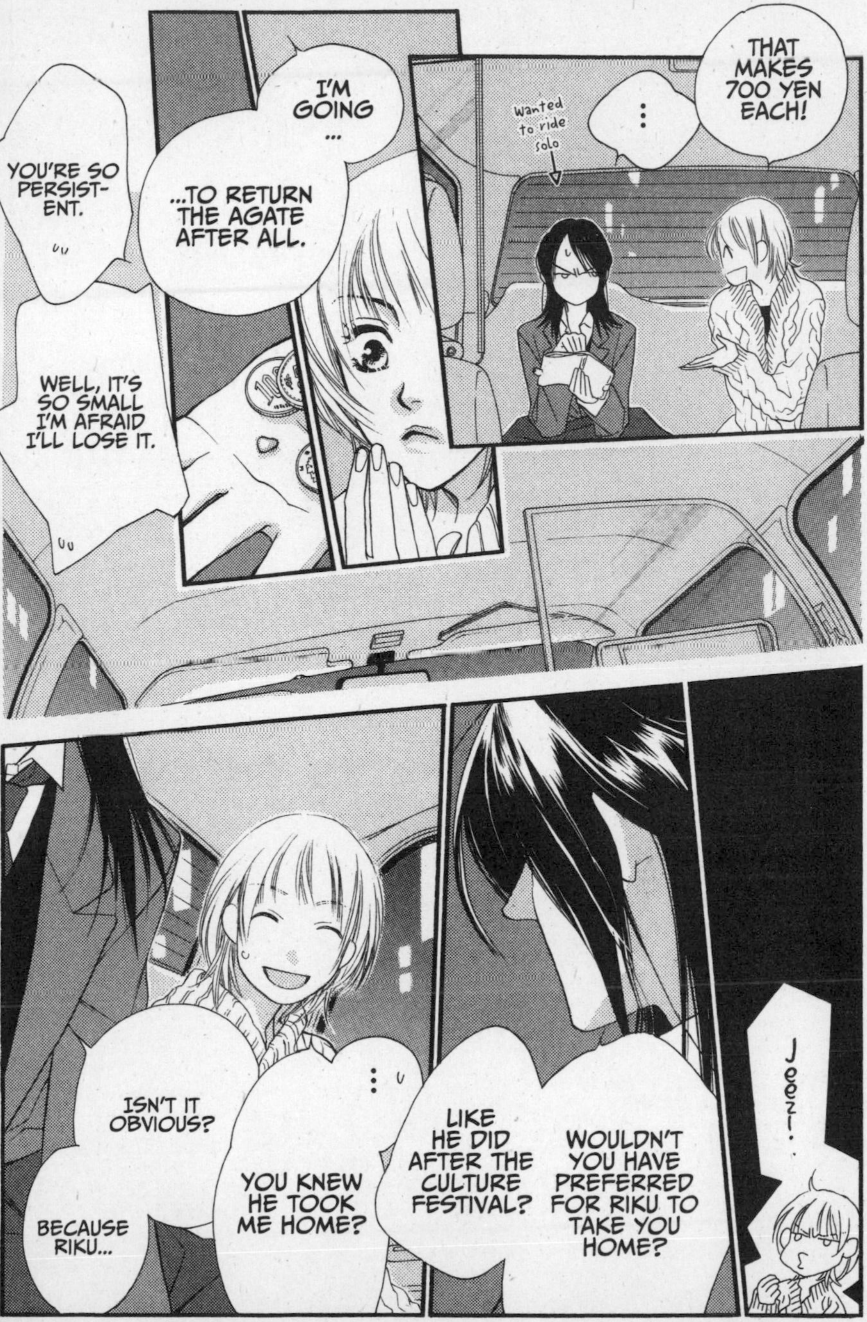
THAT MAKES 700 YEN EACH!
...
wanted to ride solo
I'M GOING ...
...TO RETURN THE AGATE AFTER ALL.
YOU'RE SO PERSIST-ENT.
WELL, IT'S SO SMALL I'M AFRAID I'LL LOSE IT.
Jeez...
WOULDN'T YOU HAVE PREFERRED FOR RIKU TO TAKE YOU HOME?
LIKE HE DID AFTER THE CULTURE FESTIVAL?
...
YOU KNEW HE TOOK ME HOME?
ISN'T IT OBVIOUS?
BECAUSE RIKU...

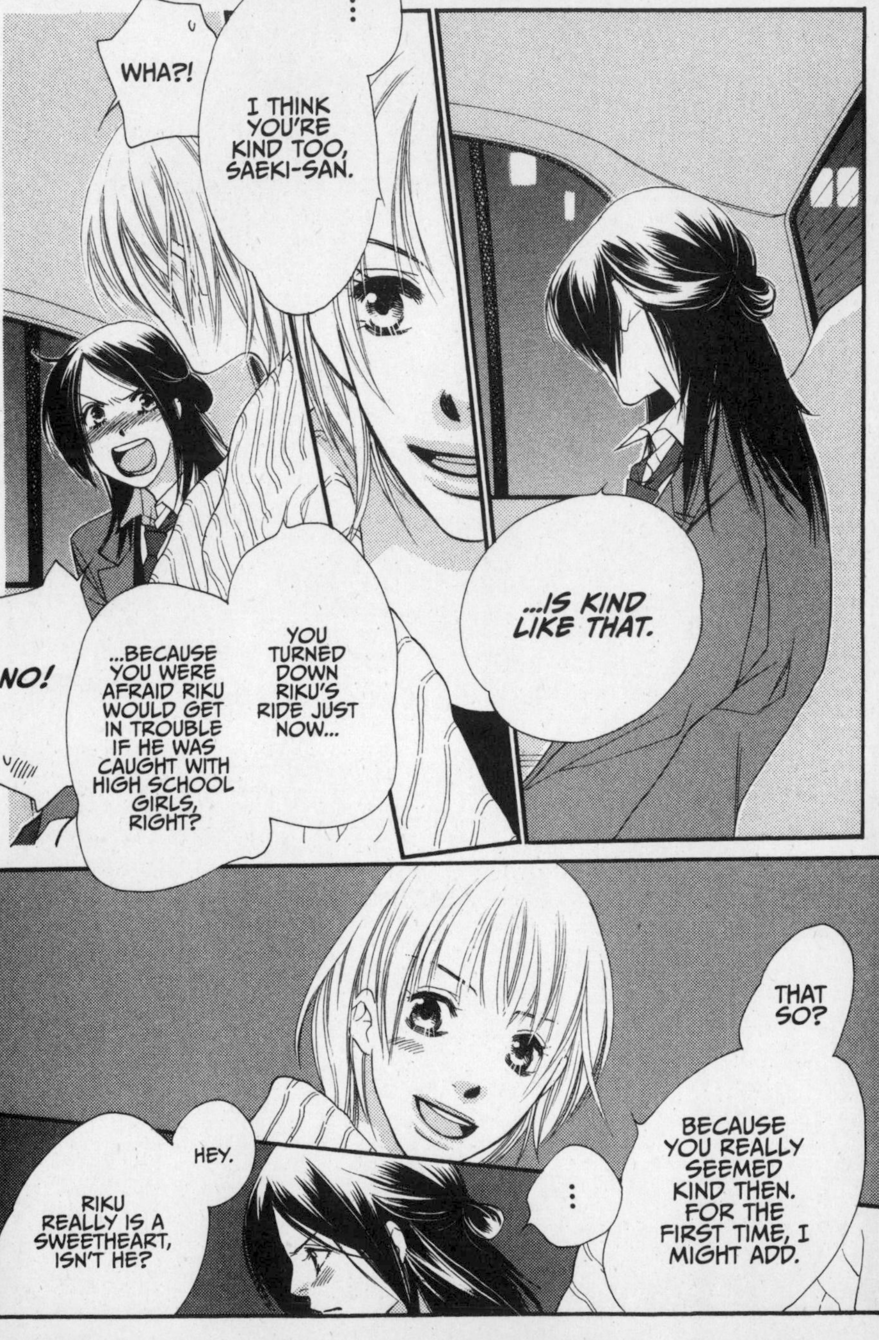
...IS KIND LIKE THAT.
......
I THINK YOU'RE KIND TOO, SAEKI-SAN.
WHA?!
YOU TURNED DOWN RIKU'S RIDE JUST NOW...
...BECAUSE YOU WERE AFRAID RIKU WOULD GET IN TROUBLE IF HE WAS CAUGHT WITH HIGH SCHOOL GIRLS, RIGHT?
NO!
THAT SO?
BECAUSE YOU REALLY SEEMED KIND THEN. FOR THE FIRST TIME, I MIGHT ADD.
...
HEY.
RIKU REALLY IS A SWEETHEART, ISN'T HE?

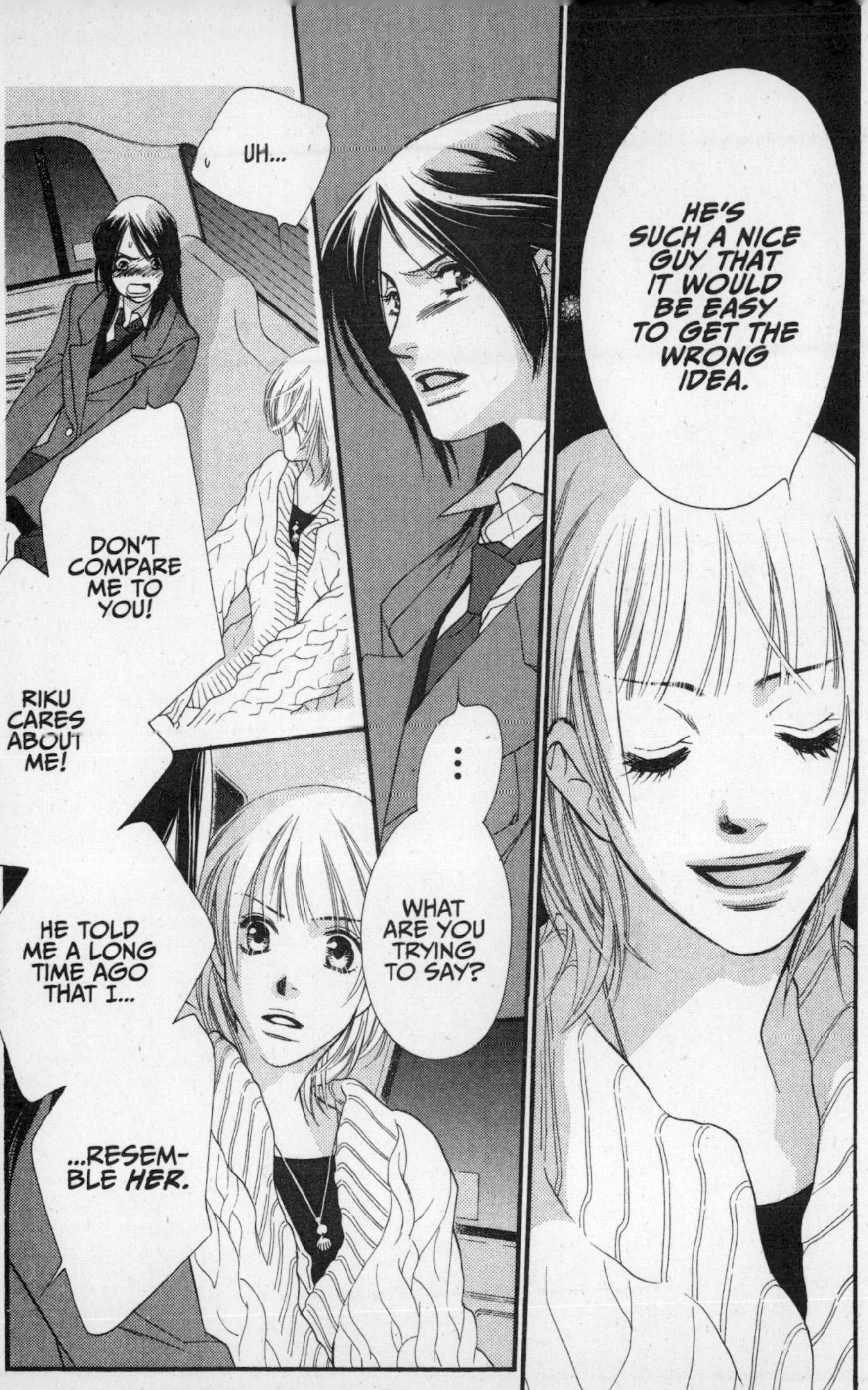
HE'S SUCH A NICE GUY THAT IT WOULD BE EASY TO GET THE WRONG IDEA.
UH...
...
WHAT ARE YOU TRYING TO SAY?
DON'T COMPARE ME TO YOU!
RIKU CARES ABOUT ME!
HE TOLD ME A LONG TIME AGO THAT I...
...RESEM-BLE *HER*.

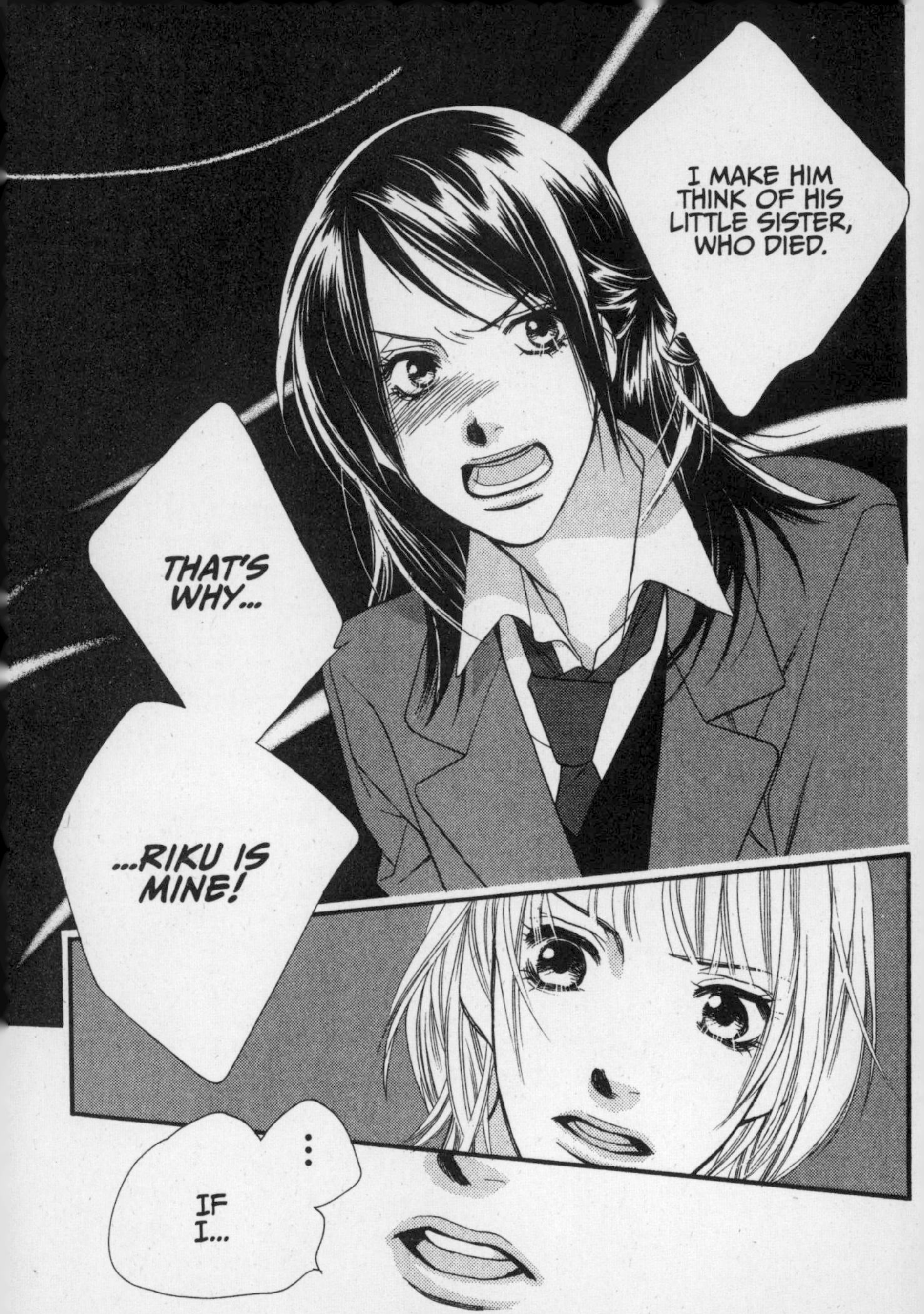
I MAKE HIM THINK OF HIS LITTLE SISTER, WHO DIED.
THAT'S WHY...
...RIKU IS MINE!
...
IF I...

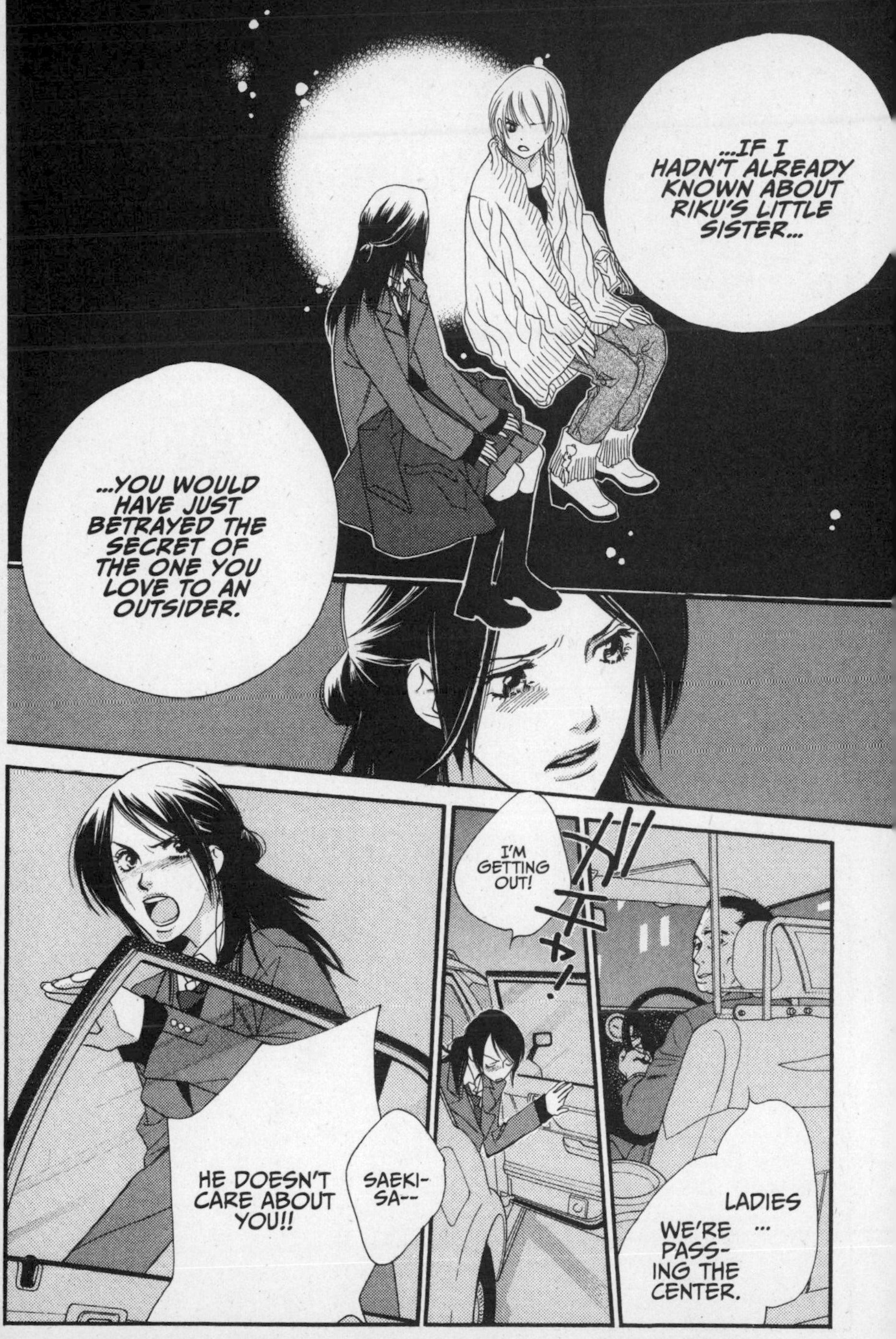
...IF I HADN'T ALREADY KNOWN ABOUT RIKU'S LITTLE SISTER...
...YOU WOULD HAVE JUST BETRAYED THE SECRET OF THE ONE YOU LOVE TO AN OUTSIDER.
LADIES ... WE'RE PASSING THE CENTER.
I'M GETTING OUT!
SAEKI-SA--
HE DOESN'T CARE ABOUT YOU!!

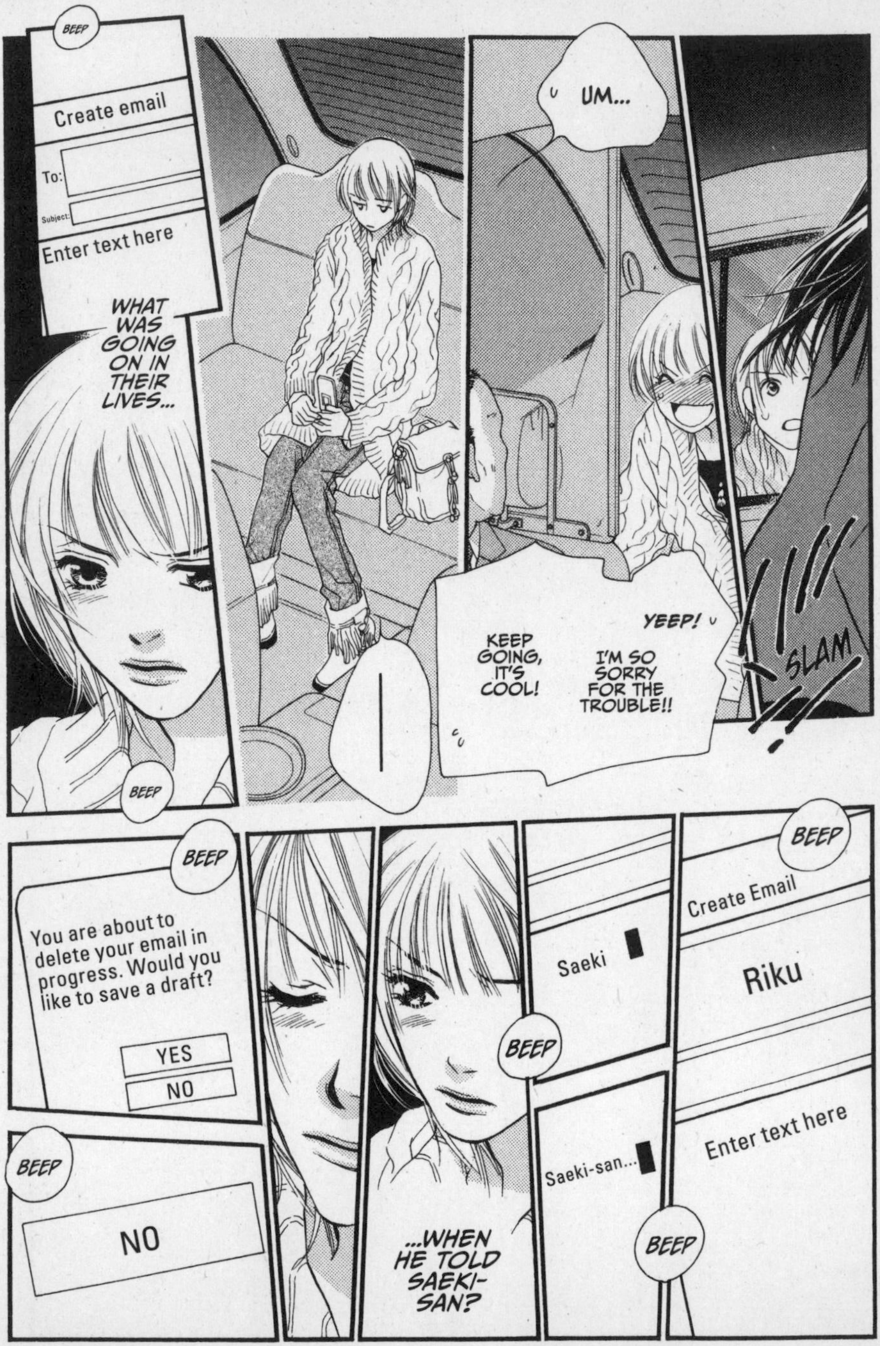
SLAM
UM...
YEEP!
I'M SO SORRY FOR THE TROUBLE!!
KEEP GOING, IT'S COOL!
BEEP
Create email
To:
Subject:
Enter text here
WHAT WAS GOING ON IN THEIR LIVES...
BEEP
BEEP
Create Email
Riku
Enter text here
BEEP
Saeki
BEEP
Saeki-san...
...WHEN HE TOLD SAEKI-SAN?
BEEP
You are about to delete your email in progress. Would you like to save a draft?
YES
NO
BEEP
NO

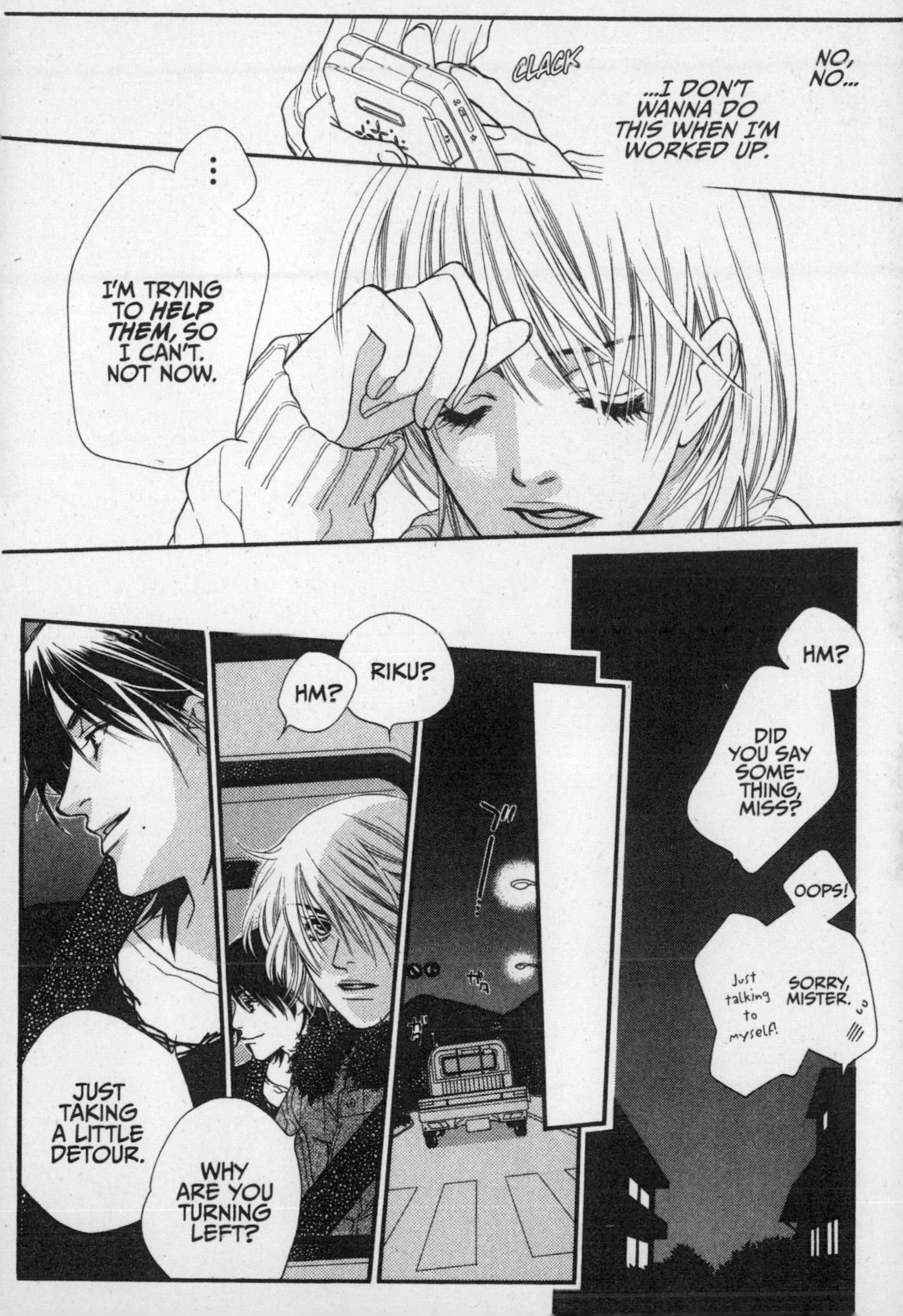
NO, NO...
...I DON'T WANNA DO THIS WHEN I'M WORKED UP.
CLACK
...
I'M TRYING TO HELP THEM, SO I CAN'T. NOT NOW.
HM?
DID YOU SAY SOMETHING, MISS?
OOPS!
SORRY, MISTER.
Just talking to myself!
RIKU?
HM?
WHY ARE YOU TURNING LEFT?
JUST TAKING A LITTLE DETOUR.

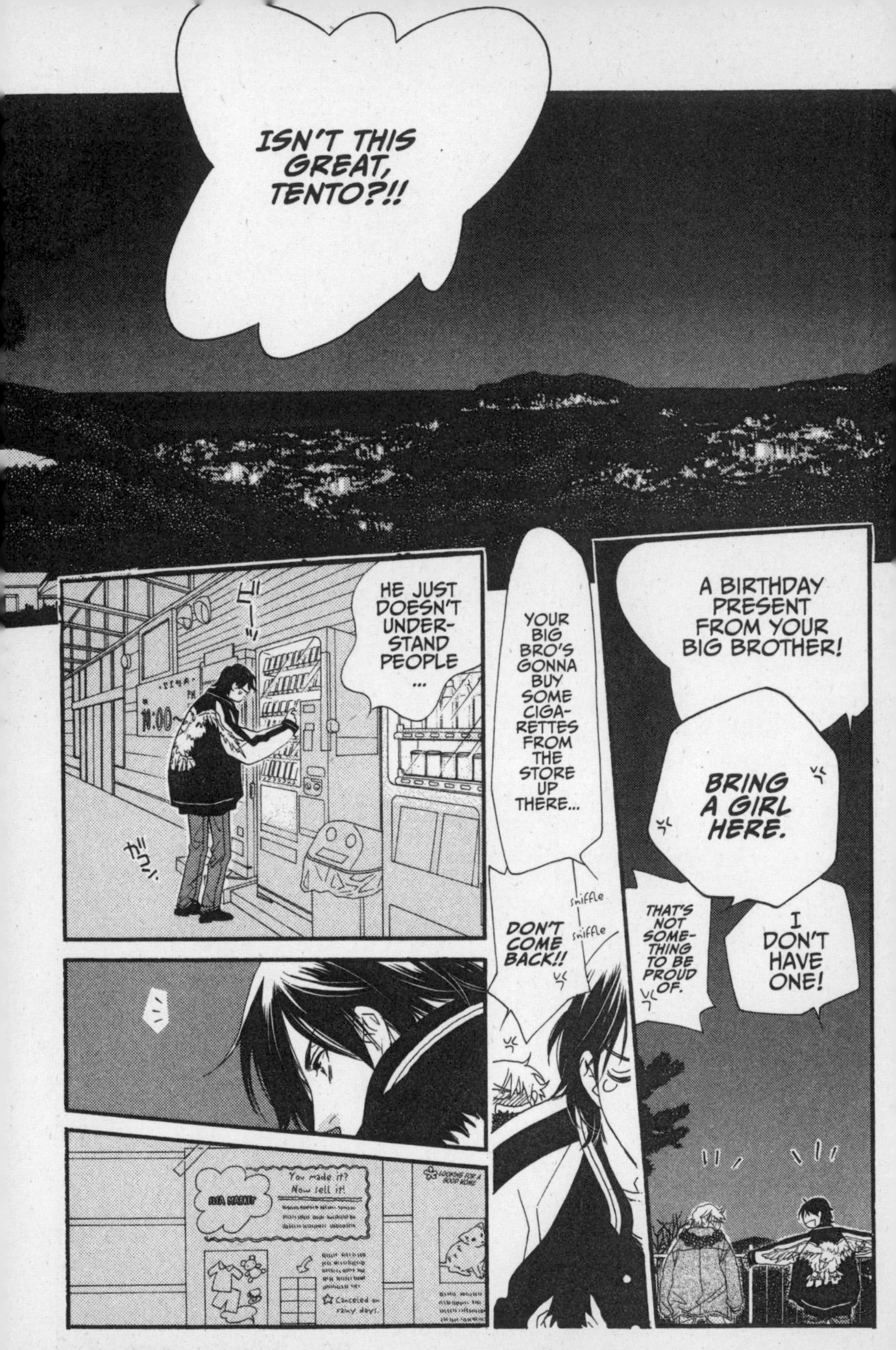
ISN'T THIS GREAT, TENTO?!!
A BIRTHDAY PRESENT FROM YOUR BIG BROTHER!
BRING A GIRL HERE.
I DON'T HAVE ONE!
THAT'S NOT SOMETHING TO BE PROUD OF.
YOUR BIG BRO'S GONNA BUY SOME CIGARETTES FROM THE STORE UP THERE...
sniffle
sniffle
DON'T COME BACK!!
HE JUST DOESN'T UNDERSTAND PEOPLE ...
You made it? Now sell it!
LOOKING FOR A GOOD HOME
Canceled on rainy days.

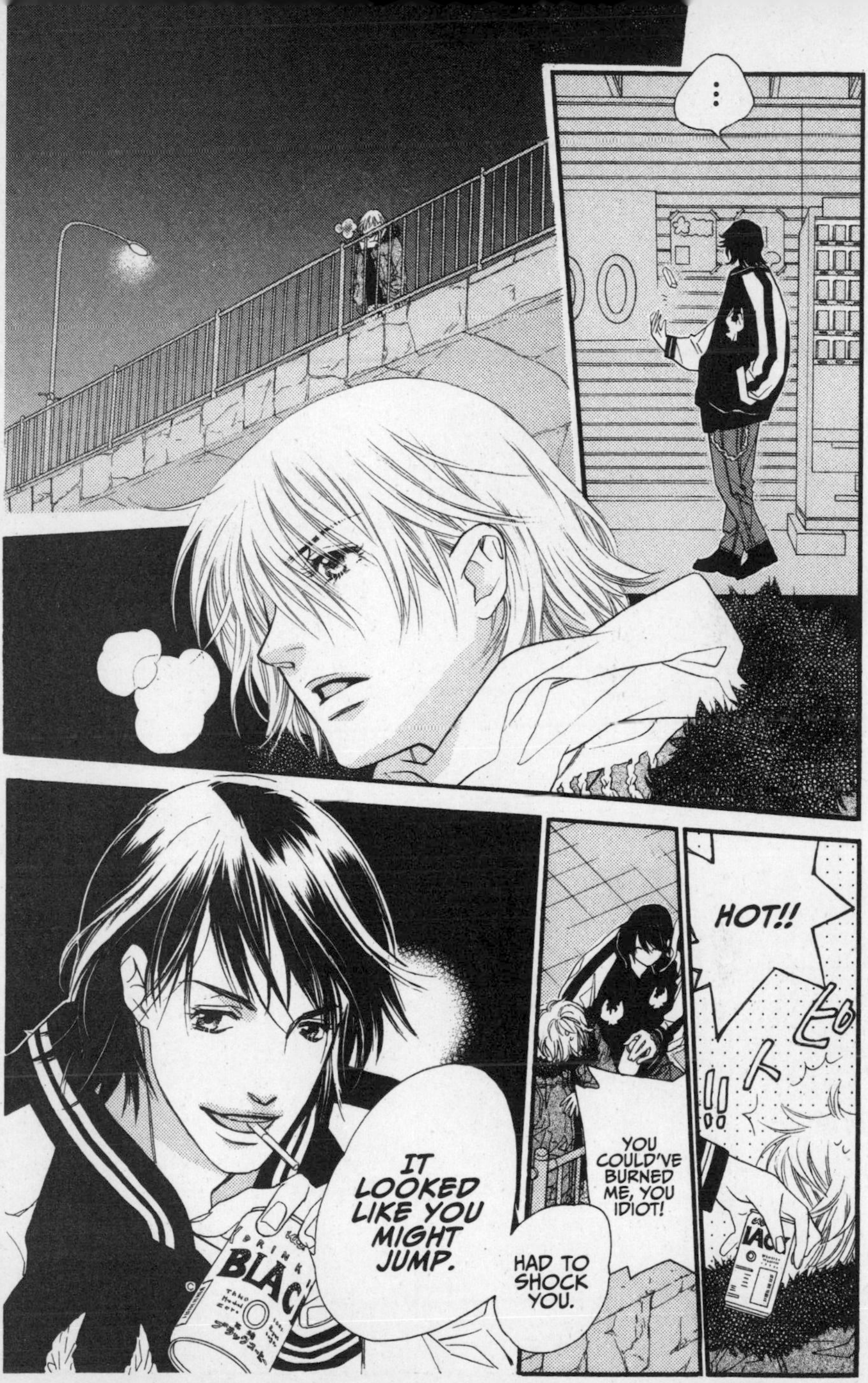
…
HOT!!
YOU COULD'VE BURNED ME, YOU IDIOT!
IT LOOKED LIKE YOU MIGHT JUMP.
HAD TO SHOCK YOU.

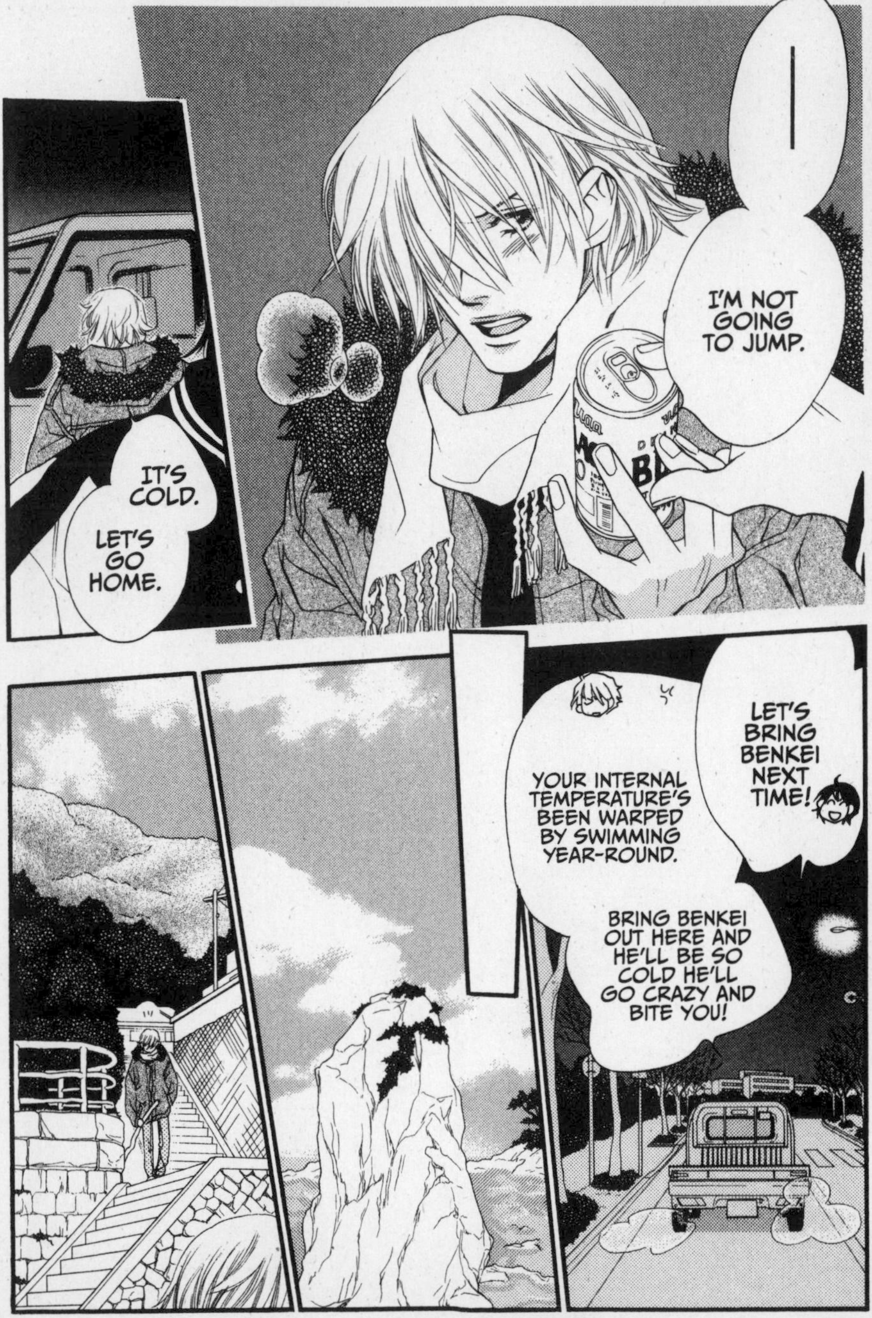
I'M NOT GOING TO JUMP.
IT'S COLD.
LET'S GO HOME.
LET'S BRING BENKEI NEXT TIME!
YOUR INTERNAL TEMPERATURE'S BEEN WARPED BY SWIMMING YEAR-ROUND.
BRING BENKEI OUT HERE AND HE'LL BE SO COLD HE'LL GO CRAZY AND BITE YOU!

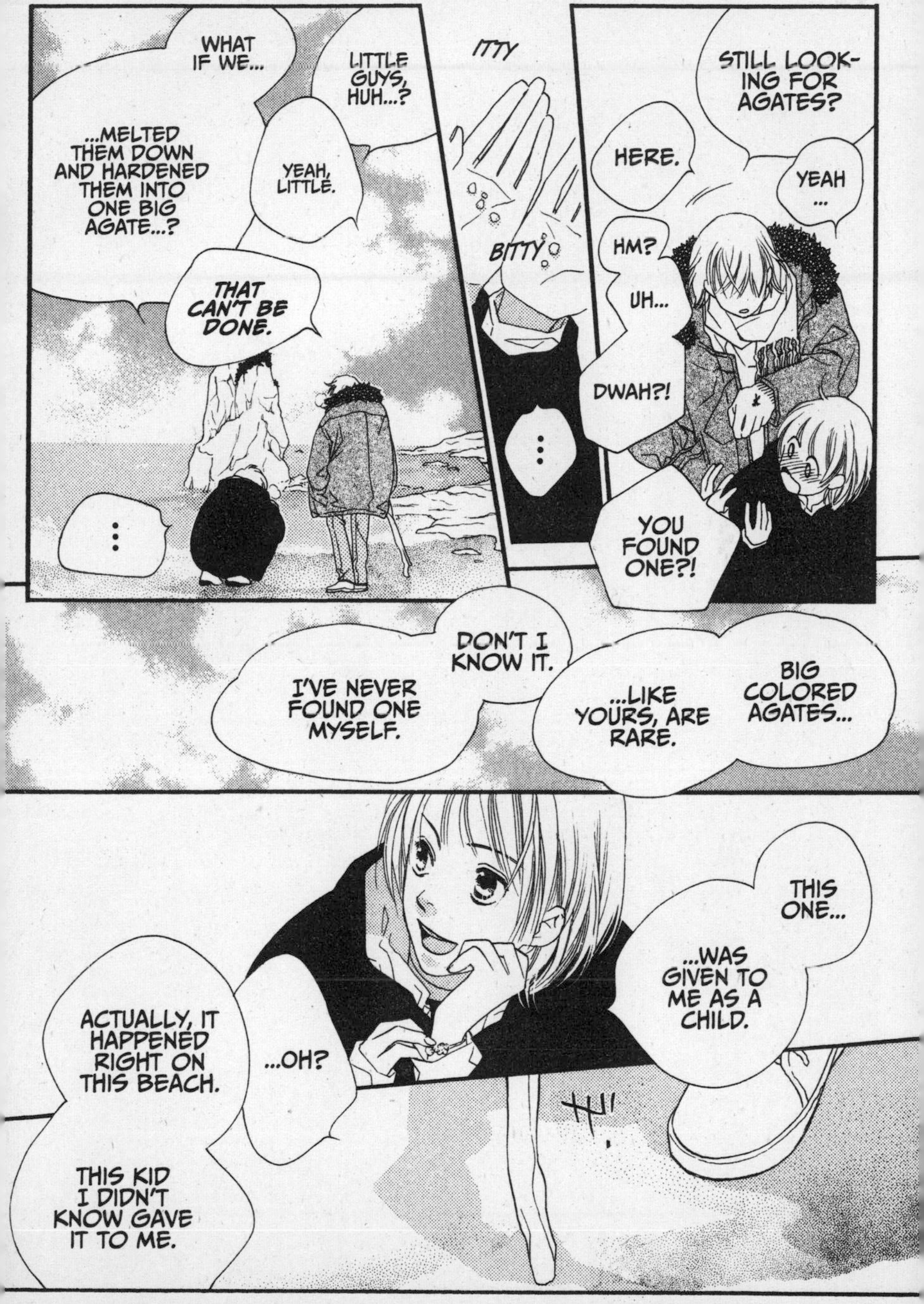
STILL LOOKING FOR AGATES?
YEAH ...
HERE.
HM?
UH...
DWAH?!
YOU FOUND ONE?!
ITTY
BITTY
...
LITTLE GUYS, HUH...?
WHAT IF WE...
YEAH, LITTLE.
...MELTED THEM DOWN AND HARDENED THEM INTO ONE BIG AGATE...?
THAT CAN'T BE DONE.
...
BIG COLORED AGATES...
...LIKE YOURS, ARE RARE.
DON'T I KNOW IT.
I'VE NEVER FOUND ONE MYSELF.
THIS ONE...
...WAS GIVEN TO ME AS A CHILD.
...OH?
ACTUALLY, IT HAPPENED RIGHT ON THIS BEACH.
THIS KID I DIDN'T KNOW GAVE IT TO ME.

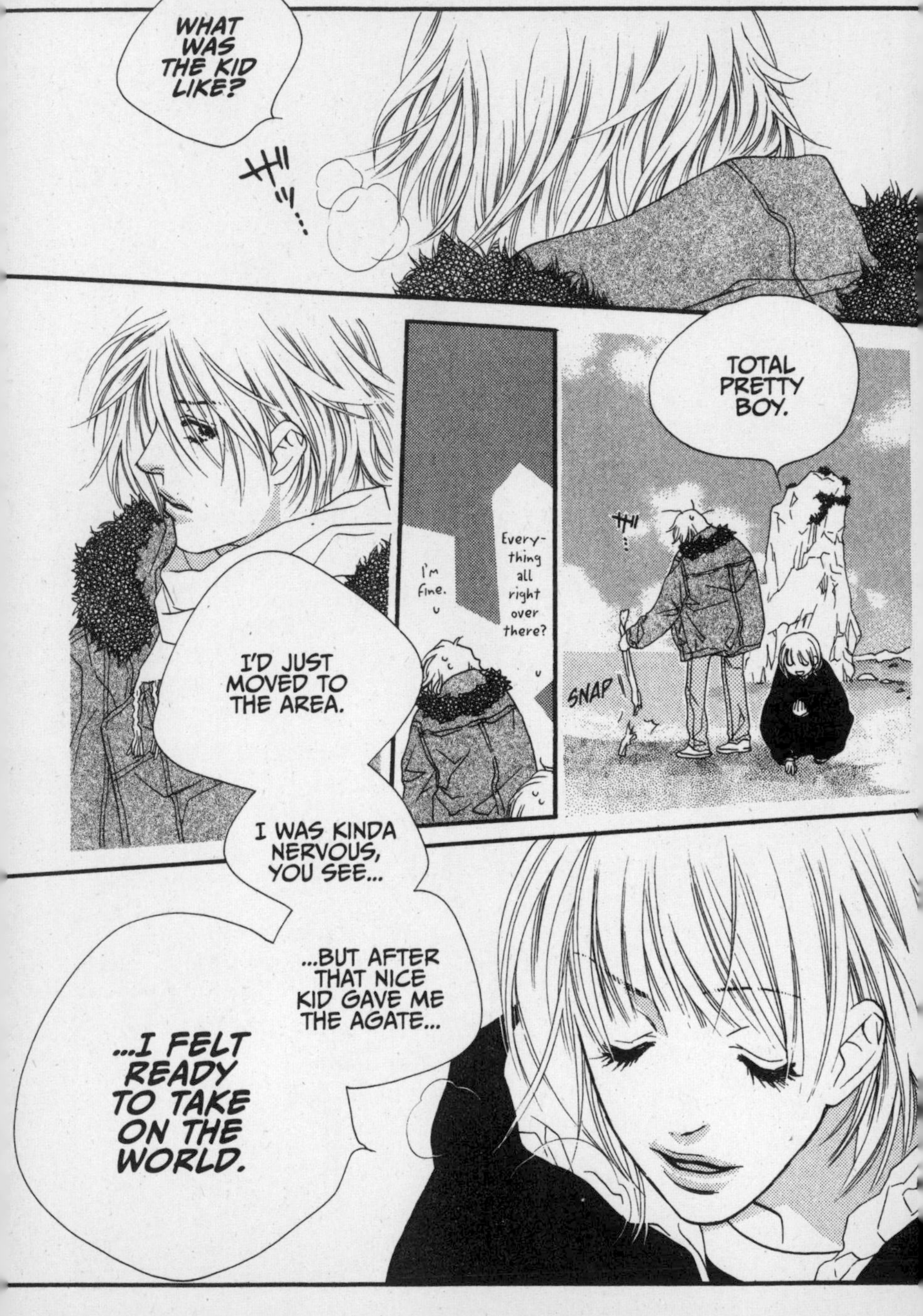
WHAT WAS THE KID LIKE?
TOTAL PRETTY BOY.
SNAP
Every-thing all right over there?
I'm fine.
I'D JUST MOVED TO THE AREA.
I WAS KINDA NERVOUS, YOU SEE...
...BUT AFTER THAT NICE KID GAVE ME THE AGATE...
...I FELT READY TO TAKE ON THE WORLD.

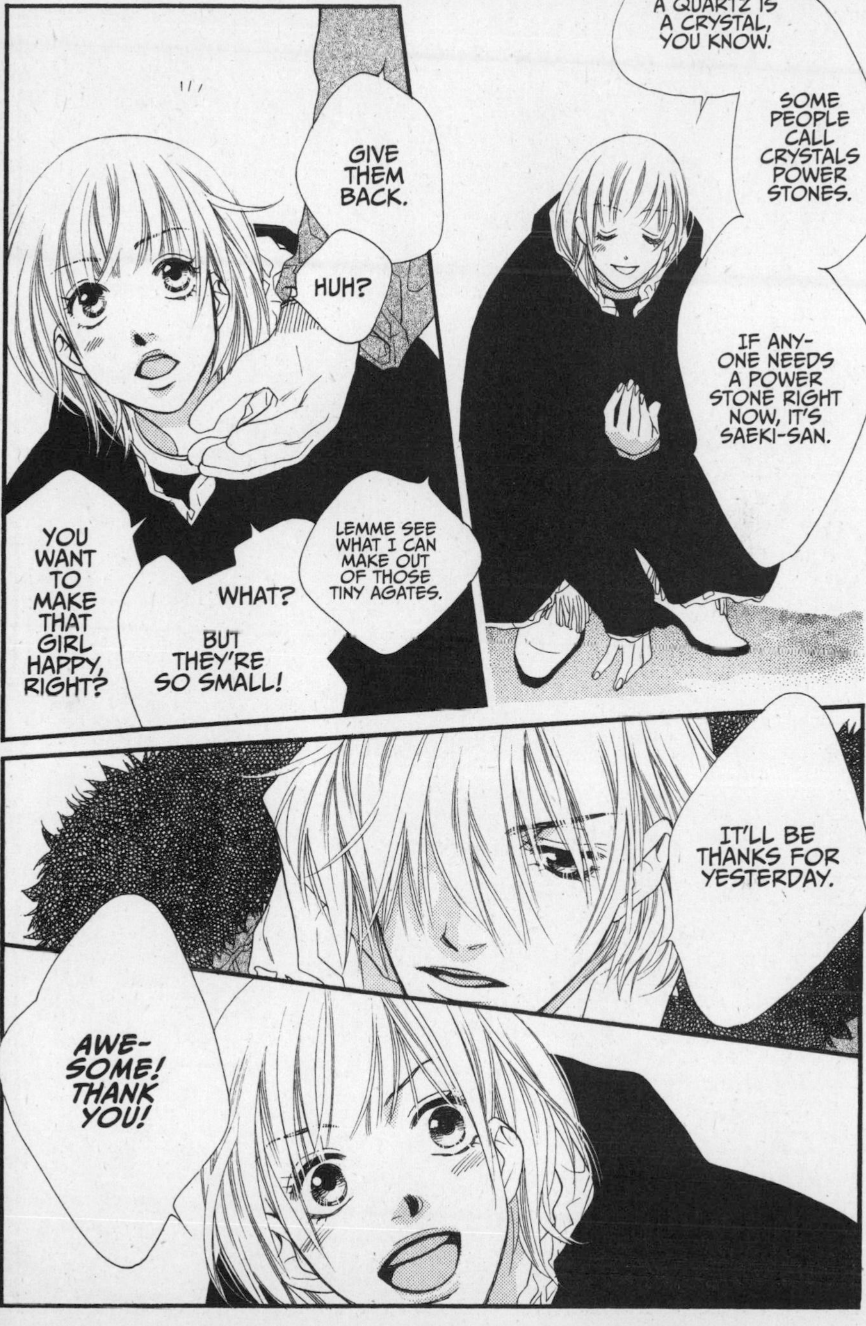
A QUARTZ IS A CRYSTAL, YOU KNOW.
SOME PEOPLE CALL CRYSTALS POWER STONES.
IF ANY-ONE NEEDS A POWER STONE RIGHT NOW, IT'S SAEKI-SAN.
GIVE THEM BACK.
HUH?
LEMME SEE WHAT I CAN MAKE OUT OF THOSE TINY AGATES.
WHAT?
BUT THEY'RE SO SMALL!
YOU WANT TO MAKE THAT GIRL HAPPY, RIGHT?
IT'LL BE THANKS FOR YESTERDAY.
AWE-SOME! THANK YOU!

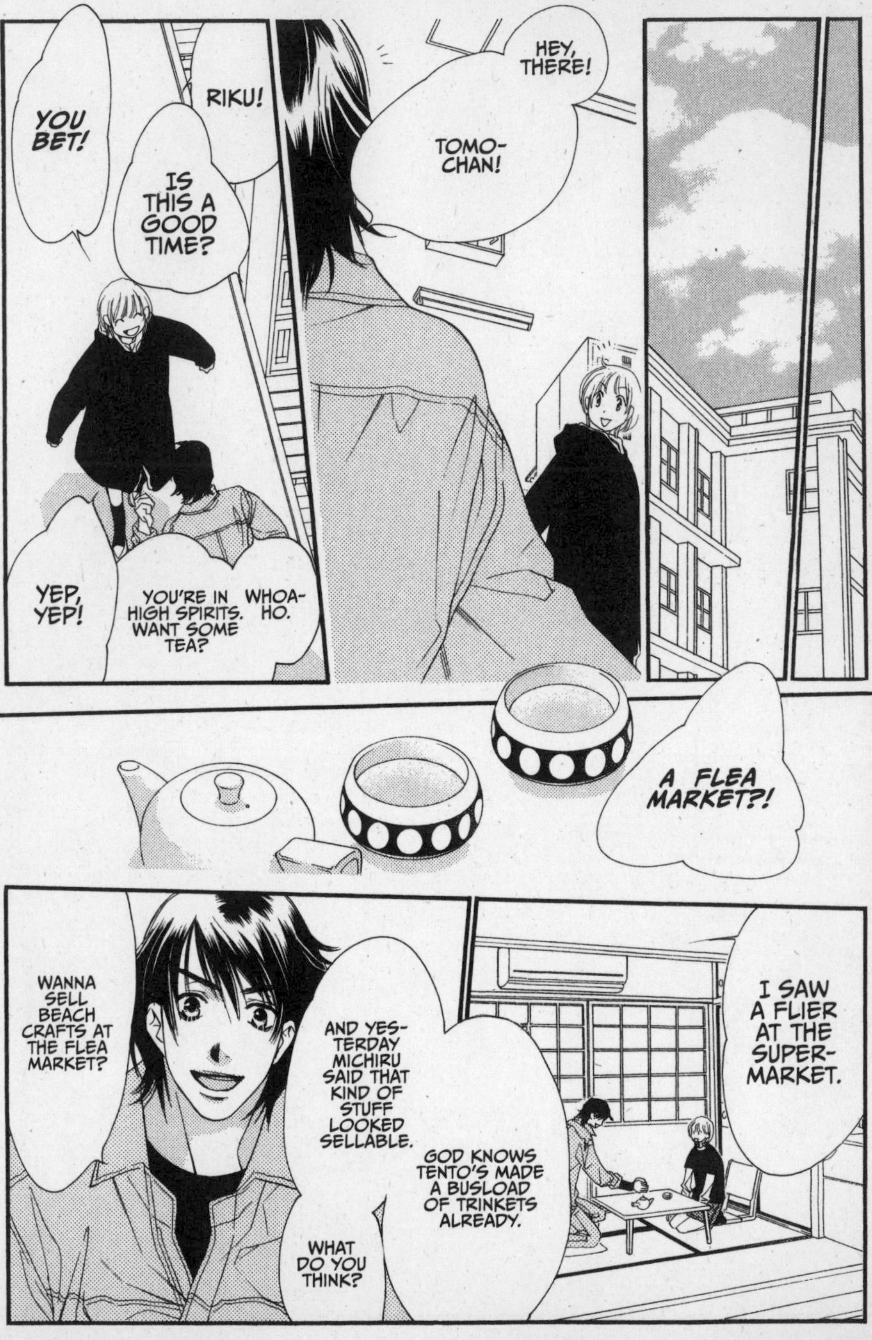
HEY, THERE!
TOMO-CHAN!
RIKU!
IS THIS A GOOD TIME?
YOU BET!
WHOA-HO.
YOU'RE IN HIGH SPIRITS. WANT SOME TEA?
YEP, YEP!
A FLEA MARKET?!
I SAW A FLIER AT THE SUPER-MARKET.
GOD KNOWS TENTO'S MADE A BUSLOAD OF TRINKETS ALREADY.
AND YES-TERDAY MICHIRU SAID THAT KIND OF STUFF LOOKED SELLABLE.
WANNA SELL BEACH CRAFTS AT THE FLEA MARKET?
WHAT DO YOU THINK?

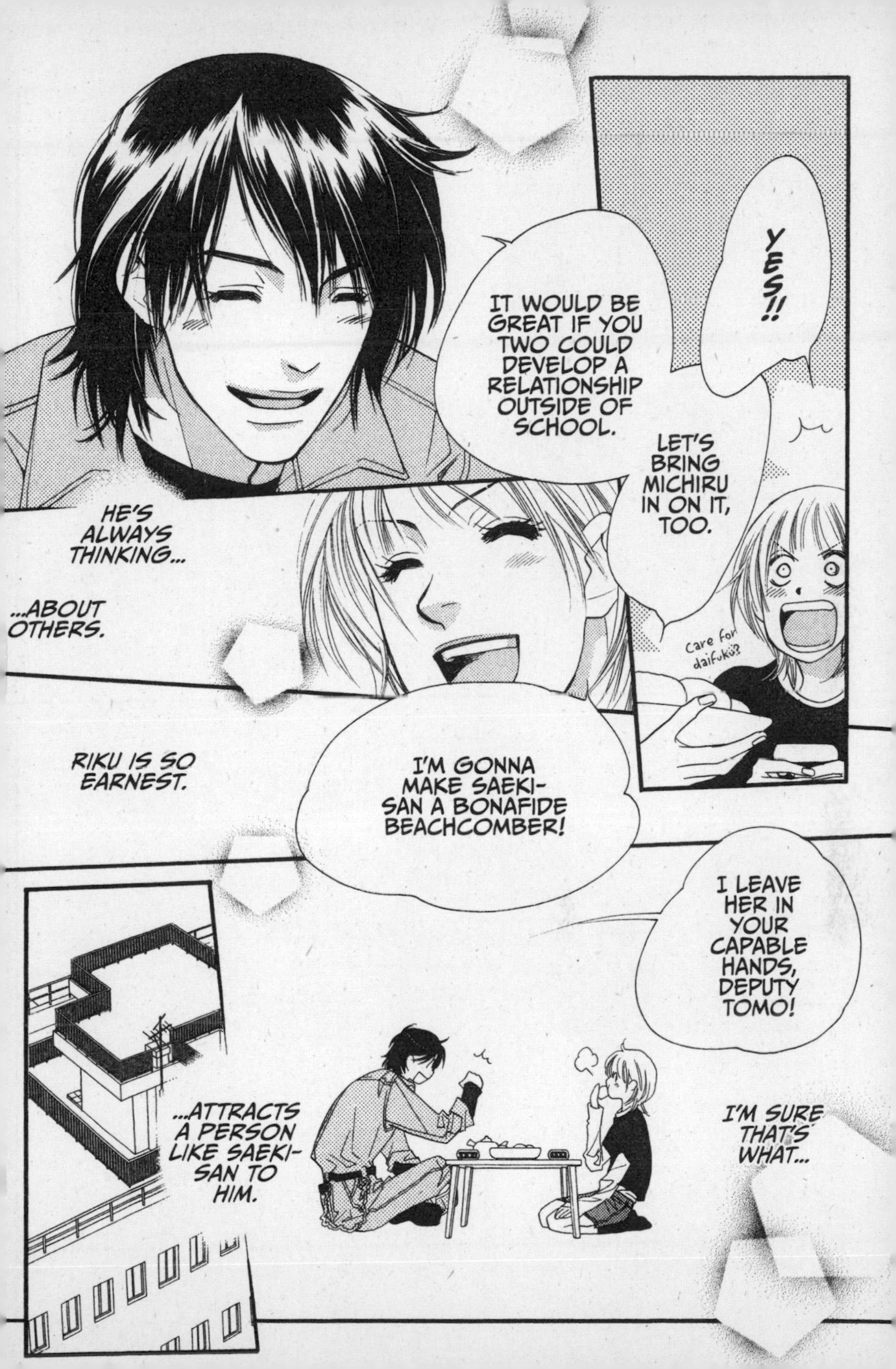
IT WOULD BE GREAT IF YOU TWO COULD DEVELOP A RELATIONSHIP OUTSIDE OF SCHOOL.
YES!!
LET'S BRING MICHIRU IN ON IT, TOO.
care for daifuku?
HE'S ALWAYS THINKING...
...ABOUT OTHERS.
RIKU IS SO EARNEST.
I'M GONNA MAKE SAEKI-SAN A BONAFIDE BEACHCOMBER!
I LEAVE HER IN YOUR CAPABLE HANDS, DEPUTY TOMO!
I'M SURE THAT'S WHAT...
...ATTRACTS A PERSON LIKE SAEKI-SAN TO HIM.

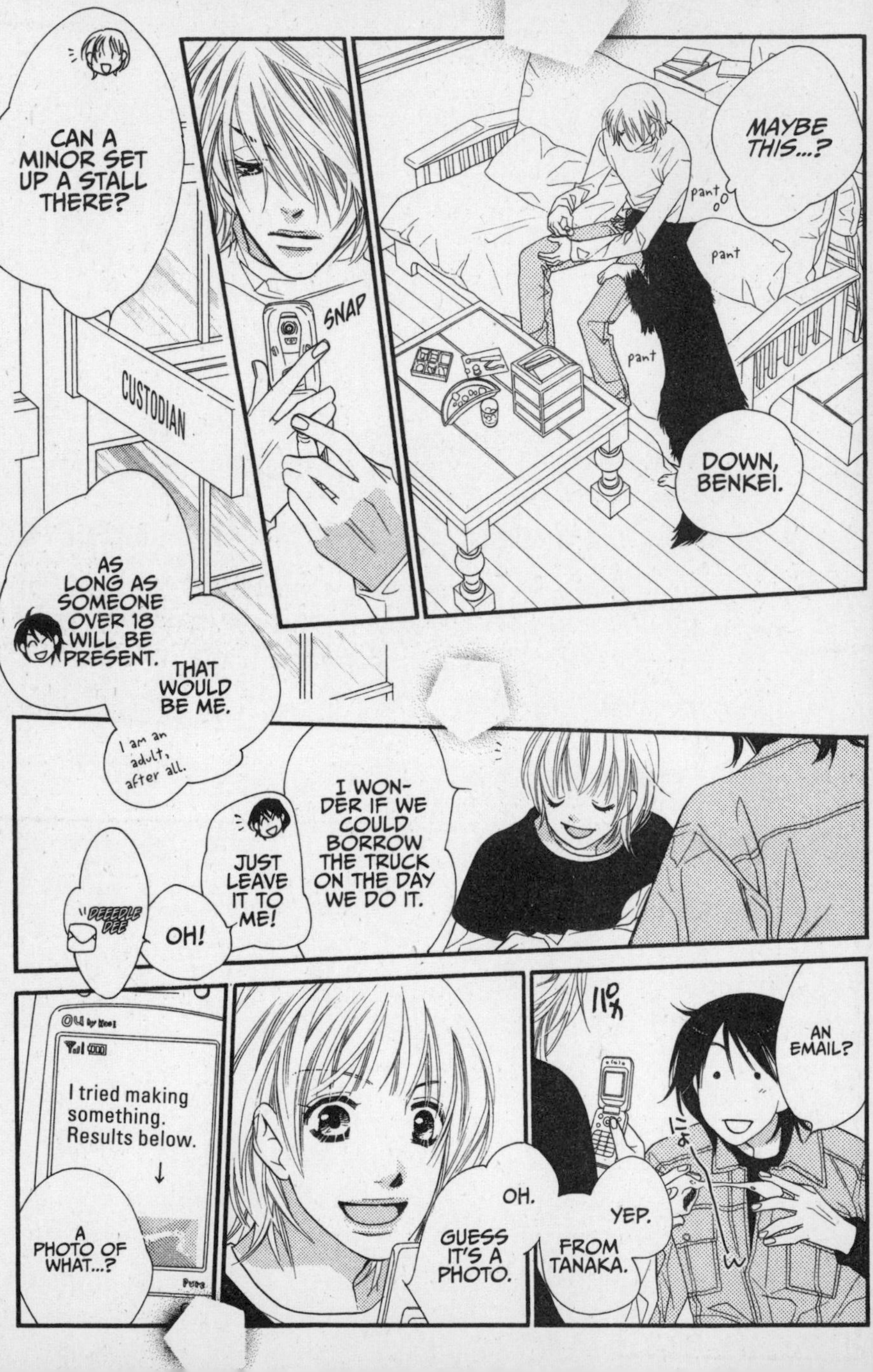
MAYBE THIS...?
pant
pant
pant
DOWN, BENKEI.
SNAP
CAN A MINOR SET UP A STALL THERE?
CUSTODIAN
AS LONG AS SOMEONE OVER 18 WILL BE PRESENT.
THAT WOULD BE ME.
I am an adult, after all.
I WONDER IF WE COULD BORROW THE TRUCK ON THE DAY WE DO IT.
JUST LEAVE IT TO ME!
OH!
DEEEDLE DEE
AN EMAIL?
YEP.
FROM TANAKA.
OH.
GUESS IT'S A PHOTO.
I tried making something. Results below.
↓
A PHOTO OF WHAT...?

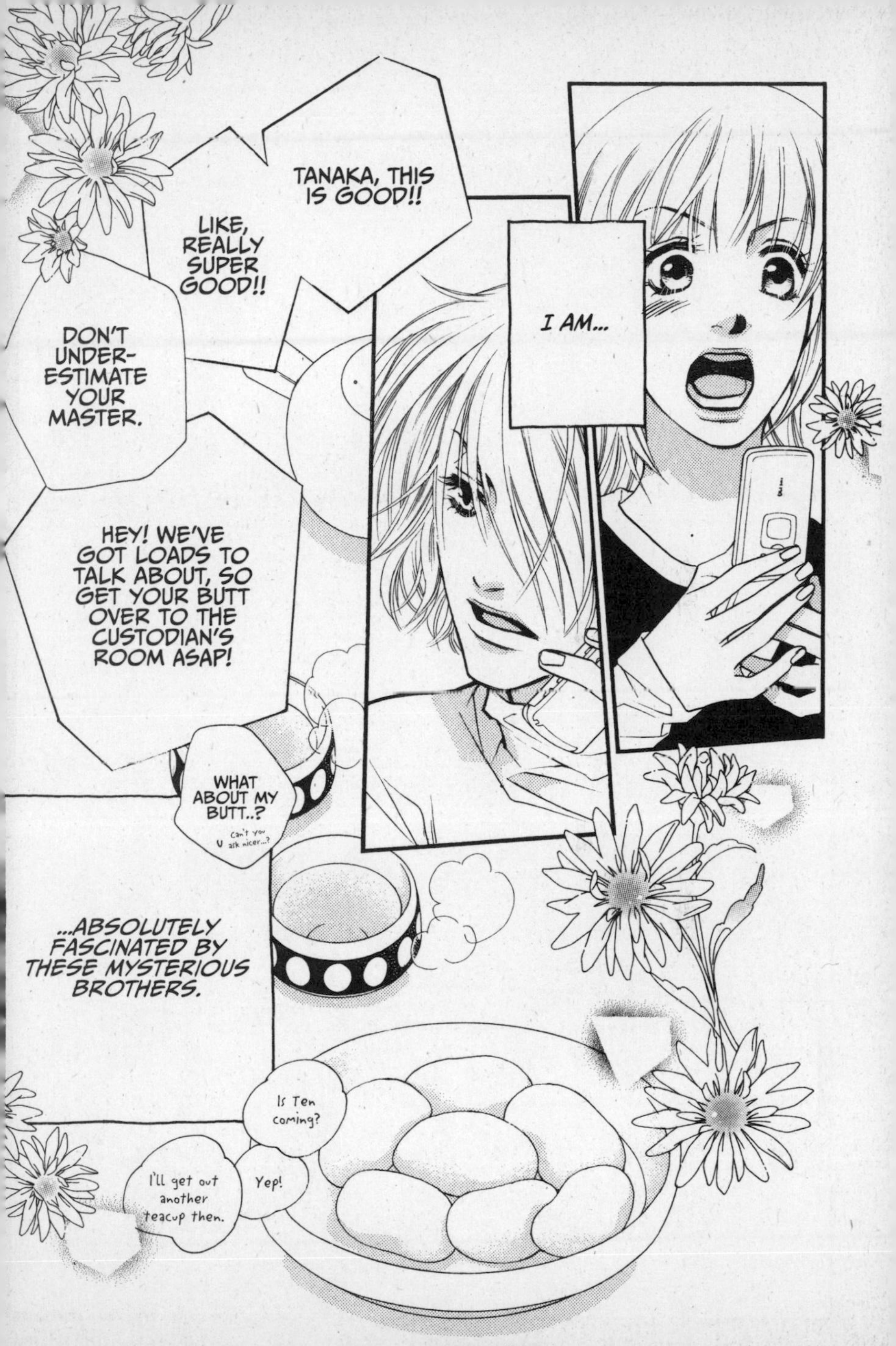
I AM...
TANAKA, THIS IS GOOD!!
LIKE, REALLY SUPER GOOD!!
DON'T UNDER-ESTIMATE YOUR MASTER.
HEY! WE'VE GOT LOADS TO TALK ABOUT, SO GET YOUR BUTT OVER TO THE CUSTODIAN'S ROOM ASAP!
WHAT ABOUT MY BUTT..?
Can't you ask nicer...?
...ABSOLUTELY FASCINATED BY THESE MYSTERIOUS BROTHERS.
Is Ten coming?
Yep!
I'll get out another teacup then.

Chapter 7 / End

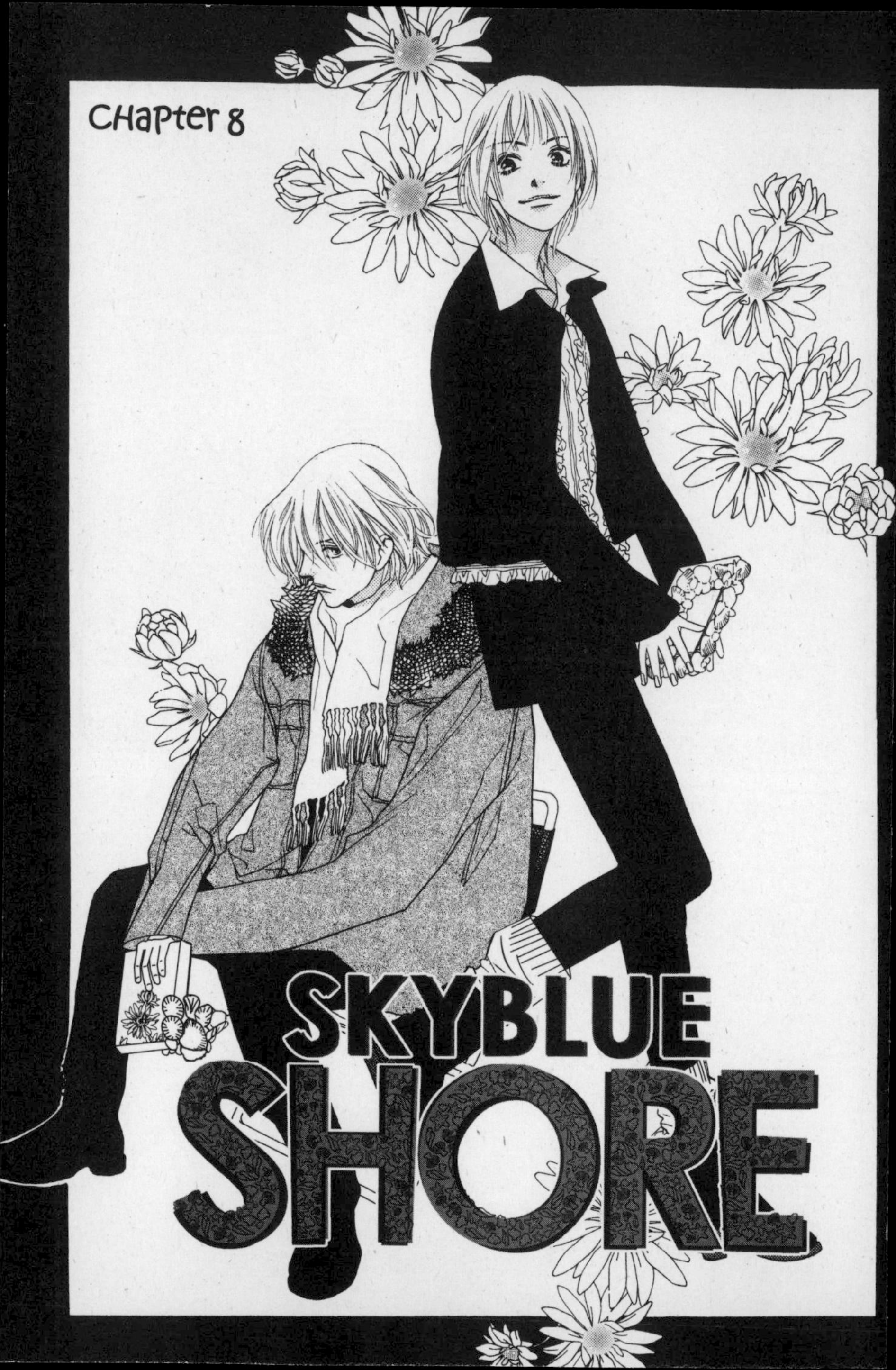
Chapter 8
SKYBLUE
SHORE

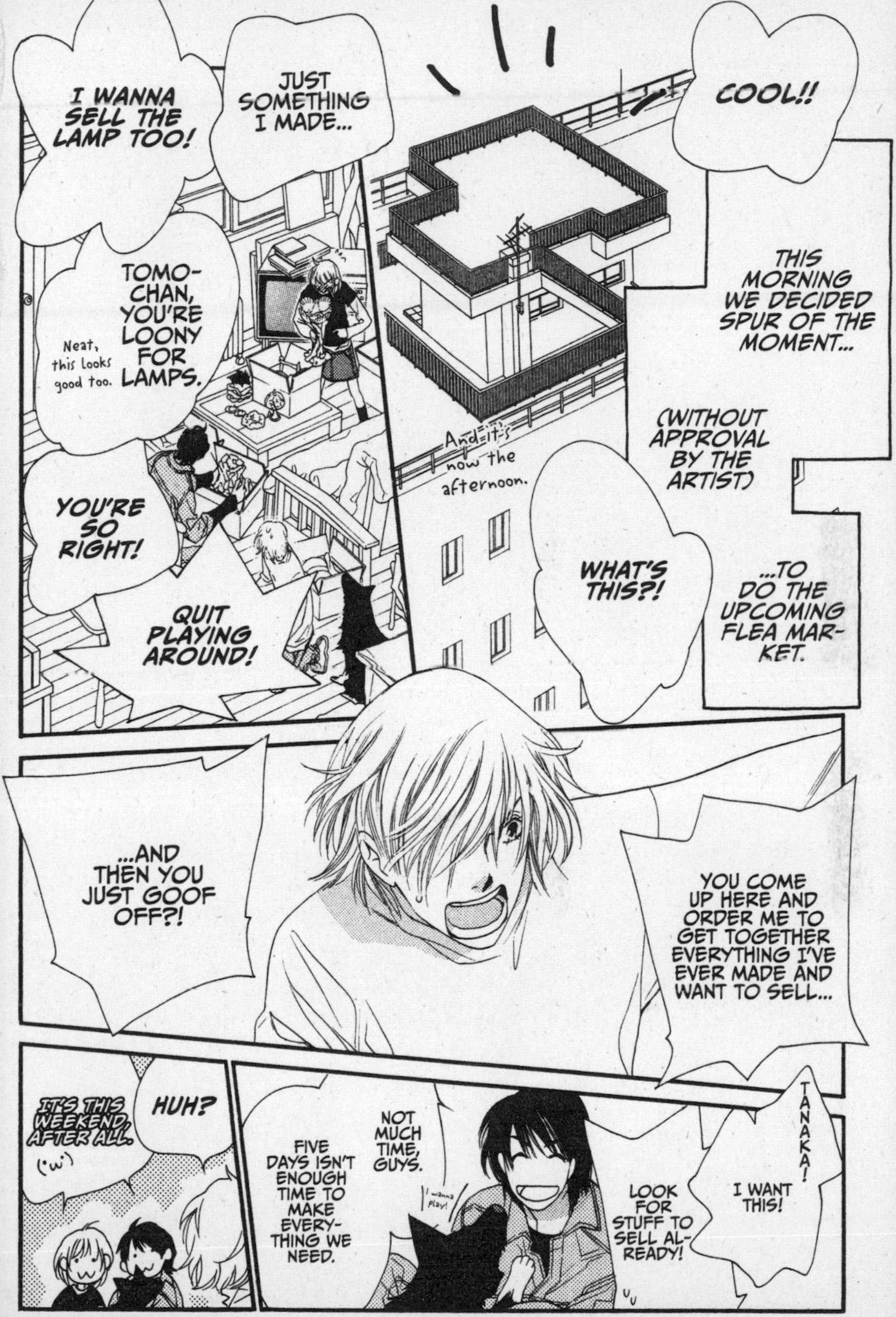
COOL!!
THIS MORNING WE DECIDED SPUR OF THE MOMENT...
(WITHOUT APPROVAL BY THE ARTIST)
...TO DO THE UPCOMING FLEA MARKET.
And it's now the afternoon.
WHAT'S THIS?!
JUST SOMETHING I MADE...
I WANNA SELL THE LAMP TOO!
TOMO-CHAN, YOU'RE LOONY FOR LAMPS.
Neat, this looks good too.
YOU'RE SO RIGHT!
QUIT PLAYING AROUND!
YOU COME UP HERE AND ORDER ME TO GET TOGETHER EVERYTHING I'VE EVER MADE AND WANT TO SELL...
...AND THEN YOU JUST GOOF OFF?!
TANAKA!
I WANT THIS!
LOOK FOR STUFF TO SELL ALREADY!
NOT MUCH TIME, GUYS.
I wanna play!
FIVE DAYS ISN'T ENOUGH TIME TO MAKE EVERYTHING WE NEED.
HUH?
IT'S THIS WEEKEND AFTER ALL.

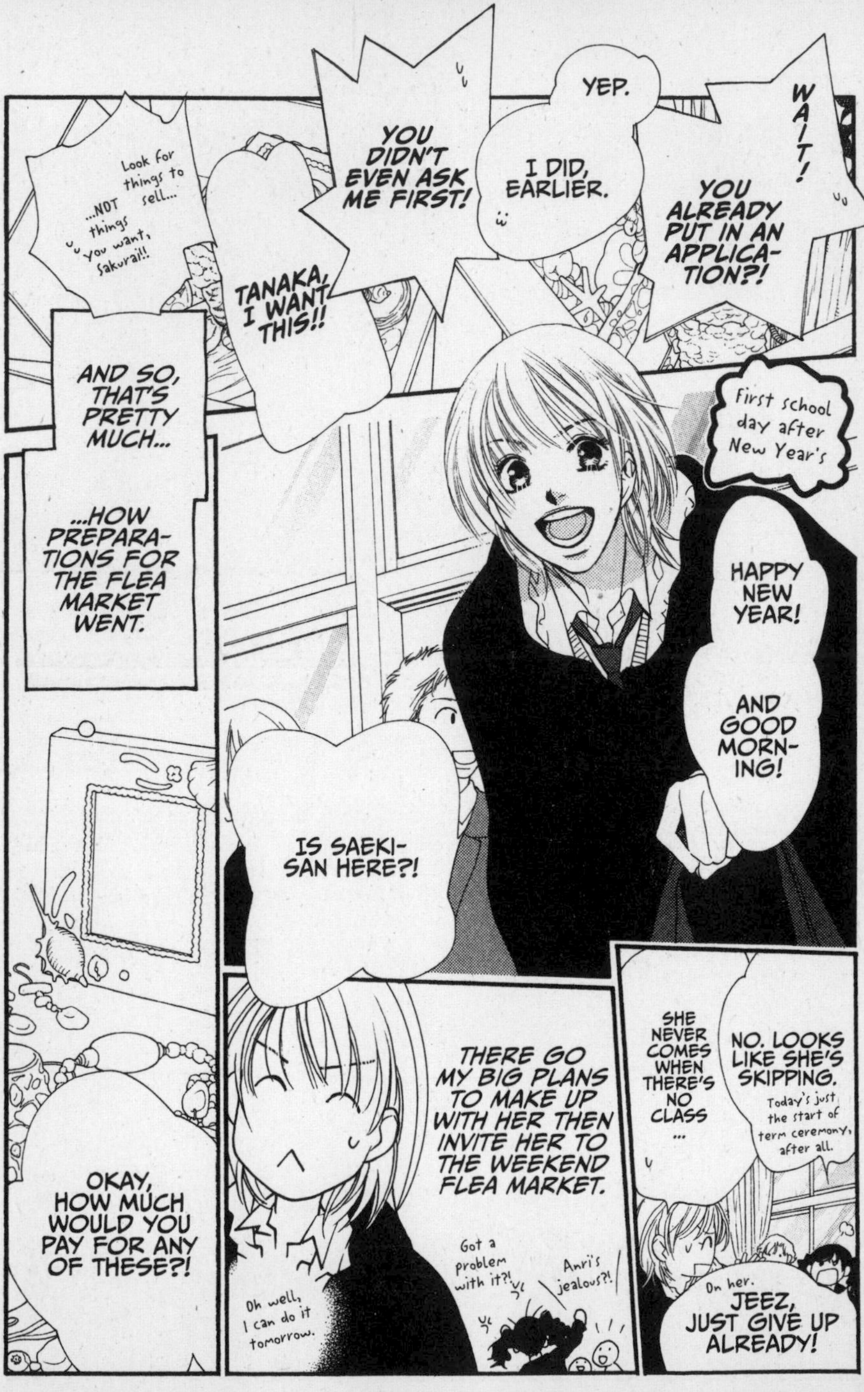
WAIT!
YOU ALREADY PUT IN AN APPLICATION?!
YEP.
I DID, EARLIER.
YOU DIDN'T EVEN ASK ME FIRST!
TANAKA, I WANT THIS!!
Look for things to sell... ...NOT things you want, Sakurai!!
First school day after New Year's
HAPPY NEW YEAR!
AND GOOD MORNING!
IS SAEKI-SAN HERE?!
NO. LOOKS LIKE SHE'S SKIPPING.
Today's just the start of term ceremony, after all.
SHE NEVER COMES WHEN THERE'S NO CLASS...
On her.
JEEZ, JUST GIVE UP ALREADY!
THERE GO MY BIG PLANS TO MAKE UP WITH HER THEN INVITE HER TO THE WEEKEND FLEA MARKET.
Anri's jealous?!
Got a problem with it?!
Oh well, I can do it tomorrow.
AND SO, THAT'S PRETTY MUCH...
...HOW PREPARATIONS FOR THE FLEA MARKET WENT.
OKAY, HOW MUCH WOULD YOU PAY FOR ANY OF THESE?!

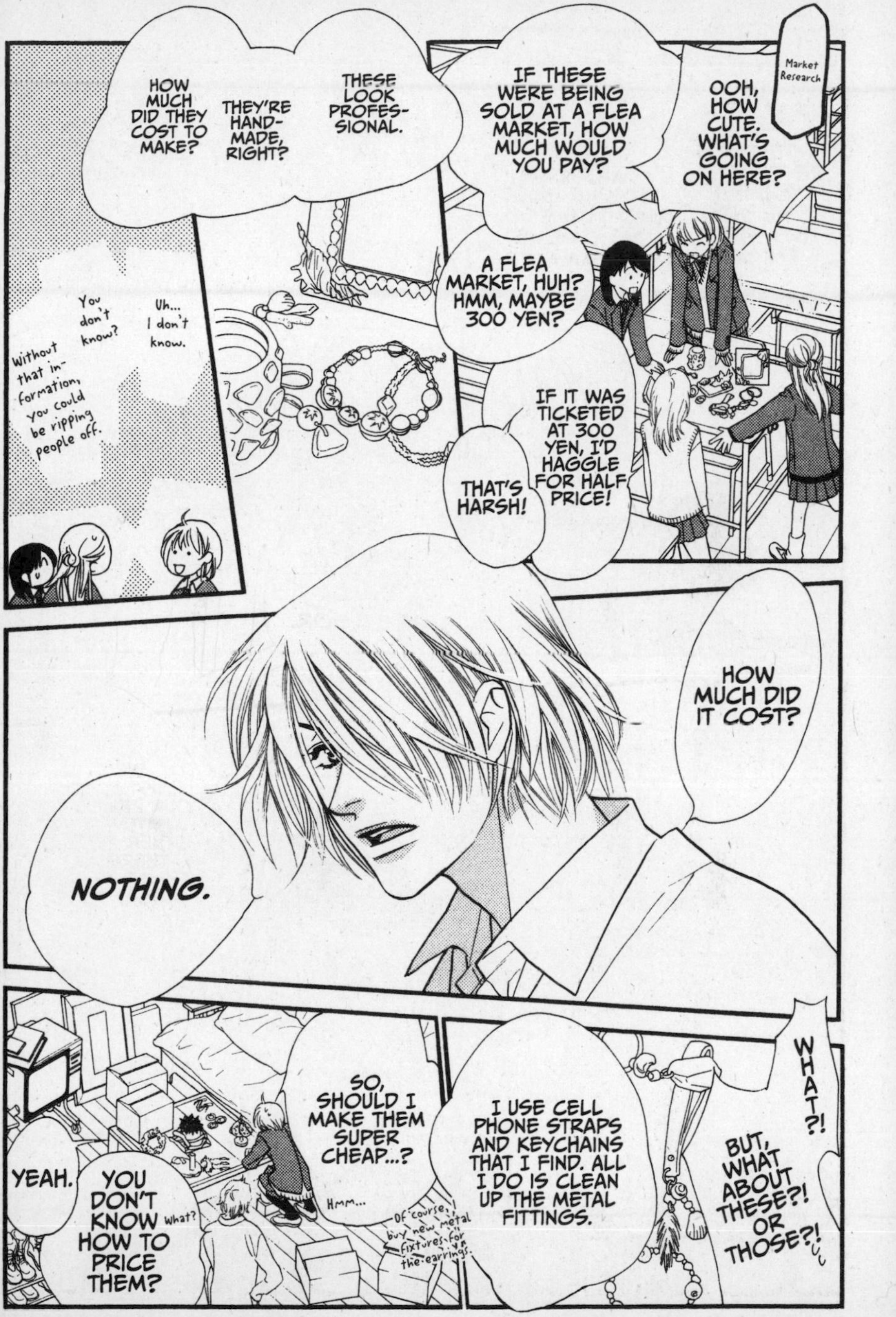
Market Research
OOH, HOW CUTE. WHAT'S GOING ON HERE?
IF THESE WERE BEING SOLD AT A FLEA MARKET, HOW MUCH WOULD YOU PAY?
A FLEA MARKET, HUH? HMM, MAYBE 300 YEN?
IF IT WAS TICKETED AT 300 YEN, I'D HAGGLE FOR HALF PRICE!
THAT'S HARSH!
THESE LOOK PROFES-SIONAL.
THEY'RE HAND-MADE, RIGHT?
HOW MUCH DID THEY COST TO MAKE?
Uh... I don't know.
You don't know?
Without that in-formation, you could be ripping people off.
HOW MUCH DID IT COST?
NOTHING.
WHAT?!
BUT, WHAT ABOUT THESE?! OR THOSE?!
I USE CELL PHONE STRAPS AND KEYCHAINS THAT I FIND. ALL I DO IS CLEAN UP THE METAL FITTINGS.
Of course, I buy new metal fixtures for the earrings.
SO, SHOULD I MAKE THEM SUPER CHEAP...?
Hmm...
YOU DON'T KNOW HOW TO PRICE THEM?
what?
YEAH.

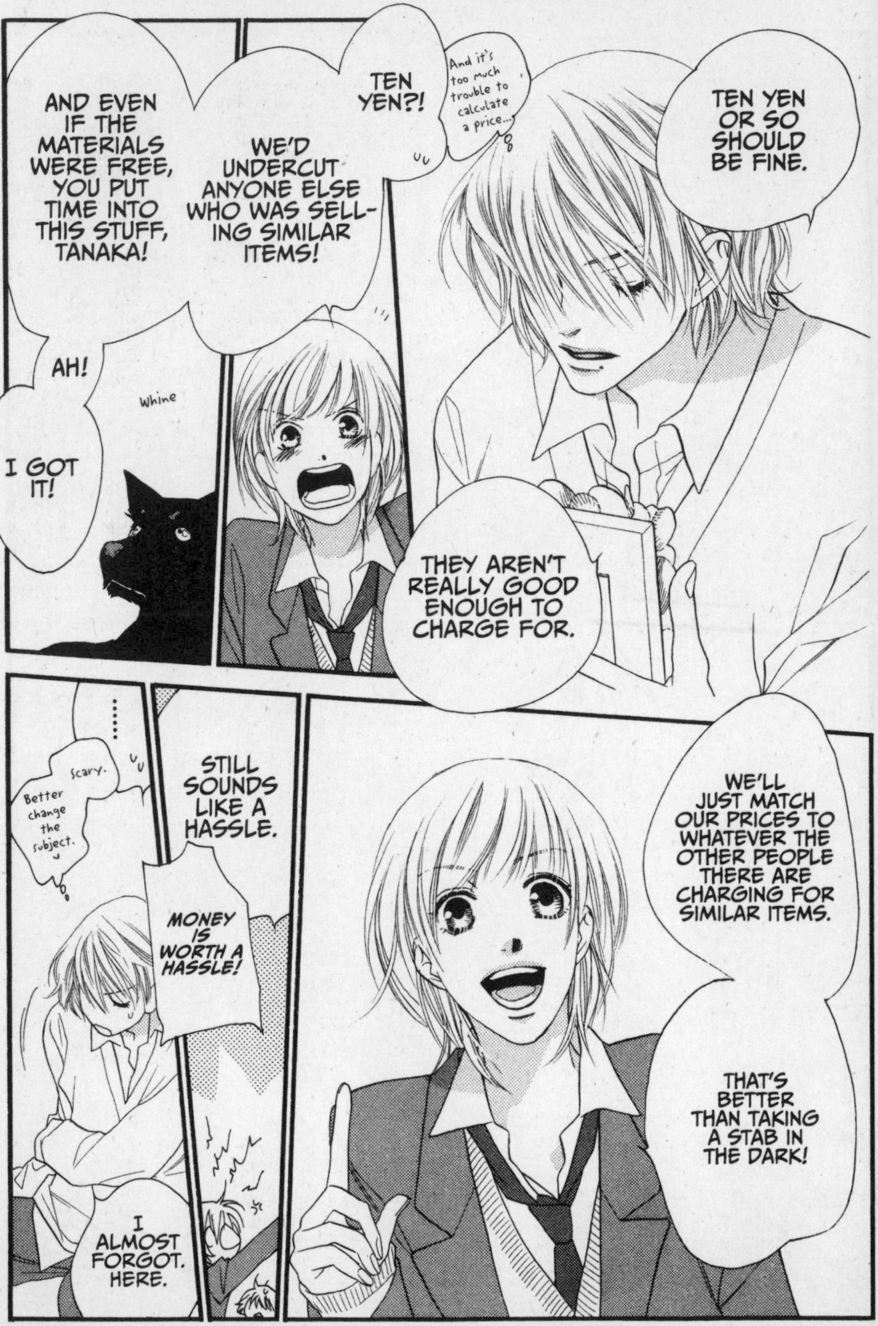
TEN YEN OR SO SHOULD BE FINE.
And it's too much trouble to calculate a price...
THEY AREN'T REALLY GOOD ENOUGH TO CHARGE FOR.
TEN YEN?!
WE'D UNDERCUT ANYONE ELSE WHO WAS SELLING SIMILAR ITEMS!
AND EVEN IF THE MATERIALS WERE FREE, YOU PUT TIME INTO THIS STUFF, TANAKA!
AH!
Whine
I GOT IT!
WE'LL JUST MATCH OUR PRICES TO WHATEVER THE OTHER PEOPLE THERE ARE CHARGING FOR SIMILAR ITEMS.
THAT'S BETTER THAN TAKING A STAB IN THE DARK!
STILL SOUNDS LIKE A HASSLE.
MONEY IS WORTH A HASSLE!
......
Scary.
Better change the subject.
I ALMOST FORGOT. HERE.

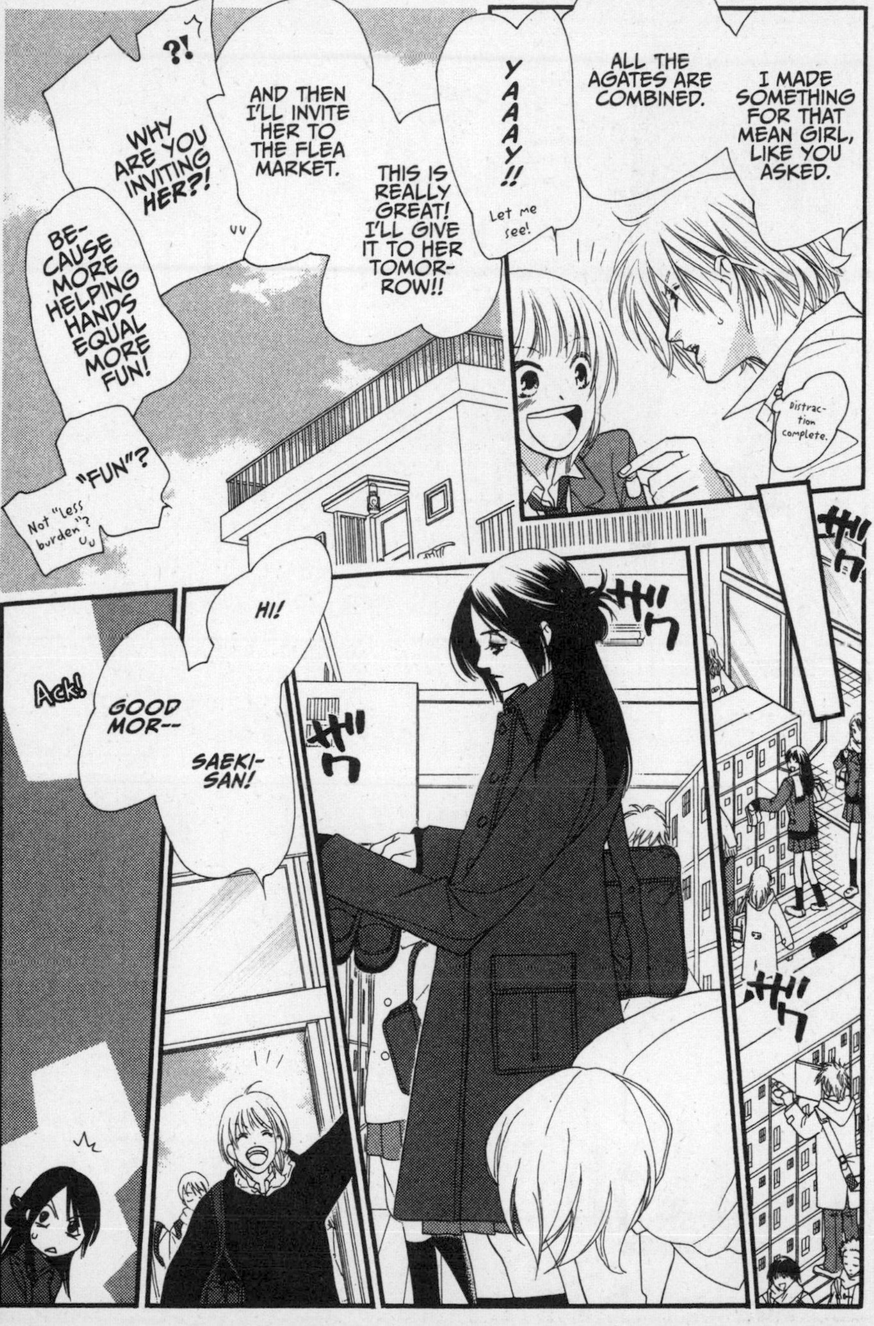
I MADE SOMETHING FOR THAT MEAN GIRL, LIKE YOU ASKED.
ALL THE AGATES ARE COMBINED.
YAAAAY!!
Let me see!
Distraction complete.
THIS IS REALLY GREAT! I'LL GIVE IT TO HER TOMORROW!!
AND THEN I'LL INVITE HER TO THE FLEA MARKET.
?!
WHY ARE YOU INVITING HER?!
BECAUSE MORE HELPING HANDS EQUAL MORE FUN!
"FUN"?
Not "less burden"?
ザワ
ザワ
ザワ
ザワ
HI!
GOOD MOR--
SAEKI-SAN!
Ack!

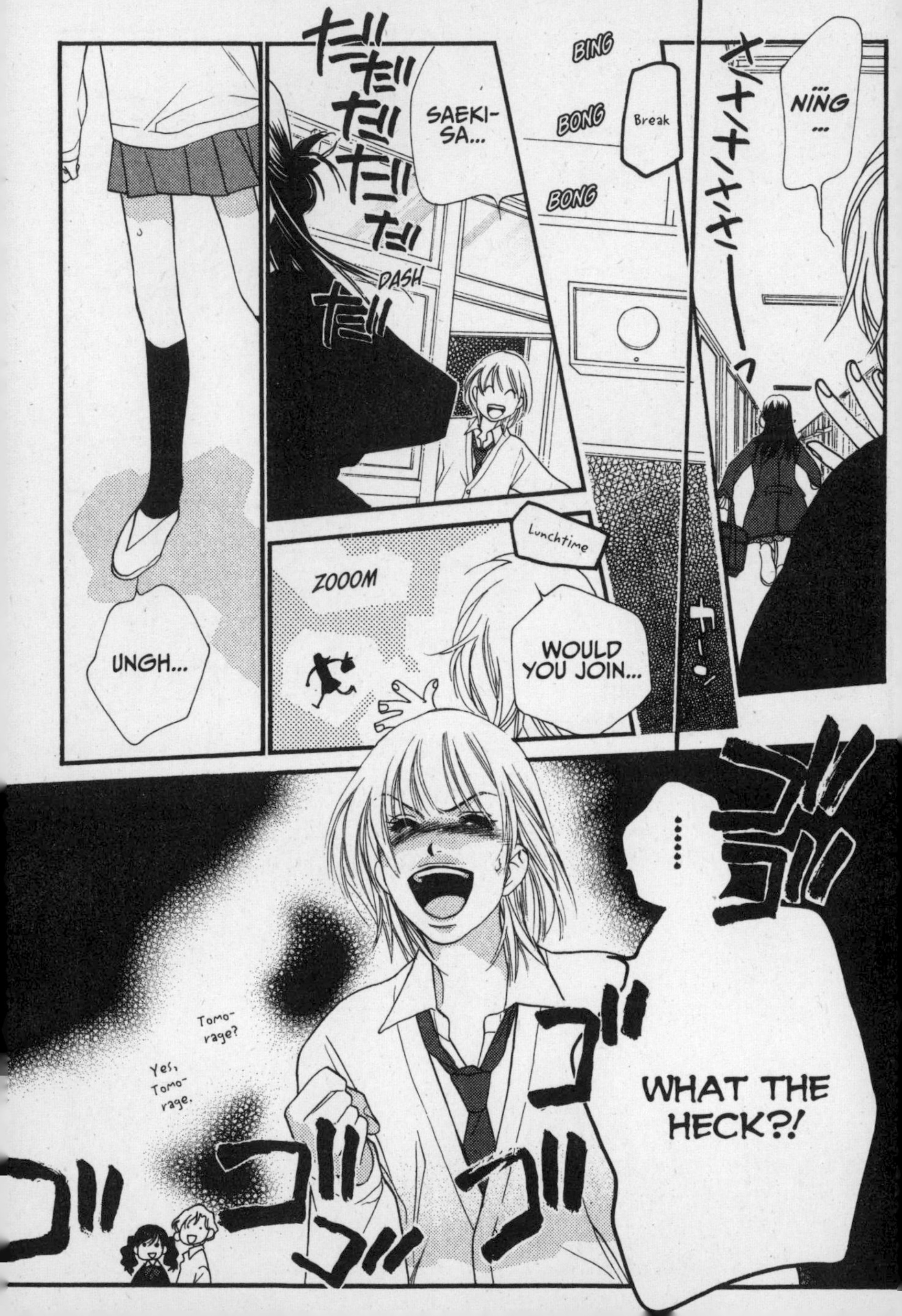
...NING...
Break
BING
BONG
BONG
SAEKI-SA...
DASH
Lunchtime
WOULD YOU JOIN...
ZOOOM
UNGH...
......
WHAT THE HECK?!
Tomo-rage?
Yes, Tomo-rage.

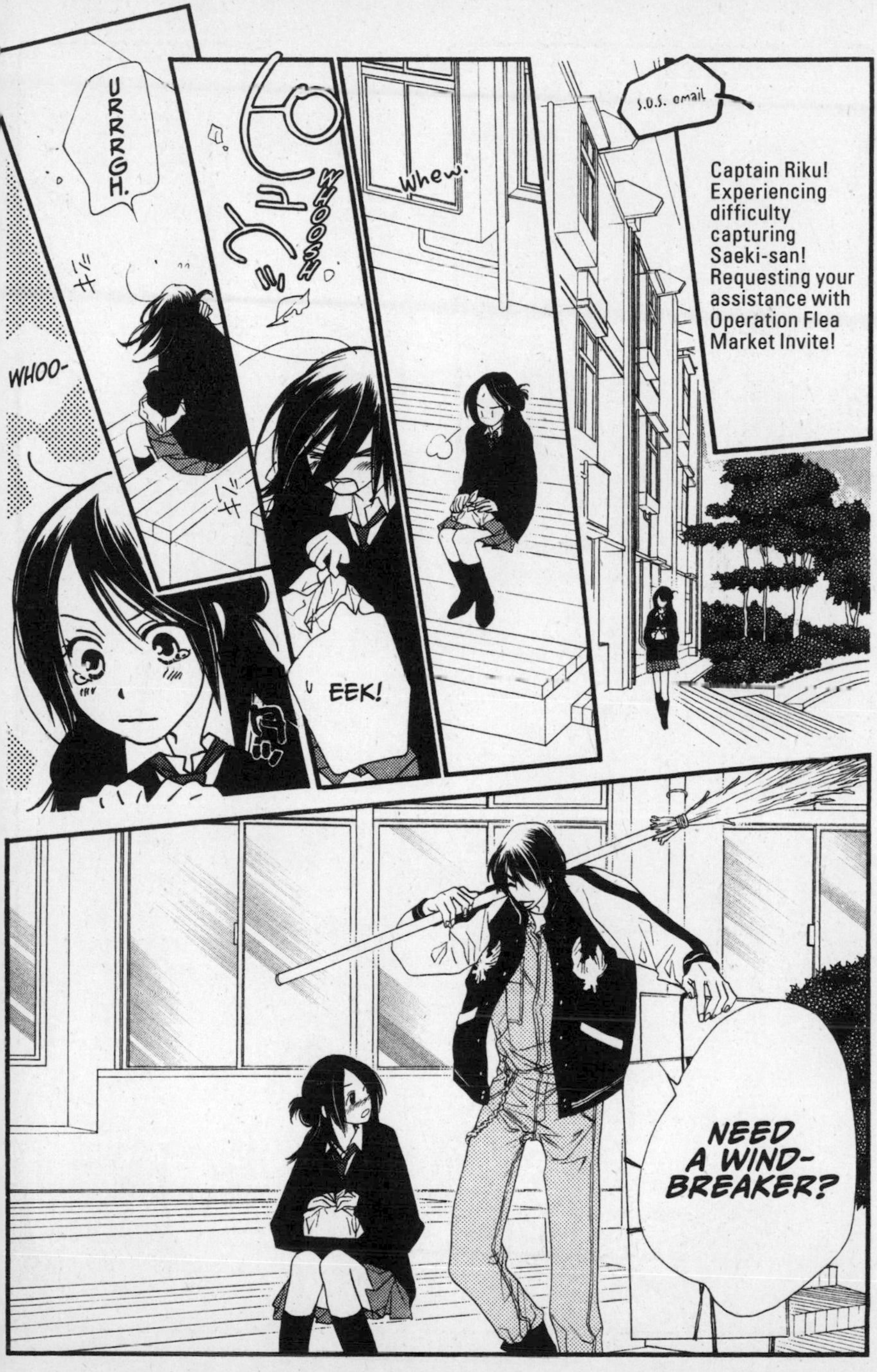
S.O.S. email
Captain Riku! Experiencing difficulty capturing Saeki-san! Requesting your assistance with Operation Flea Market Invite!
Whew.
WHOOSH
EEK!
URRRGH.
WHOO-
NEED A WIND-BREAKER?

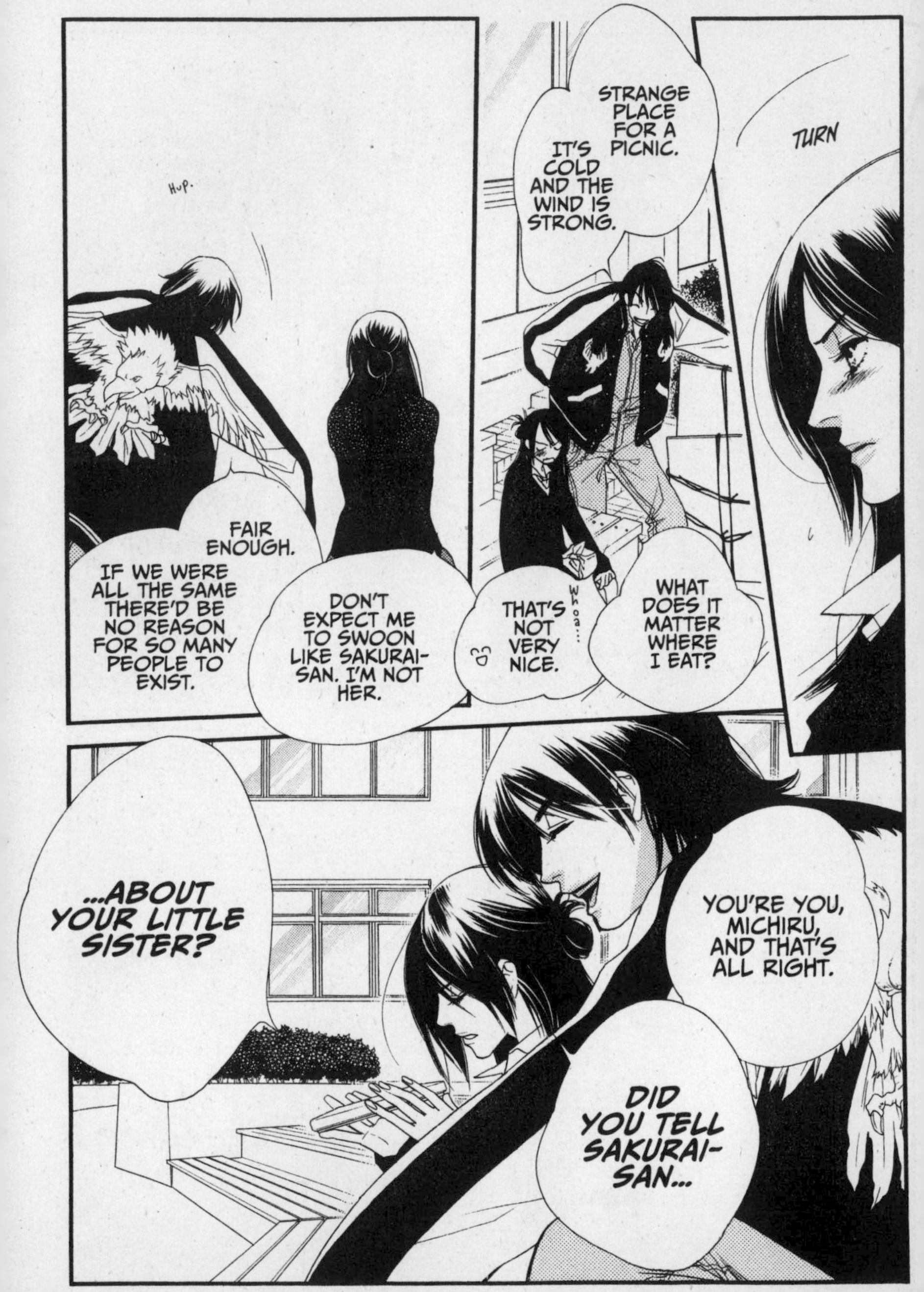
TURN
STRANGE PLACE FOR A PICNIC.
IT'S COLD AND THE WIND IS STRONG.
WHAT DOES IT MATTER WHERE I EAT?
Whoa...
THAT'S NOT VERY NICE.
DON'T EXPECT ME TO SWOON LIKE SAKURAI-SAN. I'M NOT HER.
Hup.
FAIR ENOUGH.
IF WE WERE ALL THE SAME THERE'D BE NO REASON FOR SO MANY PEOPLE TO EXIST.
YOU'RE YOU, MICHIRU, AND THAT'S ALL RIGHT.
DID YOU TELL SAKURAI-SAN...
...ABOUT YOUR LITTLE SISTER?

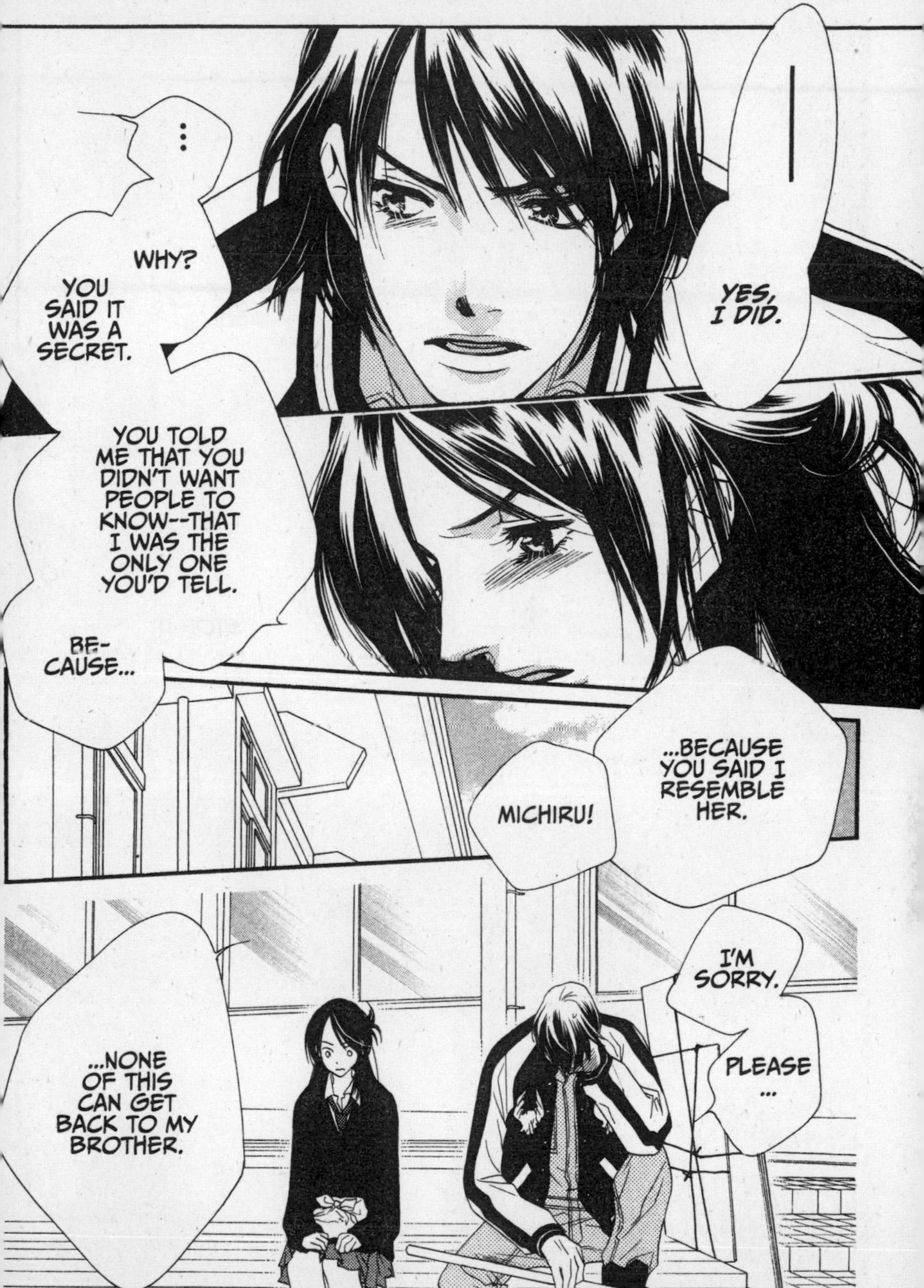
YES, I DID.
...
WHY? YOU SAID IT WAS A SECRET.
YOU TOLD ME THAT YOU DIDN'T WANT PEOPLE TO KNOW--THAT I WAS THE ONLY ONE YOU'D TELL.
BE-CAUSE...
...BECAUSE YOU SAID I RESEMBLE HER.
MICHIRU!
I'M SORRY.
PLEASE ...
...NONE OF THIS CAN GET BACK TO MY BROTHER.

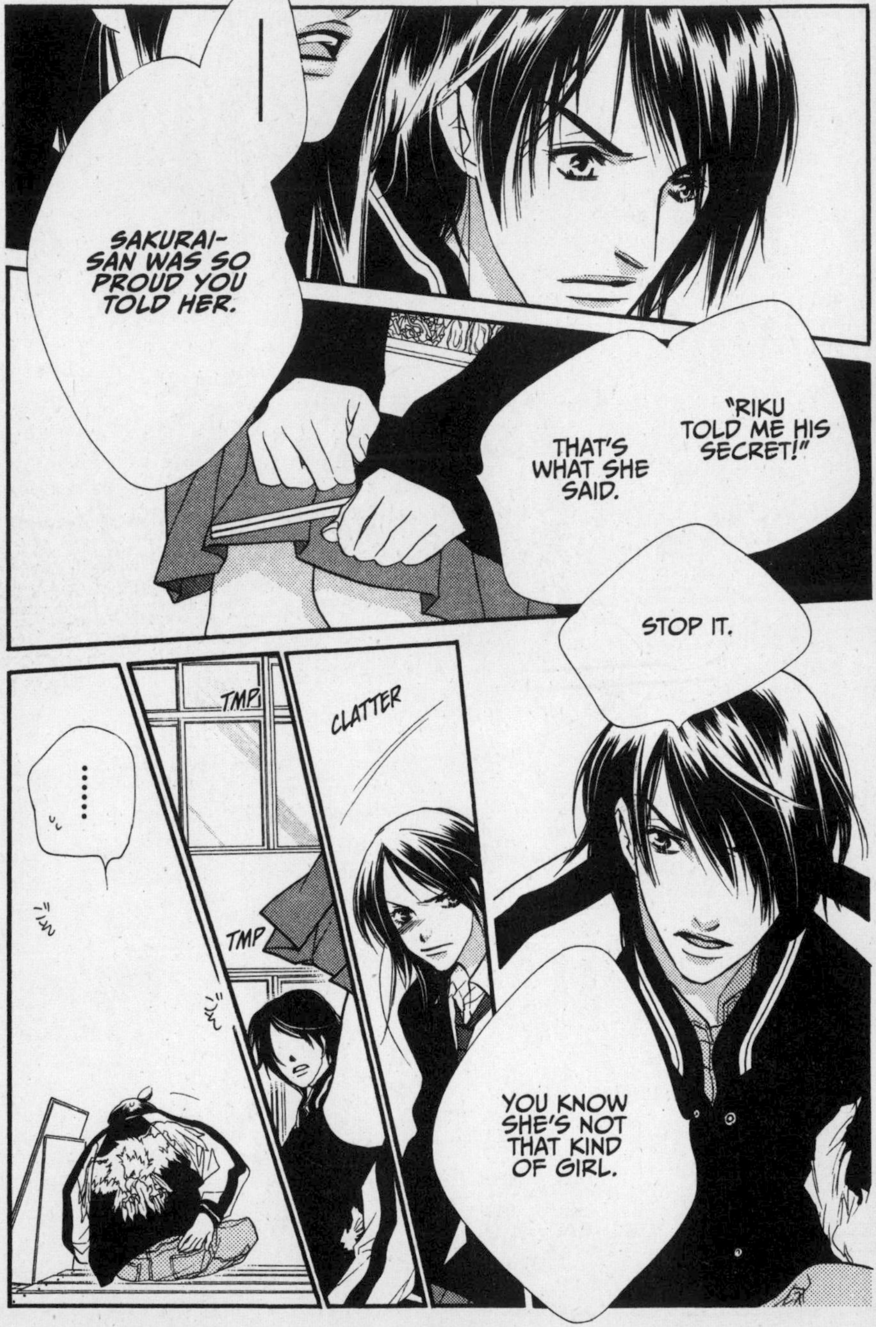
SAKURAI-SAN WAS SO PROUD YOU TOLD HER.
"RIKU TOLD ME HIS SECRET!"
THAT'S WHAT SHE SAID.
STOP IT.
YOU KNOW SHE'S NOT THAT KIND OF GIRL.
CLATTER
TMP
TMP
......

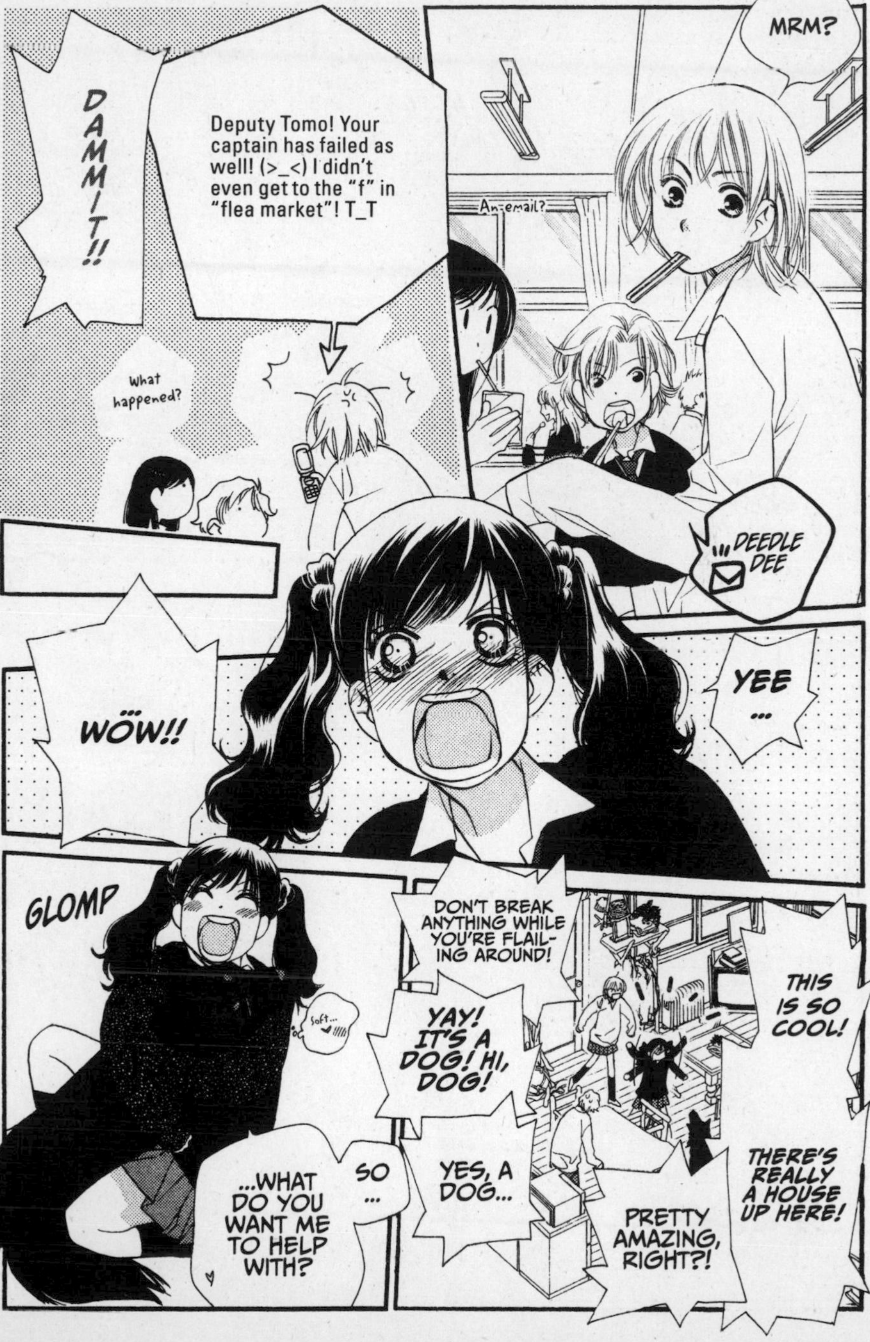
MRM?
An email?
DEEDLE DEE
DAMMIT!!
Deputy Tomo! Your captain has failed as well! (>_<) I didn't even get to the "f" in "flea market"! T_T
What happened?
YEE...
WÖW!!
THIS IS SO COOL!
THERE'S REALLY A HOUSE UP HERE!
DON'T BREAK ANYTHING WHILE YOU'RE FLAIL-ING AROUND!
YAY! IT'S A DOG! HI, DOG!
PRETTY AMAZING, RIGHT?!
YES, A DOG...
SO...
...WHAT DO YOU WANT ME TO HELP WITH?
GLOMP
Soft...

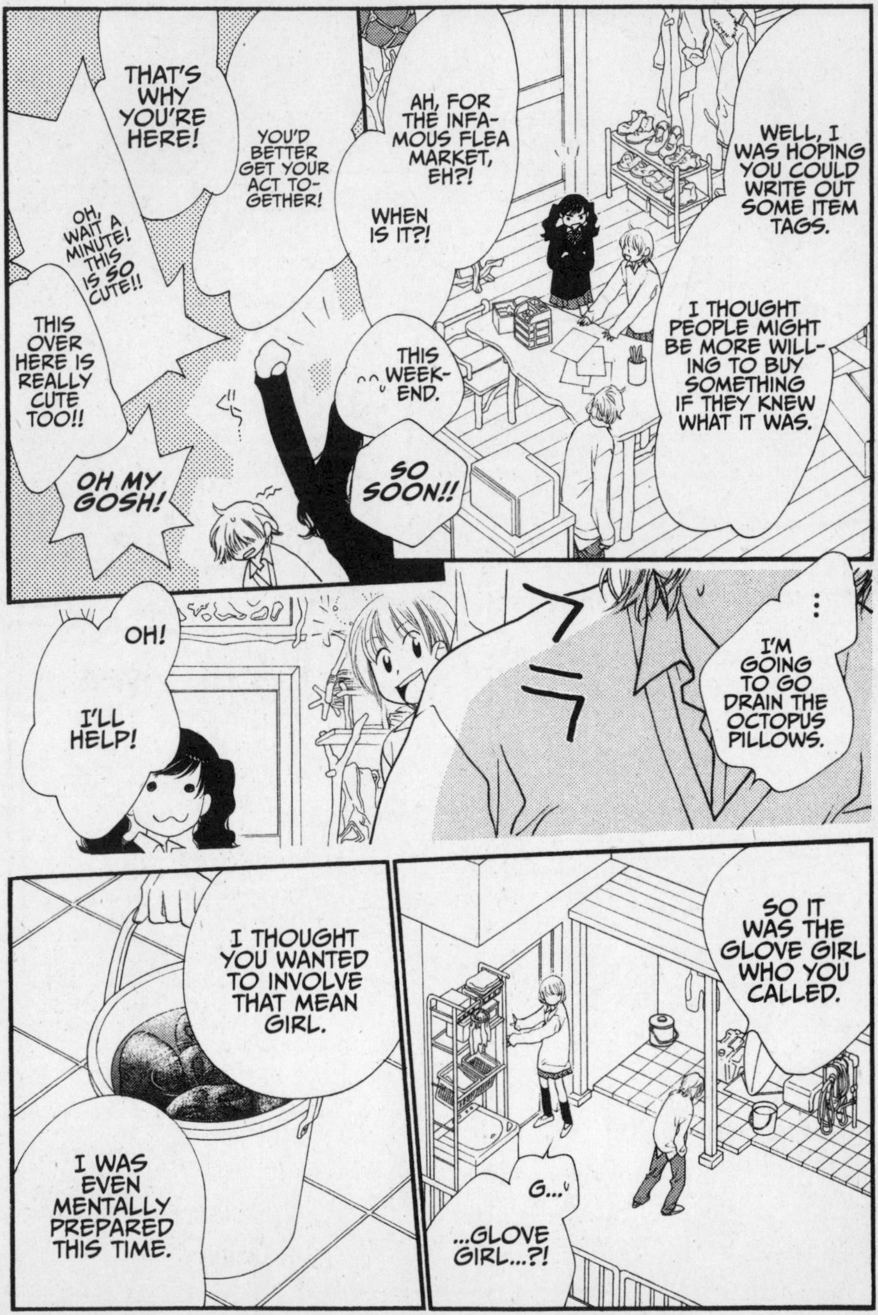
WELL, I WAS HOPING YOU COULD WRITE OUT SOME ITEM TAGS.
I THOUGHT PEOPLE MIGHT BE MORE WILLING TO BUY SOMETHING IF THEY KNEW WHAT IT WAS.
AH, FOR THE INFAMOUS FLEA MARKET, EH?!
WHEN IS IT?!
THIS WEEKEND.
SO SOON!!
THAT'S WHY YOU'RE HERE!
YOU'D BETTER GET YOUR ACT TOGETHER!
OH, WAIT A MINUTE! THIS IS SO CUTE!!
THIS OVER HERE IS REALLY CUTE TOO!!
OH MY GOSH!
...
I'M GOING TO GO DRAIN THE OCTOPUS PILLOWS.
OH!
I'LL HELP!
SO IT WAS THE GLOVE GIRL WHO YOU CALLED.
G...
...GLOVE GIRL...?!
I THOUGHT YOU WANTED TO INVOLVE THAT MEAN GIRL.
I WAS EVEN MENTALLY PREPARED THIS TIME.

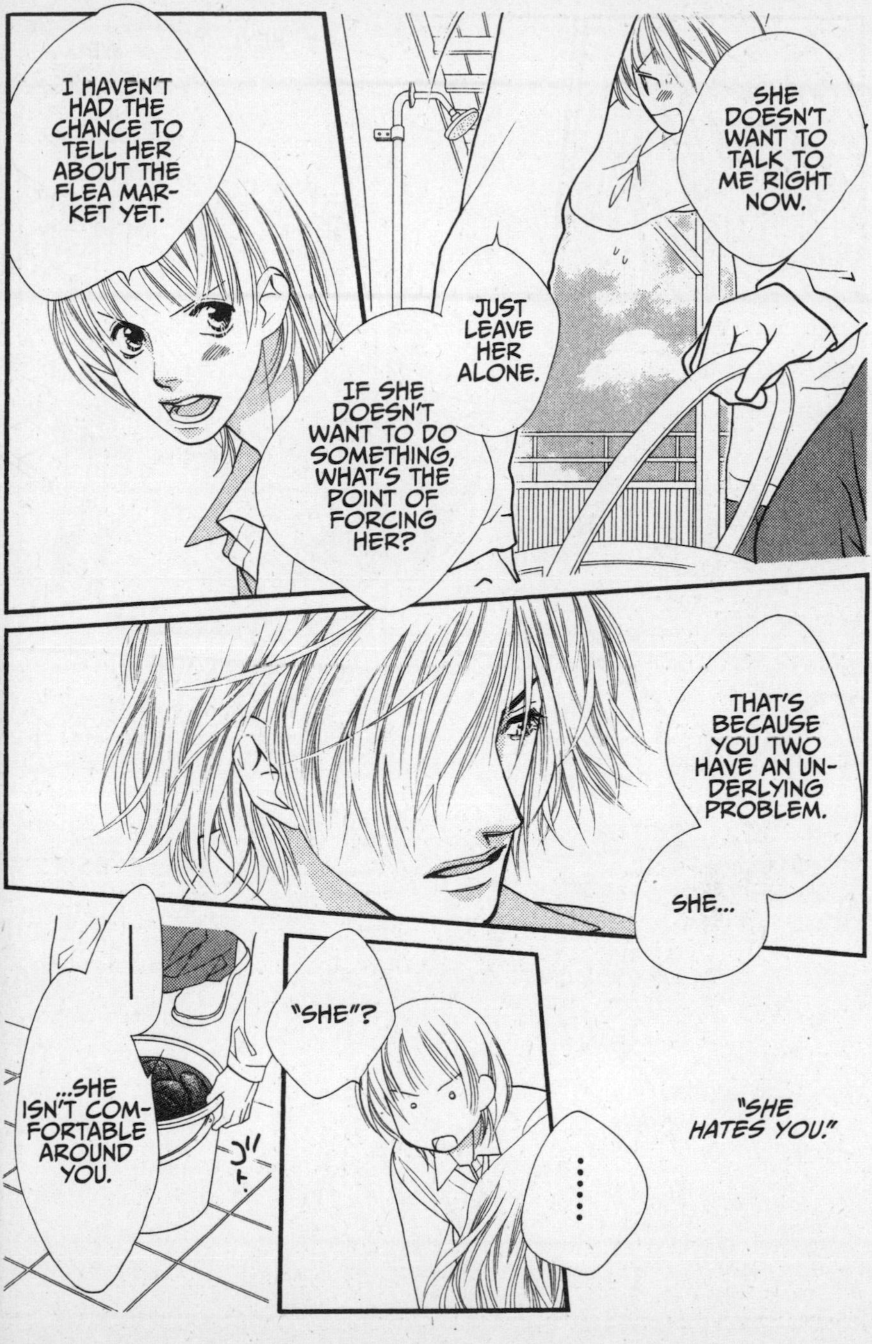
SHE DOESN'T WANT TO TALK TO ME RIGHT NOW.
JUST LEAVE HER ALONE.
IF SHE DOESN'T WANT TO DO SOMETHING, WHAT'S THE POINT OF FORCING HER?
I HAVEN'T HAD THE CHANCE TO TELL HER ABOUT THE FLEA MAR-KET YET.
THAT'S BECAUSE YOU TWO HAVE AN UN-DERLYING PROBLEM.
SHE...
"SHE HATES YOU."
"SHE"?
......
...SHE ISN'T COM-FORTABLE AROUND YOU.

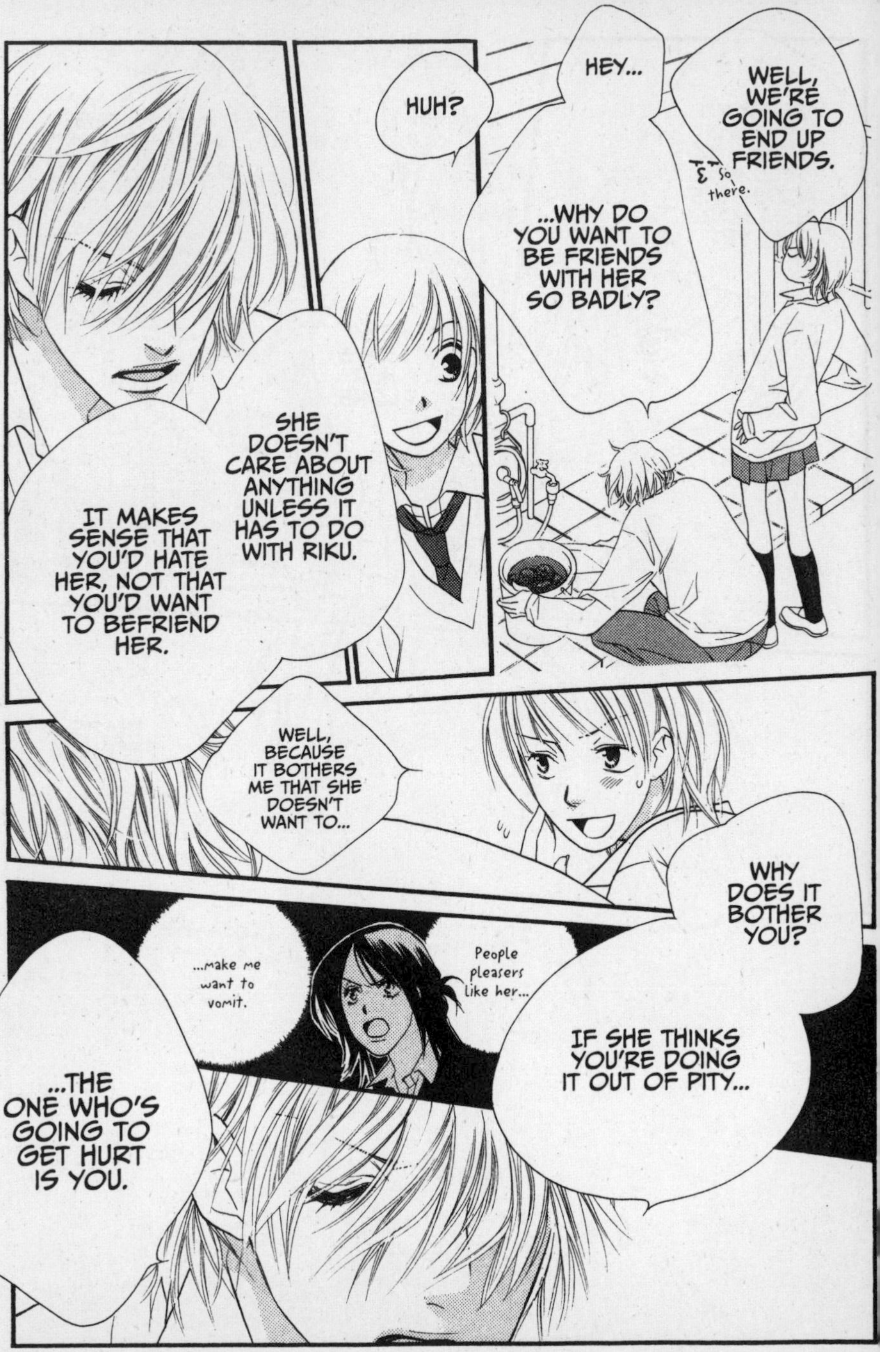
WELL, WE'RE GOING TO END UP FRIENDS.
So there.
HEY...
HUH?
...WHY DO YOU WANT TO BE FRIENDS WITH HER SO BADLY?
SHE DOESN'T CARE ABOUT ANYTHING UNLESS IT HAS TO DO WITH RIKU.
IT MAKES SENSE THAT YOU'D HATE HER, NOT THAT YOU'D WANT TO BEFRIEND HER.
WELL, BECAUSE IT BOTHERS ME THAT SHE DOESN'T WANT TO...
WHY DOES IT BOTHER YOU?
IF SHE THINKS YOU'RE DOING IT OUT OF PITY...
People pleasers like her...
...make me want to vomit.
...THE ONE WHO'S GOING TO GET HURT IS YOU.

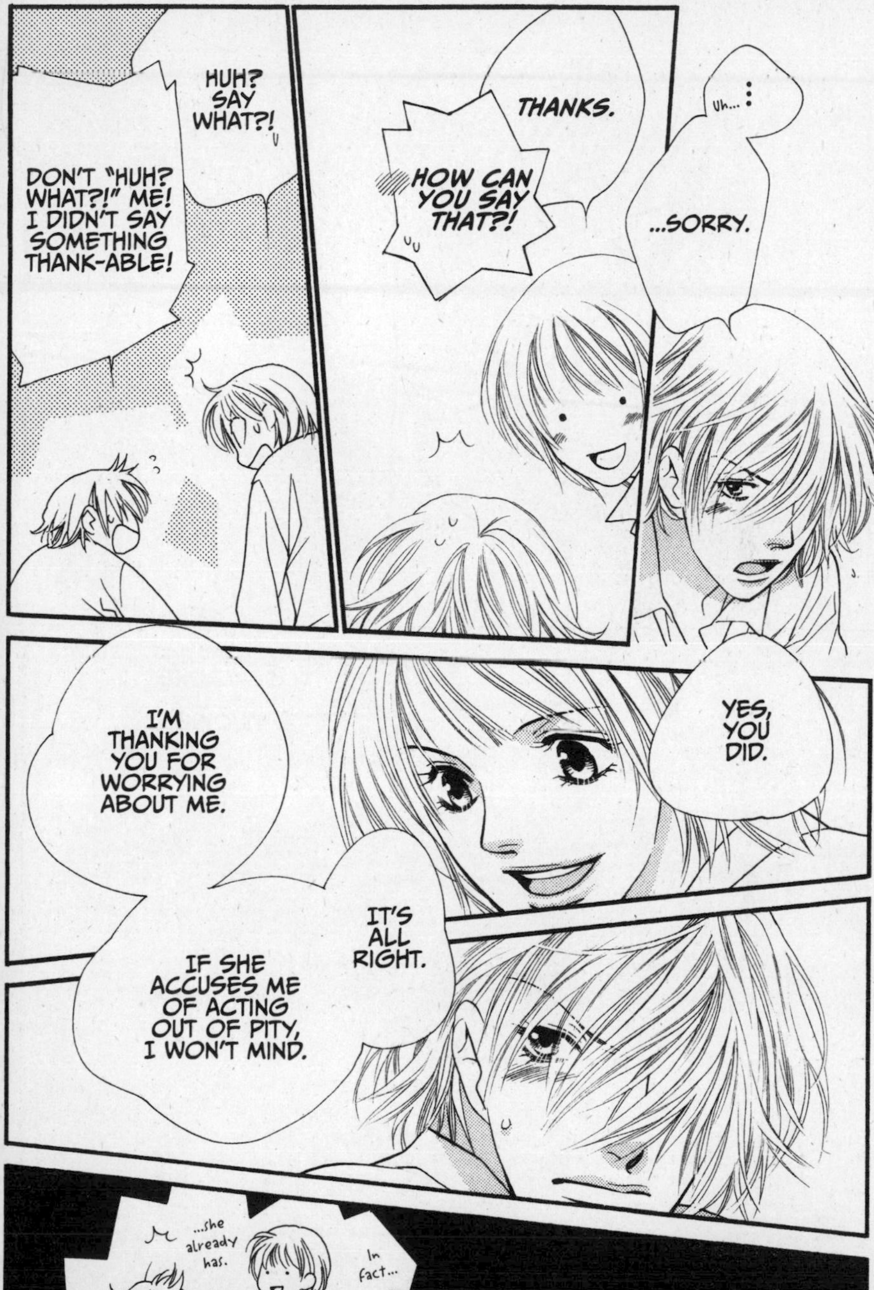
Uh...
THANKS.
...SORRY.
HOW CAN YOU SAY THAT?!
HUH? SAY WHAT?!
DON'T "HUH? WHAT?!" ME! I DIDN'T SAY SOMETHING THANK-ABLE!
YES, YOU DID.
I'M THANKING YOU FOR WORRYING ABOUT ME.
IT'S ALL RIGHT.
IF SHE ACCUSES ME OF ACTING OUT OF PITY, I WON'T MIND.
In fact...
...she already has.

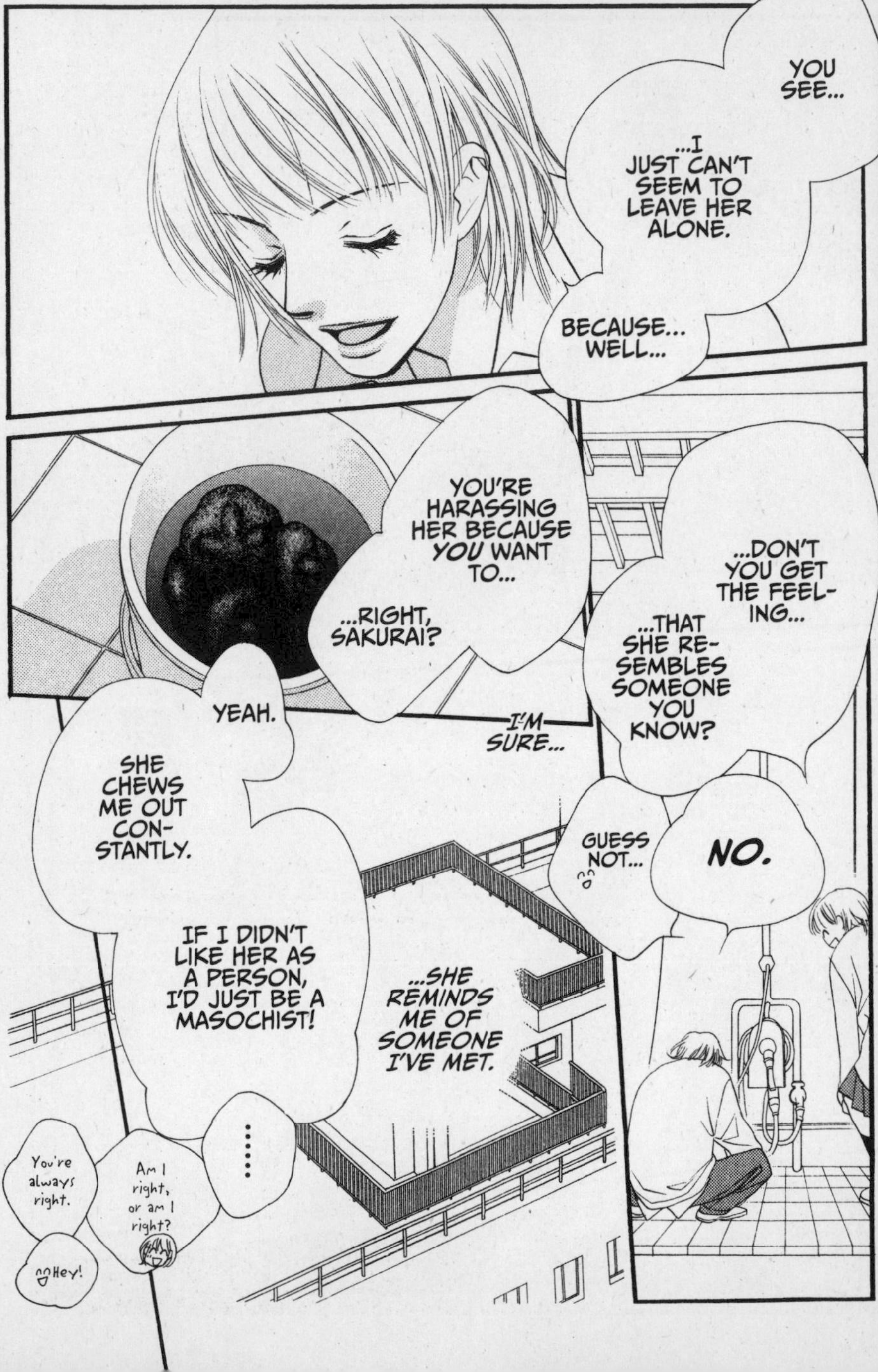
YOU SEE...
...I JUST CAN'T SEEM TO LEAVE HER ALONE.
BECAUSE... WELL...
...DON'T YOU GET THE FEEL-ING...
...THAT SHE RE-SEMBLES SOMEONE YOU KNOW?
NO.
GUESS NOT...
YOU'RE HARASSING HER BECAUSE *YOU* WANT TO...
...RIGHT, SAKURAI?
YEAH.
I'M SURE...
SHE CHEWS ME OUT CON-STANTLY.
IF I DIDN'T LIKE HER AS A PERSON, I'D JUST BE A MASOCHIST!
...SHE REMINDS ME OF SOMEONE I'VE MET.
......
Am I right, or am I right?
You're always right.
Hey!

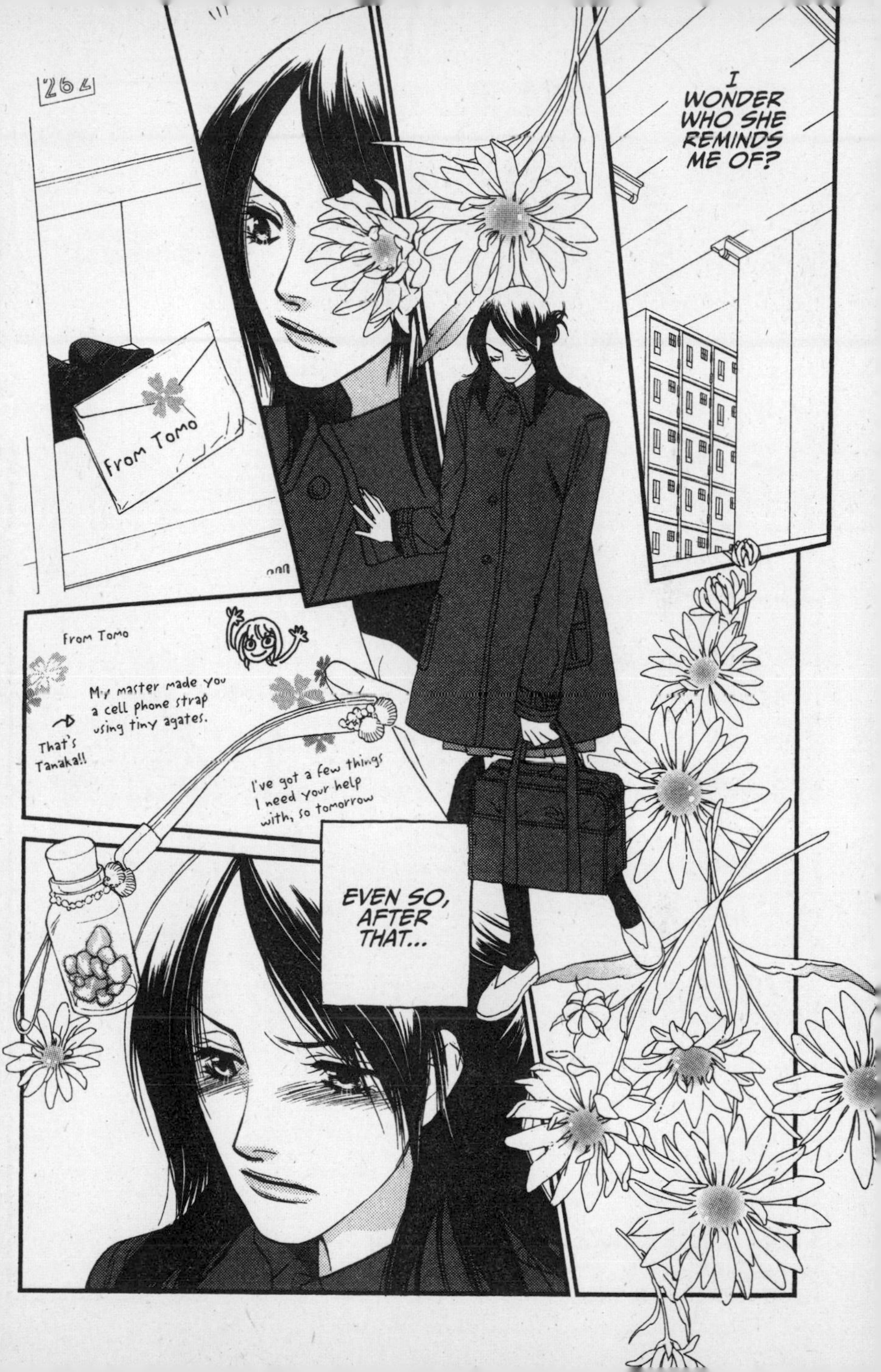

I WONDER WHO SHE REMINDS ME OF?
From Tomo
From Tomo
My master made you a cell phone strap using tiny agates.
That's Tanaka!!
I've got a few things I need your help with, so tomorrow
EVEN SO, AFTER THAT...

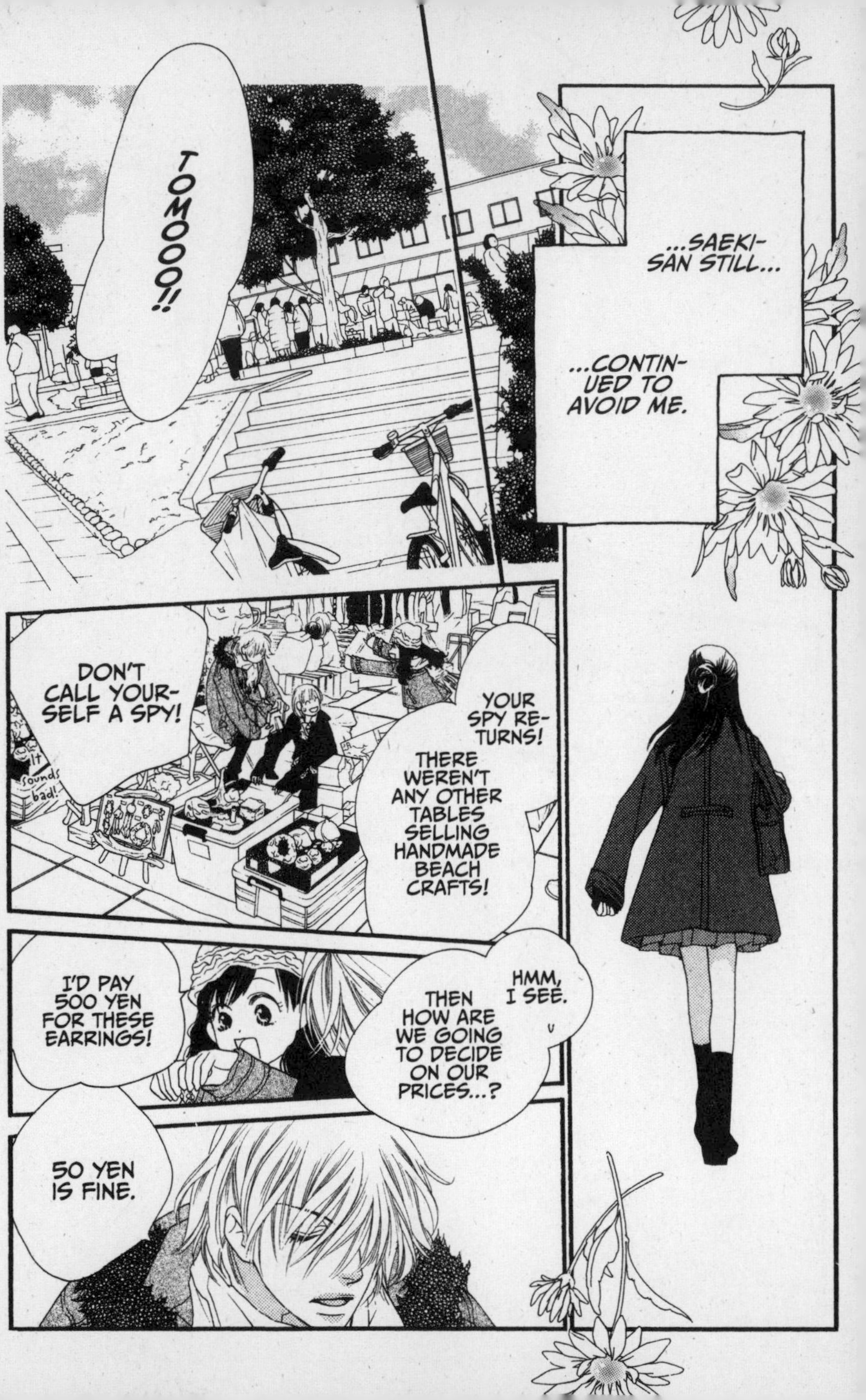
...SAEKI-SAN STILL...
...CONTINUED TO AVOID ME.
TOMOOOO!!
YOUR SPY RETURNS! THERE WEREN'T ANY OTHER TABLES SELLING HANDMADE BEACH CRAFTS!
DON'T CALL YOURSELF A SPY!
It sounds bad!
HMM, I SEE.
THEN HOW ARE WE GOING TO DECIDE ON OUR PRICES...?
I'D PAY 500 YEN FOR THESE EARRINGS!
50 YEN IS FINE.

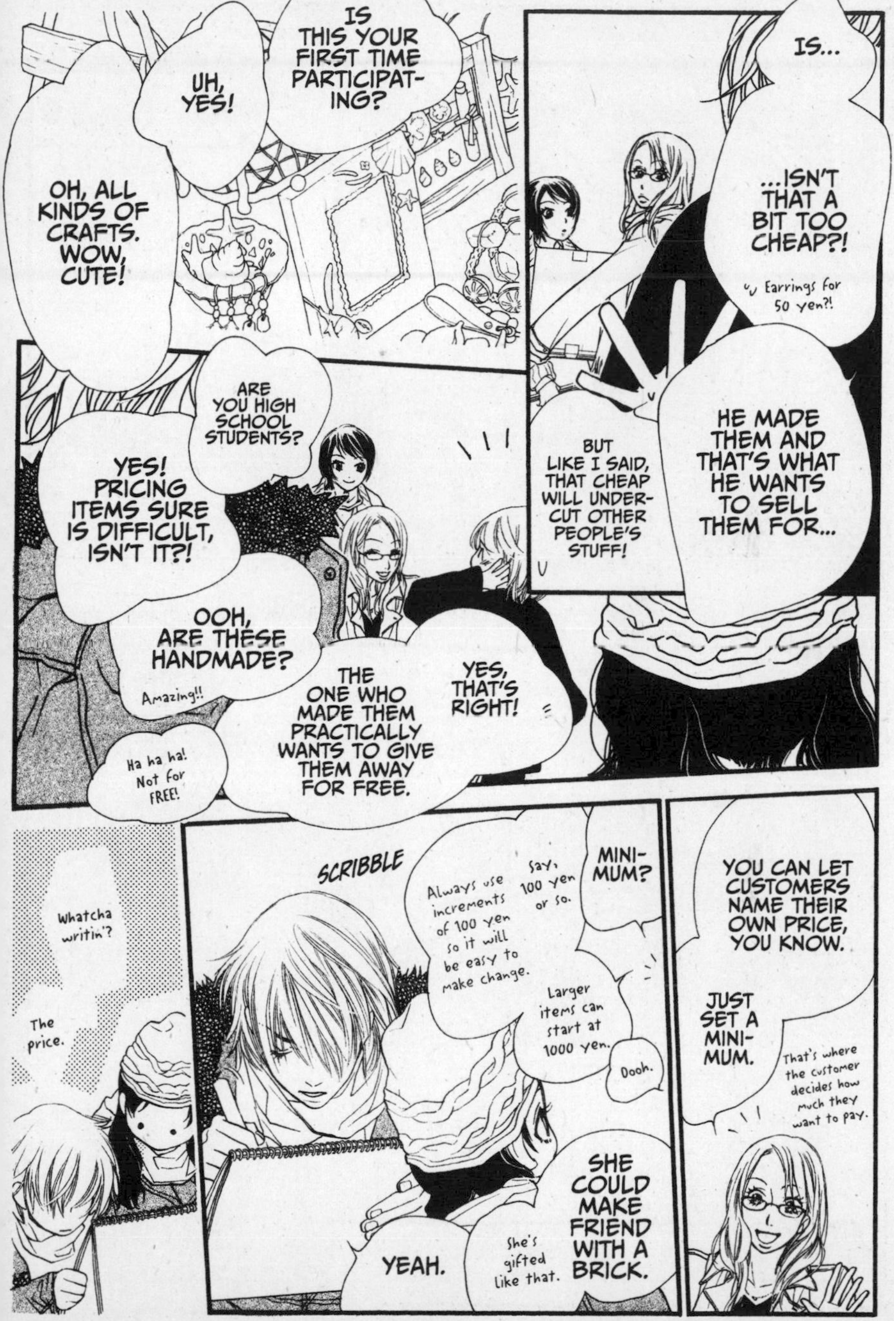
IS...
...ISN'T THAT A BIT TOO CHEAP?!
Earrings for 50 yen?!
HE MADE THEM AND THAT'S WHAT HE WANTS TO SELL THEM FOR...
BUT LIKE I SAID, THAT CHEAP WILL UNDER-CUT OTHER PEOPLE'S STUFF!
IS THIS YOUR FIRST TIME PARTICIPAT-ING?
UH, YES!
OH, ALL KINDS OF CRAFTS. WOW, CUTE!
ARE YOU HIGH SCHOOL STUDENTS?
YES! PRICING ITEMS SURE IS DIFFICULT, ISN'T IT?!
OOH, ARE THESE HANDMADE?
Amazing!!
YES, THAT'S RIGHT!
THE ONE WHO MADE THEM PRACTICALLY WANTS TO GIVE THEM AWAY FOR FREE.
Ha ha ha! Not for FREE!
YOU CAN LET CUSTOMERS NAME THEIR OWN PRICE, YOU KNOW.
JUST SET A MINI-MUM.
That's where the customer decides how much they want to pay.
MINI-MUM?
Say, 100 yen or so.
Always use increments of 100 yen so it will be easy to make change.
SCRIBBLE
Larger items can start at 1000 yen.
Oooh.
SHE COULD MAKE FRIEND WITH A BRICK.
She's gifted like that.
YEAH.
Whatcha writin'?
The price.

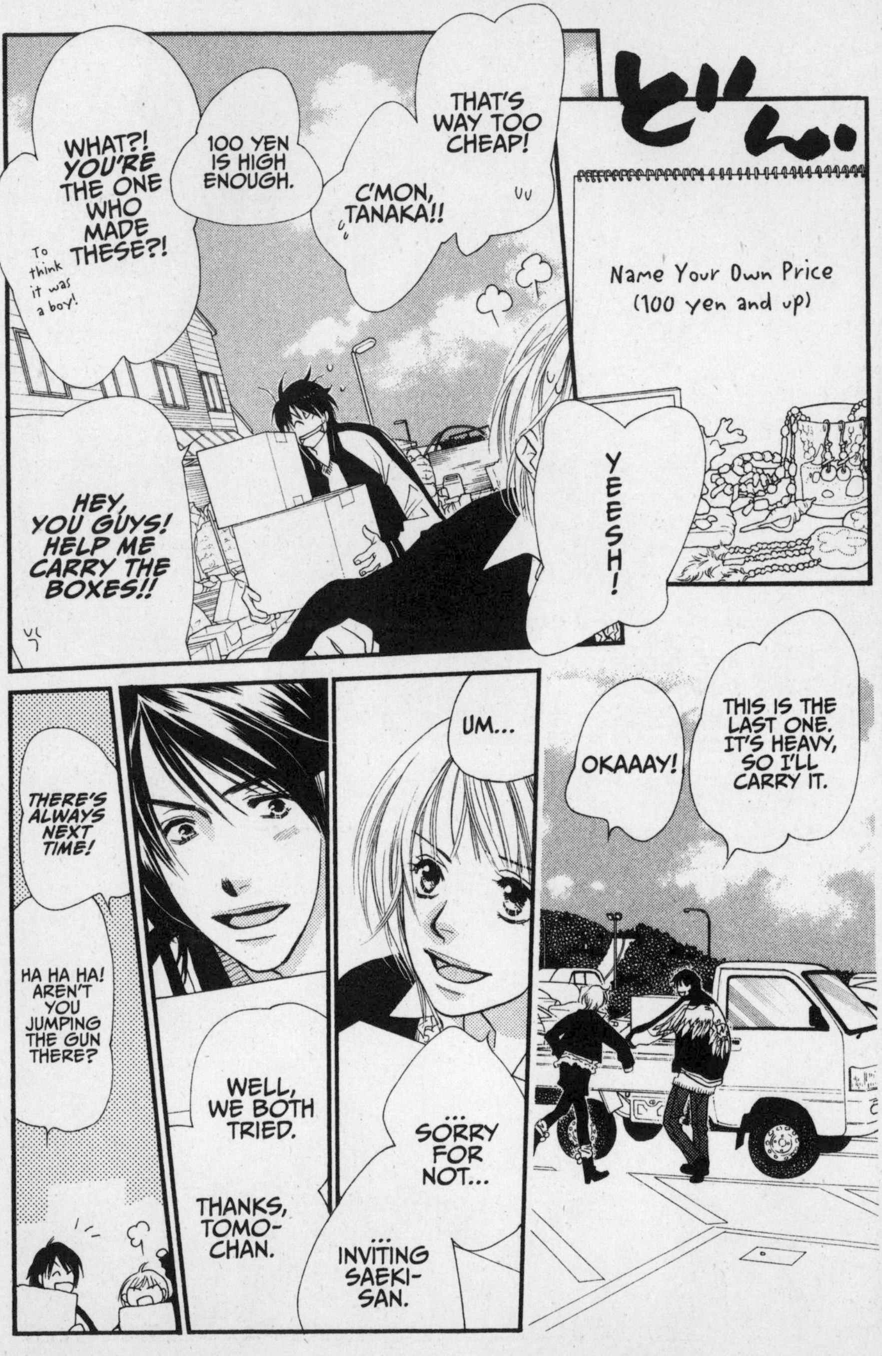

Name Your Own Price
(100 yen and up)
THAT'S WAY TOO CHEAP!
C'MON, TANAKA!!
100 YEN IS HIGH ENOUGH.
WHAT?! YOU'RE THE ONE WHO MADE THESE?!
To think it was a boy!
YEESH!
HEY, YOU GUYS! HELP ME CARRY THE BOXES!!
THIS IS THE LAST ONE. IT'S HEAVY, SO I'LL CARRY IT.
OKAAAY!
UM...
...SORRY FOR NOT...
...INVITING SAEKI-SAN.
WELL, WE BOTH TRIED.
THANKS, TOMO-CHAN.
THERE'S ALWAYS NEXT TIME!
HA HA HA! AREN'T YOU JUMPING THE GUN THERE?

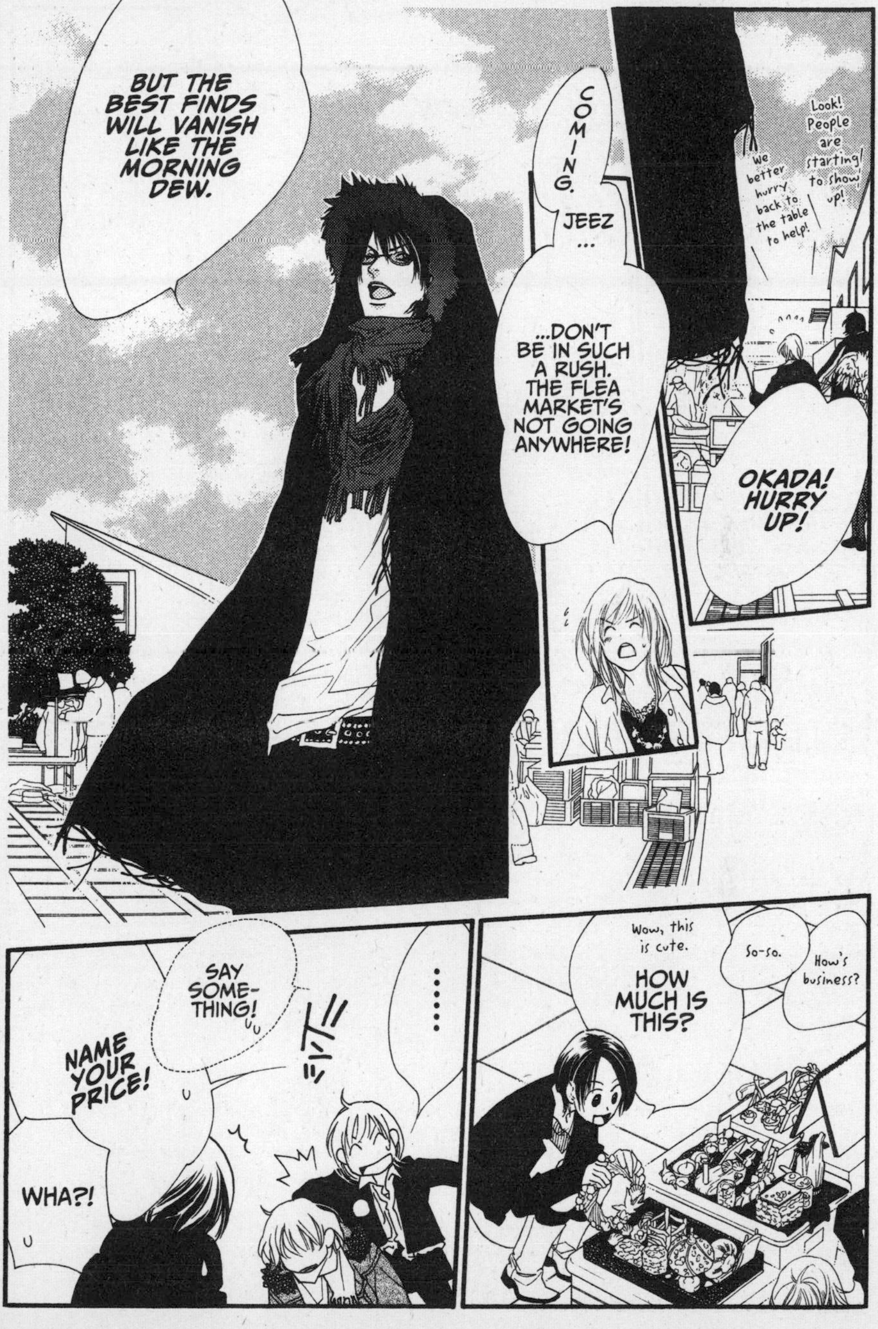
Look! People are starting to show up!
We better hurry back to the table to help!
OKADA! HURRY UP!
COMING.
JEEZ...
...DON'T BE IN SUCH A RUSH. THE FLEA MARKET'S NOT GOING ANYWHERE!
BUT THE BEST FINDS WILL VANISH LIKE THE MORNING DEW.
How's business?
So-so.
Wow, this is cute.
HOW MUCH IS THIS?
......
SAY SOME-THING!
NAME YOUR PRICE!
WHA?!

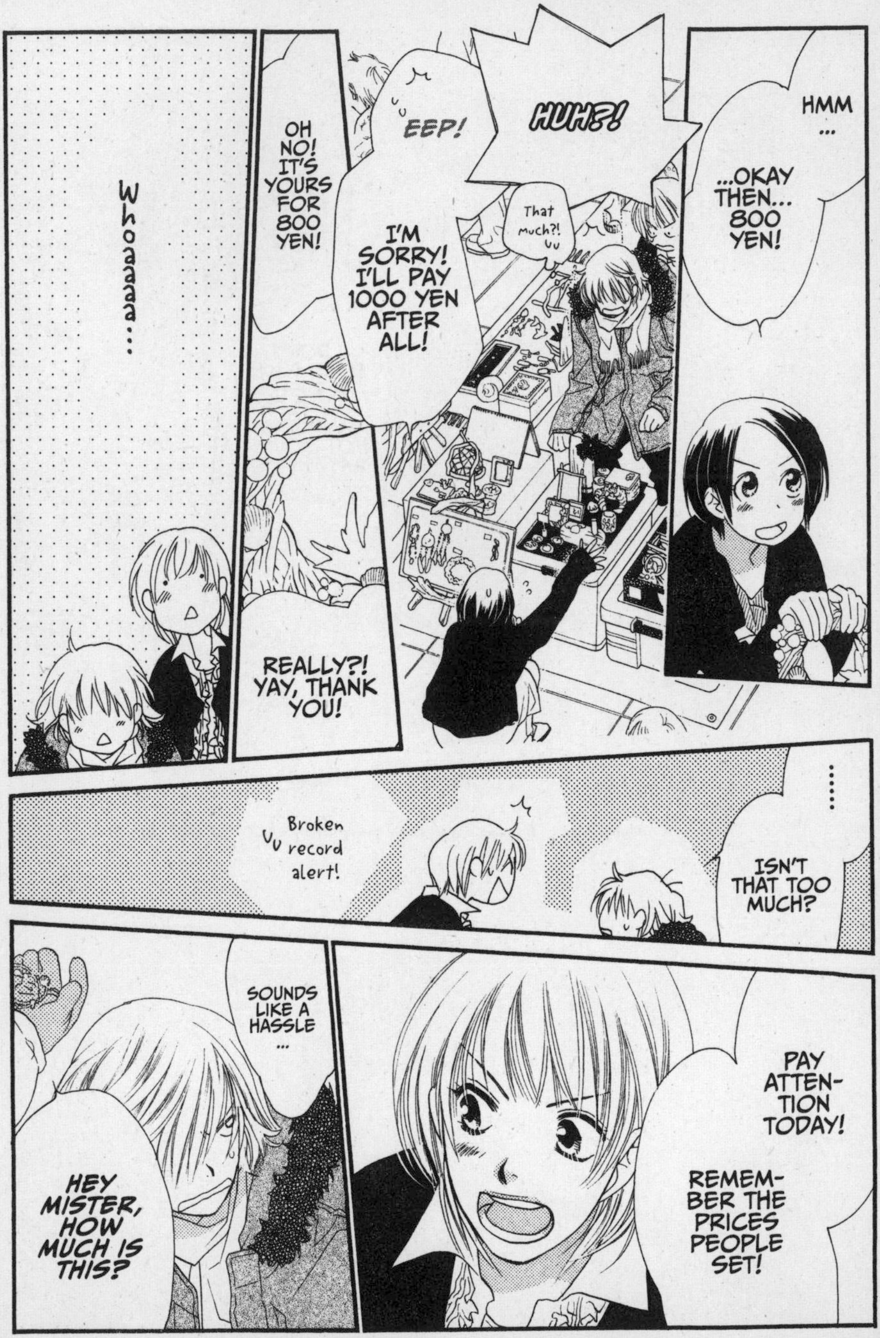
HMM...
...OKAY THEN... 800 YEN!
HUH?!
That much?!
EEP!
I'M SORRY! I'LL PAY 1000 YEN AFTER ALL!
OH NO! IT'S YOURS FOR 800 YEN!
REALLY?! YAY, THANK YOU!
Whoaaaaa...
......
ISN'T THAT TOO MUCH?
Broken record alert!
PAY ATTEN-TION TODAY!
REMEM-BER THE PRICES PEOPLE SET!
SOUNDS LIKE A HASSLE...
HEY MISTER, HOW MUCH IS THIS?

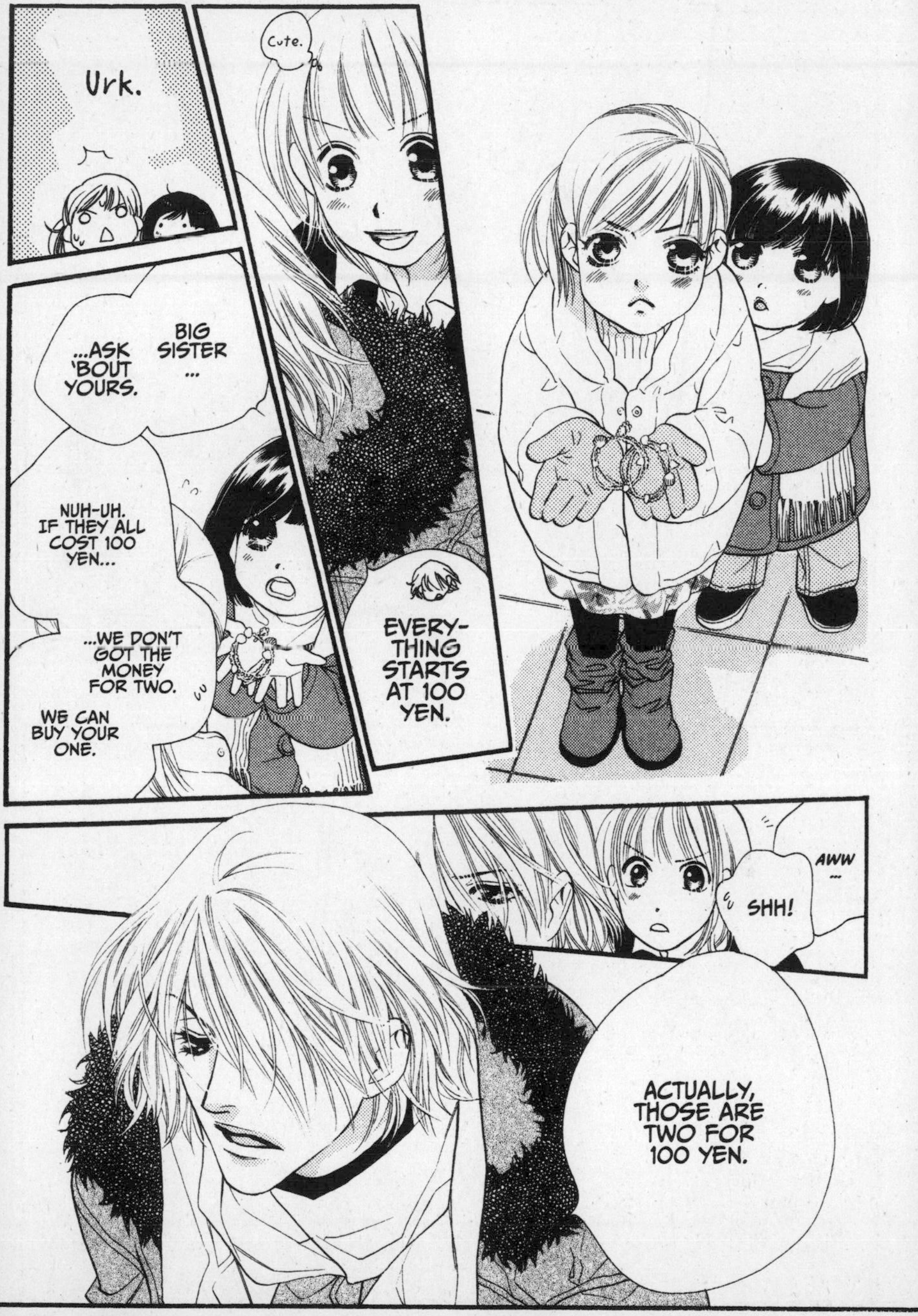

Cute.
EVERY-THING STARTS AT 100 YEN.
Urk.
BIG SISTER ...
...ASK 'BOUT YOURS.
NUH-UH. IF THEY ALL COST 100 YEN...
...WE DON'T GOT THE MONEY FOR TWO.
WE CAN BUY YOUR ONE.
AWW ...
SHH!
ACTUALLY, THOSE ARE TWO FOR 100 YEN.

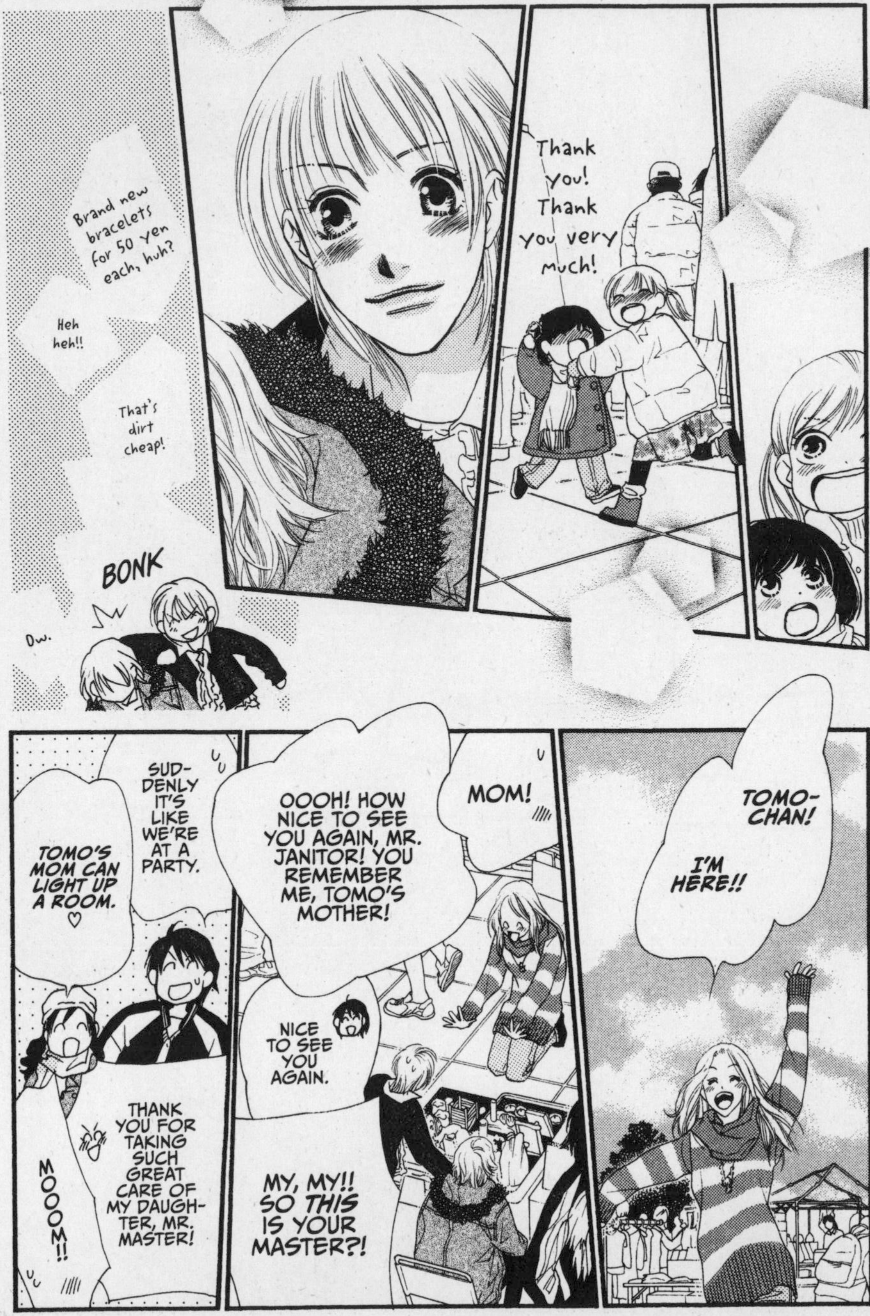
Thank you! Thank you very much!
Brand new bracelets for 50 yen each, huh?
Heh heh!!
That's dirt cheap!
BONK
Ow.
TOMO-CHAN!
I'M HERE!!
MOM!
OOOH! HOW NICE TO SEE YOU AGAIN, MR. JANITOR! YOU REMEMBER ME, TOMO'S MOTHER!
NICE TO SEE YOU AGAIN.
MY, MY!! SO THIS IS YOUR MASTER?!
SUDDENLY IT'S LIKE WE'RE AT A PARTY.
TOMO'S MOM CAN LIGHT UP A ROOM. ♡
THANK YOU FOR TAKING SUCH GREAT CARE OF MY DAUGHTER, MR. MASTER!
MOOOM!!

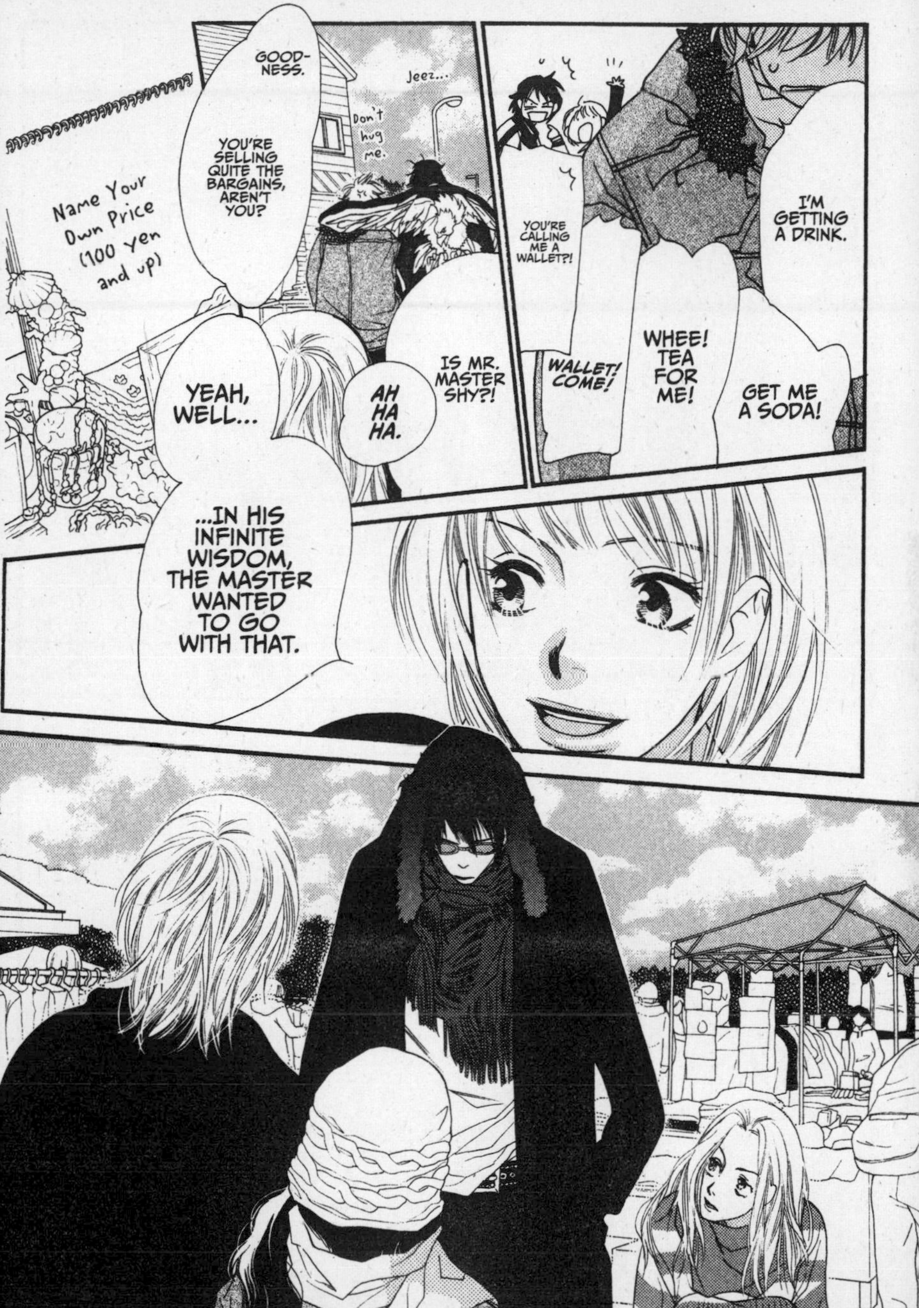
I'M GETTING A DRINK.
GET ME A SODA!
WHEE! TEA FOR ME!
WALLET! COME!
YOU'RE CALLING ME A WALLET?!
Jeez...
Don't hug me.
GOODNESS.
YOU'RE SELLING QUITE THE BARGAINS, AREN'T YOU?
Name Your Own Price (100 yen and up)
IS MR. MASTER SHY?!
AH HA HA.
YEAH, WELL...
...IN HIS INFINITE WISDOM, THE MASTER WANTED TO GO WITH THAT.

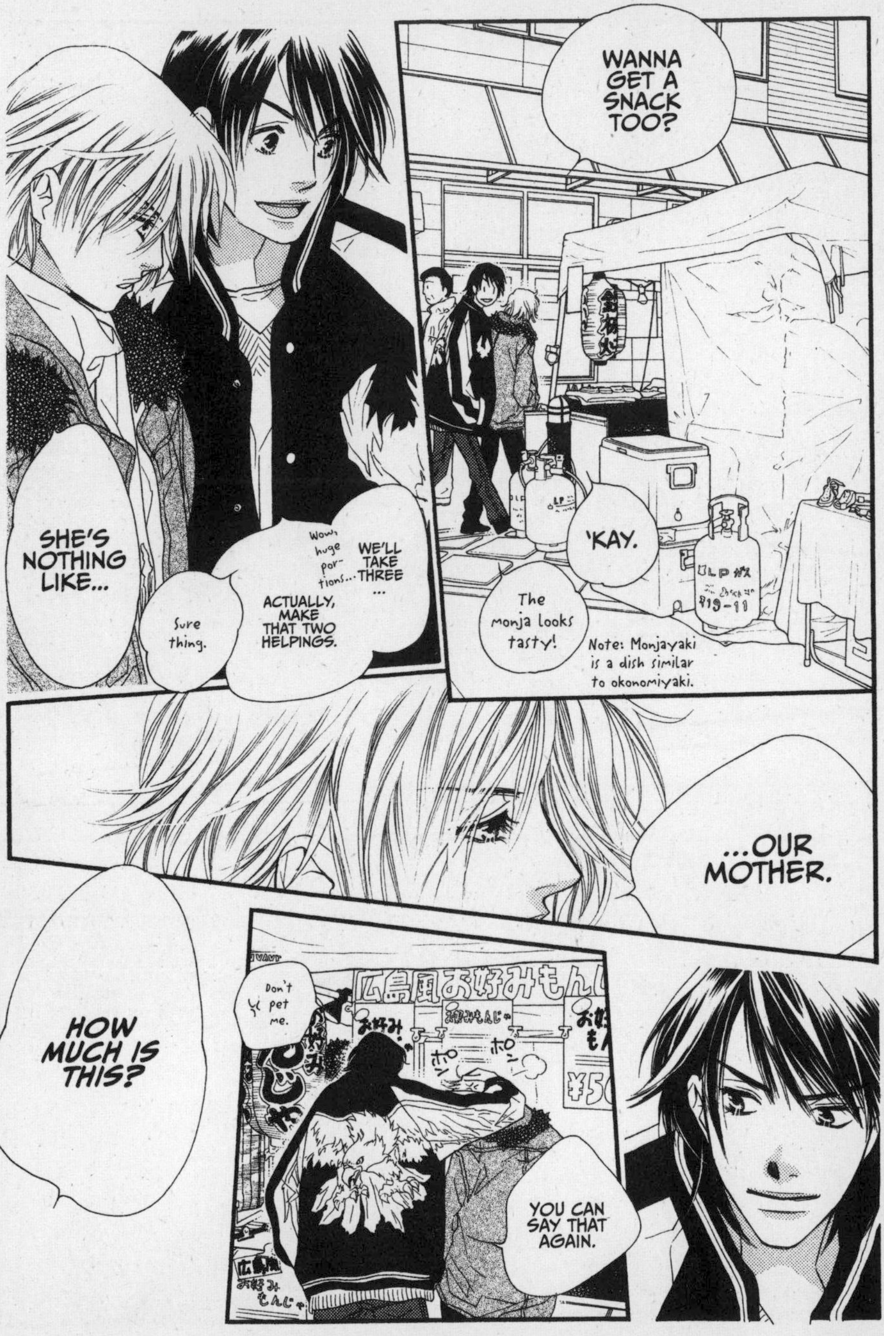
WANNA GET A SNACK TOO?
'KAY.
The monja looks tasty!
Note: Monjayaki is a dish similar to okonomiyaki.
WE'LL TAKE THREE ...
Wow, huge portions...
ACTUALLY, MAKE THAT TWO HELPINGS.
Sure thing.
SHE'S NOTHING LIKE...
...OUR MOTHER.
YOU CAN SAY THAT AGAIN.
Don't pet me.
HOW MUCH IS THIS?

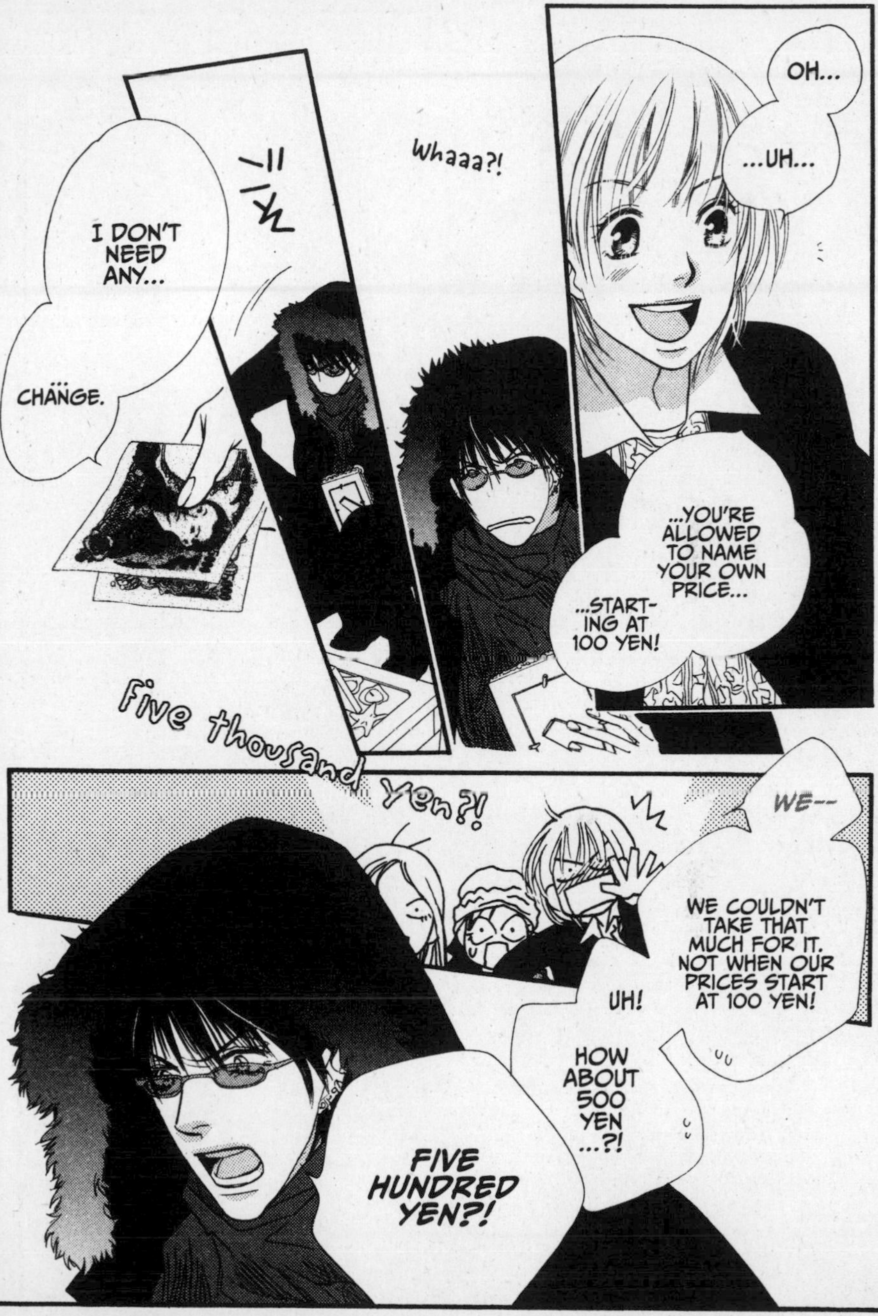
OH...
...UH...
...YOU'RE ALLOWED TO NAME YOUR OWN PRICE...
...START-ING AT 100 YEN!
Whaaa?!
I DON'T NEED ANY...
CHÄNGE.
Five thousand Yen?!
WE--
WE COULDN'T TAKE THAT MUCH FOR IT. NOT WHEN OUR PRICES START AT 100 YEN!
UH!
HOW ABOUT 500 YEN ...?!
FIVE HUNDRED YEN?!

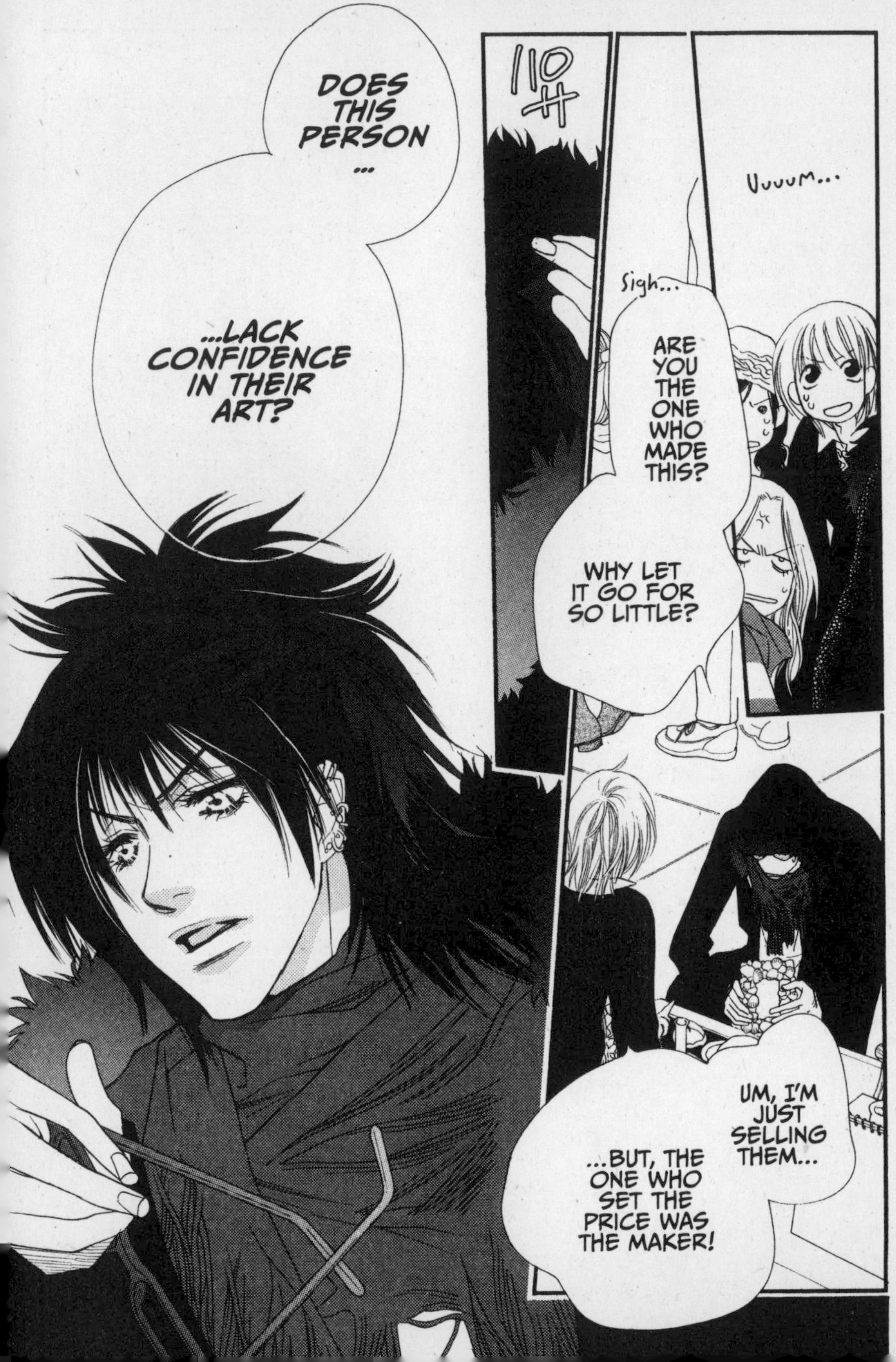
Uuuum...
Sigh...
ARE YOU THE ONE WHO MADE THIS?
WHY LET IT GO FOR SO LITTLE?
UM, I'M JUST SELLING THEM...
...BUT, THE ONE WHO SET THE PRICE WAS THE MAKER!
DOES THIS PERSON...
...LACK CONFIDENCE IN THEIR ART?

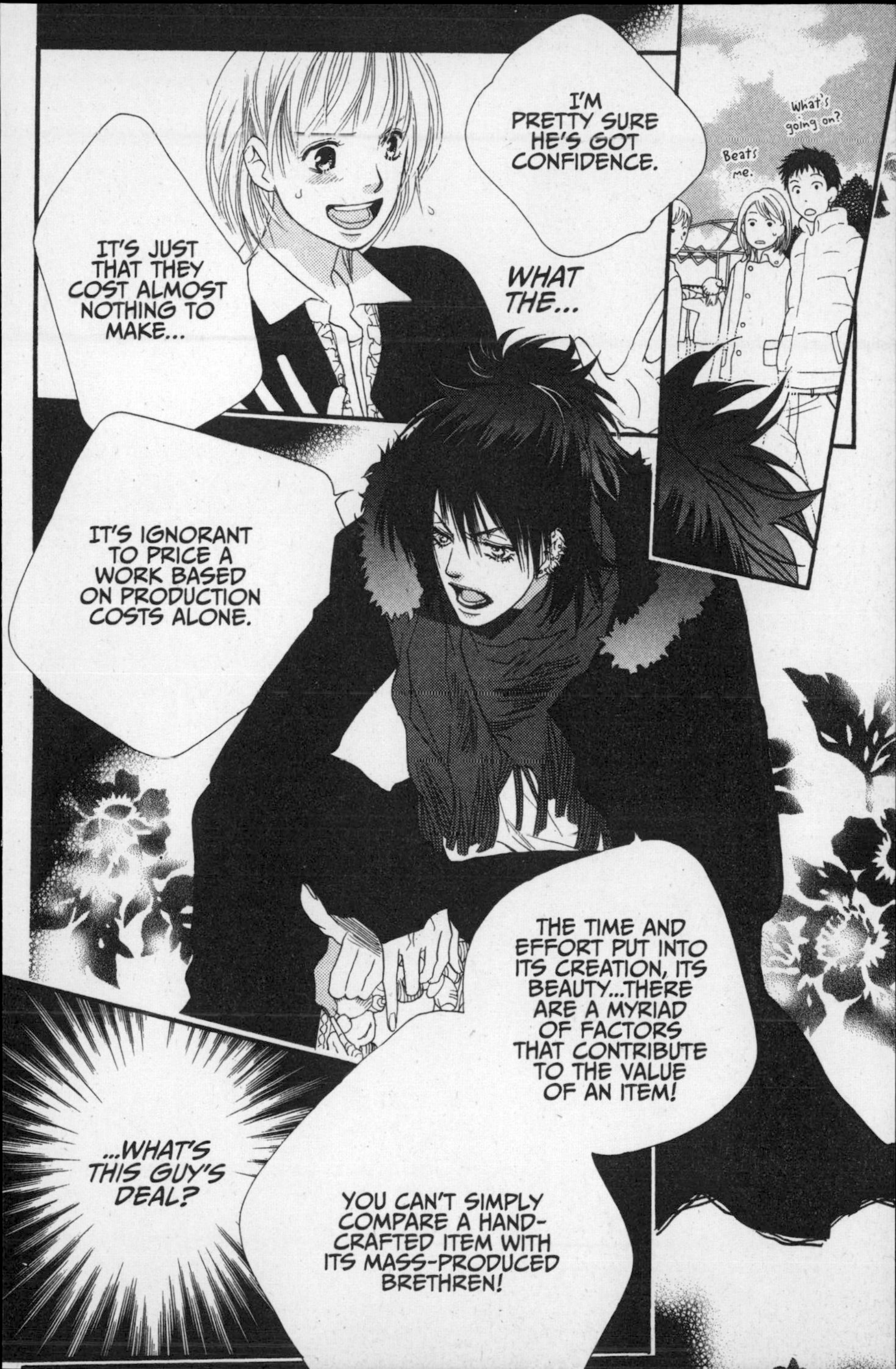

I'M PRETTY SURE HE'S GOT CONFIDENCE.
IT'S JUST THAT THEY COST ALMOST NOTHING TO MAKE...
What's going on?
Beats me.
WHAT THE...
IT'S IGNORANT TO PRICE A WORK BASED ON PRODUCTION COSTS ALONE.
THE TIME AND EFFORT PUT INTO ITS CREATION, ITS BEAUTY...THERE ARE A MYRIAD OF FACTORS THAT CONTRIBUTE TO THE VALUE OF AN ITEM!
YOU CAN'T SIMPLY COMPARE A HAND-CRAFTED ITEM WITH ITS MASS-PRODUCED BRETHREN!
...WHAT'S THIS GUY'S DEAL?

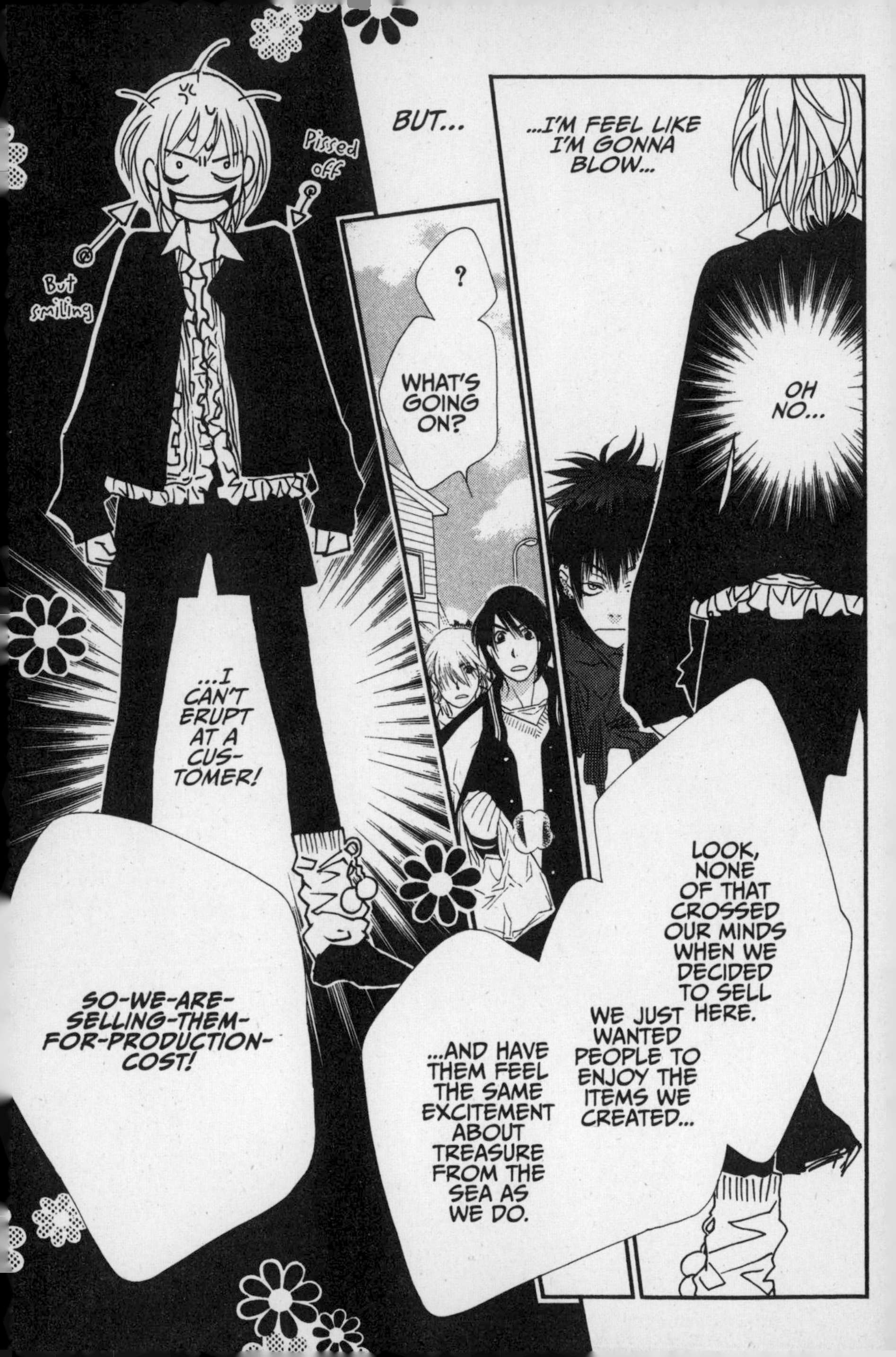
OH NO...
LOOK, NONE OF THAT CROSSED OUR MINDS WHEN WE DECIDED TO SELL HERE.
WE JUST WANTED PEOPLE TO ENJOY THE ITEMS WE CREATED...
...AND HAVE THEM FEEL THE SAME EXCITEMENT ABOUT TREASURE FROM THE SEA AS WE DO.
?
WHAT'S GOING ON?
Pissed off
But smiling
BUT...
...I'M FEEL LIKE I'M GONNA BLOW...
...I CAN'T ERUPT AT A CUS-TOMER!
SO-WE-ARE-SELLING-THEM-FOR-PRODUCTION-COST!

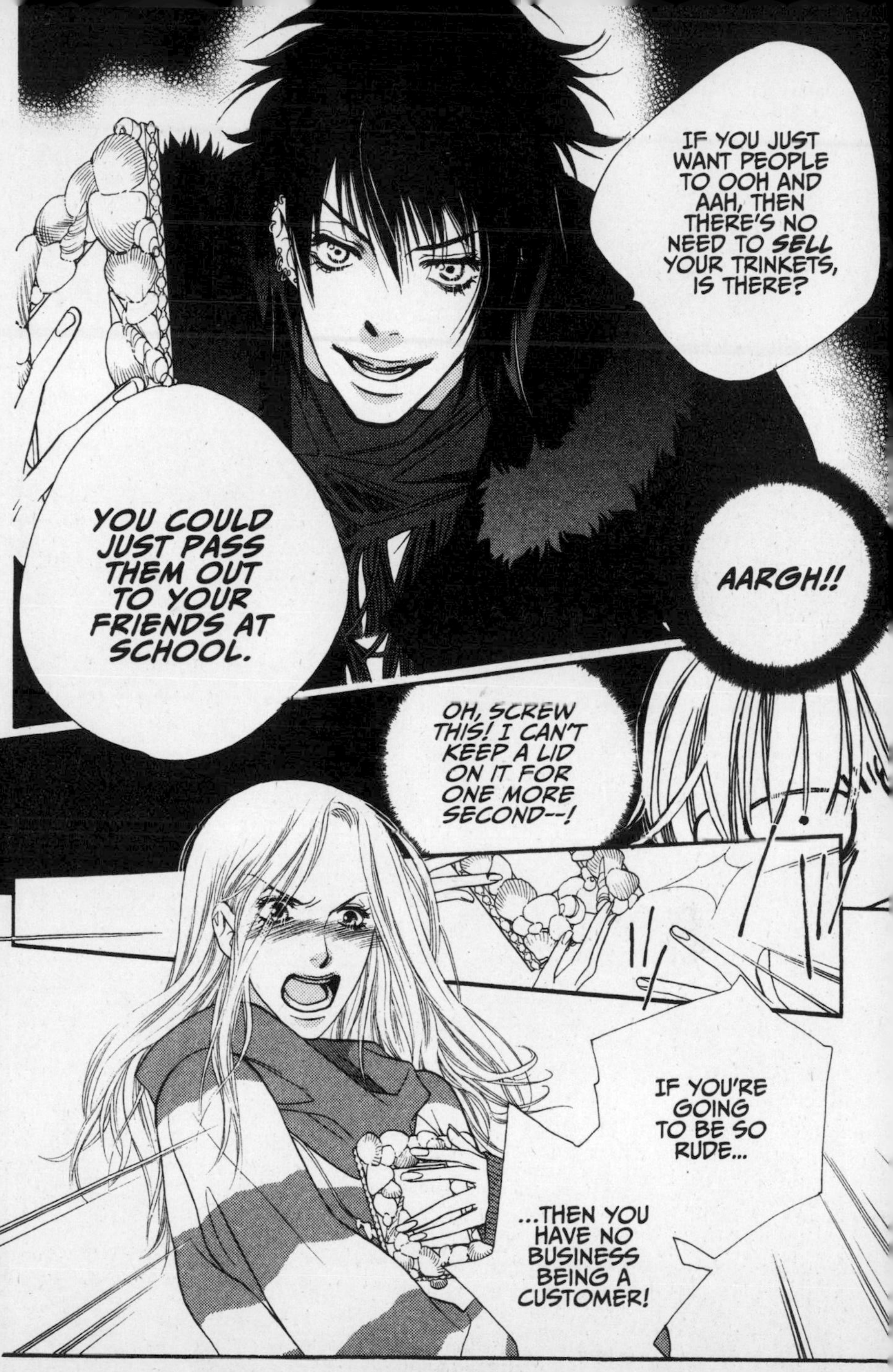
IF YOU JUST WANT PEOPLE TO OOH AND AAH, THEN THERE'S NO NEED TO *SELL* YOUR TRINKETS, IS THERE?
YOU COULD JUST PASS THEM OUT TO YOUR FRIENDS AT SCHOOL.
AARGH!!
OH, SCREW THIS! I CAN'T KEEP A LID ON IT FOR ONE MORE SECOND--!
IF YOU'RE GOING TO BE SO RUDE...
...THEN YOU HAVE NO BUSINESS BEING A CUSTOMER!

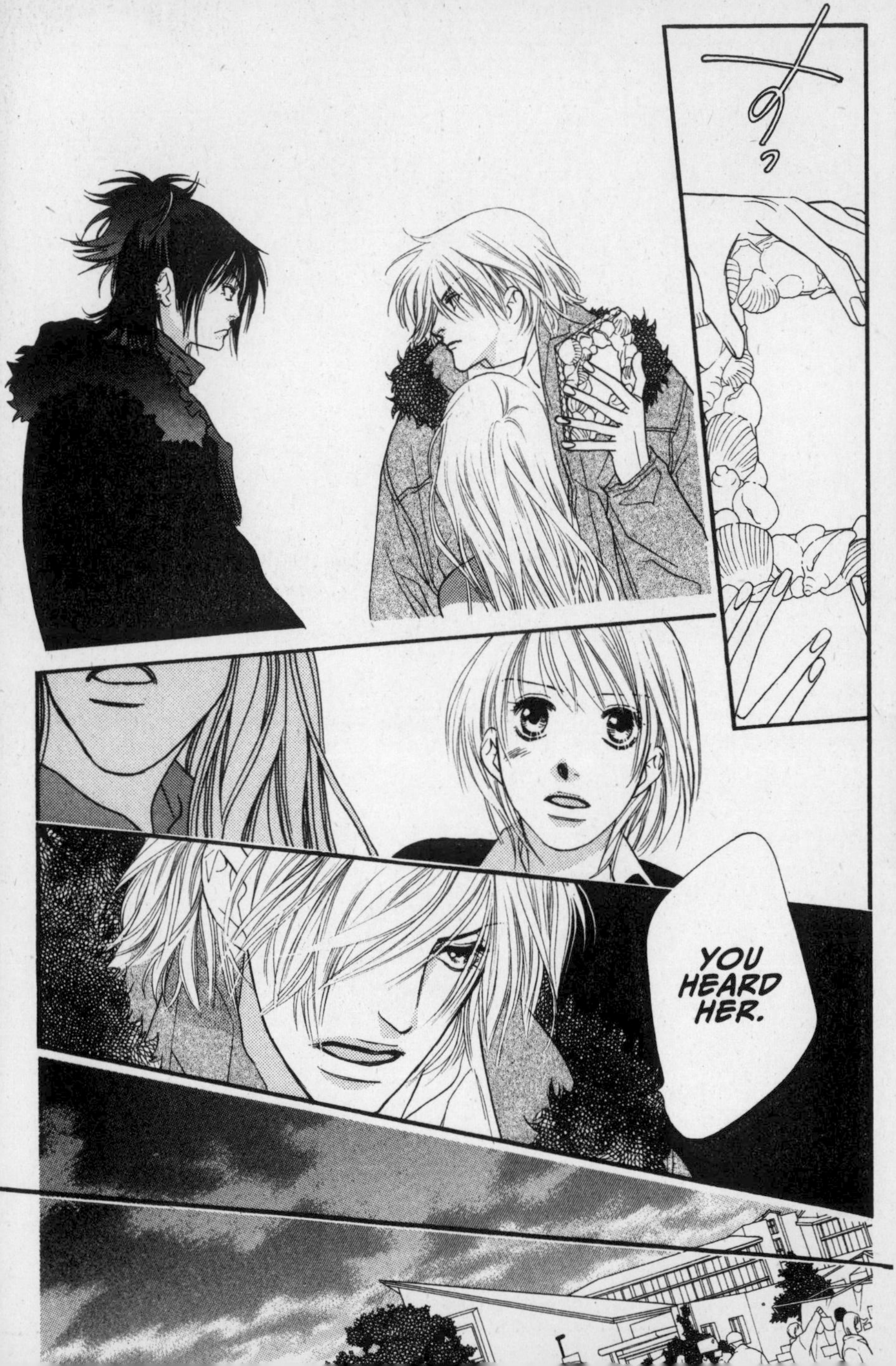
YOU HEARD HER.

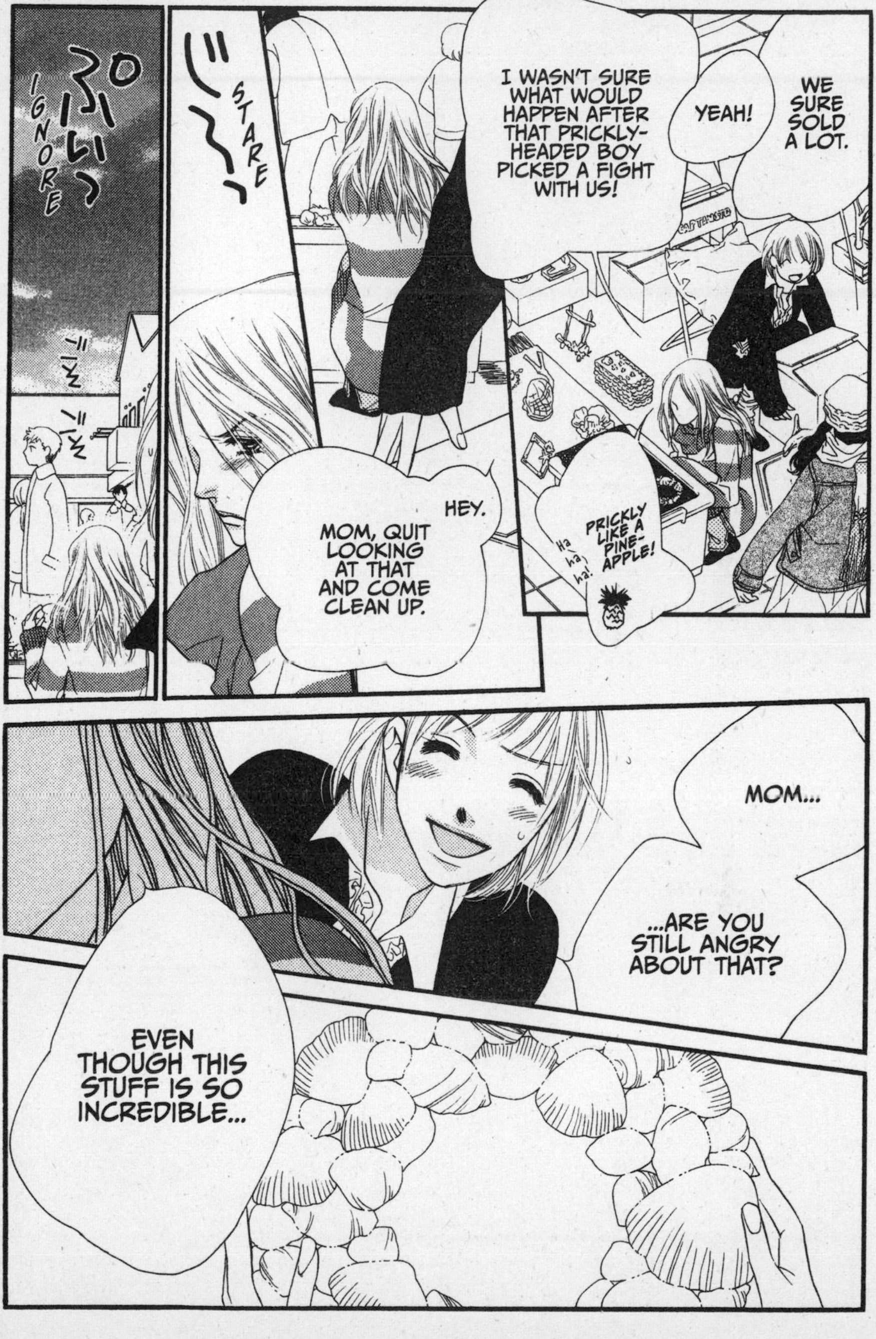
WE SURE SOLD A LOT.
YEAH!
I WASN'T SURE WHAT WOULD HAPPEN AFTER THAT PRICKLY-HEADED BOY PICKED A FIGHT WITH US!
PRICKLY LIKE A PINE-APPLE!
Ha ha, ha!
STARE
HEY.
MOM, QUIT LOOKING AT THAT AND COME CLEAN UP.
IGNORE
MOM...
...ARE YOU STILL ANGRY ABOUT THAT?
EVEN THOUGH THIS STUFF IS SO INCREDIBLE...

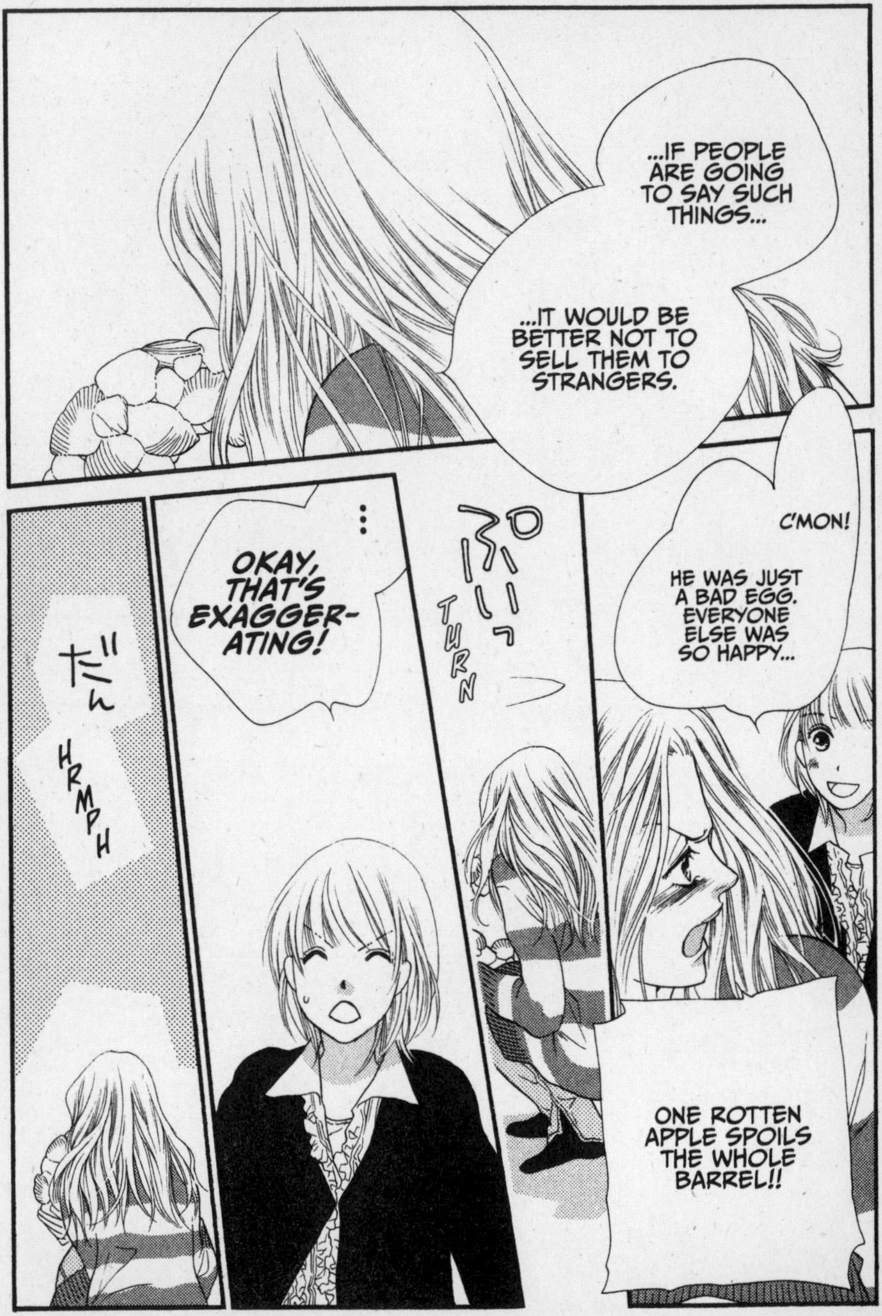
...IF PEOPLE ARE GOING TO SAY SUCH THINGS...
...IT WOULD BE BETTER NOT TO SELL THEM TO STRANGERS.
C'MON!
HE WAS JUST A BAD EGG. EVERYONE ELSE WAS SO HAPPY...
ONE ROTTEN APPLE SPOILS THE WHOLE BARREL!!
ぷいっ
TURN
...
OKAY, THAT'S EXAGGER-ATING!
だーん
HRMPH

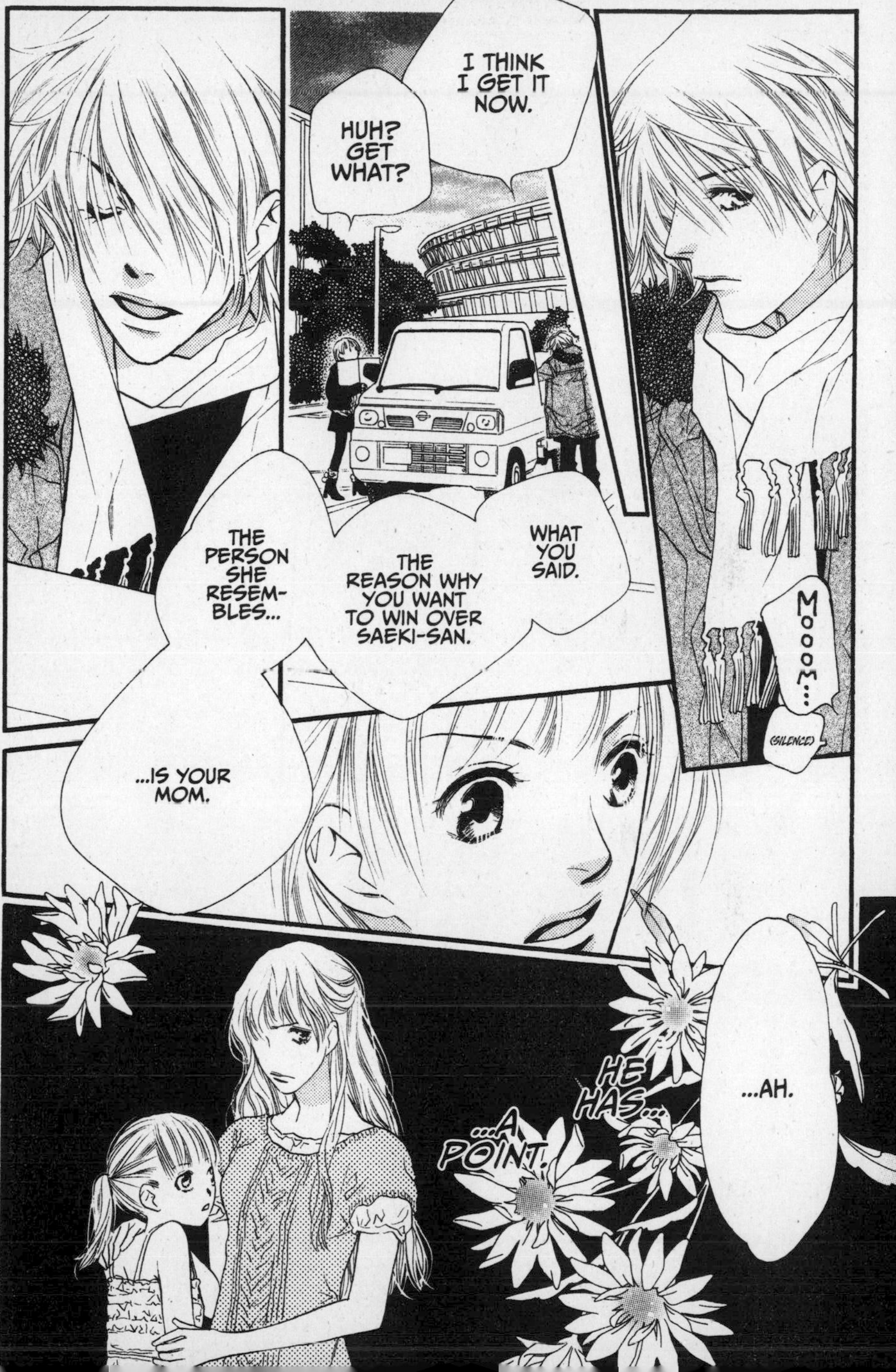
MOOOM...
(SILENCE)
I THINK I GET IT NOW.
HUH? GET WHAT?
WHAT YOU SAID.
THE REASON WHY YOU WANT TO WIN OVER SAEKI-SAN.
THE PERSON SHE RESEMBLES...
...IS YOUR MOM.
...AH.
HE HAS...
...A POINT.

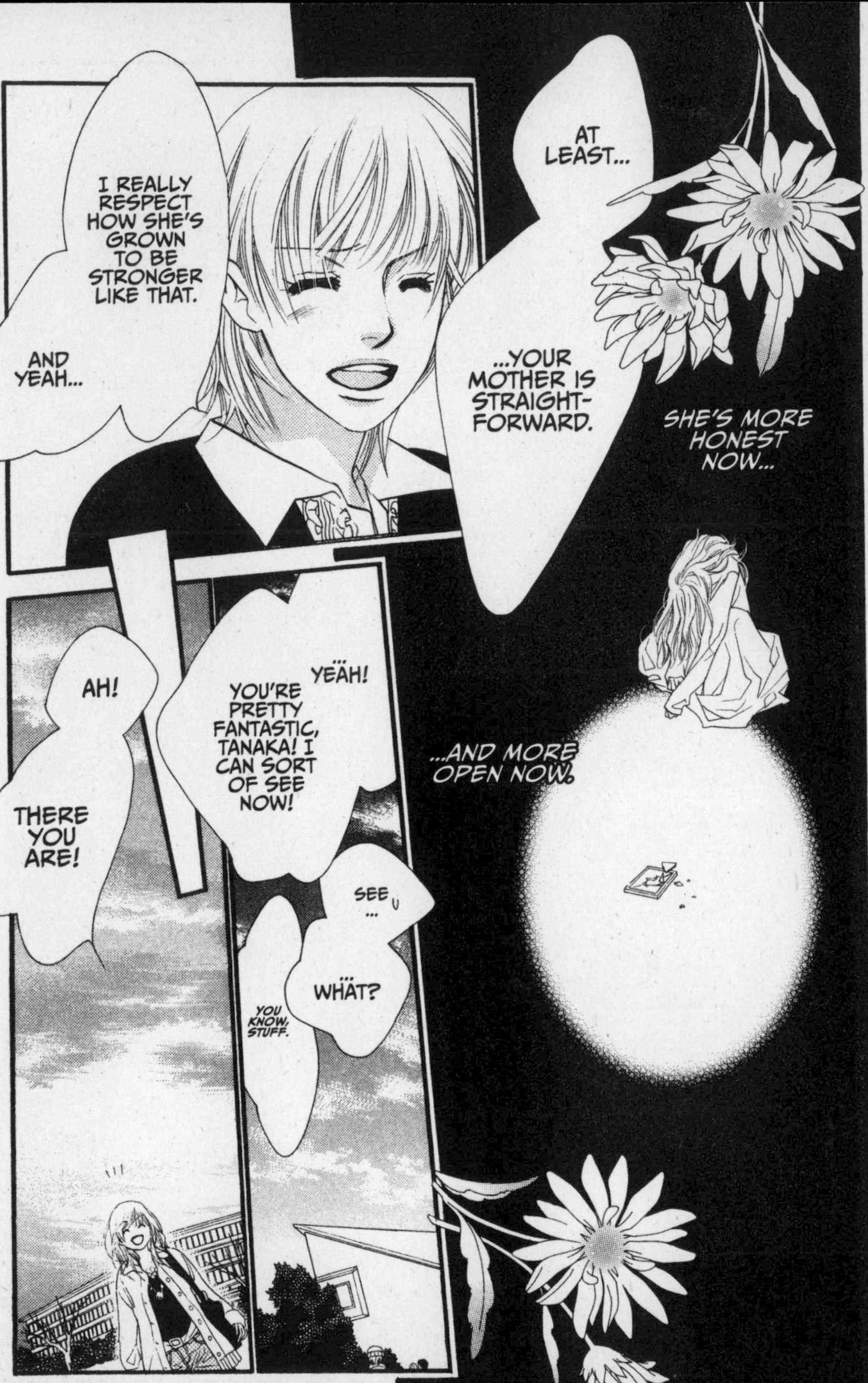
I REALLY RESPECT HOW SHE'S GROWN TO BE STRONGER LIKE THAT.
AND YEAH...
AT LEAST...
...YOUR MOTHER IS STRAIGHT-FORWARD.
SHE'S MORE HONEST NOW...
...AND MORE OPEN NOW.
YEAH!
YOU'RE PRETTY FANTASTIC, TANAKA! I CAN SORT OF SEE NOW!
SEE...
WHAT?
YOU KNOW, STUFF.
AH!
THERE YOU ARE!

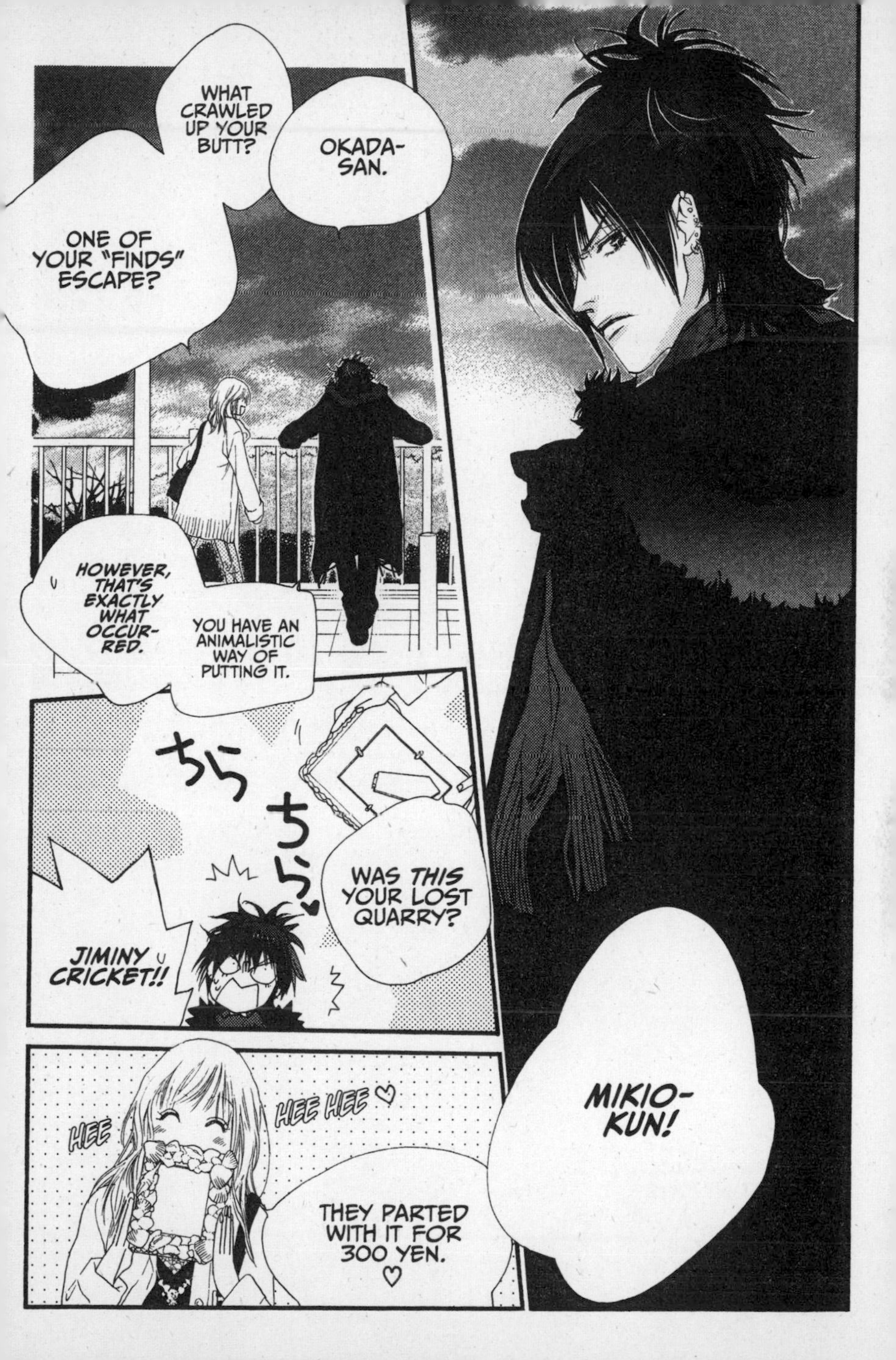
MIKIO-KUN!
OKADA-SAN.
WHAT CRAWLED UP YOUR BUTT?
ONE OF YOUR "FINDS" ESCAPE?
YOU HAVE AN ANIMALISTIC WAY OF PUTTING IT.
HOWEVER, THAT'S EXACTLY WHAT OCCURRED.
ちら ちら
WAS THIS YOUR LOST QUARRY?
JIMINY CRICKET!!
HEE HEE HEE ♡
HEE
THEY PARTED WITH IT FOR 300 YEN. ♡

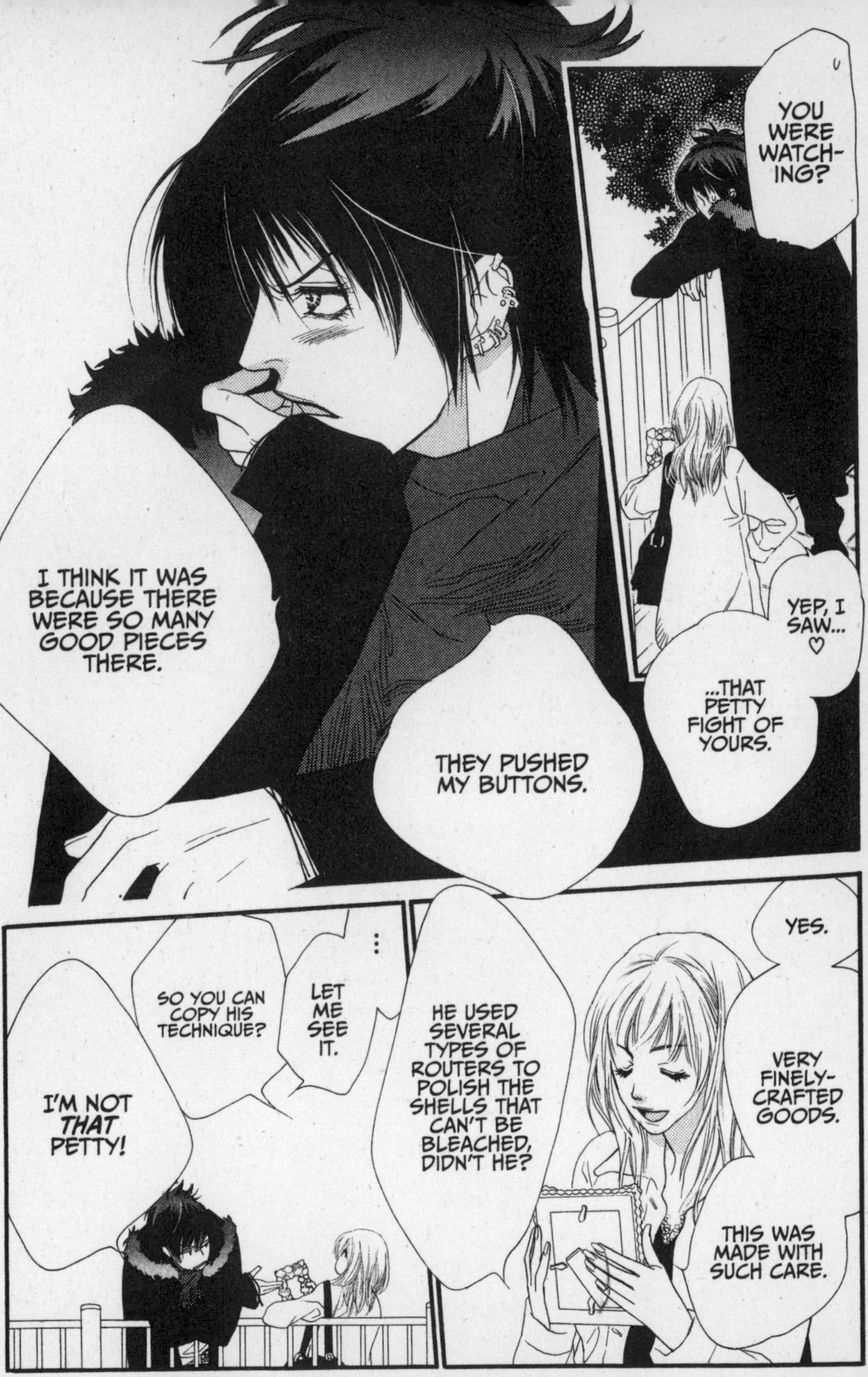
YOU WERE WATCHING?
YEP, I SAW... ♡
...THAT PETTY FIGHT OF YOURS.
THEY PUSHED MY BUTTONS.
I THINK IT WAS BECAUSE THERE WERE SO MANY GOOD PIECES THERE.
YES.
VERY FINELY-CRAFTED GOODS.
THIS WAS MADE WITH SUCH CARE.
HE USED SEVERAL TYPES OF ROUTERS TO POLISH THE SHELLS THAT CAN'T BE BLEACHED, DIDN'T HE?
...
LET ME SEE IT.
SO YOU CAN COPY HIS TECHNIQUE?
I'M NOT *THAT* PETTY!

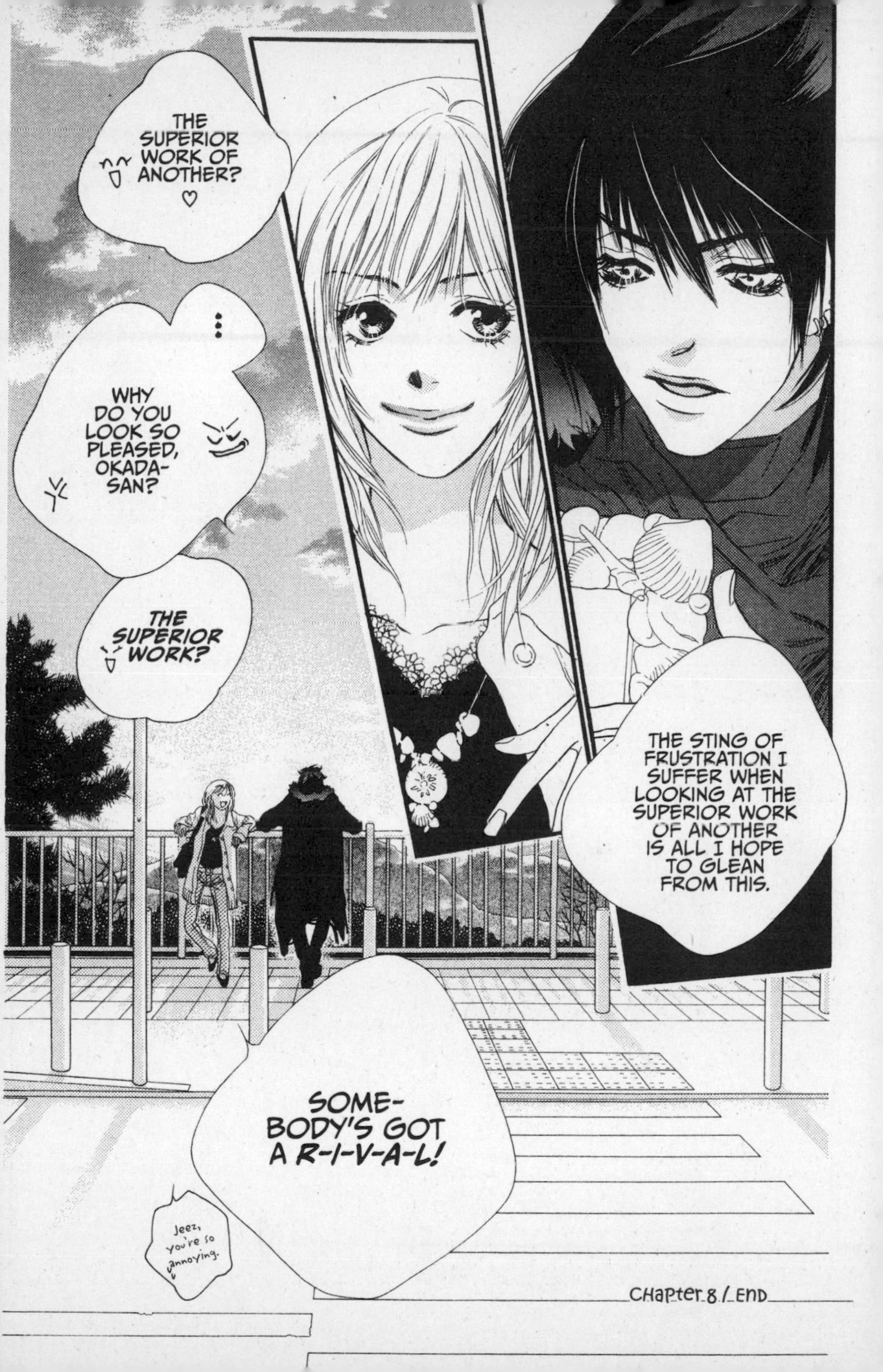
THE STING OF FRUSTRATION I SUFFER WHEN LOOKING AT THE SUPERIOR WORK OF ANOTHER IS ALL I HOPE TO GLEAN FROM THIS.
THE SUPERIOR WORK OF ANOTHER?
...
WHY DO YOU LOOK SO PLEASED, OKADA-SAN?
THE SUPERIOR WORK?
SOME-BODY'S GOT A R-I-V-A-L!
Jeez, you're so annoying.
Chapter 8 / End

Turn the page to see a comic that was created before SkyBlue Shore chapter 1!

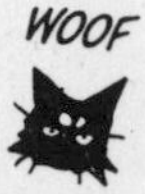
WOOF

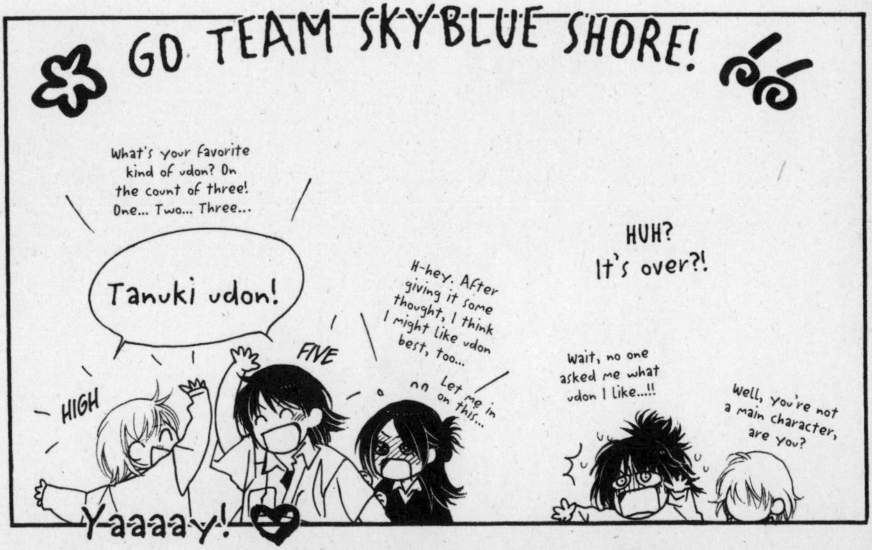
GO TEAM SKYBLUE SHORE!
What's your favorite kind of udon? On the count of three! One... Two... Three...
Tanuki udon!
HIGH
FIVE
Yaaaay!
H-hey. After giving it some thought, I think I might like udon best, too...
Let me in on this...
HUH? It's over?!
Wait, no one asked me what udon I like...!!
Well, you're not a main character, are you?

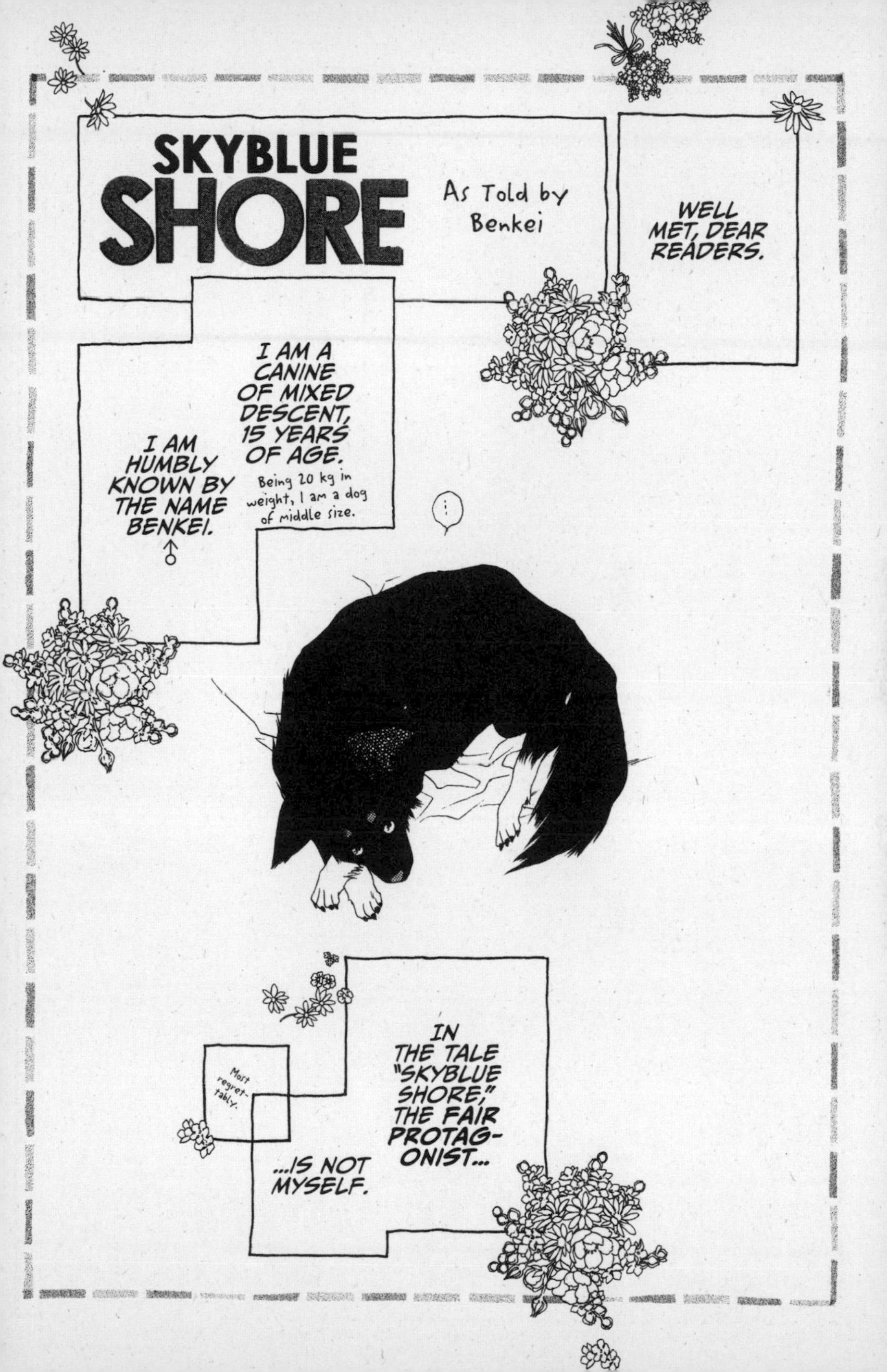

WELL MET, DEAR READERS.
SKYBLUE SHORE
As Told by Benkei
I AM A CANINE OF MIXED DESCENT, 15 YEARS OF AGE.
Being 20 kg in weight, I am a dog of middle size.
I AM HUMBLY KNOWN BY THE NAME BENKEI.
♂
...
IN THE TALE "SKYBLUE SHORE," THE FAIR PROTAGONIST...
Most regret-tably.
...IS NOT MYSELF.

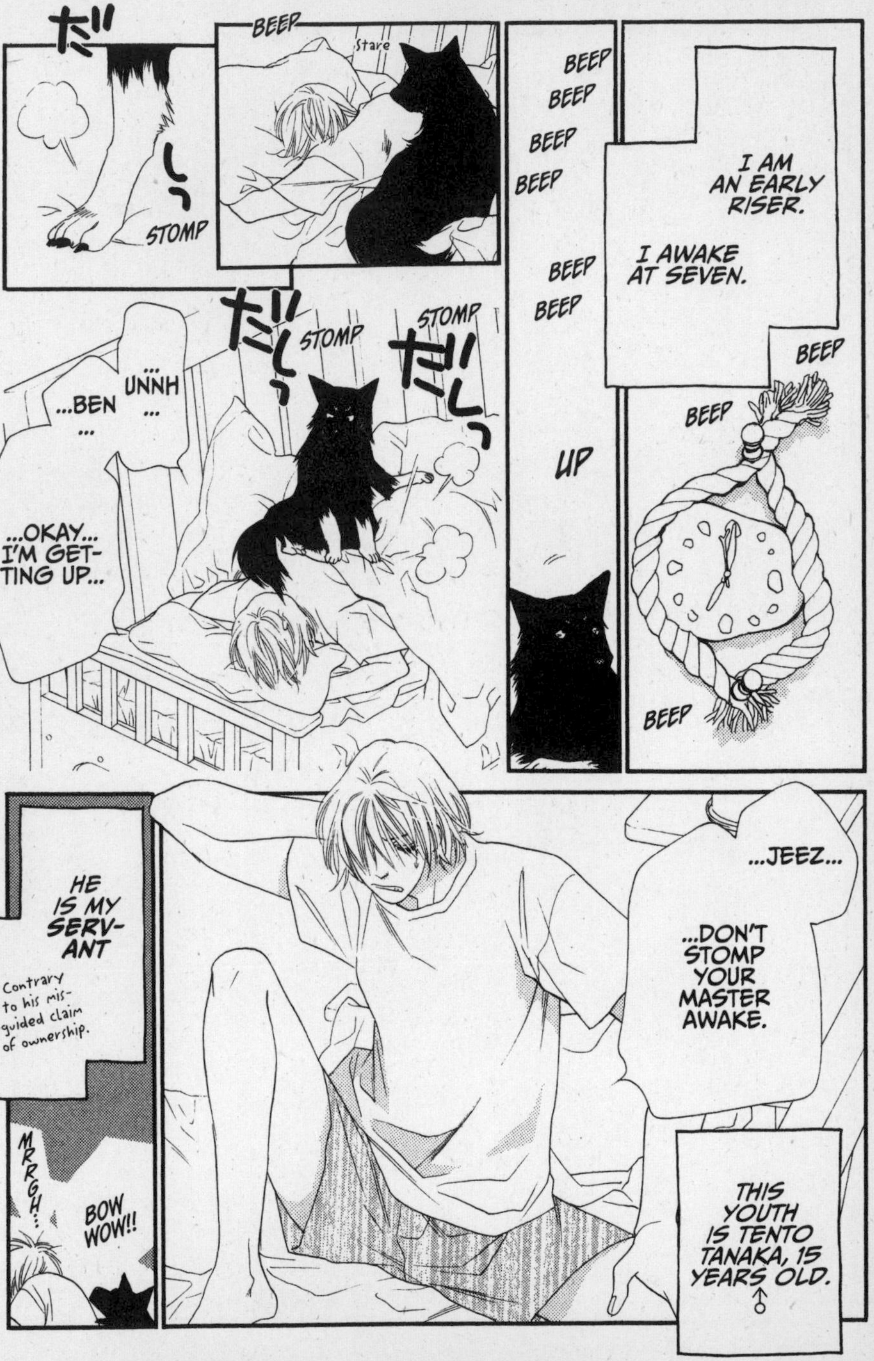

I AM AN EARLY RISER.
I AWAKE AT SEVEN.
BEEP
BEEP
BEEP
BEEP
BEEP
BEEP
BEEP
BEEP
BEEP
BEEP
BEEP
UP
BEEP
Stare
だ
しっ
STOMP
だしっ
STOMP
STOMP
だしっ
...UNNH...
...BEN...
...OKAY... I'M GETTING UP...
...JEEZ...
...DON'T STOMP YOUR MASTER AWAKE.
THIS YOUTH IS TENTO TANAKA, 15 YEARS OLD.
♂
HE IS MY SERVANT
Contrary to his misguided claim of ownership.
MRRGH...
BOW WOW!!

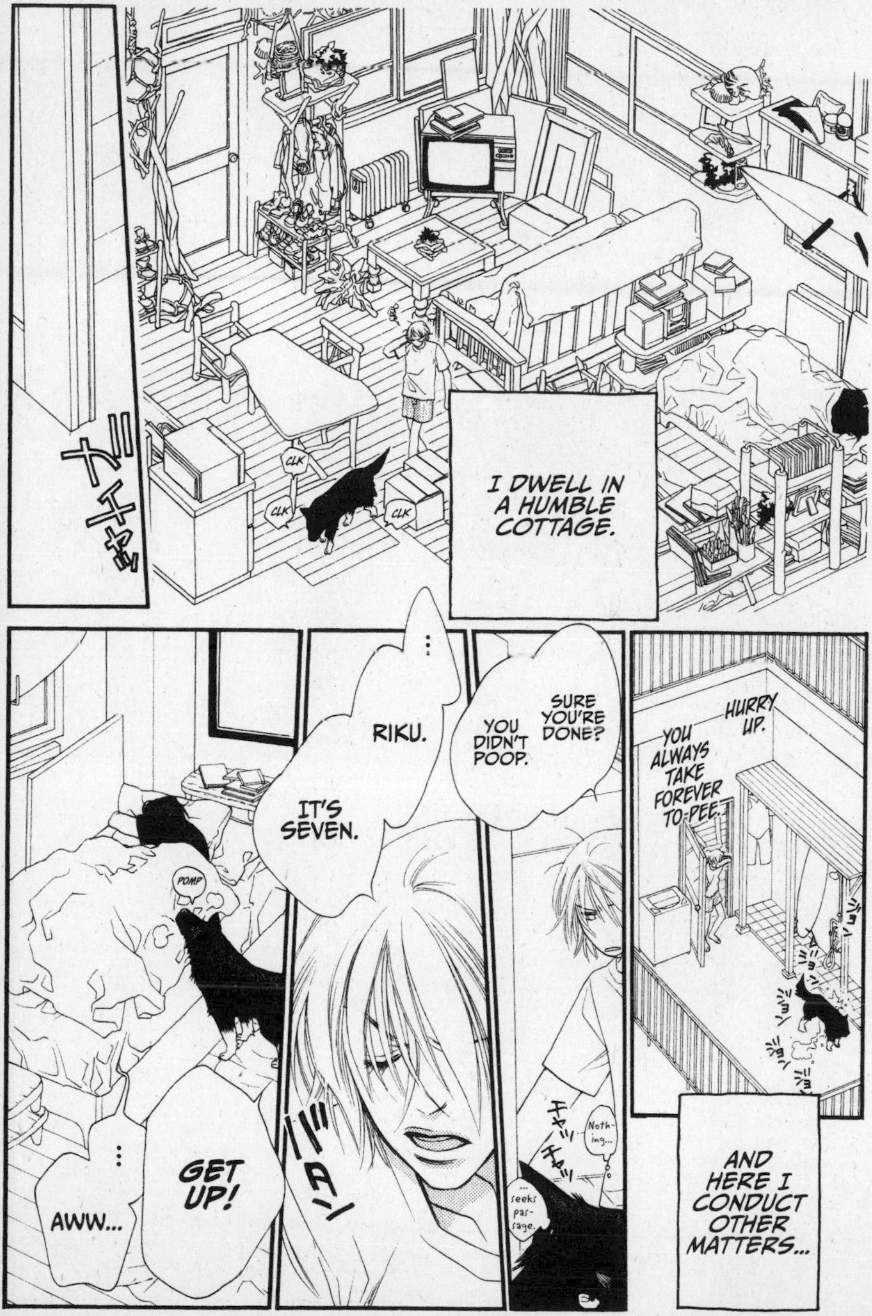
I DWELL IN A HUMBLE COTTAGE.
CLK
CLK
CLK
HURRY UP.
YOU ALWAYS TAKE FOREVER TO PEE.
AND HERE I CONDUCT OTHER MATTERS...
SURE YOU'RE DONE?
YOU DIDN'T POOP.
Noth-ing...
...seeks pas-sage.
...
RIKU.
IT'S SEVEN.
POMP
GET UP!
...
AWW...

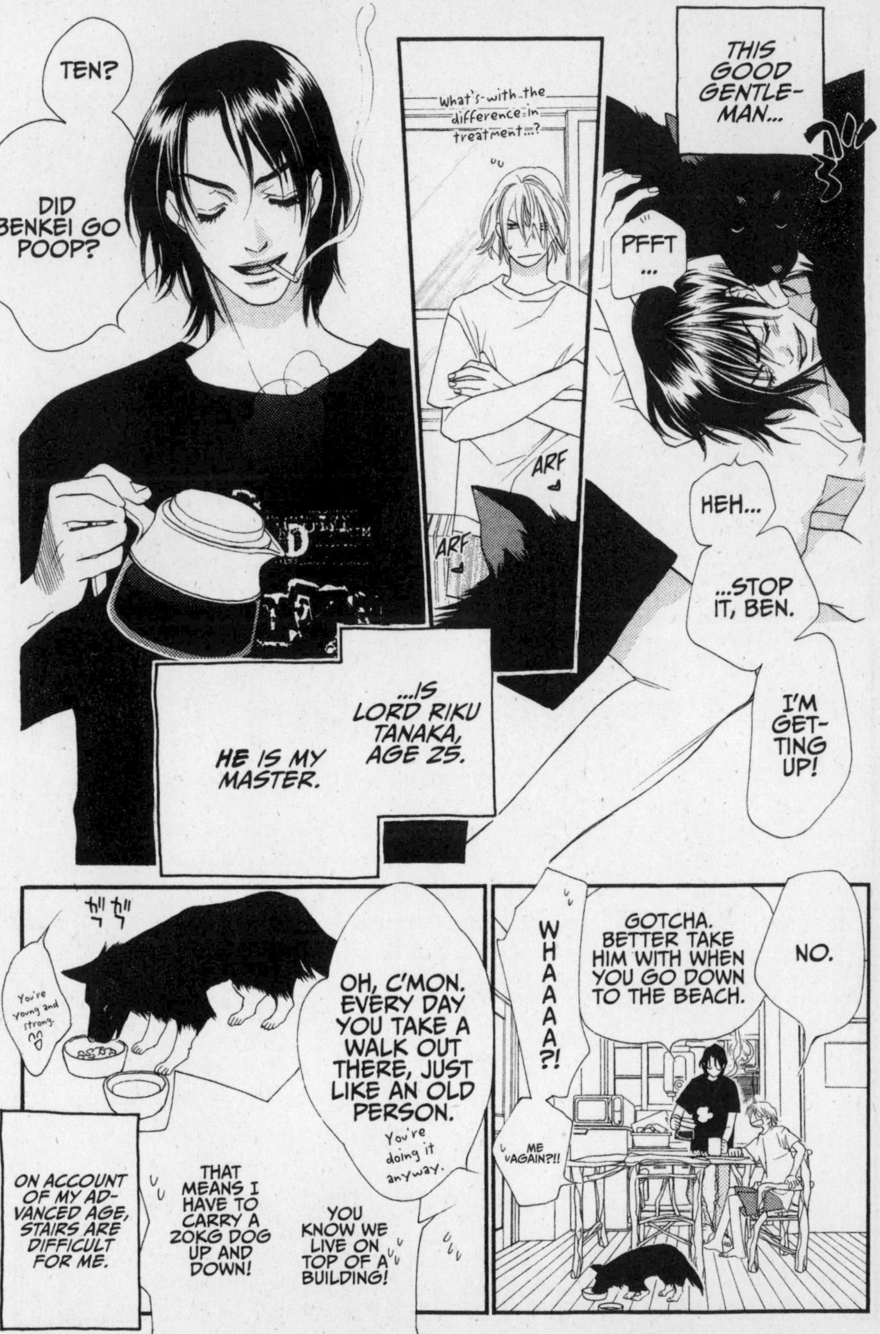
THIS GOOD GENTLEMAN...
PFFT ...
HEH...
...STOP IT, BEN.
I'M GETTING UP!
What's with the difference in treatment...?
ARF
ARF
TEN?
DID BENKEI GO POOP?
...IS LORD RIKU TANAKA, AGE 25.
HE IS MY MASTER.
NO.
GOTCHA. BETTER TAKE HIM WITH WHEN YOU GO DOWN TO THE BEACH.
WHAAAAA?!
ME AGAIN?!!
OH, C'MON. EVERY DAY YOU TAKE A WALK OUT THERE, JUST LIKE AN OLD PERSON.
You're doing it anyway.
You're young and strong.
YOU KNOW WE LIVE ON TOP OF A BUILDING!
THAT MEANS I HAVE TO CARRY A 20KG DOG UP AND DOWN!
ON ACCOUNT OF MY ADVANCED AGE, STAIRS ARE DIFFICULT FOR ME.

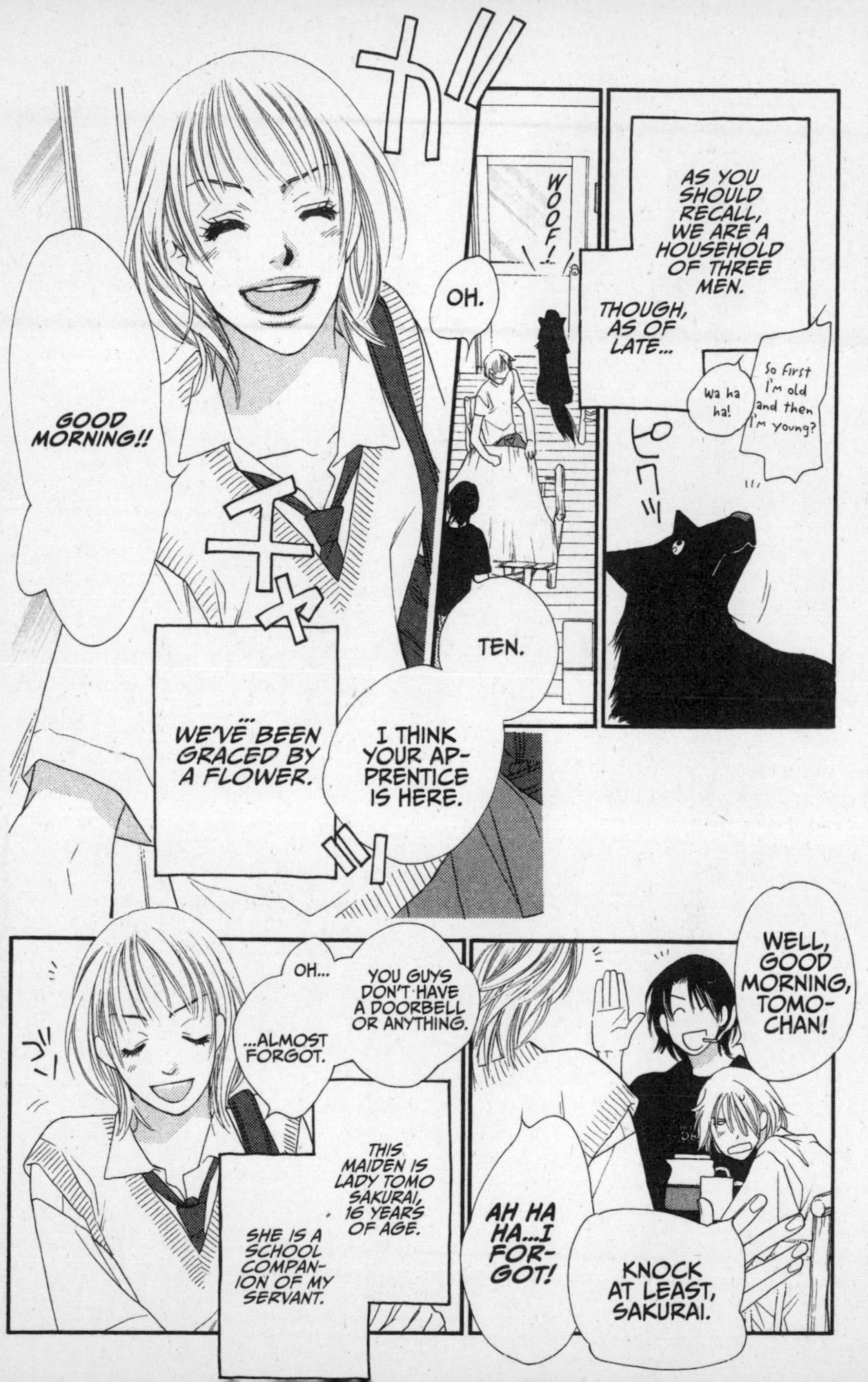
AS YOU SHOULD RECALL, WE ARE A HOUSEHOLD OF THREE MEN.
THOUGH, AS OF LATE...
So first I'm old and then I'm young?
Wa ha ha!
WOOF!
OH.
TEN.
I THINK YOUR APPRENTICE IS HERE.
...WE'VE BEEN GRACED BY A FLOWER.
GOOD MORNING!!
WELL, GOOD MORNING, TOMO-CHAN!
KNOCK AT LEAST, SAKURAI.
AH HA HA...I FORGOT!
YOU GUYS DON'T HAVE A DOORBELL OR ANYTHING.
OH...
...ALMOST FORGOT.
THIS MAIDEN IS LADY TOMO SAKURAI, 16 YEARS OF AGE.
SHE IS A SCHOOL COMPANION OF MY SERVANT.

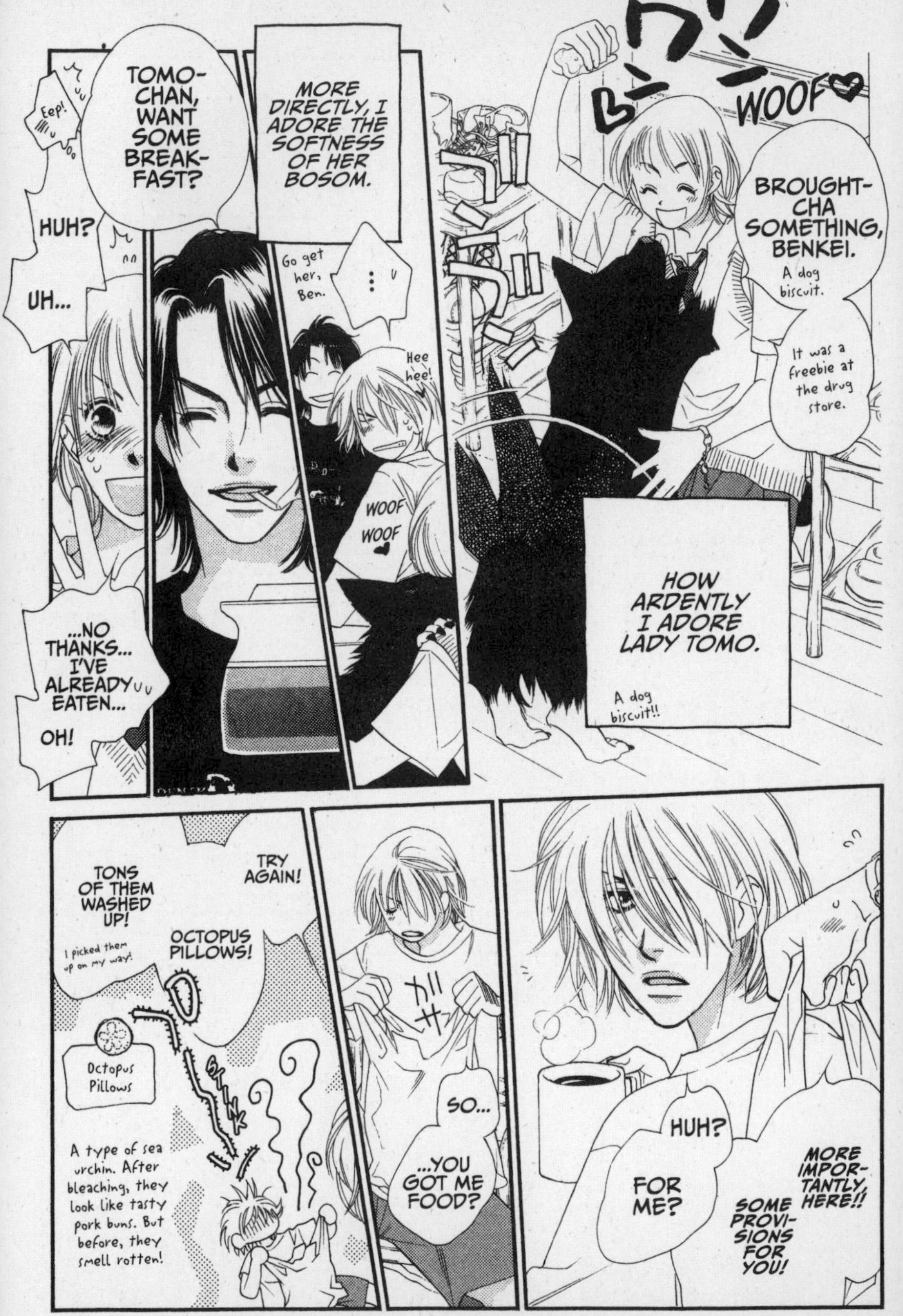
WOOF♥
BROUGHT-CHA SOMETHING, BENKEI.
A dog biscuit.
It was a freebie at the drug store.
HOW ARDENTLY I ADORE LADY TOMO.
A dog biscuit!!
MORE DIRECTLY, I ADORE THE SOFTNESS OF HER BOSOM.
...
Go get her, Ben.
Hee hee!
WOOF WOOF♥
TOMO-CHAN, WANT SOME BREAKFAST?
Eep!
HUH?
UH...
...NO THANKS... I'VE ALREADY EATEN...
OH!
MORE IMPORTANTLY, HERE!!
SOME PROVISIONS FOR YOU!
HUH?
FOR ME?
SO...
...YOU GOT ME FOOD?
TRY AGAIN!
TONS OF THEM WASHED UP!
I picked them up on my way!
OCTOPUS PILLOWS!
Octopus Pillows
STINK
A type of sea urchin. After bleaching, they look like tasty pork buns. But before, they smell rotten!

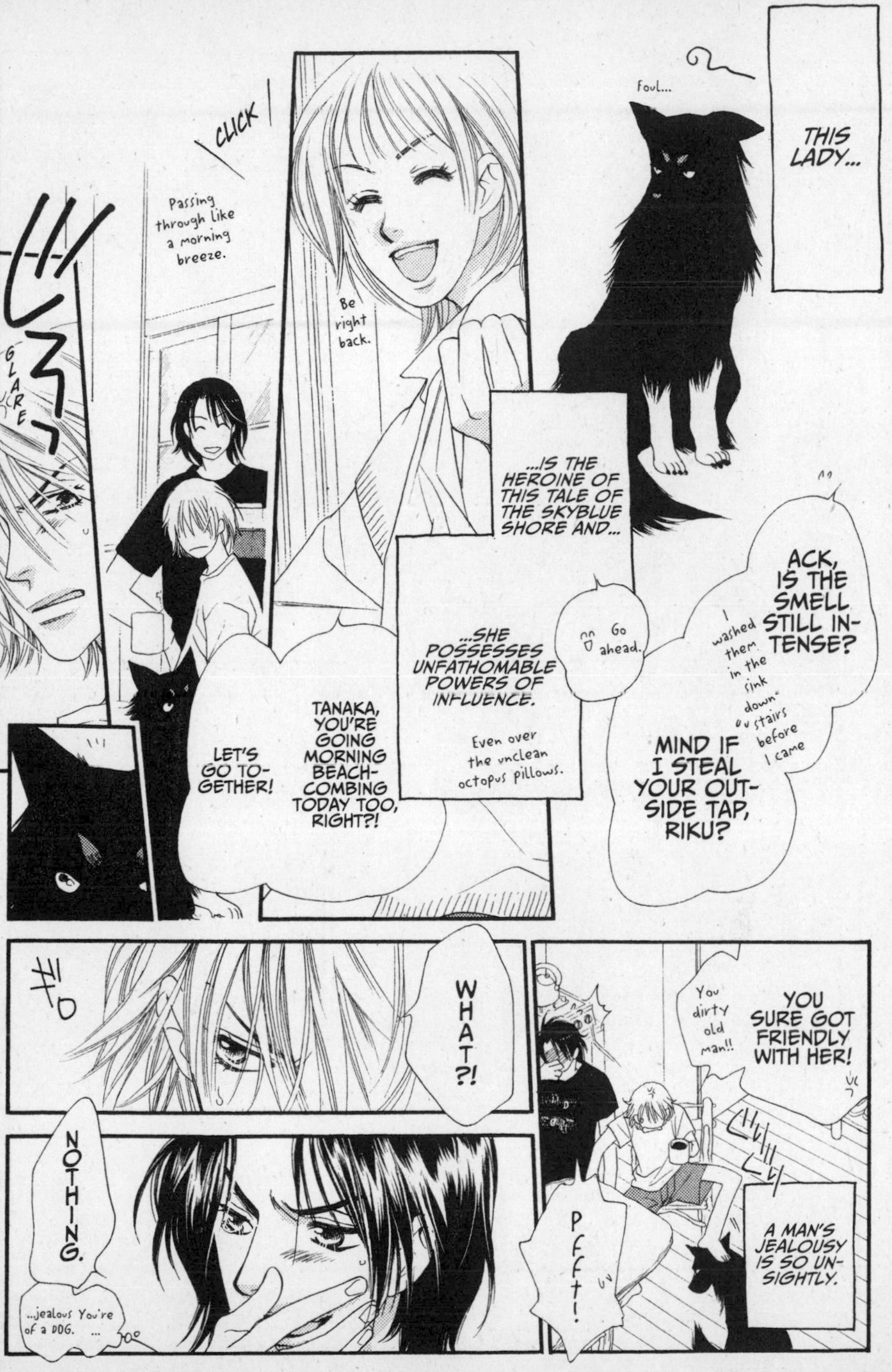
THIS LADY...
Foul...
...IS THE HEROINE OF THIS TALE OF THE SKYBLUE SHORE AND...
ACK, IS THE SMELL STILL IN-TENSE?
I washed them in the sink down-stairs before I came
MIND IF I STEAL YOUR OUT-SIDE TAP, RIKU?
Go ahead.
...SHE POSSESSES UNFATHOMABLE POWERS OF INFLUENCE.
Even over the unclean octopus pillows.
Be right back.
CLICK
TANAKA, YOU'RE GOING MORNING BEACH-COMBING TODAY TOO, RIGHT?!
LET'S GO TO-GETHER!
Passing through like a morning breeze.
GLARE
YOU SURE GOT FRIENDLY WITH HER!
You dirty old man!!
A MAN'S JEALOUSY IS SO UN-SIGHTLY.
Pfft!
WHAT?!
NOTHING.
...jealous You're of a DOG. ...

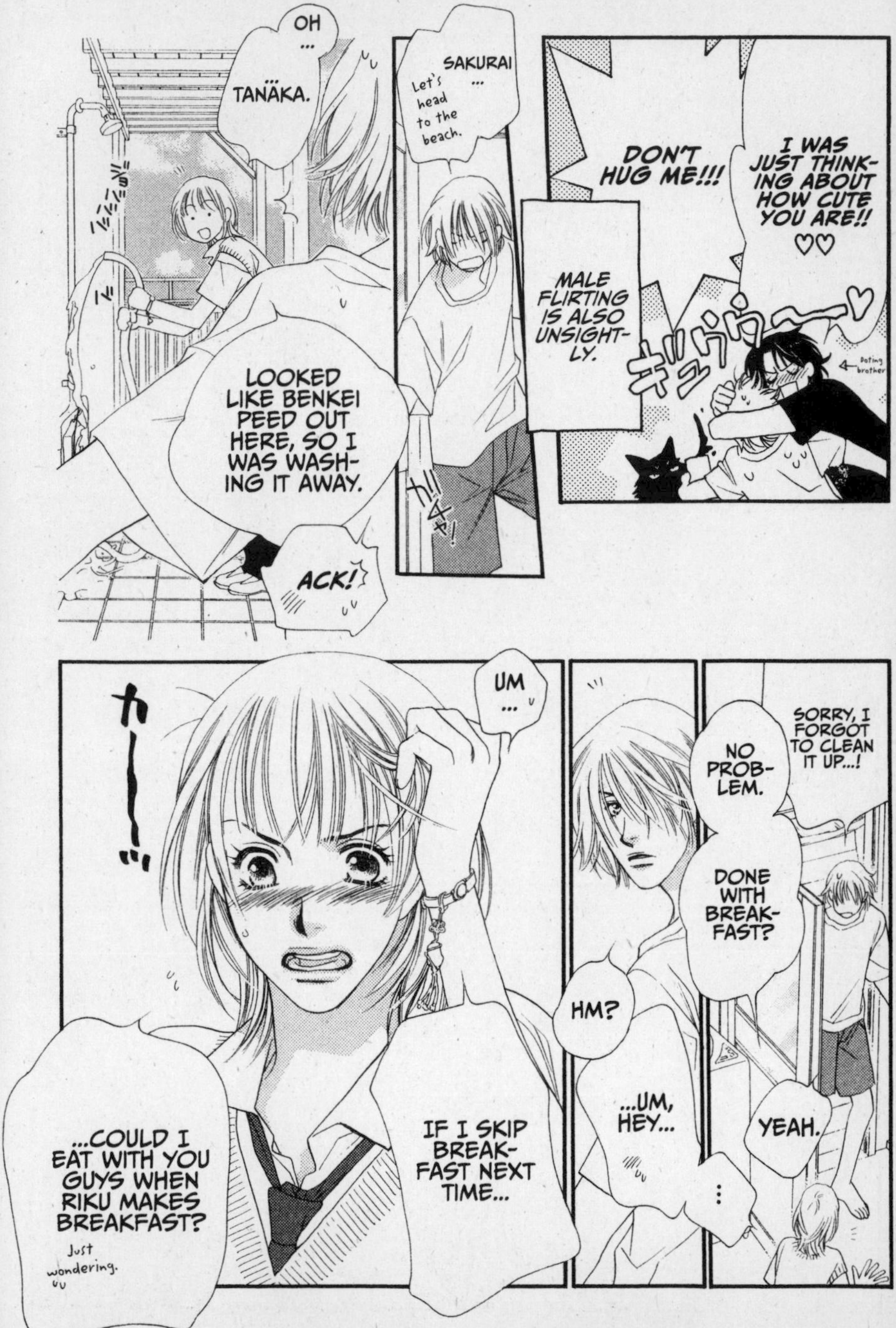
I WAS JUST THINKING ABOUT HOW CUTE YOU ARE!! ♡♡
DON'T HUG ME!!!
Doting brother
MALE FLIRTING IS ALSO UNSIGHTLY.
SAKURAI ...
Let's head to the beach.
OH ...
... TANAKA.
LOOKED LIKE BENKEI PEED OUT HERE, SO I WAS WASHING IT AWAY.
ACK!
SORRY, I FORGOT TO CLEAN IT UP...!
NO PROBLEM.
DONE WITH BREAKFAST?
YEAH.
...
HM?
...UM, HEY...
UM ...
IF I SKIP BREAKFAST NEXT TIME...
...COULD I EAT WITH YOU GUYS WHEN RIKU MAKES BREAKFAST?
Just wondering.

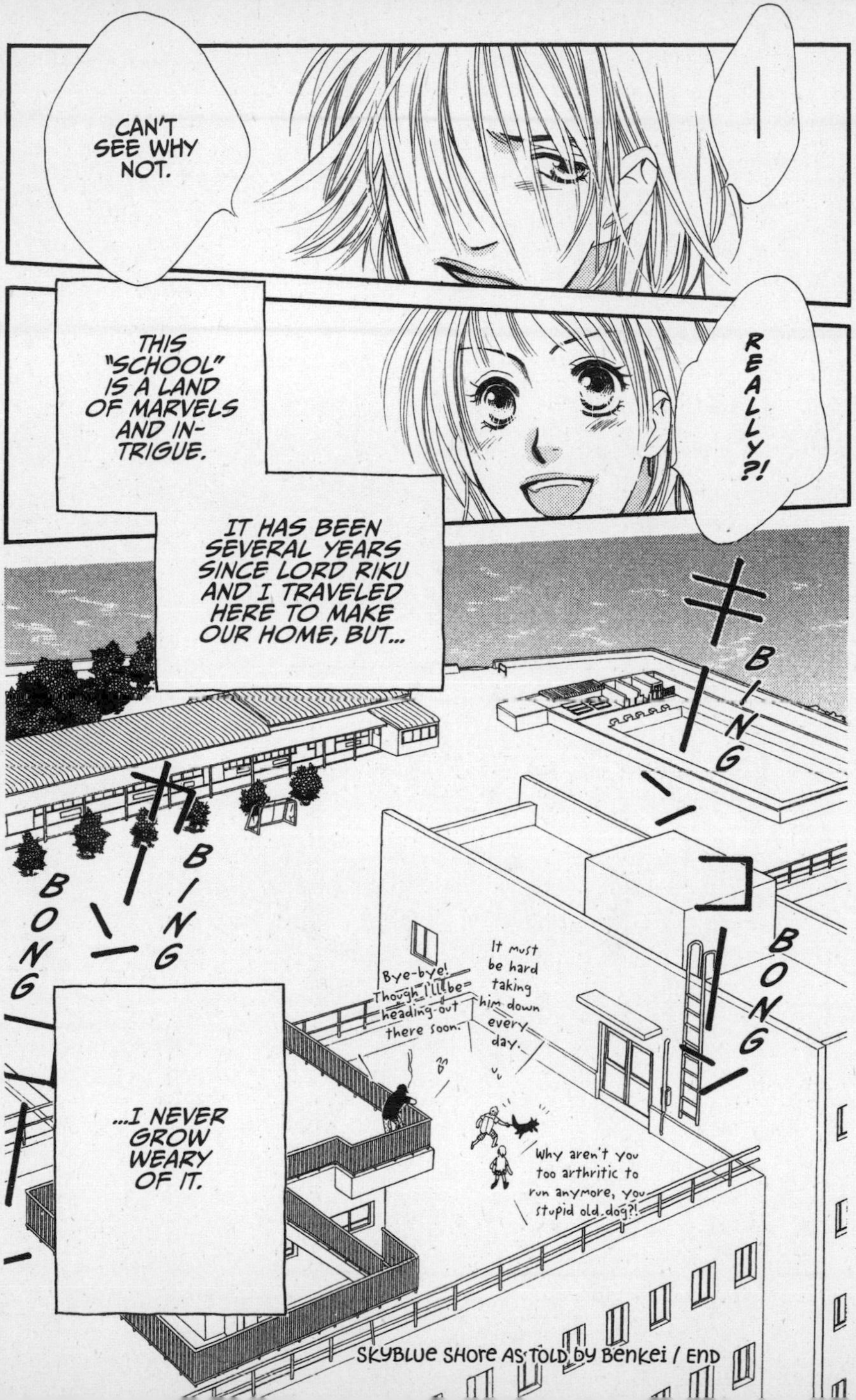
—
CAN'T SEE WHY NOT.
REALLY?!
THIS "SCHOOL" IS A LAND OF MARVELS AND IN-TRIGUE.
IT HAS BEEN SEVERAL YEARS SINCE LORD RIKU AND I TRAVELED HERE TO MAKE OUR HOME, BUT...
BING BONG
BING BONG
It must be hard taking him down every day.
Bye-bye! Though I'll be heading out there soon.
Why aren't you too arthritic to run anymore, you stupid old dog?!
...I NEVER GROW WEARY OF IT.
SKYBLUE SHORE AS TOLD BY BENKEI / END

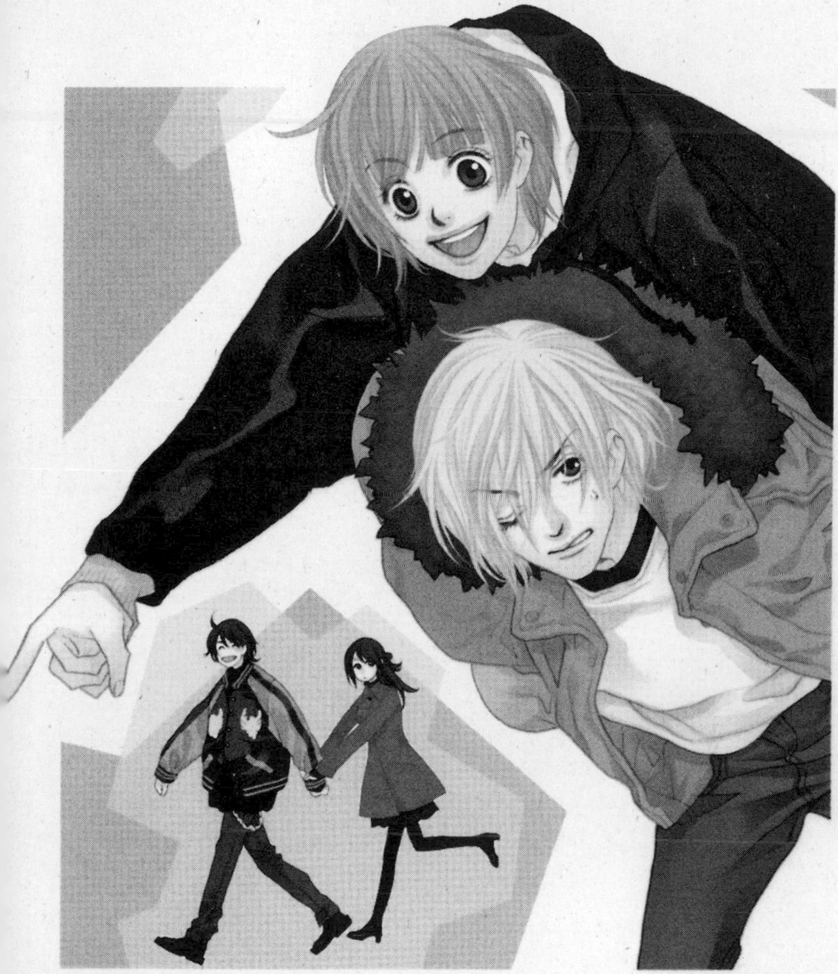

IN THE NEXT VOLUME OF...

SKYBLUE SHORE

AFTER THE FLEA MARKET, TENTO'S GRUMPY, NEW RIVAL KEEPS SHOWING UP EVERYWHERE! AT SCHOOL, PESTERING MICHIRU, EVEN MEETING UP WITH TOMO'S MOM! WILL HE BE ABLE TO BOOST TENTO'S CONFIDENCE IN HIS WORK OR WILL THEY CONTINUE TO CLASH? TOMO SEEMS TO BE GETTING THROUGH TO MICHIRU, BUT GETTING HER TO PARTICIPATE IN THE SPORTS FESTIVAL IS TOUGH. ON TOP OF ALL THAT, TOMO MANAGES TO SNAG A DATE WITH RIKU! CAN SHE FINALLY MAKE HIM HER BOYFRIEND?

DOWNLOAD THE REVOLUTION.

Get the free TOKYOPOP app for manga, anytime, anywhere!

TOKYOPOP MANGA SUPPLEMENT

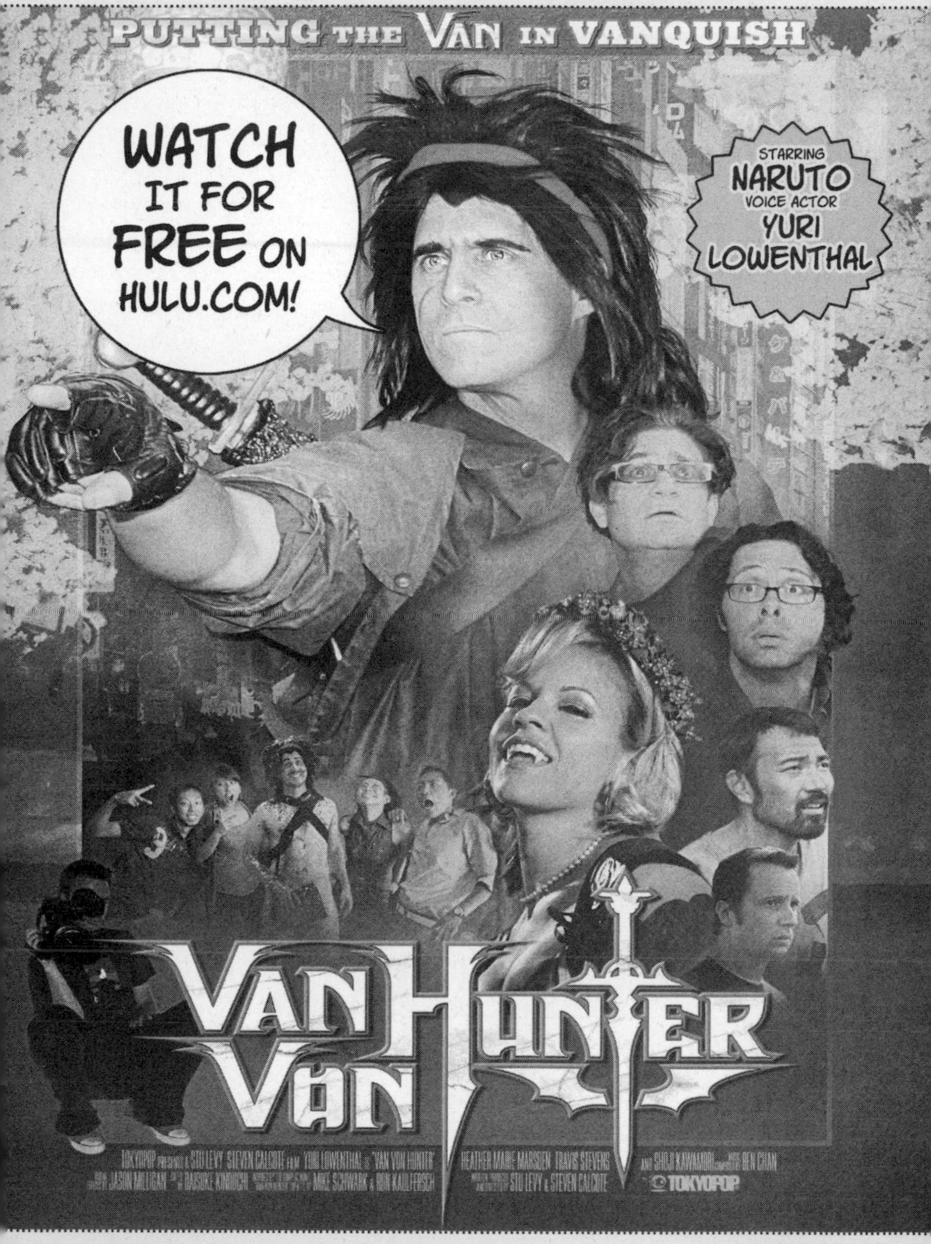

OFFICIAL SELECTION FANTASIA 2010

hulu

TOKYO POP